A Weal
HAPPII
and
MANY BITTER TRIALS

Frontispiece: *Studio portrait of Alfred Edward Pease as a young man.*

A Wealth of
HAPPINESS
and
MANY BITTER TRIALS

The Journals of
Sir Alfred Edward Pease
A Restless Man

Joseph Gurney Pease

William Sessions Limited
The Ebor Press
York, England

ISBN 1 85072 107 6

Printed in 11/12pt Times New Roman by
William Sessions Limited
The Ebor Press, York, England

CONTENTS

LIST OF ILLUSTRATIONS

vi

Acknowledgements

The production of this book is the fulfilment of a personal ambition, made possible only by the encouragement I have received from others.

Particularly I thank my sister, Anne, for her examination of my first draft, and her forthright advice to get the whole thing "tightened up" - which in so doing, has ended with me extending some chapter lengths. Further thanks go to my brother, Vincent, for extra snippets of information; to my son, Charles, for his assistance over the illustrations, and whose added advice I have heeded; to my daughter, Jane, whose constant encouragement and enthusiasm for my project has never flagged; but most of all to my wife, Shelagh, who has patiently read endless revisions, indicating omissions on the way, and who has in addition suffered three years of chaos in our home, cluttered with journals, letters and discarded attempts, and who has throughout given her unstinted support to me in my endeavours.

Last but not least I owe a great debt of thanks to my publishers, and Richard York in particular, who replied very positively and with unexpected speed to my initial approach and without whose enthusiasm and subsequent help and advice, my manuscript would, in all probability, have been left to gather dust among other family papers.

Joseph Gurney Pease
November 1992

INTRODUCTION

In 1907, my father published *The Diaries of Edward Pease (1767-1858)*, his Quaker great grandfather. Before doing so, he pondered at length about - as he put it - *"placing my prosy old ancestor in the public stocks, perhaps to be pelted by scoffers and critics."*

I have pondered, I suspect, at still greater length about 'going public' with extracts from the diaries and journals in my hands, principally those written by my father and, so far as they overlap the period covered by him, those of the diaries of my grandfather, Sir Joseph Whitwell Pease. Lest some explanation for this exposure be considered necessary, I give it at the outset to this preamble.

It is of lasting regret to me that Edward Pease's diaries, or such of them as had survived for my father to refer to for his biography, have either disappeared or been destroyed. The diaries of his son Joseph Pease (1799-1872) are incomplete, an unquantifiable number of them having disappeared during the past fifty years. It is therefore, not just that the journals forming the subject of this book are an almost complete record of a fascinating life, but also my fear of any similar fate awaiting my grandfather's and father's diaries, that I give as the only explanation for what follows.

Background to the Diaries and Journals

Before my father Alfred Edward Pease's time, five generations of the family had been Quakers living and working in Darlington, Co. Durham.

During the forty years before Alfred was born, that is to say from about 1820, many changes and additions to the family's business interests had come about. The foundation enterprise was in woolcombing in Darlington. This concern became known as Henry Pease & Co's Spinning and Weaving Mills, and from 1761,[1] a small banking sideline was operated in conjunction with the mills.

This sideline, later referred to as the Counting House, grew into a separate business, but in one respect differed from other banks. As it developed, the Counting House partners discontinued the practice of taking deposits from the general public. As a bank, it issued its own cheques and the numerous members of the family all held their accounts there. As the Pease's range of activities expanded, the role of the Counting House grew in importance as a generator of finance to aid further growth in the new developing family concerns. In time, a few isolated largish companies, ones over which the Peases had some influence but without exclusive control, also held their accounts there. The first of these was the Stockton and Darlington Railway.

By about 1820, Alfred's great grandfather, Edward Pease, while still in his early fifties withdrew from active business, and handed over the management of the Mills to his three sons. John Pease, the eldest of these three, was a recorded Minister in the Society of Friends. It was, however, Edward Pease's two younger sons Joseph and Henry, particularly the former, who later evidenced great business drive.

With the Mills left in the disciplined and capable young hands of his sons, Edward Pease turned his attention to other matters. The problem of finding an easier means of transporting coals from the South Durham coalfields to the port of Stockton interested him. He advocated a tramway. Others preferred a canal from Stockton to a point just north of Yarm-on-Tees, and a tramway from the coalfields to the canal. Edward was joined in this debate by his second son Joseph, who argued fiercely against the alternative canal plan both because it would add greatly to the construction costs, and, of still greater importance, because a canal and a tramway would involve the unnecessary double handling of coals.

George Stephenson, learning of Edward's interest in a tramway, called upon him at Darlington one day in 1821, and suggested a track where wagons were drawn not by horses but by a steam locomotive of a kind that he had perfected. Edward became enthusiastic about this idea, and in due course put up a good share of the money for the Stockton and Darlington Railway, and also became a partner with George Stephenson, and George's young son Robert, in a locomotive manufacturing business at Newcastle. This business continued with Stephensons and Peases in partnership, (or as directors after incorporation) for two more generations, Stephensons providing the day-to-day management and the majority shareholding.

Joseph Pease was elected as the first Quaker Member of Parliament, an event that caused his father, Edward, very much distress at the time, since he saw his son's entry into politics as the

"... giving way to displays of popular feeling, drinking and lampooning!"

Edward's fears were groundless, and Joseph, who promised that he would not canvass for support, nor ask any man for his vote, nor go to any expense to promote his own election, was duly elected and remained Liberal M.P. for South Durham for nine years from 1832-1841. In time, Joseph's eldest son, Joseph Whitwell Pease, came to represent the same constituency, or after boundary changes, some part of it, a seat which he retained for 38 years eventually becoming the Father of the House of Commons. For a period in between, Joseph Whitwell Pease's uncle, Henry Pease, held the seat.

In 1827, five years before launching himself into politics, Joseph Pease embarked upon the purchase of collieries in South Durham, and it was not long before the Peases were the largest colliery owners in the county. Twenty or so years later - by the 1850s - when ironstone deposits were found in Cleveland, the family joined in the scramble to exploit this discovery. During the period 1823 until the mid 1850s therefore, and at the point where the story begins, the Peases' business activities had developed to embrace:

1. The Darlington spinning and weaving mills, (Henry Pease & Co.) generally referred to simply as *The Mills.*
2. *The Counting House* (J. & J.W. Pease) - otherwise known as the Banking Department, and which assumed greater importance after it came to hold the banking account for the Stockton and Darlington Railway.
3. *The Collieries* (Joseph Pease and Partners).
4. *The Ironstone Mines* (J.W. Pease & Co.). Later, in 1882, the colliery and ironstone mining operations were brought together under the single management of *Pease and Partners Ltd.*

Now in addition, in 1828, Joseph Pease, seeing that advantages would accrue from building a port closer to the mouth of the River Tees - thereby supplanting Stockton in importance - joined forces with his relatives to buy 520 acres of land at Middlesbrough. This place was then no more than a community of about 40 souls, a few dwellings and a farm house. The price paid for the site upon which the town now stands was £35,000[2], and the partnership (incorporated at a much later date) was known as

5. *The Middlesbrough Owners* (following incorporation known as *The Owners of the Middlesbrough Estate Ltd., or in short, O.M.E.* The partners set about building docks, wharves, houses, roads and streets and attracting other industries to this new site, and extending the Stockton and Darlington Railway to the infant town. Coals could now be shipped from Middlesbrough, and by the time that the Cleveland ironstone deposits were opened up, the ore could be transported from their workings to the smelting furnaces in Middlesbrough and County Durham.

In four of these five concerns, Joseph Whitwell Pease sooner rather than later held the dominant overall position. The Darlington Mills were the domain of his uncle, Henry Pease, and his son Henry Fell Pease. But Joseph Whitwell Pease became drawn into the muddled affairs of this business.

There were two secondary ranking concerns, (in the sense only that they were not exclusively Pease controlled) in which the family had a substantial stake, and these were:

1. *The Stockton and Darlington Railway* itself, until it became amalgamated in 1863 with the North Eastern Railway. Thereafter five members of the family held N.E.R. directorships at different times, and were large holders of railway stock in that undertaking.
2. *Robert Stephenson & Co.,* - locomotive and marine engine manufacturers at Newcastle, and shipbuilders at Hebburn.

To these two, we may add a few companies majority-owned and managed by Pease relatives, but in which Joseph Whitwell Pease and his brothers had some stake. These were more in the nature of satellite interests:

3. *Wilson Pease & Co.,* were ironmasters in Middlesbrough. A recent potted history of this company may be summarised as follows:

Between 1865 and 1883 the firm was known as Hopkins Gilkes & Co., Tees-side Iron & Engine Works. Isaac Wilson (the Liberal M.P. for Middlesbrough, a North Eastern Railway director and cousin of Sir Joseph Whitwell Pease) was (with Edgar Gilkes) a partner in this company.

At some stage the company ceased the manufacture of engines and directed all efforts towards bridge building. Hopkins Gilkes & Co. had taken over the completion of the Tay Bridge which, because of a design fault and bad workmanship, collapsed in a storm plunging a train and carriages into the swirling waters below - taking with it seventy-five passengers to their deaths. Following the disaster, Edgar Gilkes (totally distraught) pulled out of the company. Four years later, in 1883, the works closed, but re-opened the following year as *Wilson Pease & Co.*

4. *Isaac Wilson & Co.,* - Middlesbrough potteries.
5. *William Whitwell & Co.,* Ironmasters & foundrymen, Thornaby-on-Tees.

Joseph Whitwell Pease, whose continuous diary entries start in 1856 when he was aged twenty-seven, had four years earlier started to take on the responsibility for the day-to-day conduct of family business affairs. His father at some time in the 1850s began to suffer from diminishing sight.

This book, then, has its beginnings in days when the family was near to the pinnacle of business success through the expanding railway system, the colliery districts of South Durham, the ironstone district of Cleveland and the developing Middlesbrough. The once profitable Mills were from the early 1870s kept going at a fearful cost, not for any rational business reason (unless hope for better times be counted as one), but partly out of sentiment. To abandon the foundation business would be a kick against family roots in Darlington. A further reason for keeping the Mills going, would be their awareness as considerable employers of labour in the town, that the social consequences and hardship resulting from closure would be extreme.

As Quakers, a very small and tightly knit body of people, who in the early days, 'married out' only in the certain knowledge of being 'disowned', it became inevitable that over several generations of marriages between families of Friends, they frequently created double, treble, or more complex relationships in all manner of directions - at times positively brain-spinning and confusing.

The more obvious consequence of this was a great trellis of very close inter-family community of interest. With so many Quaker connections, the Peases had a shared, parallel, or else complementary identity with the business concerns of many other Quaker families who were universally dubbed "cousins" - no matter how remote the relationship. The Pease Quaker relationship directly or indirectly embraced Backhouses, Barclays, Fowlers, Fox's, Frys, Gurneys, Lloyds's, Richardsons, Whitwells, Wilsons, and a whole host of others.

Mixed up with generating success in business, was the philanthropic aspect of the Quakers. In the Peases' case, this was manifested by the gratuitous building of schools, libraries, institutes, missions, alms houses and other good works for the benefit of the community generally, and the families of their employees in particular. Joseph Pease had been a prolific and generous provider of all these, as had his father before him, and Joseph Whitwell Pease saw it as a duty to follow in this tradition. An extension of this 'giving' came with financial assistance to any of the family in difficulty - business or otherwise - and it didn't stop there, but at times, and in the interests of the district, extended to aid to the business undertakings of others outside the family and the Quaker fold.

Though Alfred's journals start in 1880, when he was twenty- three years of age, by recourse to random notes he made in 1916-17, we can reach back further, to glimpse briefly some of his first impressions, and to things that influenced him for life.

The period covered by this book is an almost unbroken one of eighty-three years, from 1857 to 1939: from wealth and unbridled success to catastrophe and financial ruin. From that point on, when in middle life, Alfred, in a display of great adaptability to very changed circumstances - not simply making a virtue of necessity - continued to live, much as he had before, a life of unchanging interest. Indeed, he saw the loss of his anticipated inheritance as 'salvation', and any serious attempt to regain the former position of wealth ranked pretty low on his scale of priorities. His was a life of riches of another kind; that which comes from variety of experience and which can never be lost or taken away.

In matters of faith, Alfred moves from the Quaker tradition to the established church, and though not altogether willingly embraced, it was an attempt at compromise; to achieve inward spiritual satisfaction on terms acceptable to him, without accepting the strict ordinance of either Church or Friend.

My original intention was to publish only my father's journals, believing that his life provided all the material for a long enough book. But re-reading in conjunction, through the 23 years of diary overlap (1880-1903) of my grandfather and father, I felt that, if I could handle it, a more complete picture could be given, by extracting some of Joseph Whitwell Pease's entries.

The principal location for this narrative is in Cleveland, (at that time a district in Yorkshire); that part of the north east bordering on the river Tees to the north and the Cleveland Hills and the North Yorkshire Moors to the south. *"A little scrap of country"* as Alfred called it, but one which had a tremendous and powerful pull over him - a magnetic intangible, the secret of which may I hope be found somewhere in this book.

It is a most difficult thing to express atmosphere in words alone. Words convey ideas, and express feelings and emotions, and then it is left to the reader to draw upon experience to conjure up something of what is meant. The real recipe to recreate atmosphere is not just sight and sound, but the sense of smell to overlay everything. To me, a mental re-awakening of childhood impressions returns (without proper regard to the seasons of the year) by a kind of kaleidoscopic heady mixture from the scent of daffodils, sweet peas, lilac, and roses - the smell of one suggesting the smell of others - the intoxicating pungency of each and all of them - a garden and house heavy and loaded with the fragrance of flowers - add to that the odour from burning methylated spirits (to keep the silver tea time kettle hot) mixed with the warm fresh smell of new mown lawns (breezing through the open library window) and - dare I say it - the aromatics of the finest mild Egyptian cigarettes. That was something of the flavour of my father Alfred's home.

Though in his published works Alfred touched upon some of the events in this book, his anecdotes were drawn frequently from other supplementary material or memory. His journals are more crowded with revelations of his inner feelings than any of his published works. His complaint about his father's diaries was that Joseph Whitwell Pease revealed all too little of his true self.

The directness with which my father sometimes addressed his journals has created for me a difficult problem in making material selection. Frequently he put to paper views formed in haste, which sometimes after due reflection were revised or modified, and his extravagant excesses he either obliterated or cut out with scissors. In that sense then, he has edited them. So is what I am doing right and fair? Another thought - one overriding the fear of misused trust - is that I feel it was my father's view, my mother's also, that placed in the 'right hands', there was much material for a book far beyond the scope of his own publications.

It is not that I consider mine to be the 'right hands' to do this, but because of an undiminished love and almost obsessive admiration for the man and father and his extraordinary life, that I took it upon myself to record, I hope in complete sympathy with him, what I see as the most interesting parts of his life, told so far as possible in words of quote.

Throughout his life, Alfred seems dogged by controversy, friction, irritation and difficulty of one sort or another - but rarely could it be said of him that he was unhappy. He had the facility to cope well with adversity, and would quickly draw out some redeeming feature from the blackest of situations.

Exposing to public light any family antagonisms is something about which I am acutely sensitive; but in part, such is the story, and I have no choice - and avoidance would simply render the whole undertaking worthless. It is only with the passage of time when all the dust of storms has settled, that I feel publication is possible. Nevertheless, from what is written, some impressions gained should at least be tempered by charity, and I feel it necessary to single out for particular mention my father's attitude to his sister-in-law, his brother Jack's wife, Elsie, daughter of General Sir Henry Havelock-Allan. Perhaps it was not without valid reason that Alfred came to be rather scathing about her.

The selected references to Elsie are not many, but from such as there are, an impression may be gained that from start to finish, she was a snob, a determined, quick-tempered and manipulating woman ambitious for herself socially, and for her husband, Jack, politically. True, she did have these characteristics in varying strengths, and at a distance it delights and amuses me too.

There is however another aspect to the paradoxical Elsie - one to be found nowhere in these journals - and it is this. My mother, who would brook no criticism of Elsie from any quarter, and who as my father's third wife, was cut dead by many of my father's relations in the early years of her marriage, always said of her that *"She at no time showed me anything but the greatest kindness and friendship"*. My mother maintained a total silence to the grave about the sea of hostility through which she herself had once lived, and of what hurt she endured, and it is when I think of Elsie in the context of that period, that this very simple truth of kindness shown speaks volumes of an endearing quality in her that without mention now, would most unfairly remain concealed for ever.

Such was the strength of family bonds over all the years, that though some bitter feuding rears up through the pages of this book, when all was done, and in the end, in every possible instance I can find, either relationships were mended, or a friendly gesture made, an indication that past animosity was put aside, peace made, an example set and the stage tidied before departing from the scene of life. I find that very right, very moving and most gratifying, and the magnanimity and appeal of it all serves only to increase my enormous pride in the family to which I belong.

In compiling this record I recall many locations where earlier events in the book took place. Quite by chance I came to know Hurstbourne Park (eleven years after her death) where Beatrice Countess of Portsmouth lived and died, and the experience made fascination more engaging, the thought of the conflict between the two homes, the one, my grandfather's at Hutton, in Cleveland, the other, his niece's at Hurstbourne in Hampshire.

My inadequacies have proved no deterrent to the task of sifting and selecting from a mass of material, in an attempt to conjure up for Alfred's other descendants something of him, his sense of values and influence, a little of which spilled over into the lives of all his children. But the book is also in great measure a tribute to the three women in his life, each having in very different ways great burdens to bear.

By daytime and evening for many months, I have travelled in my mind with my father to many places, and all has given me boundless pleasure and enjoyment; and if in my own case, I shared his life for but a short eleven years, my memory of him is long, vivid, and my gratitude great, just to have been born one of his.

Notes:
1. Sir Alfred E. Pease in "The Diaries of Edward Pease" gives the starting date of the Counting House as 1765, but closer examination reveals 1761 as the earliest entry of a deposit taken.
2. The Deeds show £30,000 as the purchase price, but the terms of payment were £10,000 on 13th May, 1829 and £25,000 on 13th May, 1830.

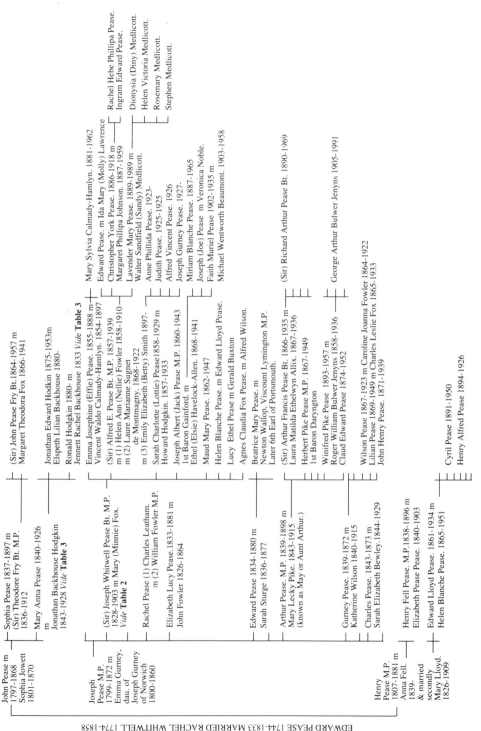

EDWARD PEASE 1744-1833 MARRIED RACHEL WHITWELL 1774-1858

Table 2 Connections through the (Falmouth) Fox Family

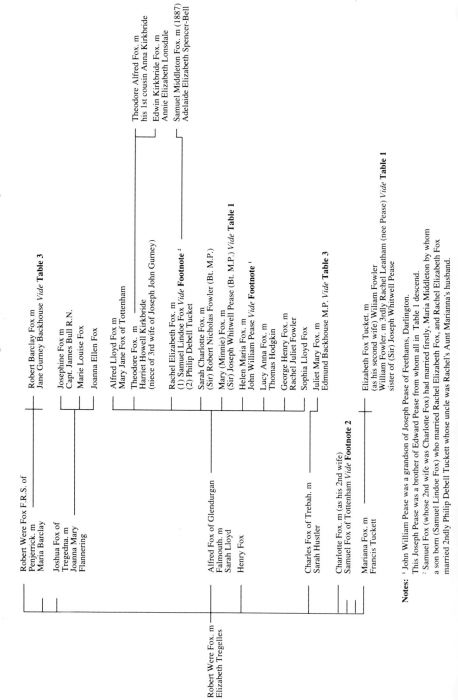

Notes:
[1] John William Pease was a grandson of Joseph Pease of Feethams, Darlington. This Joseph Pease was a brother of Edward Pease from whom all in Table 1 descend.

[2] Samuel Fox (whose 2nd wife was Charlotte Fox) had married firstly, Maria Middleton by whom a son born (Samuel Lindoe Fox) who married Rachel Elizabeth Fox, and Rachel Elizabeth Fox married 2ndly Philip Debell Tuckett whose uncle was Rachel's Aunt Marianna's husband.

Table 3   Connections through the Backhouse Family

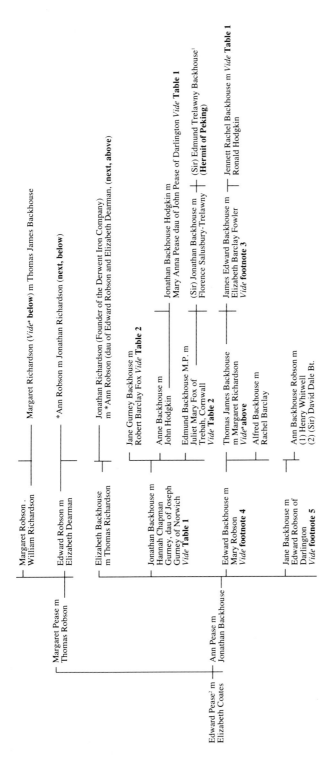

Margaret Robson .
William Richardson

Margaret Richardson (*Vide* **below**) m Thomas James Backhouse

Margaret Pease m
Thomas Robson

Edward Robson m
Elizabeth Dearman

*Ann Robson m Jonathan Richardson (**next, below**)

Elizabeth Backhouse
m Thomas Richardson

Jonathan Richardson (Founder of the Derwent Iron Company)
m *Ann Robson (dau of Edward Robson and Elizabeth Dearman, (**next, above**)

Jonathan Backhouse m
Hannah Chapman
Gurney, dau of Joseph
Gurney of Norwich
Vide **Table 1**

Jane Gurney Backhouse m
Robert Barclay Fox *Vide* **Table 2**

Anne Backhouse m
John Hodgkin

Jonathan Backhouse Hodgkin m
Mary Anna Pease dau of John Pease of Darlington *Vide* **Table 1**

Edmund Backhouse M.P. m
Juliet Mary Fox of
Trebah, Cornwall
Vide **Table 2**

(Sir) Jonathan Backhouse m
Florence Salusbury-Trelawny

(Sir) Edmund Trelawny Backhouse[1]
(**Hermit of Peking**)

Edward Pease[2] m
Elizabeth Coates

Ann Pease m
Jonathan Backhouse

Edward Backhouse m
Mary Robson
Vide **footnote 4**

Thomas James Backhouse
m Margaret Richardson
Vide **above**

James Edward Backhouse m
Elizabeth Barclay Fowler
Vide **footnote 3**

Jennett Rachel Backhouse m *Vide* **Table 1**
Ronald Hodgkin

Alfred Backhouse m
Rachel Barclay

Jane Backhouse m
Edward Robson of
Darlington
Vide **footnote 5**

Ann Backhouse Robson m
(1) Henry Whitwell
(2) (Sir) David Dale Bt.

---

1. The extraordinary life of Sir Edmund Backhouse was written by Professor Hugh Trevor-Roper and first published in 1976 under the title 'A Hidden Life: The Enigma of Sir Edmund Backhouse', published by Macmillan London Ltd 1976, and first published in the United States of America by Alfred A. Knopf Inc., 1977. A later edition with revisions was published by Penguin Books 1978 under the title 'Hermit of Peking'.
2. Edward Pease who married Elizabeth Coates was the great great granfather of Sir Joseph Whitwell Pease.
3. Elizabeth Barclay Fowler was daughter of Henry Fowler and Ann Ford Barclay. Henry Fowler was son of John Fowler of Chapel Knap who was brother of Thomas Fowler, father of (Sir) Robert Nicholas Fowler Bt.
4. Mary Robson was the elder daughter of Edward Robson (1763-1813) and Elizabeth Dearman.
5. Edward Robson (1791-1819) was the elder son of Edward Robson (1763-1813) and Elizabeth Dearman.

An extract from *Random Notes* written circa 1916:

"The physical and moral diversity of mankind is infinite. Yet it is easier to understand, that from the first man to the last on this earth, there can be no two human beings identical in either form or character, than to conceive the variety in human experience. No two lives can ever be the same, no two brains think about, no two pair of eyes observe, no two pair of ears hear nor two tongues tell in identical manner the things of the time in which they pass, from the mystery of birth to the gateway of death ...

I have not been remarkably successful. Where my life has failed in distinction (for which I really have not had much ambition) it contained a wealth of happiness and many bitter trials and experiences ...

The year of my birth was 1857, the twentieth of the reign of Queen Victoria - It was the year of the Indian Mutiny, the massacre at Cawnpore ...

Alfred E. Pease.

CHAPTER ONE

Casting the Die (1857-1884)

Early Years (1857-1879)
Alfred Edward Pease was the second in age in a family of eight children
of Joseph Whitwell Pease[1] and his wife Mary, (Minnie). Of course his
parents were a great influence upon him, especially his mother. She
came from Falmouth, one of the Fox's of Glendurgan. Of his mother
Alfred says:

> "She was all her life a most lovely sweet sympathetic and charming clever
> woman. She was full of joy and never for a moment anything but perfect in dignity
> and manner and engaging womanliness."

She was just a few days beyond her nineteenth birthday when she
married in August, 1854 from the Bank House at Falmouth, and Joseph
was twenty-six:

> "He possessed the highest spirits, was full of energy, enjoyed everything, was
> keen in business, politics and sport. He was a fighting, persevering, indomitable
> man in most ways, like his father before him, impatient of opposition and given
> rather to baiting those with different opinions. He was 5'10½" high, very erect,
> held his head well up ..."

Joseph's home was then Woodlands, situated on the western edge
of Darlington. At the time of his marriage, the town had a population of
about 12,000. Darlington was Quaker-dominated with its affairs in the
control of Peases and Backhouses, the two families being related. The
Backhouses were bankers in Darlington, their offices situated in the
main thoroughfare on High Row.

We have seen from the introduction something of the range of the
Peases' main business interests at the time of Alfred's birth in 1857.
After the Stockton and Darlington Railway amalgamated with the North

1

Eastern Railway in 1863 (upon which event his father was made a director) railways took on the aspect of a more impersonal business involvement, and played no part in Alfred's later life.

Of Joseph's five brothers alive in 1857, three had died by the time twenty-three years later that Alfred started to write up his journals. This left Joseph (b 1828) the eldest, and the next two brothers in age, Edward (b 1834) and Arthur (b 1837). In addition to these two surviving brothers, Joseph had four sisters, two of whom were married.

As a child Alfred was more in awe of his Uncle Arthur than any of the others:

> "One fault he had, of staring at you, a sort of religious glare, and he was fond of talking, gossiping and anecdote ... After every good story he told he would stare or glare at you with a smile & say 'What? ... What? ...' or just stare - till you showed you had fully appreciated it."

The person next in importance to his mother in his childhood years was his nanny, Sarah Wilson. She was a small, plump, very strict but loving woman, born in 1818, and brought up at Runswick Bay in Cleveland; *"a typical Cleveland woman in every way"* who spoke the dialect; a most devout practising Wesleyan, who lived in the fear of God and impressed upon the children under her care, how she had been "saved" for the Lord. Her discipline was imposed less by her hand than by a reminder to her charges of the fate awaiting the wicked upon the awful Day of Judgement.

Alfred loved his father's Darlington home, but he had a greater love for old Hutton Hall near Guisborough. This was a house to which Joseph took the family for a month or more each summer. Quite early in his married life Joseph had rented the old Hall together with the shooting over a large surrounding area. He had though another interest there, having bought in the 1850s the Royalties to mine for ironstone at Codhill on the hills above Hutton. In the year of Alfred's birth, the output from these Hutton mineworkings alone was 314,789 tons, but within a decade of that date they had ceased production.

One of Alfred's early childhood memories of the old Hutton Hall was of summer evenings:

> "... watching the mine horses trooping down the hill behind our house in the afternoon, going to the farm walled in pond *(sic)* beyond the snowberry belt, & then returning past our schoolroom window down to the great red roofed stables, (where there was stabling round the great yard for perhaps 80 horses) all flagged round with (a) red alum shale centre."

2

In 1862, Joseph bought an estate at Pinchinthorpe two miles west of Guisborough. During the next three years he added to this by buying the adjoining Hutton Estate (of summer visits) and other farm lands. These combined properties were in extent some 2,700 acres. But home was still Darlington and remained so until 1867.

When Alfred was eight years old in 1865, his father contested the two-member South Durham constituency and came top of the poll. This event meant a great change in life for the family:

> "From 1865 onwards we all went to London about Easter time and remained there until the end of July, generally with an interval of a week or two at Falmouth at Whitsuntide."

During his first years as an M.P. Joseph had a London home in Princes Gardens before finally buying a much more prestigious house, 24 Kensington Palace Gardens[2] which became home during the long parliamentary sessions.

Whilst Alfred was still a small boy, Joseph had already taken the lead from his father in carrying the burdens and responsibilities for the various businesses in which the family was engaged. He was later described by one source as having become, among a family of merchant princes, *"the industrial king of South Durham"*.

During these early years, Joseph was establishing himself in a rather more elevated style of home and estate than any previously embarked upon by other members of the family. Emulating other Victorian industrialists, and being greatly attracted to country living, he had bought his Cleveland properties with the resolve to remove from Darlington and to make his permanent home at Hutton.

Here in the new surroundings, in a quiet fertile valley edged to the south by pine - oak - and birch-covered hill slopes, and with great tracts of moorland heather above, he could indulge in country pursuits whenever free from the demands of business and politics.

Guisborough, little more than a mile from Hutton, had at this time about 2,000 inhabitants; a small market town shielded by the Eston Hills and Barnaby Moor from the smoke and industry of Middlesbrough nine or so miles distant by road to the north.

Only the northern night sky above the Eston Hills betrayed the immense activity beyond the valley. In winter, the clouds in the night sky billowed bright orange from the blast of the furnaces over the hill, the colour reflecting downwards to make even snow appear warm, the

1. Sir Joseph Whitwell Pease at Hutton Hall.

brilliance slowly diminishing until a few minutes later a fresh blast would illuminate the sky.

In early life, Alfred quickly came to form a very definite view about his father's and grandfather's involvement in the great business enterprises of Middlesbrough and County Durham:

> "I disliked from childhood the spoiling industrial hand of my family, who thought they were always doing good work in providing more and more employment for the people. I could see as a boy that the more they did this, the more families of boys would be produced for whom more and more mines and pits and factories would have to be made, till our lovely world would be ash heaps and chimneys and hideous houses under smoke clouds."

All that his father was doing in business was in awful contrast with Hutton, its surroundings and Alfred's summertime childhood country impressions, and of the old Hall which had

> "... the charm of antiquity, and of old gardens and in a sweet corner of the Cleveland Hills.
> Old Hutton gardens were old world. Our nursery door and window opened onto a rose garden with China, York and Lancaster gloria mundi and old fashioned roses interspersed with little box edged beds of verbena, blue salvia and such things ... The side of the house was half covered by an enormous jargonelle pear tree, the leaves of which flapped against the window of the bedroom in which I and my little brother Jack[3] slept."

From the time that Joseph bought Hutton, he started to make sweeping changes. A plan of grand design was put into execution. A new Hutton Hall of dramatic proportions was to be built on a carefully chosen site, and the old Hall that Alfred so much loved demolished.

> "By 1867 a new Hutton and new gardens had sprung up, the old corn fields and whinny pastures were laid into park, the old hedgerows disappeared, fine roads took the place of old lanes and bridle paths and bridges replaced fords and stepping stones."

The new Hall, built in domestic gothic style, of brick with stone dressings, architected by Alfred Waterhouse, had two halls, a billiards and five reception rooms, 40 bed and dressing rooms, five bathrooms, a conservatory, a winter garden ninety-one feet in length with central tiled walk, and a fernery. In the vast cellars reached by any of three staircases was a completely equipped Turkish bath with tiled and marble walls and floors, cooling room, weighing room, dairy, scullery, and laundry with washing and drying rooms, furnace room, and wine and beer cellars.

The garden and grounds were attractively laid out with weeping elm and cedars of Lebanon, clumps of rhododendrons and other flowering shrubs, and had a broad terraced walk which led to the Italian garden.

There was stabling for twenty-four horses, bothy house, head gardener's house, coachman's house, thirteen greenhouses - six or seven of these free-standing - and in time, these and the extensive kitchen gardens yielded up grapes, melons, oranges, bananas, pineapples, figs, apricots, peaches, nectarines, plums and pears. Beyond the Hall there was created a miniature lake called "the pond" which was stocked with trout. "The pond" was complemented by a boat house with a tea room above.

All this was worked into a modest fifty-four acres of private grounds.

Close by, a mere three or four minutes' walk from the new Hall, was Hutton Railway Station. Alfred's father and grandfather had promoted the railway line from Middlesbrough to Guisborough[4] in 1851, and to improve the new Hall facilities, Joseph uprooted the old station, shifting it a few hundred yards to the end of his back driveway. He gave it distinctive embellishments befitting the private station of a railway director.

With the accumulated wealth of three or four generations of family enterprise, and expectations of greater fortune to come, it may be that Joseph's new and immense residence and appendages were created to symbolise commercial success to date. A luxurious style of living was justified, so it might be argued, not simply for its own sake, but because show was 'good for credit,' 'standing' and all that kind of thing. But a more truly shocking display of ostentation quite contrary to "Quaker principles" it was hard to conceive. The advice given by Joseph's grandfather, old Edward Pease, himself a wealthy man, had always been for keeping to quiet and modest containment in matters of this kind.

When he was a small boy at Hutton, Alfred's chief friends were the old estate mole-catcher called Blanchard, and the estate gamekeeper, William Briggs.

Blanchard was an uninstructed naturalist. He fascinated Alfred with his knowledge, and taught him all the local names for birds such as cuddies, throstles, linnies, green-linnies, bull spinks, jenny-hullots, peckatrees, nanpies, and those beyond habitation, upon the hill tops, the moor bods. These colourful local names gave a greater depth of meaning to what he saw and learnt.

William Briggs, Joseph's head gamekeeper, had come to Hutton from Northumberland in the late 1850s. He spoke with a broad Northumbrian accent which gave added emphasis to the curses he directed at the dogs when they disgraced themselves on shooting days. He had a whistle which he blew furiously when grouse driving on the moors, and his whisper could be heard over a vast distance. Joseph had to speak to Briggs about the cursing, but his rough cut way was the greater part of his amiable character, and these singular traits would bring a smile to the face of any who heard him.

"There was no-one like him to look on. Sturdy, sinewy, as he stood by the kennel door in his knee breeches, muscular legs encased in thick worsted stockings, his shirt sleeves turned back displaying his brown brawny arms and his determined intelligent face bordered with a short grizzled beard. I think shaving his upper lip added to the expression of will about his face, and even his hands were quite his own down to the stiff jointed crooked, crippled little finger upon which, as a small boy I looked with wonder and thought somewhat uncanny."

It was Briggs who first taught Alfred and his brother Jack to handle a gun in the days of the old Hutton Hall before all the changes had been brought about, and

"... who initiated us into all the secrets of shooting and the kennel, who was our constant companion for weeks in every year from our schoolroom days ... I can see him at the old kennels at Hutton where 'the pond' is now, coming in from his days work, carrying my father's gun and followed by four weary pointers, and I can hear him silence a noisy occupant of the kennel at a word, and later on, when he removed to the cottage under the hill, how I used to meet him there and watch him load the muzzle loader, hand it to me and tell me to 'hold that fast' and laugh as I staggered under the recoil and watch master cocksparrow fly away none the worse."

"I didn't get on intimate terms with Briggs till the time came when I was able to shoot rabbits in the summer evenings ... and with what eagerness I rushed out to meet Briggs waiting at the back door with the gun and game bag and his retriever 'Sam' ... He used to walk behind me down the green rides and cover sides and sometimes touch my elbow and point a bunny out to me and whisper 'tak t'ium sir' or 'give it him'. I can go those rounds again in my mind and feel all the surroundings. The close warm, sunny evening, the bothering myriads of flies, the perspiration running down my face."

Joseph always made time for his children at the end of a day's work. Though he loved them all equally, of his two sons he came in time to view Jack as the one more moulded in his own image. Jack was simply

7

a nickname given by his father to Joseph Albert Pease *"owing to some fancy that ... he resembled a cob named Jack-a-Dandy,"* - so Jack he became, and the name stuck with him through life, though Joseph alone reverted to calling him Albert after he grew up.

The new Hutton Hall, its grounds and stables, was almost completed by December, 1867, when the first of the furniture was moved in from Woodlands, Darlington. So it was from here each morning by an early train that Joseph went the twenty miles to his work in Darlington.

Until the amalgamation of the Stockton and Darlington Railway with the North Eastern Railway, it was Joseph's habit to go first to the railway offices, and then to the Counting House - J. & J.W. Pease's Bank. He very regularly went to the collieries and gave close attention to the day-to-day business at these places.

After Joseph's election to Parliament, the management of the collieries was largely undertaken by David Dale, who had been brought into the colliery business some twenty years earlier in about 1845, at a time before the Derwent Iron Company at Consett, founded and run by Jonathan Richardson - a Pease relative - ran into financial difficulties. Joseph put David Dale into the Derwent Iron Company to re-establish it on a sound footing, and it was renamed the Consett Iron Company.

From 1864, during August each year, Alfred's father took a Scottish moor for the grouse season. That year it was Farr, then two seasons at Clashnadorroch and then Cluny until finally for twenty-two seasons, from 1870 until 1891, he rented Corndavon Lodge, near Crathie from the Invercauld Estates.

There was an established routine to Joseph's life throughout each year. Christmas and New Year were spent at Hutton Hall where there was always a huge family gathering. At Easter time the family moved to London, to 24 Kensington Palace Gardens. Here they remained until Whitsuntide when Joseph took his family to his Falmouth home, Kerris Vean. This was a house he had bought in the 1870s together with a farm at Bosveal. The holiday at Falmouth was taken chiefly for sea fishing, and here Joseph kept his steam-yacht *'the Roseberry'*, skippered by Capt. Green, who always had a fourteen-foot boat in tow.

After two or three weeks at Falmouth, the family returned to London until the summer, when Hutton Hall came back into its own until about 10th August, when bag and baggage was packed off for Scotland and Corndavon Lodge for the grouse season, deer stalking and some

2. Hutton Hall and 'the pond'.

fishing. The family then returned to Hutton.

Between these regular perambulations, and where they could be fitted in, there were holidays taken abroad. From his Hutton and London homes, whichever served as base according to the calendar, periodic trips were made to York for North Eastern Railway Board Meetings frequently combined with visits to the Darlington Counting House, the collieries, Mills, Middlesbrough Owners and Stephensons Locomotive works at Newcastle.

In 1872, Alfred's grandfather (Joseph Pease senior) died at his home at Darlington. His grandmother[5] had died when Alfred was three years old, in 1860.

He makes little mention of his grandfather as an influence in his life except that

> "He could be peevish & irritable in his home and latterly his ill health and blindness were some excuse for this - He could not be called a very happy man, his piety had not made him that, whatever of joy & comfort it gave him, but with children his face lighted up & he became playful with them ..." .

The year 1873 was a most prosperous one for Alfred's father, one in which his income was £154,000. During the twelve years from

1867-1878 he added a little over £400,000 to his capital out of income. There were, however, variations in fortune during the whole of this period, and for the last two years, 1877 and 1878, as trading conditions deteriorated, his domestic expenditure exceeded his income, but not to any appreciable extent.

Until 1867, when Alfred was ten years old, he and the older children had a Swiss governess, and for the last two years before going to boarding school he and his brother Jack had an Irish tutor. These two years, 1867-1869, Alfred came to regard as the most important in his life because

"They gave me, at a receptive age, an intimate acquaintance with my own locality and everyone on the estate. I picked up a great deal of knowledge about farms and farming, knew something about the various breeds of stock, poultry, pigeons, about gardens, forest trees, game, vermin and wild birds - and knew my parents and sisters far better than if it had been my lot to go school at the age of ten.
Probably these two years were the ones of the most unbroken happiness in my life. The one drawback was that it made me love my home, my pony, my dogs, my family life that it was one of the most terrible times in my life when I realised that it was ended for ever, that only holidays, as a sort of visitor to the old scenes should I ever taste its joys again."

Of his early days at Grove House School, Tottenham, Alfred had little to say except that

"I was quick at learning anything that interested me at all, but though I have never been a really lazy man at any time, I avoided doing any work I disliked as much as possible. I read books and devoured all that the school library provided. I collected stamps, eggs, butterflies, kept silk worms, a racing stud of caterpillars and some fighting spiders. I fought a few battles and generally got well hammered. I was not quarrelsome but often a plague and provocative."

After leaving Grove House School and taking his Trinity College Cambridge entrance examination, he was sent off to Embleton in Northumberland to read for the summer with the Rev. Mandell Creighton.[6]

"He (Creighton) had not long been married and had recently taken this living in order to have more time to write books. He had already one pupil, Trevor Berrington ... who became a great friend of mine for life.
Creighton was a short tempered man with a great confidence in himself, a great delight in outrageous propositions and great powers of a certain sort in conversation and argument. He appeared to despise everyone around him save the visitors he hospitably entertained which hailed from Oxford. He had all sorts of

people there from time to time who appeared to me to be most weird and dull ... I never regarded him in any way a religious man but rather as a good actor in the different parts he played. I was always fond of him. He had a warm heart and was faithful to his friends. The things which shocked me were his violent quarrels with his wife alternating with such demonstrations before Berrington and me of affection for Mrs Creighton as I had never seen before. He would have her on his knee in our study or library and they would fondle and kiss each other. No doubt it was a bore to them to have two boys with them in their first years of married life."

Alfred went up to Cambridge in October, 1876. He had decided to go for an honours degree in History.

He took a fairly desultory interest in the subjects he had to read up, spending as much time as possible with the Cambridge Drag Hounds, of which he later became Master, and followed any other pack within striking distance. In all, he enjoyed Cambridge, made a great many friends for life, and only in his last year gave himself up to any serious study, and then worked hard. By the time he was into his last year he had been joined by his brother Jack.

At Whitsuntide, 1878, he went to the Creightons at Embleton together with Jack. Also there were Hugo Charteris and Lord Lymington. The former, *"a nice fellow but bit his nails and told lies but was very clever,"* and the latter, Alfred dismissed as *"a continual joke."*

That year, 1878,

"Hutton was in its glory, & in every way a paradise of perfect felicity in a scene of beauty - we were all young eager & happy ... I was made much of at home & my parents filled the house with visitors between July and January with ... shooting & hunting parties - All the country houses about were full of prosperity, gaiety & young life."

For five or six years prior to his Cambridge days, his first cousin Helen Ann Fowler (always called Nellie) whose mother died a few days after Nellie's eighteenth birthday, was a constant visitor to her aunt and uncle at Hutton. During this time there grew up between Alfred and Nellie a great companionship.

June, 1878, marked Alfred's coming of age, but it wasn't celebrated until 3rd August. There were about 800 at the celebration on that Saturday at Hutton Hall; it included all the department heads from the Collieries, the Counting House, the Mills and the Middlesbrough Owners, farm tenants and legions of relations, all brought to Hutton by special train.[7]

*3. Helen (Nellie) Ann Fowler
as a girl.*

Everyone was feasted in a marquee, and speeches followed. Alfred had been dreading what he thought would be an occasion when he would be made to look a grand fool. That Saturday passed but there was a further celebration on the following Monday, 5th August, to which another 300 had been invited.

In the weeks preceding Alfred's coming of age celebrations, he had fallen in love with Nellie. She was only nineteen years old. Alfred had never entertained the idea of marrying so young, and in any case there were other girls he thought attractive.

What pushed him faster than perhaps he had wanted to go, was alarm at discerning that Trevor Berrington - currently a long stay visitor at Hutton - was falling in love with Nellie. Just as much and more, Alfred could not be certain that -

> "... she did not like both Trevor, Jack and one or two more who showed her marked attention to myself. I talked this over with Trevor who told me more than I shall record, but it came to this. He could not marry. He wished to go to Burmah (sic), and feeling that, he gave up all claim and really wishing I should 'try my luck'.
> On Sunday, August 4th, in the evening at sunset, about 8.30, in the Home Woods, I asked her to become my wife some day, and not without some persuasion and insistence on my part, I got a 'yes' for my question, and I walked back with her over the dewy grass my heart bounding with joy."

The following day, Monday, 5th August, Nellie left Hutton to stay with her Aunt Helen in Northumberland.

"On Tuesday, I got a note from Nellie which induced me to break the news to Mother, which I did after breakfast. She was sweet. In the afternoon I did the same to Father as we were riding along the road past Pinchinthorpe Hall where I summed up my courage to say -
'Father, - I want to tell you I am engaged!!'
'Nonsense boy - nonsense - ridiculous!!'
He evidently was surprised and alarmed. Then he said -
'Well - who is it?'
'It is to Nellie.'
We rode on in silence for a while and then he said -
'I was horribly frightened you were going to say it was your landlady's daughter or someone at Cambridge. I am much relieved. You are too young to think of marrying, but I know no-one who is sweeter than Nellie.'
Then he said had I asked her father? I said 'No,' -
'But you ought to have' &c."

Soon they were in Scotland and in the grouse butts at Corndavon, and Briggs, the gamekeeper from Hutton, attributed all Alfred's misses on 12th August to his happy condition.

"Our engagement was a long one of unbroken trust and happiness at Corndavon, and at Hutton and at Cluny during shooting and deerstalking, in the mountains, by the lochs, on the moors and under the great firs beneath the crags of the Bullochtine."

Back at Cambridge, now joined by Jack that October, 1878, together with a groom and valet, three hunters and terriers, they were lodged at 19, Trinity Street. They both joined the University Polo Club and hunted with the Cambridgeshire, the Fitzwilliam, the Puckeridge, Hick's Harriers and the Drag, and worked hard in between.

Alfred was all his life a bold crashing rider. He loved nothing more than setting a straight course and jumping every obstacle in his path - fence, gate, hedge or ditch. His love of hunting was in the rough exhilarating chase in the company of others, all of which called for quickness of eye and speed of decision. A good hunter needed to be part man, part horse and part hound to make instant communication and understanding possible, bridging the barrier of species. This intimacy with horse and hound, a perfect tripartite relationship, was one of the great joys of the chase, and though it may be purely academic to suggest it, "control" rather than "killing" the justification for the pursuit of the fox. He liked fair play and abhorred the stopping up of a fox's place of refuge and often, if he thought a gamekeeper had stopped an earth for a hunting day, with his intimate knowledge of the country to be hunted, he would rise extra early and open out the earth again.

Alfred spent his last long at Embleton with Hugo Charteris, Lord Lymington and Jack, and then took his degree. There were no first-class honours, but he secured third place in the list of five for second-class honours, and was second of his year. James Mellor Paulton, who was known as 'Harry', and a firm friend of Alfred's, delightful company, a clever actor and very popular, had treated Alfred as an ignoramus, and was *"overpowered with astonishment at the result,"* he having only got his B.A.

1880

Alfred and Nellie Fowler were married on 10th February, 1880 at the Parish Church at Corsham, Wiltshire, where her father, Robert Nicholas Fowler had his home. Fowler was a banker and six years earlier had been a Tory M.P.

Mandell Creighton officiated at the wedding. Nellie's father had left the Society of Friends in 1857 and his children had all been brought up in the established church.

Alfred and Nellie left for their honeymoon touring partly in France but chiefly in Spain, where in the sixth week of their tour news reached them that Parliament had been dissolved.

He had been thinking that at the first opportunity he would seek adoption as a Liberal Candidate. That opportunity now presented itself. The honeymoon was aborted, and they made full speed for home. Upon arrival, making known to his father his wish to stand, he was bluntly told that he had quite enough to do in setting up home this spring. He was however detailed off to help his father and Lord Lambton in the two-member South Durham constituency.

With hindsight, Alfred came to view this decision made by his father as one of two great mistakes of paternal judgement. If it was an understandable decision on Joseph's part, it prevented Alfred from entering Parliament at the most propitious time for the Liberal Party when they swept the country. Joseph comfortably retained his South Durham seat, and Joseph's brother Arthur Pease won at Whitby. Alfred's father-in-law, Robert Nicholas Fowler, now re-entered parliament as Tory M.P. for the City of London, while William Fowler[8] became Liberal M.P. for Cambridge.

With the election over, on Sunday the 11th April, 1880, Alfred was astonished at being told by his father that he was to start his business career - at once - the next day, Monday 12th April.

The second mistake of paternal judgement as Alfred saw it, was not that he was to start work immediately - even though

"I had looked forward to a days hunting after hard election work when my father sprung his decision that I was to begin work at 'the office' the next morning -"

but that

"... He insisted on my going into what he called the Counting House which was really the banking department of which Arthur Pease and he were the partners. I begged to go into the mining or colliery office, but No. I was to go into the place he selected, with Charles Fry."

Charles Fry was not one of the Quaker Fry relations of the Peases. But he

"... was a first class accountant (and) had everything at his finger ends, and would not budge from any of his preconceived ideas and methods - he was very loyal to his employers and to his work - but without any notion of policy or plans - My father relied absolutely upon him after himself in all financial transactions."

So, that Monday morning, with suppressed disappointment, Alfred dutifully went to the Counting House in Northgate, Darlington, and signed his name in the office book for the first time.

Alfred had a restless nature and, having come down from Cambridge with a good degree, he had wanted as soon as possible to be given a sphere of *real* responsibility to show his capabilities. The Counting House didn't match up to his expectations in this respect.

"There was nothing for me to do. I took up each clerk's work in turn, from the bottom to the top, and every one of these poor fellows had a more monotonous and soul killing occupation than the other, from the bottle washer, who had to address envelopes and lick stamps and enter addresses in a book, and the stamps to account for, to the keeper of the ledger, who all his life totted up columns of figures and 'called over' at 3.00pm."

Joseph's motive for putting Alfred into the Bank could have been, that it was both a thoroughly good business grounding, and would give his eldest son an overall view of the various businesses in which his father was engaged.

As part of his wider apprenticeship, he was encouraged to go to the mines, collieries, and mills and to sit in at the meetings of partners. Also delegated to him were such tasks as other members of the family didn't particularly wish to perform, such as prize-giving at the firms' schools and institutes, or opening bazaars and foundation-stone laying. This last was a not infrequent event, consequent upon the proliferating Methodist and Wesleyan chapels, institutes and schools abuilding in and about the countryside and the scattered mining communities of South Durham. The insight gained thereby into other people's lives was something he came to value enormously.

Alfred and Nellie had settled in at their home, Pinchinthorpe House, in April, 1880. Joseph had adapted the house, formerly a farm, into a gentleman's residence - not, it may be said, on the scale of Hutton Hall, from which it was separated by about one and a half miles by the shortest route, through the wood contouring the hill, and past the gamekeeper Briggs's cottage.

If Pinchinthorpe House was much more modest a home, it certainly had the merit of cosy homeliness combined with size enough in which to spread oneself. It had twelve bed and dressing rooms and (at that time) four reception rooms. The delightful main gardens, with lawns, shrubs and flower beds, divided into four parts of unequal size, shape and level, included amongst copper beech, cedar, laburnum, lilac and others, an old apple tree that was the sole survivor from the original farmhouse orchard. The enclosed rose garden was an elysian feature, down the centre of which was a pergola, about a hundred feet in length festooned with heavy scenting roses - and more in the beds to the side. Beyond was a high-walled kitchen garden, in area about 36,000 square feet. In addition, there were plenty of farm outbuildings, and more stabling than Alfred could expect to fill for a good few years.

In June, 1880, came the news of the death of Joseph's brother Edward Pease at Lucerne. This left Joseph and Arthur Pease as the only surviving brothers of Alfred's father's generation. Edward was a widower, his wife Sarah having died in 1877. They had only one child, Beatrice, who now at the time of her father's death was aged fourteen. She came to live with and be brought up by her Uncle Joseph and Aunt Minnie at Hutton Hall, and being in the middle of the same age group as Joseph's three youngest daughters, was treated as another daughter. Indeed she thereafter always called Joseph "Father" - something that seemed to come easily to her.

Beatrice's father had been a good kind uncle to Alfred:

> "... rather curious and eccentric in some ways, and jerky in his manner, but refined and courteous."

Because the deaths at earlier dates of two other brothers[9] had placed great burdens on those remaining, through the survivors having to buy out deceased partners' shares, Edward had given his executors and trustees for Beatrice the widest possible powers to work his assets during the years of Beatrice's minority. The state of his affairs at his decease was such that had his estate been wound up immediately, there would most likely have been nothing left. He had liabilities of about £230,000, and though his business assets were nominally very much in excess of this, as partnership shares, and in the shaky business conditions prevailing since the mid 1870s, they were very much of an unmarketable nature. Joseph and Arthur were their brother Edward's Executors. They were also Trustees for Beatrice.

Alfred attributed the early deaths of his several uncles to their having been teetotal. Arthur, on the other hand

> "... too had been a teetotaller in the earlier part of his life. His health suffered from this abstinence, and his life was prolonged by his having the courage to give up this practice."

Alfred was fairly economical in his references to business in his early journal entries. It was simply routine, and not worth recording except by mention of where he had been - 'Darlington' or 'Middlesbrough' &c. He gave the greatest space to his extra-business activities, and therefore gives a false impression of someone who did little work. That said, there were occasions, as his father noted, when Alfred (and Jack at a later date) sat in at partners' meetings dressed in red hunting-coat, boots and spurs, clearly impatient to get business over.

On a wintry day, 15th December, 1880, Nellie presented Alfred with their first-born, a son who was named Edward. By tradition the eldest son had to be either a Joseph or an Edward.

On New Year's Eve, 1880, while travelling back home in the train from Darlington, Joseph announced to Alfred

> "... that he proposed making me a Partner in J. & J.W. Pease."

Beside this last entry, but many years later, Alfred was moved to add the emphatic comment,

17

"(and the worst thing he ever did for me in his life!)."

Continuing on this theme he said,

"I never had a day or an hour's responsibility, was never once consulted on any matter of importance, and nothing I ever proposed or suggested was ever of the least account with my father or his factotum Charles Fry."

That year 1880 was a follow-on year from Cambridge when many of his university friends were very much in evidence at Pinchinthorpe. In October of that first year of his marriage he became a J.P. for the North Riding of Yorkshire.

The following year, 1881, there was much the same routine pattern in his life, so that the main landmarks only need to be noted:-

1. In mid-summer, his eldest sister "Effie",[10] who had married the previous year, had a daughter. The new-born was christened[11] Mary Sylvia Calmady-Hamlyn. Effie's husband, Vincent Waldo Calmady-Hamlyn, came from a Devonshire family with a long ancestry. He had been studying law at Balliol and was called to the Bar in June 1881.

2. Jack came down from Cambridge and started his business life at the collieries, living at his grandfather's former house known as Southend, in Darlington, with two maiden aunts.

3. On 6th October, 1881, Middlesbrough had a Jubilee to celebrate its half-century as a town. Joseph went to the dinner. Alfred did not:

"I don't see much to jubilate about. My grandfather and his contemporaries managed to lay the foundations of a huge hideous town, a den of misery, dirt and debauchery planted on the once green fields by the banks of the Tees. Out of this place have come huge fortunes and many more lost - we have never made much out of it."

There was a lot of truth in this last statement. In the early years of the partnership in the Middlesbrough Owners, it made but did not distribute profits, and ploughed everything back into building schools, places of worship, roads, drains, streets and lighting and such like, and generally functioned as a very benevolent developer.

1882

On 10th April, 1882, Alfred went with his father to Darlington, for a meeting at West Lodge, the home of David Dale. Those present at the meeting in addition to Alfred and his father were Jack, Arthur Pease, David Dale, Henry Fell Pease and Edward Lloyd Pease (these last two were Joseph's first cousins). After detailed discussion, it was decided to turn the collieries and ironstone departments into a private limited company to be called Pease & Partners with a capital of £2,250,000.

> "I only hope they will turn it into a public company and Father will get rid of some of his shares. He has been looking about & pulling up his expenditure the last day or two as we have shown him his financial condition is not very satisfactory."

In the four years between 1876 and 1880 the Peases' ironstone and limestone business had lost over £60,000 in bad debts, with eight of their customers going to the wall with liabilities of over a million pounds. Now, in 1882, with trading conditions unsettled for the last few years, this led into a very severe depression which lasted, with a few false dawns, until the end of the next decade.

On 13th April, three days following the meeting at David Dale's home Alfred writes:

> "Had an important Mill meeting - this dreadful sink swallows up on average (taking last ten years) £7,000 a year - and ought to be wound up ... the trade prospects are very bad indeed, so it was agreed only to carry them on the very lowest & most limited footing consistent with keeping them going, so that if it was decided to part with them at some not distant time, it could be easily done."

When not attending to his duties at the Counting House, Alfred followed his sporting interests at every opportunity. A further diversion from work was in the time and energy he devoted towards getting a badger colony established on the hills opposite his house, and also at Hutton.

This month, April, 1882 he went off to Hereford to dig for badgers to populate the Pinchinthorpe hillsides so as to be able to observe them closely and learn more about their habits. The day before setting off on his expedition with six terriers, was a Sunday, and after Quaker Meeting at Guisborough, he and Nellie went to lunch at Hutton Hall. There Joseph informed his elder son that in a letter from the Prime Minister (Gladstone) he was being offered a baronetcy, which honour Joseph accepted. Of this Alfred states:

> " ... I am not sure that I like it altogether. Mr Pease has been a good name and a brand new title is rather humiliating & it will take some time getting used to it. They said something about taking it for my sake & Edward's, but I don't feel as I

should outlive my father as I am still troubled with palpitation of the heart & a disordered stomach in spite of a temperate and healthy life."

Alfred had a miss of every fourth heart beat - sometimes more pronounced than at others - sometimes it alarmed him and at others, when totally absorbed in what he was doing, he wasn't greatly conscious of any defect but:

"I shall consider myself fortunate if I live till I am 40 - but whether I do or whether I do not, I trust and hope that death will bring me life. May wealth and prosperity prove a blessing and not a hindrance - & may we, if they are taken away from us, feel thankful that we are driven to more enduring joys. Wealth must be a help to withstand temptations, or rather an assistance to negative virtues, but is rather a hindrance to positive virtues. It is easy to be respectable if rich, but poverty must be the supreme test & discipline."

There was the usual gathering at Corndavon from 9th August, Alfred returning home on 5th September, when Charles Fry went from the Counting House for his annual holidays. By 6th October, Alfred and Jack had returned to Corndavon with their retrievers staying for a further fortnight. This became the customary annual pattern.

1883

On New Year's Day, 1883, the Cleveland Hounds met at Guisborough Cross. This day Alfred had a very bad hunting accident when his horse in jumping a fence fell on top of him into a lane. He broke several ribs, one penetrating a lung, and his collar bone was fractured, and he spent six weeks strapped up in plaster during which time he reflected upon his careless life.

On 8th February, 1883, by now back on his feet but going carefully,

"... dressed warmly & put on an Ulster & was driven down to the train & went to Darlington, to the first Annual General Meeting of Pease & Partners. Jack ... & I were made directors, I having engaged, & Jack similarly, to hand over to Father all dividends over 5%, so that I shall be in no better position, except for the sake of signing than before, as all profits are cut off my allowance."

Alfred received no salary at the Counting House, but instead received an annual allowance of £1,000 a year. It was only in 1890 that he was given a salary of £200 a year. Many years later, family fiction had it that Alfred's allowance had been £10,000 annually, on the supposed grounds that 'he could never have done what he did on less.'

By mid-Summer, 1883, one Smith, from Glasgow had been brought in to report and advise upon the loss-making Peases Mills. On 6th August, 1883,

> "Father and I met Smith, Clarke (Mills Manager), Dale & Hy. Fell (Pease) at Darlington to consider the state of the Mills. We adjourned before making any definite plans In order that Smith should report on the whole concern. They show a heavy loss & I would give up the whole lot ..."

Alfred's mother was unwell this Christmas, and remained in London with Joseph, who saw she was in need of a change in climate when fit to travel.

1884

In February, 1884, Joseph caught a fever (it was thought from defective drains at Hutton) and he and Minnie set out for Biarritz at the end of March, and a few days later joined by Alfred and Nellie. Nellie had miscarried in March, and was also in need of 'recruited health', while Alfred had had another hunting accident in February when his mare had run him into a tree.

Before setting out for Biarritz, Alfred's sister Helen Blanche Pease and Beatrice Pease, both now 18 years old, were presented at Court, and in Joseph's words, *"... both looked sweet - Beatrice quite done up by night - a large party to see them in their war paint."*

Alfred set out with Nellie to join his parents at Biarritz in April:

> "I preferred home to these hardworking tours with my father - he loved methodical sight-seeing, travelled hard & fast to get as much done as possible & always with a courier."

From Biarritz the family party travelled via Toulouse and Carcassone to Nimes at which place they found a telegram from Alfred's cousin Edith Fowler. She was in Algiers with her brother John Fowler. He had gone there for his health but the telegram indicated that he was dying and urged,

> "Please come by boat leaving Port Vendres tomorrow."

It took only minutes to decide that Alfred, a sister (Lottie[12]) and Nellie should proceed at once to Port Vendres close to the Spanish border, from where they could catch the regular steamer to Algiers.

"We arrived at Algiers at 4 a.m. - I shall never forget this, my first view of a new
continent and of this most beautiful bay and old Arab stronghold - it looked
indescribably beautiful at dawn and in the loveliest of hot sunrises - Everything
exceeded dreams of Oriental beauty and colour."

At that time, the Arabs slept with their camels on the quays, there
were white sails within the mole, and the caravans were stringing past
one another in the narrow streets. With the old Arab town shining white
against a backdrop of the blue Djurjura mountains, this scene registered
with tremendous impact on his mind.

Upon arrival at Algiers on 22nd April, 1884, they found that John
Fowler had died the previous day, and Alfred made immmediate
arrangements for the funeral, after which they rejoined (now with the
addition of Edith Fowler in deep mourning) Joseph's maelstrom tour,
which had reached Marseilles and was sweeping on fast for Cannes and
then Genoa where

"As a sample of the way my father worked us after our railway journey, we 'did'
Palazzo Doria - Realedell Universita - Durazzo Rosso - (here are Titian, Andrea
del Sarto, good Van Dykes &c &c) - Marcello Durazzo (some fine pictures noted
and the staircase) - San Lorenzo, Romanesque and Renaissance style (black and
white marble) - San Ambrogio (gaudy) - San Annunziata (fine inlaid columns -
gaudy) - Zoological Garden - Birdseye view of Genoa - The Quay - Monuments,
Columbus, Mazzini &c - the Exchange - and left the same afternoon for Milan."

Alfred and Nellie arrived back at Pinchinthorpe on 9th May, and
were followed a week later by Joseph who resumed his parliamentary
work in London.

On 24th June, a certain Dr M. presented his card at 24 Kensington
Palace Gardens. Who he was we shall never know, save that he was most
probably known to Joseph who noted that day:

"Had to get rid of Dr M------ who came after Beatrice's fortune. A note sent him
away."

Corndavon was sub-let for the start of the grouse season this
August, 1884 - financially it was another tight year - so Joseph and his
sons shot over Hutton moor for the 12th and a week later Joseph went off
to the Lake District and stayed with Theodore Fry who had married his,
Joseph's, first cousin, Sophia Pease. Theodore Fry, born in Bristol, was
Liberal M.P. for Darlington where he lived, but he had another house,

Glen Rothay, by Rydal Water.

Joseph, following his return from the Lake District, had gone to York on 22nd September, and here we find Alfred's name being canvassed as a Liberal candidate; Henry Tennant, a City Liberal and General Manager of the North Eastern Railway was most anxious that he should stand. Alfred was already taking an active part in political affairs and was chairman of the Liberal Association in Cleveland.

The next day, when Joseph returned from a day's partridge shooting at Great Ayton (four or five miles west of Hutton), he found that Newton Wallop, Viscount Lymington, had arrived. Joseph simply states he was there when he got home, recording neither surprise, nor pleasure - or anything but the fact of his arrival.

At whose invitation Lymington had arrived at Hutton has never been made clear with certainty. At all events, his purpose in coming was soon transparent as he set to work with lightning speed.

Notes:
1. In the text, the name Joseph must always be taken as a reference to Joseph Whitwell Pease. There are few references to J.W. Pease's father Joseph Pease but distinguishing notes will make such references apparent.
2. The houses in Kensington Palace Gardens were, for some reason unknown, renumbered at a later date.
3. Joseph Albert Pease b. 1860.
4. In the 1860s, at the time of "railway mania", in addition to the ten mile track promoted by Joseph and his father between Middlesbrough and Guisborough, Ralph Ward Jackson, a competing railway promoter, had also driven a railway line on the northern flank through this quiet valley, in places running in parallel with Joseph's track and separated by only two fields. Jackson was fighting for a share in the lucrative ironstone traffic. A wider motive was an attempt to prevent the Peases from controlling everything in the whole district.
   In Alfred's view, his father being the first to desecrate the valley, he derived not a little wry amusement from an entry in his father's diary in August 1861 which reads: "... much struck by the damage & unsightliness of Jackson's line!"
5. Née Emma Gurney, daughter of Joseph Gurney of Norwich.
6. Later Bishop of London.
7. Joseph frequently ordered up special trains for himself, in much the same way as ordinary mortals hail a cab. Because we come across other instances in the narrative, an early explanation is called for.
   It had been the practice in the days of the old Stockton and Darlington Railway to allow the directors free travel on the company's line, and since the amalgamation, the privilege was continued insofar as travelling on the old S & D railway track was concerned. A special train on the original N.E. Railway track was re-charged at a concessionary rate.

8. William Fowler had married secondly Rachel Leatham (née Pease) Joseph Whitwell Pease's sister, and thus had become Alfred's uncle. Rachel Leatham was the widow of Charles Albert Leatham. William Fowler and Alfred's father-in-law (Robert Nicholas Fowler, created a baronet 1885) were first cousins.
9. Charles and Gurney Pease, who had been business partners with particular and separate spheres of responsibility. Charles had been at the Counting House and Gurney at the Ironstone Mines. In Alfred's view both were useless and made a great mess of things.
10. Emma Josephine Pease b. 1855.
11. There are no christenings in the Quaker sect. Although Vincent Hamlyn was not a Quaker, Effie of course was at the time of her marriage. Even so, she had been married at Guisborough Parish Church but soon afterwards she left the Society of Friends - the first of the family to desert - and joined the established church.
12. Sarah Charlotte Pease, Alfred's sister.

CHAPTER TWO

A Calculating Visitor
& a Leap Into Politics

There must be a place here for the legend, trumpeted in later years by Sylvia Calmady-Hamlyn (at this time aged three) that upon arrival at Hutton, Lord Lymington first singled out for attention, Alfred's sister Helen Blanche Pease, until - as Sylvia put it,

> "Jack *(Alfred's brother)*, always the cynic - told him, 'you're on to the wrong one - that isn't the heiress'"

So, Lymington switched targets like a fox in a hen house, and the flapping we imagine, if brief, would be frenzied.

Of his five full days at Hutton, Lymington spent one out shooting, another out hunting on a mount supplied by Alfred from his enlarged stable, and three stalking different female prey. Suppose that chasing Blanche occupied one day only, that would leave two in which to bring Beatrice into full focus. On the fifth day we find Joseph's entry reading:

> *(29th September, 1884)* "Then had a serious chat with Lord L about B. Told him a great deal, but generally about her parentage, E'*(dward)*s weakness, & he said I had dealt frankly with him. He asked us to come and spend a Sunday at Hurstbourne when we were in town."

Immediately following this chat, Lymington left to stay and shoot at Sir Frederick Milbank's place at Thorp Perrow.

That Sylvia in time got to know Lymington and Beatrice very well is certain and she summarised her view of them thus:

> "She was always stupid *but very nice* with a pleasant voice."

And of Lymington:

"His mother always viewed him as the coming Prime Minister. Others didn't. He had brains - but conceit beyond description."

He spoke with an aristocratic lisp, his hair which he wore long was red, and a temper similar.

It might be assumed that someone of Lymington's standing was very wealthy. He was a new and young Liberal M.P. in the days when Members of Parliament received no pay, and he was heir to his father the fifth Earl of Portsmouth. His home at Hurstbourne Park, Whitchurch, Hampshire was a very substantial house, and all outward appearances suggested considerable affluence. But this concealed much.

True, Lymington's father had an estate in Hampshire, another at Eggesford in Devon, and a large estate in Ireland. A few years later it was revealed that the Hampshire property carried the encumbrance of a £106,000 mortgage. The annual interest on the mortgage was about £6,000, the property repairs annually about £3,000 and Portsmouth's own annuity was £2,000 making a total of £11,000 out of an estate rent roll of £12,000. What the situation was with the Devon and Irish estates was not revealed, as the relevance of the issue which brought this information to light was confined to Portsmouth's Hampshire affairs.

Lord Lymington was the eldest son in a family of twelve. Settlements on each out of his father's estates would have made him see with some urgency the need to take for himself a wife of some substance. It may not be taking presumption too far to suggest that the Rev. Mandell Creighton, a mutual friend of Joseph and Lymington, played a role in pointing the latter towards Hutton. Shortly before Lymington's sudden appearance, Creighton had warned him - at Joseph's bidding - that Beatrice's substantial trust colliery shares were highly speculative in character. That much is admitted. Though Joseph, if no one else, was mindful of the possible intent behind Lymington's visit, the latter was not at Hutton by his invitation.

A little more than six weeks after Lymington had been at Hutton, Joseph, Minnie and Beatrice went to stay two nights at Hurstbourne Park.

The house standing atop high ground in 600 acres of parkland, landscaped by Capability Brown, was approached from the Whitchurch end by a long pleasant uphill front drive of a little over a mile in length.

4. Beatrice Pease (later Countess of Portsmouth) as a young girl. Also pictured l. to r.: Joseph Whitwell Pease, Alfred Edward Pease and infant son, Edward Pease.

27

The lower part of the park, as it sloped away down in the direction of the village of Whitchurch, was woodland.

The other guests at Hurstbourne that November week-end included Mr Russell Lowell (the American Ambassador), Sir Thomas E. May and Mr F. Levison Gower, M.P. The party shot Lymington's parkland during the Saturday afternoon, but Joseph contained himself in comment to:

> "The house is ugly enough, but very comfortable inside and all seems quietly and nicely appointed."

Between the time of Lymington's sudden appearance at Hutton and now, Alfred had gone to meet York City Liberals to be interviewed as a possible parliamentary candidate. He had a grilling for his views on all important issues of the day and was invited to become one of the candidates.

York was a single constituency with two M.P.s. The other Liberal candidate was to be Frank Lockwood, Q.C., who had already fought a by-election the previous year and had lost by 21 votes.

With his chance at last, Alfred's adoption meeting soon followed, and Joseph went through to see how his elder son made out, recording

> "... to a great Liberal meeting where Alfred made an excellent speech and was, with only one dissentient adopted. He spoke wonderfully well ..."

and the following morning Joseph was still aglow with pride:

> "Alfred's reception last night was most striking. It was a most excellent meeting. His speech reads well in the papers."

Five days after Joseph had been to stay at Hurstbourne, and now back in London, we find the Countess of Portsmouth appearing on the scene at 24 Kensington Palace Gardens. She had

> "... come to see Beatrice and had a good chat with her & with M*(innie)*. She seemed a very sweet woman, quite taken with B and gave L a very good character as a pure young man. She was very loving; said L had never offered to anyone before and kissed both M & B on leaving. It was arranged for L to see B tomorrow."

Joseph then adds a cryptic note:

> "M was to tell her" *(Beatrice)* "as they went to Tottenham during the afternoon and also about S.M.F."

5. Mary (Minnie) (Lady) Pease née
Fox, wife of Sir Joseph Whitwell Pease.

That is, tell Beatrice that a formal proposal would be coming from Lymington at the arranged meeting the following day. But who was S.M.F. and why was his name brought forward if not thought at least an equal, if not a better suitor?

The answer to this could lie only in the person of Samuel Middleton Fox, now aged twenty-four. His qualification in a matter of this sort was unassailable. First he was Minnie's nephew, her sister Rachel's son, so there would be no direct blood relationship in such a match; but of overriding importance would be that by such a union, the Pease business and financial interests would be kept within a closely related Quaker family enclave. Alas, we are not privy to Samuel Middleton Fox's views in the matter - still less whether he was aware that his hat had been snatched off his head and flung into the ring.

Beatrice, by now alerted to what tomorrow held in store for her, became feverish and agitated. When Lymington came the following day at noon, he went into the drawing room:

> "M watched the drawing room door faithfully whilst he made his offer. He would not stay *(to)* lunch - she off her feed! and all the afternoon a good deal excited not knowing what to do. M thought she was almost ready to refuse him off hand."

Beatrice delayed a decision for 24 hours and then

"Seems to have made up her mind to accept Lymington."

After communicating her acceptance, Joseph wrote:

"I quite hope the right thing has been done. All we hear about him & his seems right in the best sense of the word. Lady Portsmouth especially took my judgement as an excellent woman, fearing God & bringing up her 12 children well!"

The next day, now 26th November, 1884, Joseph and the family returned to Hutton where on 2nd December, Lymington telegraphed to say he was coming up - and did - arriving only a hair's breadth behind the telegram.

Six days later, Joseph wrote:

"Much annoyed to get a letter from Lucas which said that Beatrice & L were at their proposal coming to see him. I went and saw them and told them I had nothing to hide, that I knew all her affairs &c."

Arthur Lucas was the Darlington solicitor for Beatrice's trust affairs, the trustees being Joseph and his brother Arthur Pease. Joseph was sorely affronted. Why hadn't they spoken to him instead of going to Lucas behind his back?

After reproaching Beatrice and Lymington, Joseph had his horse saddled and went to the meet of hounds at Great Ayton to get his annoyance worked off. But the remedy didn't work, and he returned in the afternoon still needled, for a second go with the two of them

"... on Beatrice's property showing him the difficulty of the entire position."

Joseph pointed out that Beatrice's income was of a very variable fluctuating nature. The variables could range from years of no income to ones of very high dividends. This was as regards her investments in Pease & Partners. This was where the greater part of her fortune lay, and represented the sheet anchor of her trust estate. The character of Beatrice's trust investment in Pease & Partners had of course changed since her father's death, from partnership shares to those in a private limited company. These were very difficult and hard times. Pease & Partners during the last twelve months had paid a dividend of only $1^1/_4$ per cent, and the further outlook was grim. Mortgage and overdraft interest payments had prior claim on income before anything could be paid over to Beatrice, and it was not possible to rearrange her investments so as to provide for a known and stated income, for the very good reason that nobody was likely to buy shares in an undertaking paying such a trifle in dividend - and paying possibly nothing at all during the current year. The situation called for patience to await an upturn in trade. In any case any eventual sale of shares would have to be sufficient to discharge the considerable trust liabilities of approximately £230,000, none of which liability was of the trustees' making, but which they had had to take on as found at the time Beatrice's father died.

The day following Joseph's lecture to Beatrice and Lymington, he had two or three interviews with them

"... on their, or rather her affairs. I think he has a decided notion about the main chance."

In the space of a fortnight then, the atmosphere had changed from one of hope at the right thing being done to one of decided unease.

Events are now starting to move at hurricane speed. On 13th December, Joseph, Minnie, a daughter (Blanche) and Beatrice went up to London, Minnie and Beatrice to get the trousseau, and Joseph to arrange about settlements. That business arranged, they travelled on, taking Beatrice to Eggesford in Devon to meet Lymington's father the Earl of Portsmouth. This was an altogether very favourable experience and Joseph enjoyed his visit. He had a day's shooting and a day's hunting and was most appreciative, saying:

"They have all been most kind to Beatrice giving her jewels &c &c &c."

On 23rd December, Lymington joined the party on the same train for the return journey to Hutton from King's Cross, but travelled north with Beatrice separately in a smoking compartment. The day before departure, Joseph had been to see Lymington's solicitor, Mr Preston Kurslake, on making provision for Lymington and Beatrice to draw on capital within certain specified limits, in years when there might be a shortfall in income, such drawing to be paid back during years of high income. This was agreed upon generally.

On Christmas Eve, Joseph, his brother Arthur, and Lucas the solicitor had a discussion over Beatrice's settlement.

"The main points are, Lymington a life interest and her full power to will as she would have the latter under her father's will at 21. The moral power to prohibit it seems gone."

Clearly, what most troubles Joseph, is that the future course of events is going to risk Beatrice's commercial interests going out of the Pease family - unless at some future time, those interests could be bought out.

On New Year's Eve, 1884, Joseph closed his diary on a note of muted enthusiasm:

> "Lymington's engagement to Beatrice seems alright though not what one expected."

and on business:

> "This year has been one of steady bad trade. Large quantities of iron and coal produced at little profit. We parted 31st May with our Mills, an old family business which made our family and which has cost my father *(and)* Henry Pease and their sons £200,000 loss."

The Mills had been leased - not sold - and Smith from Glasgow and Clarke the manager had taken them over.

1885

On New Year's Day, Lord Lymington went south and within the week Joseph

> "Met Lucas on Beatrice's Settlement. There seem two main points, both only arising in case of no children and her death. Should Lymington have a full life interest. Should she have full power of devise. I say £5,000 is enough in the first case. That she should be practically limited to her father's family in willing. Wrote Lymington that I would abandon the latter point if he would abandon the former. He seems 'all in' for the fortune."

and a week later -

> "Got a little of my own way! Still, it is much in his *(Lymington's)* favour."

With that detail more or less settled, Joseph turned on 23rd January to affairs in general. This month was the time when he drew up his private balance sheet each year, and for 1884 this had turned out badly. Even two of his managed Hutton farms had lost money, and mulling over Beatrice's balance sheet this same day, he could only consider it a poor one - £4,000 loss on the half year - concluding:

> "Everyone poor & grumbling. Went to bed tired and in bad spirits."

At the beginning of February, Joseph saw Minnie, a daughter (Lottie) and Beatrice off to London to make the final wedding arrangements - no long engagement this one. The skies must have seemed leaden when he wrote on the day Beatrice left:

> "B's marriage comes on fast and makes leaving home a grave affair."

Foreboding was not lessened on 7th February, still at Hutton and dealing with his correspondence that morning:

> "What disturbed me about M & Lymington's letters, L evidently wants to live out of B's fortune. I don't like it! Wrote L at length showing him that if there was not income - it would be a bad time for selling the securities, that all our trouble would be thrown away."

The last week before the wedding and the days were dragging. Joseph remained at Hutton, though kept in touch with the arrangements being made and

> "I wish the whole thing was at an end and over."

For solace, he went to Pinchinthorpe quite tired out and sick at heart, but greatly enjoyed just being there. It was no good brooding on the now inevitable, and to dispel his father's gloomy thoughts, Alfred got him out to Marske and Upleatham with hounds, and for a few hours they went racing across country. This both knew to be the only prescription likely to blow away all feelings of anxiety.

On Saturday, 14th February, Joseph set off for London. Alfred, Nellie and Jack were supposed to go on the Sunday, but Alfred was delayed by a dose of colic. When he did arrive in London on the Monday, Joseph thought his son looked *"washed out."* In fact Alfred looked what Joseph felt. However, the Portsmouths gave a large dinner party that night which passed very pleasantly and Joseph felt supported.

The Wedding day arrived. Joseph was awake early and was very sick. He was churned up and remained in bed till noon when he at last got up, and the family set out for St Mary Abbot's, Kensington. Beatrice was securely married by five clergy, including (now) Canon Mandell Creighton. The reception followed at 24 Kensington Palace Gardens. The happy pair left for Hurstbourne in the late afternoon before setting out for a honeymoon in Tasmania.

After everyone had gone, Joseph went to bed, but before doing so, went as always to his writing table last thing, and after expressing satisfaction at the day's arrangements, wrote:

> "Most anxious does one feel for this dear girl. She seems to have her happiness in her own hands"

adding, perhaps in self-reproach at his earlier clouded thoughts which, on this of all days, he must banish from his mind:

> "and to have married a good pure earnest man."

Beatrice was three days from her nineteenth birthday and Lymington just turned twenty-nine when they married.

At the end of March, Alfred went off to Eggesford with Will Nichol, the huntsman to the Cleveland, to collect some of the Earl of Portsmouth's draft hounds. He stayed three nights before returning with six and a half couple. Of Portsmouth's pack Alfred wrote:

> "A grand level lot, heavy boned, hard looking and with nice shoulders, not heavy as heavy hounds shoulders are apt to be, and on short good legs."

Writing of Lymington's father he says

> "... he is devoted to hounds and withal a jolly Squire and good all round sportsman, but when talking of hounds he is slow, halting, hem-hemming and 'don't ye know,' 'I mean' and 'you understand what I mean' and difficult to follow."

Before setting off this May for his Falmouth house, Kerris Vean, for his annual fishing holiday, Joseph did his final round of his Hutton stables and gardens, and especially when he was going away made a point of seeing and chatting with Briggs at his house on the hillside, and Simpson, the coachman at the stables. Joseph had a high and affectionate regard for these two long-serving employees, and this month he felt concern about them both. Simpson was certainly not well, and Briggs

> "... has been very ill & is still so I fear. Quite affecting to see him & feel his warm attachment to me & to us all."

Joseph also knew that in Falmouth, his father-in-law Alfred Fox was terminally ill.

While in Falmouth, he wrote asking Dr Hume of Newcastle to attend on Briggs. Just as Minnie's father seemed within hours of his end a telegram came announcing the death of William Briggs. Joseph felt this very keenly, but couldn't leave, so Alfred and Jack headed north for the funeral. Alfred, writing of the man who had been king pin in his life from childhood to manhood, paid this tribute:

"Yesterday, the 20th June, 1885, my brother Jack and I followed the hearse that bore William Briggs from his sunny red tiled cottage on the hillside to his last resting place in Guisborough cemetery. We have been to many funerals Jack and I, but I believe never to one which made us, as this one did, cry like a couple of children.

We had all got attached to him and his ways. Out shooting I shall miss his cheery voice & the whistle he used to blow too loudly & too frequently. We shall have no such candid critic to tell us to 'hold straighter' or to exclaim 'Whatever in the world is the matter!' or to give us the benefit of his opinion which was always given with the preface 'Beg pardon Sir Joseph. Now how wad it be ...'

And now his pretty home with the well kept garden has lost its master, and when during the last few weeks I have gone there, I have not stopped outside & shouted 'Briggs!' at the top of my voice till he came out to chat over things with me, but I have walked in, and entered noiselessly and waited till 'the mother' as he always called Mrs Briggs, came to tell me I might see him. I looked at the view of Hutton, Guisbro' & the sea from there & wondered if Briggs had looked on it for the last time & thought of his last weary painful walk from the station to his house the day he was taken ill.

When I entered his sickroom, there he was, the same Briggs, the same strong voice & the still strong grasp of the hand, but his tanned face turned pale, his eyes sunken & his cheeks so fallen in ... and so died after a fiery trial in which he proved the metal he was made of, the most upright, faithful and much loved servant of my father."

Three days later Alfred Fox died. Joseph regarded him as one of the most admirable self-denying men he ever knew.

Turning to the political scene, in early June the Liberal Government foundered on the budget vote. The Cabinet was in any case in total disarray on the Irish Home Rule question. The Queen sent for Lord Salisbury to form an administration, and it was clear, a General Election could not be long delayed.

In October, Lord Salisbury asked the Queen to dissolve Parliament and the General Election of 1885 started to get under way. Joseph's brother, Arthur, was already very busy in defence of his seat at Whitby. Alfred and Frank Lockwood were hard at work in York where a large army of reinforcements came on 28th October. Included in this force were Lord Lymington, Arthur Pease, Hugh Bell, General Sir Henry Havelock-Allan and his wife Lady Alice, together with their daughter Elsie, and Vincent Calmady-Hamlyn.

After dinner that evening there was a great meeting in the Exhibition Building with Lord Ripon in the chair and a crushed attendance (put by Joseph at between seven and eight thousand) *"A grand sight."* Lord Ripon spoke for 1 hour and 20 minutes and other speakers followed, including Lord Lymington, Arthur Pease and Sir Henry Havelock-Allan, and of course the candidates.

In those days, in order to hold the attention of the audience, it was usual to interpose between the speeches the most uproarious entertainment - comic turns and songs - so that these lengthy meetings were in no way considered dull. There was always terrific competition between the Tories and Liberals to put on the best show.

Alfred and Lockwood worked at a cracking pace paying particular attention to the Irish quarter of Walmgate, the contentious issue of Irish Home Rule being the dominant one at this time. Joseph went off to his new Barnard Castle constituency, adjoining which was that of Bishop Auckland which Alfred's great friend of Cambridge days, "Harry" Paulton was fighting. This was a very winnable seat being the other half of Joseph's now carved up old South Durham constituency. It had been offered to Alfred just at the time that he was committing himself to York, and he felt therefore bound to decline it. York he knew would be a much tougher fight than Bishop Auckland.

During the campaign, Alfred and Joseph met for a week-end at Pinchinthorpe and discussed their respective campaigns. Everything seemed to be going all right at York as far as anyone could tell. Ethel, another of Alfred's sisters, at this time aged seventeen, was fearful not for him but for Lockwood, and would rather Alfred lost than that Lockwood, having lost in the by-election the previous year, should suffer a second defeat.

During the final week, Joseph broke away from his own fight to dash to York to examine the canvass returns which looked well enough. *"Steam is up in York"* - *"Great excitement"* and he set about throwing in everything to help his elder son to victory. He sent carriages and 51 horses to York to whip up the electors on polling day, something from which Lockwood had been disadvantaged the previous year and which materially contributed to his defeat.

"Hope to see Alfred landed on Wednesday 25th Nov. is my main anxiety"

wrote Joseph. Polling day arrived, and Alfred telegraphed his father begging him not to come until after the poll in case of stirring up jealousies, not as between Lockwood and himself, but with Lockwood's supporters. Joseph paid heed to this request, arriving in York by the night mail train, being met at the station by his son-in-law Vincent Hamlyn, who gave confident accounts of the day. Jack was with Alfred watching the count.

Joseph and Vincent walked from the station over Lendal Bridge and they fought their way through the gathered multitude to the Mansion House. At about midnight, the Under Sheriff came out with the result. Pease 5,353, Lockwood 5,260 - both Liberals elected, the nearest Tory rival being 670 votes behind.

Joseph was jubilant.

> "We could hardly believe it. The mob made so much noise that the Sheriff couldn't be heard. Jack threw up two orange handkerchiefs which soon brought tremendous cheering."

The two victors left the Mansion house and went to Councillor Foster's to speak and thank supporters, *"Alfred did it well,"* before going on to the Liberal Club and then in the early morning, to bed.

In those days, not all constituencies voted on the same day, so that some time elapsed before all results were known. Joseph won comfortably at Barnard Castle with almost 71% of the vote against the Earl of Strathmore's son, Patrick Bowes-Lyon. Henry Fell Pease won in Cleveland with about the same margin as Joseph, and Theodore Fry held Darlington. The one great disappointment came at Whitby where Arthur Pease lost by 340 votes. Other victors for the Liberals were "Harry" Paulton (Bishop Auckland), Sir Henry Havelock-Allan (South-East Durham) and Lord Lymington who won the South Molton constituency of North Devon with a 2,001 majority. The result in the country was a Liberal majority over the Tories, but they needed the support of the Parnellite Irish M.P.s.

Joseph, Alfred, Jack and "Harry" Paulton converged on Hutton Hall after all the fighting was over, and went down to the cellars where the Turkish Baths were located, and there, all in a lather of steam and sweat, fought over their recent battles anew.

The religious significance of Christmas was not lost this year by the recent political success, which made an additional reason for celebration, and at Hutton Hall there was a house full with all the family gathered including the two grandchildren, Edward Pease and Sylvia Hamlyn.

1886

As we move into the New Year, Joseph is casting around for economies after another dismal showing in business during 1885, and he resolved that, if he could get £35,000 for 24 Kensington Palace Gardens, he would sell it, and find a place nearer the House of Commons. While Joseph was thinking of moving down market, Lymington had hopes of a modest start in the opposite direction, and with Beatrice called at 24 KPG with the aim of getting Beatrice's trustees to finance the purchase of a lease on a house in Mayfair. Joseph talked them out of that scheme.

In the middle of January, 1886, Joseph, now back at Hutton, was with Jack, and again down in the Turkish Baths. Jack told his father that he had offered to Elsie Havelock-Allan who was 'thinking about it':

> "He told me a great deal about Sir H*(enry Havelock-Allan)* who seems mad. I have always liked Elsie. There is something very charming about her."

In due course we shall come across evidence of General Sir Henry Havelock-Allan's sometimes bizarre behaviour, but let it be said at this juncture, that he had been, like his father (General Havelock) before him a great soldier, and had won the Victoria Cross at Lucknow.

Elsie Havelock-Allan communicated her acceptance of Jack's proposal a few days later.

With the new Parliament assembled, Alfred took his seat for the first time on the government side below the gangway.

He soon set down his general views on Gladstone's Irish policy, noting that many of his colleagues were genuinely apprehensive about Home Rule for Ireland. As for himself, he was very much in favour of the experiment being tried, but was mindful that since Lord Hartington had refused to join Gladstone's cabinet and had many followers in the party, it would be difficult for Gladstone to keep a united party behind him. Alfred felt his own views on Home Rule were those shared by only a small minority of Liberals, in which minority his father could not be counted as one!

Joseph was sounded by Lord Richard Grosvenor as to whether he would take office if it were offered to him. He did not jump at the opportunity, and was therefore passed over, and when Edward Heneage was appointed to the Duchy of Lancaster we find Joseph saying:

> "Saw Heneage had got the Duchy of Lancaster. I should have liked it - I dare say I have plenty to do - nous verrons."

This February, Alfred attended to some minor financial pruning, in conjunction with which he went to Tattersalls to see three of his horses sold, but also bought in one in to keep as a park hack.

"After seeing them sold, I walked down to Brooks's with Father. While there, someone came into the front drawing room where I was writing & said 'there's an enormous crowd coming up the street.' I went to the window of the Club with Father & several more who happened to be in & saw a mob running up the street. About 500 men running, first loosely packed then a dense mass led by two men carrying small flags, one a red one on the end of a stick. As we looked at them out of curiosity, all of a sudden we realised they were dangerous for a volley of stones through the windows drove us under cover. Some members got under the furniture & we found ourselves undergoing a hot bombardment with all kinds of missiles. It lasted perhaps ten minutes, forty large panes of glass being smashed to atoms and the whole floor right to the fireplace strewn with glass & stones, pieces of pavement, books &c knocked off the tables.

There had been a meeting of the unemployed in Trafalgar Square, and taking advantage of this there had been a meeting of the Socialists & the criminal classes had joined in.

I was amused with an old gentleman lying on his face on the sofa on which I stood at Brooks's, shouting 'this'll do 'em no good' as the first windows were smashed, and as the work grew worse he went on from denouncing them in stronger & stronger language, to vowing he would 'STOP HIS SUBSCRIPTIONS'!! It was curious to see the damage in the streets. I sallied out with Houghton & saw the small beginnings at the Carlton in Pall Mall, more windows smashed at the bottom of St James's, all smashed at the top of Piccadilly - the shops wrecked in S. Audley Street and looted."

After Joseph's disappointment at being overtaken by Heneage in the matter of the Duchy, and after a day or two of reflection he decided to write to Lord Richard Grosvenor 'on his ambitions'. Though he did not not disclose what these were, we do know from Alfred's journal, that what he hoped for more than anything else, was to be appointed a Privy Councillor. He had been in the House for twenty years, and had been a hard working conscientious member. In Alfred's view, it was Joseph's involvement as President of the Peace Society, his almost 'peace at any price' attitude, his leadership of the crusade against the opium trade with China, as well as being a capital punishment abolitionist, that had all been factors militating against his having been offered office before. And now, when the opportunity had been presented to him, he had simply let it go.

Having written to Lord Richard Grosvenor, he turned next to reply to a letter from Lymington

"... on B's affairs. He seems never at rest about them. I fear she has an ill time with a fortune hunter! though he always seems happy with her."

Alfred made his maiden speech on 23rd March 1885 during the debate on Local Taxation, but as it came during the dinner hour it was to a rather empty House. He had had no intention of speaking beforehand, but as the subject interested him he thought he would take the plunge and see what it was like. Joseph came in and stayed when Alfred told him he was going to speak, and he rose from the second place from the front bench, just below the gangway.

"It was worse than I expected, and I was so nervous that fluency suffered very much at several points. I however got out most of what I intended to say. On the whole it was not at all a brilliant beginning, but then it was not an occasion for shining, nor did I want to make an effect. If I had, I should have made my first start on the Irish question or something exciting. The Speaker told Balfour who repeated it to my father that he considered it was a speech of great promise. My father said 'the effect on the House was decidedly good. You were more than usually cheered, your matter was excellent but you were hardly fluent enough.' The feeling one has, is of *(a)* critical lot of sneerers listening to you ... this feeling makes you inclined to skip points, skim over your most precious arguments and fills you with a longing to get it over & sit down. As a matter of fact, the House is very tolerant of and indulgent to beginners."

Spending a few days back home in April, when out hunting with the Zetland, Alfred was

"... well abused and insulted by my acquaintances for my Home Rule tendencies - which grow stronger the more I think of the failures of the past and the strength of the Irish sentiment on this question & the need of winning their loyalty."

When he returned to London and Gladstone brought forward his proposals on Ireland to a crowded House,

"I went, expecting to be very much excited at the prospect of having, sooner or later, to have to vote for or against this tremendous proposal, but bringing as I am, thoroughly conscious of a perfectly unbiased mind to bear on the subject, I believe I shall vote for it with satisfaction, and with no little hope for a brighter future for Ireland, & a better Union of real and lasting value between the peoples of Gt. Britain & Ireland ..."

Joseph's view on Gladstone's proposals this same day was:

"To my mind it has very many flaws. It has no security for the minority; it puts Ireland out of the Imperial comity, and it leaves us to collect taxes, customs & excise with Irish tools. It puts full confidence in those in which I place none."

During the week-end, on 11th April Alfred reflected:

"My mind full of the Irish question and feel deeply the fact that Father takes an opposite view to myself. I have to differ on 9 most vital questions with him, and as this almost unknown to us, it is quite an affliction to me. But on a question like this, every private feeling & interest must never be thought of for a moment; the happiness of generations, the fate of an Empire may depend on our vote. I wish to God I had not the responsibility laid on me, it is a grievous burden that is worrying me and others I believe night and day. Nellie is one great help in these real troubles."

As the debate continued, on the Monday following we have Alfred's view of the Tory Lord Randolph Churchill:

"... his speech as a whole was sham and trivial."

Joseph, however, thought

"Randolph Churchill made a good speech on Gladstone's Irish Bill."

Alfred, in making his assessment of voting intentions on the Liberal side, included among a list of forty-eight members under the heading "almost certain to vote against it to a man," Havelock-Allan, Heneage, and Lymington. A second list, numbering twenty-one members headed "against the Bill & probably vote against it" he included his father. In a further list numbering seven, rated as undecided, "probably for the Bill but rather shaky" he included Henry Fell Pease.

Returning to London after the Easter recess he laments the passing of his short break with:

"It was pleasant to get back to my wife, but I wished as I left the north that I was once more living my old country life, and watching the spring turn into summer, instead of being worried to death with political anxieties, & the insults of Conservatives & malcontent Liberal society in this dirty cockney town, where the political atmosphere is as fetid as the foul air of the place.
I found all well in the north though trade was very bad. Father is letting the two farms at Hutton (Codhill & Bousdale) over which he has dropped so much money & reducing hands on the estate. Jack & Elsie have been staying at Hutton and seem very happy.
I enjoyed my holiday, though the difference of opinion between myself and Father on the Irish question *(is)* a source of worry to myself. He confines himself to criticising the details of the Bill & will not say anything of the principles or an alternative policy. He reads nothing but one side and will not listen to any other & dismisses the whole subject by some sweeping condemnation of the Irish race ... I took the chair on Wednesday (28th Apl) at Guisbro' at a Home Rule meeting

41

when H.F. Pease addressed his supporters & announced his intention of voting for the second reading."

During the recess Joseph had attended to business. He felt he was being drawn back into the Mill affairs which seemed short of money and going badly. He also gave serious thought to the formation of Robert Stephenson & Co. into a private limited company, and after discussing finance with Charles Fry and David Dale at the Counting House, went home

"... heartily tired & things don't seem going quite straight with our lives."

In early May, Alfred and Frank Lockwood held a meeting in York to gauge the temperature of feeling on the Irish issue. Henry Tennant, who had been instrumental in getting Alfred to stand, was one of the seceders. This was a keen loss to Alfred and to York Liberals, but even so, at the meeting held in the Festival Concert Rooms,

"Six weeks ago I should hardly have expected half the party to support the views I hold and we found them practically unanimous - I spoke for 55 minutes - we supped at 11.30 & returned by the night train."

Gladstone's Manifesto on Ireland came out about the same time in May which prompts from Joseph:

" - it looks like a howl of despair. He seems ready to chop the Land Bill and to let the House make what it can of Home Rule. Much chat and no one speaking well of Gladstone's measures but a breaking up of the Liberal Party."

The division on the issue between Joseph and Alfred was a reflection of the divisions within the Liberal Party.

11th May saw a further conflict of attitude on a different issue.

"Father brought in his Capital Punishment Abolition resolution. He made an excellent speech but he cannot persuade the House nor me at present that there is no protective deterrent effect in the death penalty - I believe the word gallows has a deterrent effect, & capital punishment places the crime of murder in a different category in the public conscience, and preaches the sanctity of human life. I listened to the debate and absented myself from the division."

In the division the Bill was lost 62 - 117.

With ever deepening concern, that the sharp internal divisions over Irish Home Rule was going to wreck the Liberal Party, the Bill had either to be dropped or a compromise found acceptable to both factions.

6. Pinchinthorpe House (circa 1937).

However it was not long before there was clear and open Liberal revolt. Lord Hartington held a public meeting at which £100,000 was raised to fight all Liberal Home Rulers at the next election. This marked the beginning of the "Liberal Unionists" as a party and Alfred at any rate was outraged:

> "What a savage fight we shall have. I would spend my last shilling in the (Home Rule) cause, and we feel most bitterly the conduct of those who will not help, in what we have wished to make a calm and careful settlement on a safe basis of the Irish question - We shall win in the end - How the country will resent this action of 100 peers, baronets & millionaires."

On 27th May, Joseph and Alfred went to a clandestine meeting called by Gladstone and held at the Foreign Office. The carefully worded circular excluded all Liberals not in favour of any concessions of any kind. Of this meeting Joseph's account is dismissive:

> " - it took him $3/4$ of an hour to tell us that he would try for a 2nd reading of the Bill - and then let it drop, leaving till the autumn a new Bill in a fresh session."

Alfred's account is euphoric:

> "He was in splendid form, clear, cheerful & sparkling & handling the delicate & complex question in the most masterly & wonderful manner ... the effect of his

speech was at once evident for several prominent dissentients proclaimed their 'salvation,' ... He has allowed the party to go on finding out its weakness - he has let each dissenting part of it discover its own bent, & then taking the dividing line which separates those in favour of the *principle,* and those who oppose it."

The Hartington dissentients were, in Alfred's view, staggered and depressed once the news of Gladstone's meeting was out. They had anticipated the crisis being resolved by Hartington becoming Premier and the main body of the party wheeling round to his support.

On 1st June, Joseph worked at the House on an address on the Irish question. After this, and as the result of a chance meeting with Joseph Chamberlain on the stairs, he went to a meeting called by him. The upshot of this meeting was the passing of a resolution by 38 to 9 for fighting the Home Rule Bill, Joseph having voted with the majority! This resolution had a profound effect in the lobby and Joseph felt it now looked like the end of the Bill.

Within twenty-four hours he was regretting having supported the resolution, and now fearful that the split would become irrevocable, and in a solo attempt to repair the damage and keep the party stitched together, he framed a letter to Marjoribanks, the government Chief Whip.

The substance of this letter advocated -

1.   To state that the best way to keep the party together was to withdraw the Bill altogether leaving the autumn session free but
2.   If this could not be done, could not Mr Gladstone in asking for a 2nd reading state that those who voted for it, voted on the *principle* of granting Ireland legislative powers on specifically and specially Irish affairs, leaving open the question of Ulster.
3.   That all Irish legislation must be founded on the five principles the Prime Minister had laid down at first, (including), integrity, divisions of burdens between England & Ireland, protection of minorities &c &c leaving all detailed discussion by the House until the autumn. If Mr Gladstone could say this, Joseph and many others would support a 2nd reading.

Having penned his letter, he handed it to Alfred, with the instruction to deliver it to Marjoribanks, he (Joseph) having to dash to York on railway business. Marjoribanks took the letter to Downing Street. Later, at lunch, Marjoribanks told Alfred that Gladstone accepted the letter and would reply to this effect, and wished Joseph to be wired to return, which he did the same night.

Gladstone had written to Joseph intimating that he accepted his letter "word for word". When news of what had taken place got around, the Hartington faction were furious. The Tories were more so, and when Alfred bumped into his Tory father-in-law in the lobby he, Sir Robert Nicholas Fowler[1]

"... was also very wrath & congratulated me as his 'noble son in law' and with a loud voice proclaiming in the lobby that he heard Brassey, Bass & Pease were to have peerages for this!"

Alfred was frequently irritated by his father-in-law, a man of intimidating size and character, and had to steel himself against the overwhelming temptation to retaliate on this and many other such occasions. What drove him to almost total distraction was a hunting day with Fowler, and the return home to stables - not at the 'neck or nothing' pace that Alfred loved, not even at a trot, but at a walk, and being forced to listen to Fowler reciting endlessly whole memorised passages from the Greek classics. Otherwise there were always Fowler's *"oft repeated stories & never wearying abuse of Bright, Gladstone & the whole Liberal Govt. ..."* to test Alfred's composure.

When the Home Rule Bill came up for its second reading on 7th June and the House divided, the Government lost by a majority of 30.

Joseph, driving back to 24 KPG together with Alfred after the vote, proclaimed *"never was a thing so botched."*

Excitement now centred around whether a dissolution of Parliament would come at once or later, but in preparation, Joseph set about writing his election address, and then went for a cruise as the guest of Sir Donald Currie on his steam yacht, up the east coast from Gravesend to Edinburgh, disembarking at the Tees on the return trip.

Alfred and Frank Lockwood bolted to York. Nellie was close to her second confinement and remained in London as the election got under way, and as a new drama took centre stage.

Joseph's brother Arthur, defeated last time at Whitby, felt inclined to fight Kidderminster and went off there. Within a week he was writing discouragingly to Joseph but without revealing why. Joseph, to be helpful, pointed Arthur to Richmond (Yorks) which was without a Liberal candidate. In reply, Arthur told his brother that he had abandoned Kidderminster following Gladstone's Manchester speech on Irish Home Rule and had new plans. He was coming to Darlington to offer full support to the Tory candidate there, Arnold Forster. Forster

7. Sir Robert Nicholas Fowler Bt., M.P.

seizing upon this immediately had bills slapped up all over the town advertising the erstwhile Liberal Arthur Pease's support at forthcoming meetings!

At this juncture, C.B. Martin of Barnard Castle and one Robinson of Northallerton arrived in Darlington to invite Arthur to stand as Liberal for Richmond. As they walked around the town, they saw in amazed disbelief, posters everywhere announcing that the candidate they sought was supporting the Tories. In acute distress and not a little disgust they left the town and enlisted W.E.R. Turton as Richmond's Liberal candidate.

When Joseph learned about his brother's plans he became quite frantic, and implored Arthur to abandon this reckless folly. It was embarking upon an offensive and unthinkable course to support the political enemy of a relative. Moreover, if Arthur persisted in it, then he, Joseph, was coming to Darlington to support their common blood relative, the Liberal candidate Theodore Fry.

There was no stopping Arthur, and a clear family political division was opening up and, as Joseph had an unopposed run at Barnard Castle, the two brothers duly took their separate platform places alongside rival candidates.

Further mayhem followed when 'Harry' Paulton, who was again fighting Bishop Auckland, received a telegram which read "Arthur Pease is going to stand if 2,000 sign a requisition"! Alfred now joined the fray writing to his uncle and to David Dale,

> "... pointing out all the evils that must result from such a course and how Father, Jack, Lloyd Pease, Dale & perhaps Henry Fell *(Pease)* would all take our stand by Paulton."

That crisis was defused a day later when David Dale wired Alfred in York to say that Arthur Pease would not be standing.

At Darlington Arthur's support for Forster was unavailing, but only just so, since Theodore Fry scraped home by a mere 57 votes. Sir Henry Havelock-Allan switched to the Liberal Unionist ticket and was elected. Lymington also had gone over to the Liberal Unionists and held on to his South Molton seat.

Alfred was in bitter mood and felt his uncle had been mischievous. He laid the blame for Arthur's change of allegiance squarely on his wife, May, known to Alfred as "Aunt Arthur". She was an Irish Protestant, so if that wasn't enough to settle where her sympathies lay, what would add strength to her convictions would be the fact that her brother, a Conservative at the last election, had stood against, only to be defeated by, Charles Stewart Parnell, the leader of the Parnellite Irish Nationalists. Alfred however, after a day's reflection, and when he had cooled somewhat, says:

> "I have no doubt he thought it was his duty to sacrifice his personal feelings for his newly discovered political convictions. He (Arthur) telegraphed to the Whitby people when asked if he would help the Unionist candidate there against Col. Clayhills. He said 'I could not oppose Col Clayhills & my Whitby friends', though he entered with zest into opposition against a blood relation supported by his brother & family, & sacrificed every consideration for those who had been his friends & attached allies since he was born."

While all this turmoil was in progress, Alfred and Frank Lockwood went a ceaseless round of big and little meetings. They spoke at warehouses, out of inn windows, schoolrooms packed and unventilated until

> "... we really have exhausted almost the Irish question & have aroused the most extraordinary enthusiasm, so much so, that wherever we go we are cheered & followed & our drives from one place to another are like triumphal progresses."

In the middle of the election on 24th June, Alfred received a telegram from London. *"Nellie had a splendid boy at 2.30 - both doing beautifully."* He dropped everything and made a dash to London to see Nellie and the new infant. He was allowed only a few hours with them and then returned to his election. He had said in the course of the election, that should he again be returned for the city this infant, boy or girl, would have 'York' as one of its names.

The result was:

	Pease	4,816	elected
	Lockwood	4,810	elected
	Legard	4,352	
	Dundas	4,295	

and the infant was named Christopher York Pease.

"It was a more exciting count than last time. After I had moved and Legard seconded the vote of thanks to the Sheriff, the poll was declared outside & we could hear the roar of applause which came from the multitude - The Lord Mayor, somewhat unceremoniously dismissed us from the Mansion House, he being a Tory."

They were escorted by a large body of police to Councillor Foster's in St Leonards Place, where they made speeches, and at last to the Station Hotel, to bed and blessed sleep.

Note:

1. Robert Nicholas Fowler was, in addition to being Tory M.P. for the City of London, also its Lord Mayor on two occasions, and as was then customary, as the holder of that office, he was created a baronet.

CHAPTER THREE

The Irish Question & Business Worries

1886 continued

Political infighting over Irish Home Rule had brought defeat to the Liberals in the country. Gladstone resigned and Lord Salisbury became Tory Prime Minister. It seemed in Alfred's view that the new ministerial appointments augured for a weak government, with the prospect of another election within a couple of years.

That was one thing. Another was that the family political divide was simply a reflection of the split in the Liberal party over the explosive Irish question, from Alfred's unflinching support for Home Rule, through Joseph's now tepid support, down to Arthur's outright opposition. A serious attempt at mending fences must be made between Joseph and Arthur, and these political divisions must not be allowed to invade personal or business matters.

Before this could come about, however, Joseph had another worry on his hands. His wife, Minnie, was to undergo an operation in July, 1886. This was successfully carried out but her doctors wanted her to go to St. Moritz to convalesce.

"I do not see how I can leave home with business as it is. Her health is essential to me, but to go abroad is an awful affair to me."

A week later he made arrangements for a bank loan of £35,000.

"This nearly makes my arrangements complete – but money has run out fast."

Arrangements were completed by borrowing elsewhere a further £10,000 secured.

These arrangements, it need hardly be said, were to provide cover at the Counting House during his absence, to meet dividend and interest payments made by the concerns holding their accounts there. Pease & Partners had failed to declare a dividend at any time during the last two and a half years since paying $1^1/4\%$ (actual) in January, 1884.

Finances arranged, Joseph, Minnie and two daughters then set out for the Engadine. By the glorious 12th August, they were at St Moritz, the grouse neglected. In any case Corndavon had again been sub-let for a month, and Alfred alone with Cockfield (now Head Gamekeeper at Hutton) went on to the Hutton moor where he had everything his own way.

On 6th Sept. 1886 Alfred went to Hurstbourne Park, Hampshire:

"The park looked very pretty & Beatrice did the honours of the house well – Lymington was not so good in this, there being very little of the simple & kindly courtesy that distinguishes the better bred aristocracy, & by better bred I mean refinement and not breeding. However, he gave us 3 days' good partridge shooting ... The thing Lymington cares for most and does best is the kitchen department – Glad to leave."

Alfred was soon travelling back to Pinchinthorpe having first, in passing through London, welcomed his parents on their return; and his mother after a month's rest, he was thankful to record, was apparently restored in health.

The whole family gathered at Hutton Hall for the week-end of 16th October, it being Jack's last as a bachelor. He and Elsie Havelock-Allan were married at Darlington on 19th October.

In November, Alfred wrote a letter to *The Times* on Irish Home Rule just before going off for three days' shooting at Misarden Park with Ted Leatham:

"I was rather upset in the stomach whilst there, and this combined with the perturbation of mind consequent in finding what a commotion I had made by my letter to the *The Times* last Saturday. I am properly abused by *The Times* in three different leaders being held as an example of political disrepute & immorality – *The Spectator* takes special notice of my letter (on Dec 4th) calling me an intellectual & moral fanatic – private correspondents call me a Fenian & send me tracts, but I get a few warmly congratulatory letters from my friends, one I especially value from Edward Grey – I admit I wrote the letter in hot blood & used stronger language than I should have ... but I am not sorry as people want waking up."

Just before Christmas, Lord Randolph Churchill resigned as Chancellor of the Exchequer creating panic among the Unionists, and speculation began about the possibility of another general election. Between Christmas and New Year, Joseph found that Arthur (who between the election and now had been away in America) was to stand as the Unionist candidate at Darlington against Theodore Fry, and not a single family fencing rail had so far been nailed back in place.

On the very day he made this uncomfortable discovery, Joseph went with David Dale, Henry Fell Pease and Alfred to a meeting on the future of the *The Northern Echo*. This Darlington newspaper, of which Alfred was one of the directors, was in financial straits. The *Echo* took a reliable Liberal line under its Editor J.H. 'Echo' Bell. During this meeting as Joseph records,

"Arthur came in and walked out again."

Arthur must have felt that by stopping he might be intruding on something of which he no longer felt himself to be a part.

The following day Joseph and Arthur met on the train going to Newcastle for a Stephensons board meeting. They chatted on "Sturge's affairs" and other matters of mutual interest, but the political scene appears to have been carefully avoided, the better to maintain even an uncertain peace.

The Sturge affair was some appeal to Beatrice's trustees for financial assistance, the Sturges being Beatrice's relations on her late mother's side. Beatrice had not income enough to keep Lymington quiet, so an appeal from another quarter was one falling on deaf ears.

"They seem to think that Beatrice is to do everything for them and I take care that she does not ..."

This was Joseph's concluding statement on the Sturge business after the correspondence had dragged on into the New Year.

As usual, Christmas 1886 was a large family gathering at Hutton, and New Year's Eve was an occasion when Joseph and Alfred both turned to their journals to review the year and reflect. This year from Alfred's pen we have:

"... a most depressed one in trade and the anxieties which have surrounded my father I have shared to some extent, but although our private affairs have not prospered so well as usual from a business point of view, we have got on somehow

51

8. *The Conservatory at Hutton Hall.*

very comfortably ... I can say that I have had a happy year & one I am thankful for, knowing that the sunshine that has surrounded my path so far cannot last always – a want of systematic work, an irritable temper, a careless tongue & my constant tendency to idleness are the faults that I must struggle against."

1887

As the year began, Alfred went up for the opening of Parliament, and fed up with London and its loathsome fog, he had gone north again only to return once more, this time with Nellie, Edward and the baby Christopher. They settled in at 24 KPG,

"... where Father allows us to remain at any rate till Easter or till the house is sold."

There had been precious little interest shown by anyone in taking up the sale offer, and its disposal was proving to be a very slow economy in the making.

Alfred stuck to his parliamentary duties through the long debate on the Queen's address, and when the debate on the adjournment came on 18th March, it having been moved by the Parnellite M.P. John Dillon, calling attention to the death of one Hanlon, who had been bayoneted by the police at Yanghall, the Tories cheered wildly the description of the police action.

"Parnell was very violent in his language & I never saw him show suppressed rage & indignation more – He made the Tories wince as he stood quietly with his finger half pointing to Balfour, his eyes full of a determined look and denounced their talk of bloodshed in Ireland."

Alfred voted with the Irish M.P.s, – the minority, 226 – 88. There were only eighty-five Parnellite M.P.s in this parliament and

"This night Sir Henry Havelock-Allan was very drunk & made a scandalous scene."

The conduct and abusive language used by Jack's father-in-law towards Alfred was outrageous and

"... he was saved from being named, by my asking Flower[1] to tell the Speaker what was the matter – It is sad to see a man who has been a splendid soldier in such a condition – I fear it is a sign he is going off his head again."

Ireland and the Tories' Coercion Bill occupied a great deal of parliamentary time this year. Joseph now joined Alfred in expressions of great indignation, and feelings in the House on both sides were running high. The Parnellites and Liberals were incensed when reading regular press accounts of evictions, brutality and the demolition of farmhouses erected by the Irish tenants with their own hands at their own cost, who were now unable to pay the extortionate rents, exacted in many cases by absentee landlords. Alfred and Joseph, together with Jack decided to go to Ireland to see for themselves what was taking place.

Upon arrival in Dublin, 26th May, 1887, they called on John Dillon at his house in Great North George Street. Dillon was a very fair-minded man, and in his conversation he told them that they must try to see both sides; the landlords, the constabulary and especially the Protestants living in Catholic districts as well as the farm tenants. Before leaving Dublin, they called on Timothy Harrington[2] at the National League offices in O'Connell Street.

Alfred says:

"It is curious to find men like Harrington after four political imprisonments during which they have suffered terribly, quite kindly and moderate. Harrington suffered 6 months imprisonment on one occasion for having told the farmers in Tipperary, that if they did not treat the labourers well, he wd. advise them to combine as he had advised the tenants. He was arrested, and sent to solitary confinement, skilly and the plank bed 'for intimidating the farmers' – and those very farmers in that very county elected him by overwhelming numbers their member while he was in gaol for intimidating them."

27th May. "I left Dublin for Westport. From the train you see at first a rich grass country for many miles, but gradually you arrive at a great boggy plain, which stretches, covered with small holdings, across the centre of Ireland. The object that first struck my notice was roofless houses, standing amongst enclosures where the walls and fences were thrown down, & the ribs in the grass alone showed where the land had been tilled, & where the potato plots had been. The number of these objects increased till it was difficult to believe one's eyes.

After leaving Mullingar, I thought I would count how many I could see in 10 minutes – Well I tried, & in 10 minutes I counted 21, then we reached Athlone and I tried again, & in the next 10 minutes I counted 43. I had never realised as I did in passing through this country how small the holdings were, & always regarded the Irish tenants as small farmers, but really they are nothing of the sort – I had read often that:- in 1881 there were 499,108 agricultural holders, & of these, 161,029 held less than 10 acres – but it was quite another thing to see it & be amongst it as I was when I got to Westport.

In the walks & drives I took in this district, I was astonished to see extraordinary poor & boggy stony barren country covered with miniature enclosures & little houses, the people in rags, invariably bare footed & half naked, often carrying huge loads, women & children, of peat, seaweed, of manure & even of soil itself in great basket creels on their backs, up the stony paths to their hillside patches. Some had donkey's doing the same work, unshod & often unbridled, then others cutting turf in the bogs, or tilling in their potato patches – every one of which appeared to be reclaimed land, the poor nature of which, proved by the manner in which the holdings from which the tenants had been evicted quite recently, had relapsed into bog or mountain grass. I have never seen people working so hard, or living in such poverty, nor had I ever seen so courteous & kindly a population.

We enquired how they lived & found that here, as throughout the west, they subsisted for 9 months of the year on three meals of potatoes and salt a day, & the other months, April, May & June when the old potatoes were over, & before the new came on, on 3 meals of Indian meal & water, & if they could pay their rents, and had plenty of potatoes & meal to supply them thus, they were perfectly content.

I next made enquiries of people living in the town of Westport, including the parish priest, as to the rents, & found they varied from 20/- & 25/- to £2 an acre – & this for land that on the Yorkshire moors would not find tenants at 2/6 or 5/- – I found that the town park lands, or what we should call accommodation land round the town, poor as it was, let for £5 an acre, & up till 3 years ago was rented at £6 & even £7. The fact is that here as elsewhere, the landlord takes from the tenant, not a rent from the land, but a rent that has no relation whatever to the soil or its capacities, but simply what a tenant will pay for bare existence – or put another way, the price a man will undertake to pay rather than starve to death, go into the workhouse or leave his country for America."

Turning his attention to the landlords, he singles out for particular attention

"... three monsters *(who)* own the land, about 300,000 acres, Lord Sligo, Lord Lucan and Sir R. Palmer – three absentees who have evicted many thousands of people & thrown down many thousands of houses & villages & one or two towns ..."

Lord Sligo raked in £20 – £25,000 a year from his tenants.

"I travelled through part of this estate & a scene more truly frightful I never looked *(upon)*, hundreds & hundreds of houses still standing without windows doors or roofs, gaunt grim monuments in every direction of an exterminated people. These wretched beings decimated by famine, were ejected with every circumstance of the grossest cruelty. I was told the dead were during that time to be seen lying outside the houses & in the roads – What these people had already suffered no tongue could ever tell, nor will history ever record."

Almost immediately upon his return from Ireland, Alfred went up to London, the House, and back to the Coercion Bill, more than ever convinced about the rightness of Home Rule for Ireland, but by 25th July,

"Getting very weary of the session & London. London always hateful to me – public wrangles worry me and when these are added to personal and private cares I long to be once more quietly at home pursuing the regular routine of country life like that I lived before 1885."

He now mentions that the *York Herald,* a newspaper hitherto the mouthpiece for the Liberal Party in that city, had gone over to the Unionists, and on 7th August,

"I have all the past week played truant from my place in parliament, but I was so nearly knocked up that I think I should have broken down if I had stayed. I have enjoyed my week at home very much, tho' I have not had as much rest as I hoped for. The *York Herald* having gone over to the enemy has brought a heap of correspondence upon me, & I fear circumstance will cause me not to follow Gladstone's advice ... 'not to have anything to do with newspapers in your constituency.'
Two schemes seem possible to me. Pressure on the *York Herald* from the 'Gladstonian' shareholders & directors to accompany either:-
1. Try to raise £30,000 to run a paper against the *Herald* on the same line. This I fear we cannot do.
2. To run our evening Liberal paper & a weekly one looking to working up to a morning paper."

Joseph was away fishing at Falmouth and Alfred wrote to him setting out his ideas. By the 11th August, following a talk with J.H. 'Echo' Bell at Darlington, Alfred was at a meeting in York on the subject of starting up a new newspaper. Lord Ripon was in the chair and 'Echo' Bell was there also to give his advice.

The Gladstonian Liberals on the *Herald* were in a hopeless minority, so they were in no position to regain the advantage. One thing irking Alfred was the fact that his father had handed £2,000 to the *Herald* to save it from bankruptcy and to serve the Liberal Party, and now it was acting against that party and against the son of its benefactor. Apart from making public the underhand conduct of the Liberal Unionists, no particular course of action was decided upon at this meeting.

By September, Joseph and Alfred had started in earnest to examine ways of launching a new Liberal newspaper in York. This much at any rate had been resolved upon, however it was to be financed. About the same time Joseph and Arthur had journeyed to Newcastle to a Stephensons meeting after which Joseph contemplated the change in relationship between them:

> "It is amazing how differences in political party (I don't say view) close(s) up matters that used to be of mutual interest!"

Corndavon had been sub-let again this year, but there was some shooting around Hutton and Pinchinthorpe, and in November Lymington suddenly appeared, but received only a day and a half's mention as one of the guns – nothing more – just came and went like the wind.

By December, Alfred, taking his brother Jack and Harry Paulton with him, returned to Ireland to witness the Massereene evictions. Other witnesses on the first day were P. Stanhope, M.P., The Countess Tolstoy, Theodore Fry, M.P., and Sir W. Wedderburn.

Captain Keogh, the magistrate who was directing operations, was insolent and tried to get the observers removed. He told Stanhope that he had no business being there and needn't look to him for protection. But the divisional magistrate Cullen, also present, treated the observers with courtesy and told Stanhope, that if the party stayed with the police they should see everything.

On the second day of evictions, with Captain Keogh in sole charge, the lanes leading to the holdings had been barricaded by felled trees. Stone walls had been set up on the road and a bonfire started to slow the progress of the police and crowbar men. When Captain Keogh tried to get permission to cross neighbouring land to detour the obstacles in his path, permission was refused. Captain Keogh then mounted a car opposite a tree from which was suspended an effigy of Judge Keogh, (the deceased and detested brother of Captain Keogh). Brandishing a stick he shouted at the quiet orderly crowd, "Forthwith everyone must disperse". And first addressing the police, and then the crowd – "Disperse the people forthwith – I won't tolerate it, you must be suppressed. County Inspector, disperse these crowds. The people may be armed and may fire on my forces."

The constabulary went about their business in a less excited manner, hacking away at the trees, but soon gave up at the hopelessness of the task. Keogh then gave orders to march across the fields, which they did, and the people set alight to the whin bushes on the banks leading to the holdings. When they reached the dwellings, (there were two side by side) Captain Keogh placed a double cordon around the houses and the crowbar men set about their business, and the tenants came out of their houses without resistance.

The observers this day, Alfred, Jack, Theodore Fry and Sir William Wedderburn held a meeting at which they made speeches expressing sympathy with the people in their sufferings and constitutional struggle for free speech, a free press, and Home Rule.

On 11th Dec. Alfred went to Arklow, to the Catholic Church there, and after the service went with Father Dillon to see tenants who had been evicted and who were now living in National League huts. On a sunny afternoon, Alfred travelled on a car with Father Dillon to where,

> "... in view of the beautiful valleys & hills of Aroca, & on the S. the rugged steep of the mountain of Tara rising out of a rich fertile undulating landscape ... are buried the remains of the insurgents who fell at the disastrous 'Siege of Arklow' June 9th, 1798."

As they travelled along the road, Father Dillon recited a dirge:

> "... in a soft musical voice full of pathos & nationalist feeling – it is shockingly rebellious, but a country without a nationalist sentiment is contemptible, and if men can feel keenly about their country, they have the stuff for valuable confederates -
>
> *Sleep ye heroes calmly sleep peaceful be your slumbers*
> *Unknown though be your hallowed names forgotten though your numbers*
> *Full well we know ye died in faith no adverse judgment fearing*
> *For fell ye not with pike in hand for conscience & for Erin*
>
> *Brave were your hearts as earnest prayers to God the just addressing*
> *And heart drawn sighs for peaceful homes & love-lit eyes repressing*
> *Ye stood whilst in your half armed ranks no step was seen to falter*
> *To strike one bold if fruitless blow for Country & for Altar*

Ye little recked by myriad foes by England's might supported
Your thoughts dwelt more on truth & right by England's craft distorted
Ye little recked of child – of wife – left fatherless forlorn
Too full your hearts of one fell name – of England – the forsworn.

Dream ye heroes, sweetly dream 'neath Tara's crags reposing
That hands, as brave, as yours today with Englands might are closing
And though no pike is borne in them, nor heard the musket's rattle
They're one with yours of '98 in fighting freedoms battle

What! though above your ashes stand no sculptured mausoleum!
What! though the sighing breezes chant your valours love Te Deum
What! though undecked your nameless graves with wealth of wreathed treasure
Your memory shrined in Irish hearts in glorys bounteous measure

Sleep ye heroes softly sleep by rugged Tara guarded
Nor fear your gallant deeds shall go by Erin unregarded
For when her radiant crownless harp o'er every hill is flying
A prayer she'll breathe for your brave hearts neath Tara's shadow lying –"

Alfred and Jack returned to England on 12th December, 1887.

As usual at Christmas, there was a large family gathering. All except Vincent and Effie Hamlyn, who were at Cannes, were there, including Effie's daughter Sylvia Hamlyn, now aged six. Nanny, Sarah Wilson, who had such a large share of the responsibility for the childhood upbringing of Alfred, his brother and his six sisters, always had by tradition a nursery tea on Christmas Eve at Hutton Hall. Attendance was obligatory, but no-one, including Joseph and Minnie, would ever have wanted to miss it.

1888

Early in the new year, Alfred received a lawyer's letter from Barlee & Greer of Dublin, threatening immediate proceedings against him for something he had said in a speech at Darlington with reference to the Kinsella case, an incident during the evictions.

"I stated that it was alleged in evidence, that Freeman the bailiff, had shot Kinsella – the passage they quote apparently represents me as having stated it on my own authority! Of course some vindictive Unionist at Darlington has done this – it is absurd how much trouble & annoyance one's political opponents can put one to about a trifle, but if they think they are going to gag Englishmen & prevent them as they try in Ireland, from exposing hideous scandals, they make a mistake."

Alfred consulted his solicitor, a suitable reply sent and there the matter ended.

The newspaper project for York was getting under way, and negotiations were started for the purchase of the *Yorkshire Chronicle*. Without a morning newspaper Unionist propaganda was going unchallenged.

"Since speaking at York on Friday night last *(13th January, 1888)*, I have been subjected to the most scurrilous abuse in the *Y. Herald* – & I am sorry to find that Uncle Arthur has been the instigator of it. He might, if he had thought I had made false statements, have given me the opportunity of correcting them – In everything they have criticised me for, I believe I have been perfectly accurate – I stated there were 2,000 evictions on Lord Sligo's property since he succeeded – I believe there have been far more – Uncle Arthur I suppose gets a telegram from Sligo's Agent denying it!"

By 24th January, the *Yorkshire Chronicle* had been bought. Joseph had been through to York and found there had been

"... some good work done. Machine agreed to be purchased, arrangements with Mr Whitaker confirmed. Saw over the premises of the *Yorkshire Chronicle*."

The premises needed a lot doing to them before production could commence.

The following day, 25th January, Joseph, Alfred and Jack were at Hutton for a full days session over Joseph's accounts. Times were very bad and a firm resolve was made to pull down expenses as far as possible. Joseph had to face a *"huge amount of interest"* on his overdraft at the Counting House. There had not been a colliery dividend during the past four years. Joseph complains that

"We get so little income that I cannot make ends meet. We went into our general position at the office and my own shortness of revenue, as there are no profits from Stephensons, collieries or iron making. They *(Alfred and Jack)* were kind and good."

At Hutton, the wages of Joseph's estate employees were reduced, some were found other work, expenditure on the garden[3] had to be slashed to no more than £500, and a smaller though proportionate economy regime was introduced at Pinchinthorpe. Doubtless Jack did likewise at his home, Snow Hall, Gainford, Co. Durham.

Alfred left for London and

"... its greasy pavements, its smoke laden atmosphere & filthy leafless trees" for the opening of Parliament. He went to 24 KPG alone, and while there he tried for the larger economy, going to house agents to urge them to find a buyer.

Now the Mills, of which Joseph thought he had largely divested himself, loomed up again, Clarke and Smith saying they were short of finance. Following a meeting between Joseph, Jack, Henry Fell Pease, David Dale and Charles Fry it was agreed to aid them by £6,000, Smith putting £2,000 worth of yarns into *"our hands."*

In March, Joseph went to a Stephensons meeting.

"Loss on year £16,000! No joke!"

This was a long hard depression. The tale of woe was the same elsewhere with all industry being hit by it, and the catalogue of company failures made cheerless reading. David Dale, who held a directorship with a Barrow-in-Furness company owning collieries in Lancashire, Yorkshire and Wales, said they had recorded a loss of £500,000 during the last year.

In April, 1888, Joseph was laid up following a relatively minor operation, which threw onto Alfred's shoulders

"... many of his affairs to see to; besides this there have been business worries and anxieties as to the future that have been a constant harass – Then again it has been a busy time in parliament, what with coercion in Ireland, local government bills at home & sensational budgets. I have had to watch carefully the government's attempts to deprive York city of its position as a county."

Compounding everything, Minnie was again unwell; Alfred's sister, Effie Hamlyn had scarlet fever, but if there was something in all this gloom that amused him during this period of stringent domestic economy, it was seeing Jack and Elsie bringing carriage horses and servants

"... up to town in State for 'the Season'."

During May, 1888, Alfred went a busy round in the north, holding political meetings at Stockton, Middlesbrough, Pickering and Darlington and elsewhere and dealing with

"... a huge correspondence which is the burden of my life. One long bombardment of begging letters, or letters plaguing me to address meetings, open bazaars or take chairs ... I have enjoyed being at home – the weather has been lovely – the birds singing all day but especially at dawn & night fall – the country looking exquisite

– I have watched the cubs opposite my house in the warm afternoon & evenings & thoroughly enjoyed the sight amidst the most beautiful surroundings."

By 9th June, after being back in London a week or so, Alfred unexpectedly finds himself having to return home to Pinchinthorpe because of political business, after which

"The last fortnight has been an anxious one; in fact for a year past I have felt that the clouds of the future have been gathering – anxieties in business matters that cannot be put on paper are harassing enough, especially when you feel that serious events may take place for which you are not in the least responsible – The advice which I have given when asked for it has only found active support from Jack. For years my forebodings & opinions on the way certain private persons were managing their concerns have been received as the views of a pessimist & a croaker, & now these persons led away by sanguine temperaments & inability to realise facts find themselves in queer street. They look and talk as if it was misfortune for which they should have sympathy, & having got themselves in what probably is an inextricable mess, expect me to do the impossible or to suggest some possible cure for an impossible case – added to this wearing bother, I have had for weeks to live without Nellie in London, a thing that agrees badly with my temper & life ... Again, Effie seems to be in a poor way and the doctors are very much alarmed at her condition. Mother who is seriously unwell has been telegraphed to for Folkestone from Falmouth."

Effie was ill at Folkestone. Alfred's mind frequently turned to her in her illness. He wrote to her almost daily, and anxiously hoped that the doctors were wrong in their belief that her case was beyond aid. She had a glandular disease and on 19th June, Alfred received a letter from his father saying:

"The day has passed nearly away – & I have I think only to prepare – if they want preparing, your minds for any tidings we may have to send."

23rd June, was Joseph's birthday and for Alfred

"A telegram was put into my hands 'Effie died at four thirty. Could Alfred & Nellie come early prepared to stay Sunday?'"

They left at once and

"... travelled down in a crowded train to Folkestone – it was a very hot & beautiful day & it was hard to realise that my sister Effie had seen the waving grass & trees for the last time & no earthly breezes or smiling summer sun would touch her cheeks again."

The first few days after the funeral were spent in helping Vincent

Hamlyn adjust to his loss. Sylvia Hamlyn, *"poor little woman"*, had come up to Hutton from her father's London home.

Soon after this, a decision was made that Sylvia would live at Hutton, but go south to London or Devonshire at all times that her father could spare from his circuit work to have her with him.

Alfred returned to town but was back at Pinchinthorpe by 21st July

"... with a secret intention of not returning."

He spent about three weeks doing some of those things he most enjoyed, attending agricultural shows at Kildale, and the Great Yorkshire, which this year was held at Huddersfield, and the Cleveland Hunt puppy show at Skelton.

By the end of August, the *Yorkshire Chronicle* at York and the *Northern Echo* at Darlington were both losing money. Of the latter Alfred says:

"The amount of anxiety and bother these non paying concerns gives me I cannot describe – I dislike Bell's way of managing the paper & takes all criticism as reflections on himself. I should like the paper cleared of all personal politics & devoted to latest & local news with each day a special article or subject given space to."

And a few days later referring to the *Yorkshire Chronicle,* about which by now, he was probably wishing he had heeded Gladstone's advice:

" – a source of trouble and annoyance this paper – Marchmont, the Editor does not seem a good business man."

A meeting held to discuss how they were to proceed profitably with the *Chronicle,* culminated in Joseph and Alfred agreeing to put up more money if Frank Lockwood and the other York directors would do likewise. Marchmont was followed as Editor by a man named Goadby who had come over to the *Chronicle* from the *York Herald.* In other spheres the collieries were showing more activity, but 24 KPG was still unsold.

Lymington and Beatrice came to Hutton 11th September, 1888, he for four days' shooting. Whilst at Hutton Joseph

"... had a funny interview with Beatrice Lymington who was most anxious for a colliery dividend! to which I would not commit myself. Saw them off to Darlington."

When Beatrice had returned to Hurstbourne, she sent Joseph what he described as a *"saucy letter"* to which he immediately set about framing a reply

"... on her want of confidence in us and her unreasonable grumblings for money."

If the grumblings were understandable, still nothing could be done at present. She just had to be patient and wait for things to improve – everyone else was forced to this view.

Alfred was back in Ireland for three days at the end of October. He went, much against all inclination, but felt he had a duty to go in answer to a request from Pierce Mahony[4] who felt he (Alfred) could do something to stop the evictions going on at Glensharold. He could do little but observe and protest at the inhumanity in all that he saw, and continue to draw attention at home to what was going on in Ireland.

Just before Christmas a by-election took place at Stockton. Joseph Dodds, a very popular and much respected solicitor in the town, had resigned his seat on account of some embarrassing financial difficulty. The Liberal candidate at this election was Sir Horace Davey, Q.C.

Alfred went with his father to help Davey and while there, saw Herbert Pike Pease, one of Arthur Pease's sons walking about Stockton sporting Tory colours, an experience they found most humiliating.

Sir Horace Davey won the by-election with a 395 majority, after which Joseph telegraphed his congratulations and sat down to write to his brother Arthur on the theme of finding a way out of their political antagonisms. In his reply Arthur gave no quarter but acknowledged their differences as being *"advocates of legislative separation."*

1889

In January, Alfred was very strongly pressed to stand as a candidate for a seat on the North Riding County Council. He had no real wish to add to his existing cares, but he allowed himself to be nominated. When he found he was to be opposed, he began to regret this further involvement. He won his seat comfortably, and in February his father was made a North Riding County Alderman.

At the end of February, Alfred was back at his parliamentary work, and once more fell foul of Jack's father-in-law Sir Henry Havelock-Allan.

There had been strong feeling among the Tories arising from the publication in *The Times* of a facsimile letter purporting to have been written by Parnell the Irish Nationalist. But it was a forgery, for which a man named Piggott, it was later discovered, was responsible. When the forgery was uncovered, Piggott fled to Madrid where he shot himself, and *The Times* which had taken sides against Parnell in all the hullabaloo, was left with 'egg on its mast head'. As to Sir Henry's behaviour on this occasion:

"O'Hanlon (Parnellite) who was sitting on a back bench, made some remark to T.W. Russell (Liberal Unionist), who was sitting in front of him, which I did not catch. Russell turned round and said 'I have nothing to do with Piggott!,' whereupon Sir Henry Havelock-Allan (L.U.) who was wandering about the back benches on our side on the war-path, deliberately barged into O'Hanlon & threw himself on top of him. O'Hanlon appealed to the Speaker and H.J. Wilson (L) corroborated O'Hanlon's statement. Sir Henry said he noticed O'Hanlon's irregular remark, but had 'not the slightest intention of touching him'!! The Speaker ordered him to apologise. Sir Henry is clever enough to make even an apology offensive, and did so on this occasion.

Later he selected me for some blasphemous and obscene insults, and dogged me to the library and back again; amongst his pretty threats was one 'to do me in on my doorstep, where he would be at 2.0a.m., when he would cut my _____ liver out'. I told him I should report him to the Speaker for a nuisance, and did, but asked him to speak to Sir Henry privately; he did this at the Chair, and Sir Henry returned to me and with profuse apologies begged my forgiveness and added, 'You see, Pease, it was because I was in *great pain* from pinching my finger in shutting a window yesterday!' I will say this for him, that he was almost as much tickled as I was with this excuse, and we laughed together sitting side by side not far from the Speaker who seemed puzzled by the reconciliation."

In March, 1889, Jack's wife, Elsie, gave birth to a son who was named Joseph Pease, a brother for Miriam Blanche Pease who was born in August, 1887. The particular reason for noting these events is to record some of Sir Henry's many quirks.

For reasons best known to himself, he viewed his daughter's husband, and it is supposed all other members of the Pease family, with the utmost contempt. His grandchildren, merely by the accident of birth, also got lumped into this category, and he referred to them, not as his grandchildren but as "the grocer's children" – Jack Pease being the "grocer." It could only be that in Sir Henry's view, the colliery and ironstone mining industries were somehow to be equated with bags of flour, eggs, tinned fruit and such like.

He refused to have his grandchildren in his house at Blackwell Grange, Darlington, so that if Alice, Lady Havelock-Allan wished to see them when Sir Henry was at home, they had to be smuggled in at dead of night, and to show no light in case he made the discovery.

When in London, he was always a tiresome obstacle to other riders who might encounter him in Rotten Row, where he led his horse by one hand while reading from his Bible in the other.

Not long after the incident in the Commons, Joseph being away at Newcastle where Stephensons were showing a £21,000 loss for 1888, Alfred in London found a buyer for 24 KPG and committed his father to a sale at £18,000!

"Too little!" was Joseph's reaction.

But a wait of two years for a sale when finances were tight was quite long enough, and with this accomplished, Alfred, thoroughly satisfied, went home to Pinchinthorpe.

Whilst there this time, he recorded the death of his constant companion since 1877 and Cambridge days, his wire-haired terrier "Worry." His animals and pets were a very important part of his life, and "Worry" had now so injured herself in fighting her way out of her kennel yard, tearing at the wire placed across the iron bars to prevent her, that she had to be put to sleep. Alfred, coming from the stables found her half way to the freedom she sought, and knowing he and help was near, she stopped struggling, and despite the most terrible self-inflicted injuries, wagged her tail excitedly. He did all that he could to staunch her wounds, without as much as a whimper from her, and he placed her gently back in the straw of her kennel.

"So I said good-bye to her, lying quietly and patiently in the straw and she now lies in the old orchard, a faithful & sweet little companion.

She was a most wonderful combination of fondsomeness and gentleness, pretty ways and perfectly reckless courage – I have had scores of wire haired terriers, but she was the fleetest killer of rats & quickest I ever saw or had, and she used often to come with (the) Drag at Cambridge, & could lead all the way & a most extraordinary sight she was, to see her racing & turn, twisting as hard as she could lick, often black with mud, her tongue hanging out and looking quite demented with excitement, & almost incredible that the little rough white thing asleep on my bed was the same creature ... Once during the last few months of her life, after all her teeth were gone, when she was quite blind & deaf, ruptured, one of her legs useless from a compound fracture in two or three places, I put her into a place where I thought there was a rat, she went in, her old style, found him, one as big as a rabbit, snacked him up, gave the old shake & chucked him up & went for the next."

"Worry" had always been with Alfred when he had been to collect badgers to populate the hillsides at Pinchinthorpe. Now in June, 1889 one evening he went up to the badger setts to

"... see if I could see anything of the fox cubs that were bred here & which I have not seen for a month – At 10.0p.m. I was astonished by seeing five old badgers, great big hoary ones, come out of one hole & within a foot of where I stood – two of them went across the ride & went into the hole where the fox cubs were bred. I was, for the first time in my life angry with them as I am compelled to believe that though before they were so many, they never interfered with the foxes, yet that now they have driven my vixen away."

While staying with Lord Rosebery at Mentmore over the weekend, on Monday, 24th June, at breakfast Alfred was handed a telegram from Nellie asking him to return sometime that day. Within fifteen minutes he was on his way to Cheddington Station. In London, Joseph wired to Middlesbrough for a special train to take Alfred on to Pinchinthorpe.

Alfred got home, half an hour after Nellie had been delivered of a baby girl. In the evening,

"I took Christopher over on his donkey to Hutton to tell old (Nanny) Wilson who was crazy with delight – after folding her hands in ecstasy & blessing heaven, kissing me, she sent a number of messages to her darling mistress – Afterwards, in her constant manner reminded me of my duty to my child & the necessity I was under of 'presenting her to the Lord' of 'blessing His name' of 'bringing her up in His fear' & added with that fervent piety & awe which made me smile when I thought of it after, looking at the sleeping babe, 'My precious Master! Another living soul!! To perish everlastingly! or to be saved. It rests with you to give her to the Lord!'"

The babe was given the names Lavender Mary. "Lavender" was a name of Alfred's choice – after one of his favourite hunters – and Mary after his mother whom we know as Minnie.

In July, 1889, he was back in London, where at 24 KPG everything was being packed up for storage pending finding another suitable town house. Charged with feeling, Joseph left the house that had been his for a quarter of his life, and with Minnie went to Falmouth. Alfred, who had been awakened early by the noisy sparrows in the ivy, was the last to leave, and after seeing the pantechnicon loaded, he took his baggage to Jones Private Hotel, Park Place, St James's, his new temporary lodgings.

In August he had a narrow escape from death when shooting Frank Lockwood's moors at Scalby, near Scarborough. There were six guns, one of whom was a man named Hutchinson.

"Hutchinson, stumbling along with his gun carried carelessly, put his foot in a deep rut on the road as I was walking with him to the butts after lunch, he stumbled sideways. I was just looking to see where his gun would go when he stumbled, saw the two round barrel ends just under my cheek & before I knew what had happened, I had staggered & fell in to the moor holding my head completely stunned for a moment, his gun having gone off close under my ear not more than an inch or so from *(my)* throat – I could not hear for a long time after, & felt as if half my head had gone – However, a miss is as good as a mile for such a man, & he shot away merrily all the afternoon after apologising for giving me, what he feared was a very dreadful fright!"

Late September and all were once more at Corndavon for a fortnight. During their stay, and at the behest of Jack's wife, Elsie, Joseph had written to the Duke of Cleveland to ask if as owner of a house known as Selaby, Gainford Co. Durham, he would consider Jack as a tenant for the place.

Sylvia Hamlyn, an astute assessor of adult character, saw her grandfather, Joseph, always as *"wax in Elsie's hands."* The day before departure from Corndavon, the Duke had replied that he didn't wish to let Selaby. Still less did he wish even to put it into a proper state of repair.

Leaving by train from Ballater, an uncomfortable journey followed, everyone being made to suffer because of Joseph's failed effort, and

"Elsie cried and sulked all the way to Edinbro' because she could not get Selaby. She is a perfectly spoilt child."

And travelling on home the following day,

"... easily to Darlington – Elsie's sulks spoiling our journey."

During November Alfred was able to snatch a few days' hunting with the Cleveland Hounds. One of these days – and after a long run, he changed to his second mount for the day, "Caress" -

"... jumping at the chance of giving her her first taste of cross country work ... soon all joined in, a quiet November evening, a sinking dull sun & the country in grand order. They flew across between Grey Towers & Rye Hill by the back of Batty's houses & then for Stanley Houses. They check(ed) at the stell[5] & our fox had gone toward Ayton. He then turned north again, but left Blackmore plantation on his right – all this time 'Caress' going like an old hunter (except the refusal of the stell at a big spot) & full of freedom and life.

Kicking off (at) a stubby fence to cover a ditch into the Stokesley road, she kicked back with such a will that the fence stubs broke & she came down and rolled with me, but we were both up in a minute, both enjoying it almost, we were so pleased with each other, & away again towards (the) Ayton (&) Stokesley road & then sharp to the right some big fences, hounds going slower towards Angrove & then, such a catastrophe.

I put her at a small fence into the high road; she jumped, landed, pecked & slipped on the flinty road, recovered, slipped again & down she went. I knew too well what had happened. The pride of my stables & my hope & pride had broken her knee. Very lame myself with a sprained ankle in starch bandages, I limped home with my mare, wishing rather I had broken both my legs than this, & my thoughts were very bitter as I held her head & restrained her, eager as she was from still going faster than a walk even on three legs, & long after in the dark I could see the white of her game but gentle eye & it made my heart ache to think what an awful blemish she would bear & how cruel & undeserved this lasting reproach on her would be. As Fred[6] said 'Your day's hunting will cost you about £300 sir'-

The only bright thing is that if she recovers completely except the mark I shall keep her ... & if she is left a stumbler by the injury to her knee, I have the best hunter brood mare in England – Last year she won 13 first prizes & 1 second in 14 shows – No more of this!"

Joseph's reaction was:

"Why will he jump a 4 yr. old into a hard lane!! "

After two days of self reproach,

"... conscious of my terrible weakness & readiness to give way to the spirit of the world – tho' I don't think I am worldly minded, yet many of those things that 'please me most' I feel I enjoy too much and give up time to that might be better used."

There happened now this November an extraordinary boom in Cleveland. Pig iron No. 3 which the year before sold at 29/- or 30/- per ton, was now 67/-. The dramatic improvement was the same at the collieries with £10,000 profit the previous month, but it was certainly all wanted. In other respects too the news was brighter than for long enough. There looked to be a sale of the *Northern Echo* coming about, and even Stephensons was well off for locomotive orders, though Joseph remained dissatisfied with the vigour of the management there.

1890

When the year began to open out, hopes were higher that in business, things were beginning to come right at last. By mid year Pease & Partners were in a position to pay a final dividend of five per cent[7] while putting £45,000 to reserves. This still left the Reserve Fund about £60,000 short of where it ought to be, but the prospects were very great that at least a further £25,000 would be added during the following half year. Beyond that it was difficult to see.

The year began with Alfred's sister Helen Blanche Pease marrying her cousin Edward Lloyd Pease at the Friends' Meeting House, Guisborough, and the year closed with another sister, Ethel marrying Gerald Buxton, son of Edward North Buxton, of Knighton, Buckhurst Hill, Essex. The Buxtons were in the brewery business, Truman, Hanbury, Buxton.

In June, Alfred absented himself from Parliament to attend the Berlin Horse Show. Before that, in March, much to his father's alarm, he entered for the House of Commons steeplechase with his grey mare "Norah Creina," and ran a close second.

Between the start and finish of the year, Alfred had taken a house in Egerton Gardens for the parliamentary session. Joseph, looking for a replacement for 24 KPG, and after viewing a number of properties, none of which came up to the exacting standards to which he was accustomed, settled finally upon 44, Grosvenor Gardens. A modernisation programme was instituted. Electric light was to be installed, and other refinements made and the house redecorated throughout, all of which would take well into the new year to accomplish.

In September, Jack and Elsie threw a large party for their friends, relations and associates at Hutton Hall, the only place large enough to entertain the 800 Elsie had invited. About 450 accepted. The refreshments were abundant and Joseph in recording the event said:

> "... the folks went through 30 gallons of champagne & claret cup and seemed much pleased."

A few days after this, Joseph was at a meeting at the Mills, where he was

> "... disgusted to find that *(the)* Mills at Priestgate[8] had lost abt. £4,000 owing, they say to the decrease value in wood in stock & to the rise in coals and oils – I am sick of these Mills!!"

In October he tried to bring about a sale of the Mills for £70,000. By November negotiations hovered around £65,000 and he gave instructions to a Darlington solicitor, Hutchinson, to do what he could, but the negotiations flickered out.

This was a year when with the exceptions mentioned above, nothing of great moment took place, but on the whole, things looked altogether brighter and improving.

In December, Joseph and Minnie went to stay with the Lymingtons at Hurstbourne Park, where Lymington politely let it be known – and not for the first time it may be appreciated – that

> "... they would like to sell out of the collieries if the way was made easy for them."

This remained an impossible request to accede to. The long bad years had to be made good, recovery in trade had to be certain, and the most exacting and continued patience was once more asked of them by Joseph.

The Hutton Christmas of 1890 was an upset with Minnie's mother dying on Christmas Eve at Falmouth, to where Minnie had gone some days before, while Joseph left Hutton for the funeral on Christmas Day.

Despite the sadness at the year's end, there was much to be hopeful about and morale was back in the ascendancy.

1891

Then calamity! On New Year's Day, 1891, the Lymingtons' Hurstbourne Park home was burnt to the ground!

Joseph learnt of this as he was travelling north from London, returning from his mother-in-law's funeral in Falmouth, and after looking in at the alterations progressing at 44, Grosvenor Gardens. Reading the newspaper account in the train it appeared that the only things saved from this disaster were books and silver. All Beatrice's and Lymington's heirlooms had been engulfed in the flames. Joseph straight away sent telegrams of sympathy and awaited clarification of the catastrophe.

When a disaster such as this strikes, the mind focuses immediately upon precautions one has neglected to take, and Joseph was no exception to this reaction. Fire drill was introduced at Hutton Hall, the estate workers were given clear instructions under his directions, so that everyone knew what to do in case of a similar thing happening there. He went carefully into the provision of modern fire fighting equipment.

Towards the end of January, Pease and Partners showed a profit for the half year of £131,000 which made £290,000 for the year as a whole. Even if this meant some improvement in income, last year's weddings had not promoted economy, and had the Mills and Stephensons been profitable this might augur well for the future.

Early in January, the miners at Pease & Partners Esh Pit had gone on strike over 10 hour working, and then the quarry men followed because Arthur Pease's son, Arthur Francis Pease

"... had declined to make the men a back payment of $^1/_2$d a ton 'frost money', but which he agreed to give them for the future."

By early March, 1891, Lymington had resolved to rebuild Hurstbourne though on a smaller scale. Before ever the insurance claim was met, Joseph advanced from his own resources sums totalling £40,000, so that rebuilding could commence without delay. Beatrice wrote to Joseph suggesting that he might write to the Earl of Portsmouth, for the purpose of proposing that Lymington be given full possession of Hurstbourne and, it would also seem, the rest of his father's Hampshire Estate. Joseph appears to have had his uses even if in other respects he was not as co-operative as the Lymingtons would have liked. However, wishing to help in any way he could, there followed two or three meetings between the Lymingtons and him before a final draft letter was prepared.

In this letter, Joseph wrote that while he in no way wished to interfere in Portsmouth's affairs, might it perhaps be best to place the proceeds of the insurance claim at Lymington's entire disposal; and secondly, that since the amount of the claim was likely to fall short of the cost of rebuilding, decorating and re-furnishing &c, (this being the view expressed by Beatrice) perhaps Portsmouth might consider making a deed of gift to Lymington of the whole Estate, and placing the responsibility for meeting the charges thereon, including settlement provisions, on Lymington. If Portsmouth so divested himself, he would be relieved of a great deal of anxiety.

Portsmouth in reply, confirmed the reduced scale of the proposed new Hurstbourne, more in keeping with the depressed land values – now down from £30 an acre to £10! He also revealed that he was being pressed hard by the Capital and Counties Bank to make repayment of a loan for farm improvements, and finally that on the question of making a deed of gift, he simply could not afford to divest himself of his beneficial interest. There were other undisclosed reasons which Portsmouth's agent said would make a surrender extremely difficult.

Joseph had a further meeting with the Lymingtons at the latter's London home, 2, Abbey Gardens, at which the contents of Portsmouth's letter were discussed. Some kind of a reply by Joseph, beyond a mere acknowledgement, must have been suggested, and following his return to Grosvenor Gardens, and after short reflection, Beatrice sent to Joseph the following letter:-

> My dear Father,
> We have come to the conclusion that it would be best to send no reply to Ld. P. It is not necessary & might do harm,
> > Yours affectionately,
> > > Btce. Lymington.

Joseph having no further role to play in this scheme, made preparations for a holiday in Venice with Minnie. It happened that the Lymingtons were departing the same day by the same train for Florence, and for a few days they travelled more or less together as far as Milan from where they went their separate ways.

Just before Joseph left, Alfred announced that for the second time he was entering the House of Commons steeplechase. He told his father that he was running no risks, and with Joseph saying that the game was not worth the candle, nor the fun worth the risk, Alfred, to please him said that he wouldn't ride another – but just this once he would. So Joseph was left setting out on holiday still wishing he was out of it, and all the way to Lucerne it troubled him.

The race was run in Pytchley country, and the stiffest course had been made out for the entrants. "Norah Creina," Alfred's mount of the previous year, was very fit, and he led off on the four-mile course. Sir Savile Crossley rode into him and cannoned him just after turning the flag for the run home, but after a while Alfred had it all his own way, and came in an easy winner, never having had to move either hand or heel. With the satisfaction of winning, he straight away wired to his father in Switzerland of his success.

Earlier this year, Alfred had introduced the first ever Wild Bird Protection Bill to the House. Herbert Asquith had drafted the Bill in less than half an hour, just following his verbal instructions given over the shoulder.

In May, we find Alfred making final preparations to go to the Pyrenees. His imagination had been fired by his sister Ethel's father-in-law, Edward North Buxton, who had been there the previous year, hunting for ibex which live in the most precipitous places, and which cannot be stalked as with deer.

Taking Nellie with him, he had in addition recruited his brother, Jack, and Ted Leatham[9]. Also on the trip was Lundie, the Scottish gamekeeper at Corndavon who for whatever reason, was sent on from London a day ahead with clear instructions to await the main party when it arrived at Pierrefitte in the south of France. It may be supposed that Lundie had no knowledge whatever of French, but that his rural Scottish resourcefulness would get him by.

However, when Alfred and the others had pulled into the station at Dax, being then about ninety-five miles short of their ultimate destination, sitting in the carriage of a northbound train, directly opposite their own compartment they saw Lundie. Alfred, Jack and Ted shouted, banged on the windows and made frantic signals to Lundie to get out and into their train, and but for the fluke of spotting him, the expedition would have started as a fiasco. Whilst the object of the trip was partially successful, they had recognised the difficulties of the terrain and the previously known rarity of encountering ibex, and had not entertained over optimistic expectations.

Leaving Gavarnie in the Pyrenees, and after a day's march, crossing to the Spanish side in deep snow, the party now strengthened by three guides (Celestin Passet, François Tresgarges and François Bernard) a cook and fifteen porters, reached their mountain hut. After the first day, success attended Ted Leatham's patience. The main excitement during the following three days, all of them blank, was in the waiting for nothing in ugly places, on ledges with terrifying drops:

> *20th May* "This morning I was top rifle in a very ugly spot, I thought, and when I had to get up to leave my rock, took about a quarter of an hour before I could work up my courage to raise myself on to my feet – but by the end of the week I found myself less nervous about sitting on the brink of the awful heights for hours."

Adventure was chiefly satisfied by being frozen in snowstorms and shifting mists and in making a way back to the hut by doubtful routes. On day five, in such a situation, none of the guides

When my brother-in-law
Gerald Buxton was hunting
in the Pyrenees - one day François
Tresgarges & François Bernard were sitting side by side
on some rocks, Tresgarges a very small almost hunch-backed
Bernard a giant, & the latter half asleep - Gerald lit his
pipe with a fusee ▬▬▬ - Tresgarges saw it thrown down
after the pipe was lit - had never seen anything like it &
picked it up & looking for a place to put it thought it would
just fit Bernhards ear hole & shoved it well in - of course
the fusee was red hot inside - Bernhard went up like a rocket
and head first over the rocks with a yell that roused all the
echoes of the valley - much to Tresgarges' astonishment - and
when I used to see these 2 sitting together. I always thought
of this story -

9. *Alfred's sketch of an incident in the Pyrenees.*

74

"... knew how to get down – we went onto gigantic snow wreaths which projected far beyond the cliff tops, but they could not find a way. At last we heard them say that there must be a way down by a certain precipice – it was the reason Celestin gave that struck terror into Ted and into me – 'Parceque j'ai vu les izards monter par la!' We began to wonder if any of us would ever be heard of again. We then went down an awful place, long drops on the face of a precipice thousands of feet deep. Where we dropped from rock to rock or terrace we generally alighted or fell on loose stones, snow falling and the ravines all bottomless abysses in the mist ... snow making it impossible not to slip, yet to slip certain death. The descent by the Salerous passage was like being in paradise after all this – we all met wet through, round the smokey chimney all happy to be at the bottom."

Ten days after setting out on this trip, a telegram from home informed Nellie of her father's sudden and totally unexpected death. With this most wretched news, the party immediately sent word for the return of the porters, and after an uneventful journey arrived in London on 28th May.

Notes
1. Cyril Flower, Liberal Whip.
2. Parnellite M.P. Dublin City, Harbour.
3. Average annual garden expenditure is taken at £2,800, of which 56% comprised wages and 10.5% coal and coke for the greenhouses.
4. Parnellite M.P. for Meath.
5. A dialect word, meaning a large open ditch, wide and deep.
6. Fred Freeman, Alfred's groom.
7. Expressed as being at the annual rate of 10%.
8. The Darlington Mills were in two parts. The Priestgate Mill was down by the River Skerne, and the Railway Mill further to the north.
9. Edward (Ted) Aldham Leatham was a brother of Charles A. Leatham, (d.1858) whose widow, Rachel, was sister of Sir Joseph Whitwell Pease. Rachel Leatham (née Pease) m. 2ndly 1875, William Fowler.

CHAPTER FOUR

Asia Minor & Exile in Algeria

1891 continued

Upon his return from the Pyrenees, Alfred met Edward North Buxton and discussed plans for a joint expedition to Asia Minor starting out in September. The object was to obtain, if possible, specimens of a large species of red deer known as soghun, which were to be found in the mountainous interior, and of which at the time, only one was known to have been brought back to England. It was perhaps considered unwise for Nellie to accompany Alfred on this rather longer expedition, and in any case the three children were too young to be left without one parent.

August and the family was once more at Corndavon, but this was to be the last visit there. The lease was up for renewal and Joseph felt disinclined to take it on again. The question of Joseph's right to sub-let had been raised, and if this was an influencing factor in his decision, another would have been domestic economy.

The month spent at Corndavon was one of appalling weather, adding to the air of melancholy. The bag this final season was 1,544 brace of grouse and 380 hares.

On the day of departure, Alfred wrote,

> "We have turned our faces for ever from the dear old place round which from boyhood I have spent so many happy days, and in which I have spent so many jolly evenings. I painted in large letters above the smoking-room chimney-piece 'Ichabod' when one pipe after another was taken away, and one voice after another was heard no more, & we were gathering the last traces of our possessions together & leaving the old snug quarters bare & vacant for the coming strangers."

10. *Edward North Buxton.*

On 18th September, Alfred, with Edward Buxton and the latter's Norwegian elk hound "Smoke", left Charing Cross for Brindisi. Smoke could be booked only as far as Dover, and at Calais, Buxton, a lean bearded man, six feet three inches in height, handed in the baggage ticket by mistake and retained Smoke's expired one. When Brindisi was reached, Buxton handed in for their baggage, Smoke's old useless ticket and feigned incredulity to the excited gesticulating Italians over such a trifle.

Buxton had a character of great appeal to Alfred. He had been Liberal M.P. for South-West Essex but gave up his seat in 1886. A great naturalist and an Alpinist, he was very absent-minded, but discomfort never bothered him. Alfred said of him that

> "... he had the poorest knowledge of medical treatment of any traveller I ever met. In a serious case of dysentery I have known him insist on a diet of sardines and jam! The patient, being a Buxton recovered."[1]

Alfred, Edward Buxton and Smoke eventually arrived at Smyrna where they were met by the English Vice-Consul, who with a little cash inducement, got the party through customs and to the British Consulate, where their rifles, revolvers and stores had been sent, clearing customs without inspection.

They were joined at Smyrna by two of the Pyrenean hunters from the expedition of three months earlier, Celestin Passet and Benjamin Vergez. In addition an interpreter (François), a Turkish cook (Yani Tragedi), and two Turkish hunters (Bouba and Mustapha), were recruited.

From Smyrna the party travelled by rail to the terminus at Dinair, and eventually, with provisions on camels, marched across the plains to the village of Homa at the foot of the mountain Ak Dagh.

After three days' tracking the slots of deer without a sighting, they moved the camp up river while Alfred and Edward Buxton went hunting.

"We had gone to sit at two passes near the top of the Ak Dagh. Whilst I was seated on the mountain, one of the great black eagles saw me under a rock and came to see what it was. He circled round a few times within about ten yards of me and looked uncommonly hungry I thought as he moved his head from side to side, but I also thought, as soon as he realised what I was, he would hurry off. Not a bit of it. He made two or three circles in the air and came with a swish within five feet of me, and then tacked off to repeat the experiment in a more businesslike way. I thought 'that's near enough!' and next time he came I had my rifle ready and was on my feet, and only kept him off by shouting and waving my rifle at him. I never was so puzzled and felt both the disagreeable possibility of being clawed somewhere like a flash of lightning and the ludicrous position I was in, in being frightened by a big bird! I was very glad when, after a look at me from 6 feet off whilst I danced a sort of demoniac's hornpipe, he sheered off to the white precipice above me."

During the evening of this same day, wandering off alone some miles up river from the new camp site,

"... and as I pursued my way in a reflective mood up a track through the trees, I suddenly saw two desperate-looking villains armed to the teeth standing in my way. They each carried yatagans, knives, several large pistols and each a long flint-lock gun. I thought I detected an impression of triumph in their grin, and for a moment thought I would take them right and left, but halted and remarked in the conventional phrase (which was hardly true) 'Hoosh geldinez' (you have come agreeably) and they returned in a little by replying 'Hoosh bouldouk!' They poured out a torrent of words in which I gladly recognised the word 'tutun' (baccy) and I emptied my baccy pouch and papers into their hands. They stared long at me and my rifle and then made off. I watched the ugly customers down the mountain and then returned to camp."

They broke camp again the following morning to try in the mountains about forty miles to the north-east, and with 11 horses emerged from the mountains on the east side and struck across the plain reaching the village of Belyuk after mid-day. From here they continued over arid and rocky mountain passes and reached the great plain of Tchul Orassi. In the evening they came to Arpessan where they took up quarters in the village 'Oda'; that is to say, a place where travellers could stay overnight and which in this instance was represented by something akin to a cattle-shed.

"We were made welcome, firing of thorns and sun dried camel's dung was brought to us, and some sweetmeat and mastic to drink. We lit our fire, warmed up the stink and made some excellent bovril, and had biscuits and chocolate for dinner. We turned in all together in this foul den. I lay between dirty old Yani and Edward (Buxton), and had Bouba close to my legs. Bouba was ill in spite of numerous quinine pills I had given him, made the most awful noises all night. I escaped my share of bites, the others being continually tormented by fleas and vermin. I oiled myself repeatedly with tar oil and had a certain amount of sleep, but had to keep my head in the blanket to keep the foul smell that blew through the open hole in the wall above my head, from the unspeakable abominations that were heaped in mountains of manure outside."

Moving on the following morning they came by late afternoon to a dirty village, Ta-Taki. The people, though, were clean, the dogs numerous, very large and savage and

"... a perpetual terror to poor Smoke. Here I saw the underground dwellings that I read about in Xenophon's *Anabasis* - most curious, nothing to be seen on the surface except on minute examination, a lid or stopper. When this was removed, a man or woman would emerge from a sort of big rat hole."

Another day's march, and long after sundown, seeing the cypresses and minarets standing out against a starlit sky, they came at last to the large town of Tchai. The travellers were now feeling foot and saddle sore, and Alfred was ill with asthma and hay fever. Following a bad night, they journeyed on to Bollawadun. They were now close to the Emir Dagh where it was hoped better luck might at last prevail.

Here they found, that except for a river-bed through a tortuous ravine, the place was waterless. Angora goats dotted the mountain sides, and having reached a ridge when almost dark, they were forced to spend a restless night at this ill-chosen site. Throughout the night the men shouted at the horses which kept fouling up the tent cords in the confined space. With so many goats on the mountain, to stay in this area was pointless, and despite being travel-sore, they decided to retrace their steps by the shortest possible route.

"Started at 9 en route for Afyon Kara Hissar[2]. Had a long ride over the plain to Kara Hissar. It was weird and beautiful, the aspect of this old city under the mountains at sunset, tints of violet and red on the plains, the mountain and rock of Kara Hissar beyond, with the blue smoke and white minarets against the black rock looked like a gigantic pillar standing out in a sea of blue mist, and right above the high rock shone the crescent moon."

By the following morning Edward Buxton could ride no more, and a Turkish officer whose acquaintance they had made, said that a good horse araba with springs could be obtained in the town, and they could ride to Sandukli on a good road.

"I accompanied Edward in this machine. How we ever got to Sandukli over these mountains is almost a miracle - driving over boulders, gully's and stream beds, often certain we could get no further. We arrived at the filthy town of Sandukli at the same time as our heavy caravan at 7.30 and had a dirty buggy room at the Khan."

The day following their arrival at their old camp, things seemed just as unfavourable as before. Buxton and Alfred split in different directions, Alfred taking with him one of the Pyrenean hunters (Benjamin) and at 4.30 p.m. miles from their base, on the wrong side of the mountain from camp, Benjamin clearly had no idea of their road back whilst Alfred believed he had a fair one:

"*(Benjamin)* was nearly silly with sciatica and could not get on at all at times. As night came on he got quite childish and his pain grew worse. He would 'never see France again,' he was 'no use,' we were 'going wrong.' I insisted on his coming on quicker knowing that if we could not reach the summit with the last glimmer of twilight we should be lost for the night. To make things pleasant, it poured with rain and when at last we reached the arête it was pitch black. Benjamin overruled me on the question as to where to begin the descent and this led us into an awful mess, as when we left the col, we should have tried to get onto the ridge, a spur of which ran down to our river, instead of which we scrambled down into the black dripping depths of the forest, fighting with thickets and arbutus scrub and having some thirty ravines and couloirs to cross. In spite of Benjamin's entreaties and moans and declarations that the camp was in another part of the mountains, I stuck to my line when once we were committed to it, and took everything as it came, pulling Benjamin along and was rewarded about 7.15 by seeing the light of the camp fire in the valley below. They were on the look out for us with a lantern and I was truly glad to get back, get wet clothes off and hot soup."

Morale was suffering badly by the following day. Buxton did nothing on the north side of the mountain, the camp was getting wet and the cook Yani was howling in his tent, and Benjamin and his sciatica showed no improvement. Four days more of useless search for deer followed, and this camp was finally broken up. Achmet, a hunter and guide recruited on their journey, was determined to try over the high mountains behind. The prospect was too much for Buxton who was footsore.

"I had three hours climb passing a most curious abyss amongst the precipitous rocks near the summit which Achmet wished me to approach and look down. For the first time I suspected Achmet, but most unworthily, for when I approached and looked down into the black depth below taking good care to have my rifle handy and keep at a safe distance from Achmet, I saw that in the bottom was snow (Kar) and he wished to explain to me how men were sometimes let down with ropes to get the snow and sell in the villages on the plain. When we reached the other side I glassed it well, but saw that it was nothing but stones, absolutely devoid of any vegetation, save a few pines."

On 23rd October they abandoned the expedition and set off back for Smyrna. They went by boat to Constantinople where customs relieved Alfred of his revolver (later returned through the offices of the British Embassy) and returned to London by the Orient Express.

During Alfred's absence, the Earl of Portsmouth had died and Lymington had now succeeded as 6th Earl.

In business, the shipbuilding arm of Robert Stephenson & Co. Ltd., at Hebburn, ran into a loss £20,000 greater than had been expected on a shipbuilding contract. They also faced a penalty of £9,000 for non-delivery. This mess was a source of great annoyance to Joseph.

Nothing much else had changed, except that Edward Clarke, the Mills manager, who owed Joseph a debt of £7,000, was pressed for payment. He was let off repayment of £1,000, but Clarke asked for time in which to pay, which was granted.

In the autumn of 1891, Alfred turned his attention to taking on, as his father's tenant, Spite Hall Farm at Pinchinthorpe, paying a rental to Joseph of £165 a year. A programme of improvements to house and buildings was commenced, and a man named Thomas Henderson was put in as farm manager.

In the last week of November, a friend of Cambridge days, Sandy Fellowes, came with his wife to stay at Pinchinthorpe. On a a cold, frosty day, out hunting, following from the dog cart with Sandy and his wife, Nellie caught a severe chill. This was the beginning of a much more serious condition, and three days later when she was showing no improvement, the doctor ordered her to remain indoors. Alfred had a talk with the doctor:

> "He frightened me a good deal and I am very anxious perhaps without cause, but the idea of anything dreadful resulting from her present cough frightens me very much."

As the year 1891 drew to its close Edward Clarke of the Darlington Mills died very suddenly leaving his affairs, and those of the Mills in a state of great confusion. A fresh start under a new manager was made. His name was Brunskill and having been promoted from within the Mills, if he was not very sanguine about future profitability, at least he would ensure that the speculations, muddles and overdraws of Clarke's tenure might be counted as things of the past.

This December, Alfred was appointed a director of the National Provident Institution, and went up to London to meet his fellow directors and attend his first board meeting.

Also this December, Beatrice and the new Earl of Portsmouth came up for a few days to reiterate their desire for a 'stated income' - in wearying reply to which, they were told that nothing had changed to render the request possible.

Joseph summarised 1891 saying:

> "... things domestic seem so gloomy, so is business - it makes me flat," and he concluded that 1891 had been a year "not very flattering to my vanity."

1892

Nellie's cough persisted through January, though the doctor pronounced her chest sound. Even so, her strength needed building up. The beginning of March, 1892 saw a very serious turn of events. The miners in the Durham coalfields were calling for an all out strike. This situation arose because the mine owners, who had put wages up in the good year of 1890-91, were now proposing wage cuts because of faltering trade and low prices at the pit head. The miners refused arbitration.

The situation was discussed at Pease & Partners board meeting on 2nd March, and as the strike looked set to be a long one, preparations were made for keeping the pits pumped.

Immediately following this meeting, Joseph went to the joyless

Mills for another, where he found

> "Most disgusting losses and revelations of fraud in taking stock, keeping back invoices and taking credit for the goods they represented."

The 82,000 Durham miners came out on strike on 12th March, Alfred observing that

> "... it is very hard on the collateral industries, as all the furnaces & ironstone mines &c have to shut up during the strike, & I fear there will be much misery and damage done. It will break some concerns - some pits will never start again & many furnaces will not go into blast."

Let it here be said, that as far as the Peases were concerned, they did what they could to bring some relief to the families of the striking miners. Alfred, for his part, gave lectures to raise money, and Pease and Partners gave to an assistance fund for the striking miners' families.

The Portsmouths must have been about half crazed at the onset of this ruinous strike, and the prospects for them of another year of financial drought. By April, with the strike continuing, Joseph now became more worried about Minnie's state of health, she having a return of abdominal pains, the root cause of which her doctors seemed unable to fathom.

> "This and financial worries take it out of me."

The next day travelling north from London with Alfred in the restaurant car over dinner,

> "... he *(Alfred)* seems low about business prospects. It can't always be sunshine - but in a gloom one gets anxious about its duration and strength."

This month, April, Joseph took Minnie down to Hastings, hoping the sea air would restore her health. Alfred went to York to commence a Liberal campaign with Frank Lockwood, but being worried about the strike, its consequences and the general state of business, and following hard reflection, he wrote to his father saying that he thought for the sake of his family and his position commercially, he ought to give up his seat in Parliament.

Joseph found this very disturbing, and though he felt that if things continued as at present, then Alfred would be right to give up York, nevertheless for the present, he wrote urging him to hold on awhile.

While Minnie at Hastings was improving sufficiently for her

doctors to suggest a three-month move to Switzerland, more anxiety came, with Charles Fry informing Joseph that the pull on the Counting House was very strong and something must be done to relieve pressure:

> "This settles all my plans!!"

On 5th May, Joseph's brother, Arthur Pease, suddenly sprang to life in great alarm at the general state of things, particularly at the Counting House, and next day, Joseph was with David Dale at Darlington where they:

> "... met Arthur who seemed quite unnerved. I showed them that the family balances between 1889, Dec 31st and 1891 had not materially altered, but we had paid off about £200,000 as *(sic) (and)* reinvested that amount ..."

It was June when at last the miners' strike came to an end, and with some reluctance, they accepted as arbitrator in the dispute, the appointment of the Bishop of Durham.

Alfred and his father had a long sit down about the collieries and finances on 6th June, which resulted in working out a satisfactory scheme, and the exercise reassured them both that things were not quite as bad as they had first thought. Joseph went to Darlington next day to put the scheme to Charles Fry:

> "The pull up until August looks heavy, but God granting in his blessing it will work out - it is the extraneous things that bother me. Mills, Stephensons &c - under paid management, Arthur sticks at nothing!"

A day's diversion from these problems took place on 10th June, when Joseph went to Barnard Castle, to the opening of the newly built chateau-like Bowes Museum. Standing on a table placed at the entrance, he made a speech, of which the *"folks were good enough to approve"* and was then invited to open the doors.

A General Election was now upon the country. Alfred, who no longer felt the same urgency to abandon his seat as he had in April, went off to York to start his campaign in earnest. Joseph who had hoped for an unopposed return found he had a contest on his hands. This was difficult since Minnie was in London where she suffered a severe setback with shivering fits, restlessness and pain. Joseph remained with her and left the fighting of his campaign in the capable hands of David Dale.

At York polling day came on 4th July and Joseph received the result at 2.30 a.m. by telegram - Alfred was out! - Bottom of the poll. Alfred, writing of his defeat said:

> "It was not until the last 5 minutes that the result was certain - It was a blow - but I don't think a soul guessed what I felt at the time - & I went through the rest of the ordeal with sufficient outside composure -
> It was strange looking at the howling, hooting, cheering mob from the steps of the Mansion House, just the same men probably who howled with delight at my two former victories. The Tories were very offensive at the Mansion House but among the common people I received nothing but civility, except one or two 'good-bye Mr Pease' as chaff - But Lady Terry to whom I said 'I must congratulate you on a very great victory' said insolently 'Yes, - you see *we* were fighting for *our* country,' I replied 'Yes I hope I was equally fighting for mine.'
> Several rude remarks were made, but it is always so. I shall never forget the condition of our committee when Lockwood and I entered it to address the crowd in St Sampson's Square. Silence, quivering mouths, broken by an excited man swearing & telling me not to come near them, that York was unworthy of me - Lockwood who accompanied me to the window, & by whose side I stood while he tried to say some broken words to the indignant & disappointed thousands, was very much cut up - His allusion to his dear colleague unmanned me for half a moment, but I was quite myself when the crowd stopped cheering me, & my turn to speak came - Then we were escorted by a large police force to the hotel - Nellie behaved like the plucky woman she is all through, & kept her tears for the bedroom."

Alfred attributed his defeat to the short-time working on the railways consequent upon the miners' strike; the York railwaymen were sore about this and the Tories had exploited it to the full,

> "... and as usual threw all principles to the winds & said here is Pease, a colliery owner, represent him as a bloated capitalist (good heavens!). Represent his father as a cruel railway director trampling on the pit men in Durham & the railwaymen in York &c.
> One libel disseminated by the York Tories was that my father had declared during the strike 'that he would starve the pit men and let grass grow in the streets of the villages before a pit should commence work again' - when, as a matter of fact he was for compromise throughout, our men allowed houses rent free & coal, & their families assisted by subscriptions, & the condition of our men & our treatment was the cause for comment on our generosity in the *Daily News* - However, perhaps it is better to lead a quiet life than to be bled, badgered and bullied for 7 years more!"

Alfred's brother Jack was busy fighting his first election at Tyneside where he came out victorious with a 450 majority, and Joseph's brother Arthur, engaged in a bitter battle with his 'blood relative'

Theodore Fry in Darlington, lost. At Barnard Castle, Alfred made the speech of thanks on behalf of his father who was now at Brighton where Minnie was alarmingly ill. Joseph had been returned with a majority of 2,413. In the country, the Liberals were back in power.

By mid-July Alfred at Pinchinthorpe was taking stock of his new situation. First he was anxious about Nellie who with a recurring cough was confined to the house. Secondly he was cut off from his political life associates and colleagues, and thirdly, business and personal finances were in a sadly depressed condition. Arnold Morley had told him that had he been victorious at York he would have had junior office. Alfred reflected that whilst he would be ready to re-enter the House, he hadn't sufficient money to *"rub along here."*

Towards the end of July, a telegram from Joseph asked Alfred to come to Brighton as Minnie's condition worsened. When he arrived and Minnie was asked if she would see him, she said *"No - I am too ill."*

> "She did however, for after lunch I walked into her room. She was lying very still in the shaded room, as white as the bedclothes and pillows. She was terribly changed & altered, so wasted and thin, so little of her sweet face left. As I bent over her, she smiled and opened her eyes which were quite bright, & she drew her little thin hand all wasted from under the clothes, it was only when I had it in mine & found how not only her face was changed, but that her arms and hands were all gone, that I realised how near death she was - She said several things to me ... I caught these words, 'My darling son, my dear pet - you have been a sweet son to me, I think so much of you.' I kissed her poor face & after lingering a moment left the room. Is this the last I shall ever see of my sweet mother is the thought that accompanies me ever since. I left Brighton & dined quietly at Brooks's, then went to Grosvenor Gardens for the night."

Minnie died on 3rd August. Alfred and Jack travelled together, and reaching Brighton found their father downstairs quietly reading. Joseph tried to say some words of welcome while Alfred, taking hold of his hand, reflected on the great change in all their lives but especially for

> "... my dear Father, accustomed to go to her with everything, to unburden himself & comfort himself with his wife who was everything to him, and in whom he was proud and happy - what does it mean to him?"

In the days after the funeral, Alfred went over to Hutton to try help Joseph regain himself, but it was too wet at the start of the grouse season to go onto the moors. A day or two later when Joseph was at Pinchinthorpe, Alfred showed his father a letter he had received from

11. Joseph (Jack) Albert Pease, later Lord Gainford of Headlam.

Lord Rosebery, now Foreign Secretary, who wanted to see him in London.

Alfred telegraphed that he would come up to London as soon as he had returned from Scotland where he was going to Craiganour, and receiving no reply from Rosebery, proceeded with his plans for Scotland. Nellie was going to her sister's place at Fincastle, and as Alfred and she parted company at Pitlochry to go their separate ways, he felt that Nellie was coughing rather worse and this made him fidgety at leaving her.

Five days later, now with the knowledge that Lord Rosebery wanted to appoint him as his Private Secretary at the Foreign Office, Alfred, after some hesitation on account of the concern he felt over Nellie's health, wrote gratefully accepting. He asked only that he be allowed six weeks a year abroad with Nellie on this account.

The following day, returning off the moors at 7.00 p.m. Alfred found his nephew Freeland Barbour at Craiganour having driven over from Fincastle. Dr Simpson, attending Nellie there, was alarmed at her state of health and asked to see Alfred immediately.

Leaving straight away they arrived four hours later at Fincastle where Alfred was glad to be back with his wife, but hardly slept for anxiety.

In the morning, he saw Dr Simpson who said Nellie had a weakness in her right lung and strongly advised going home straight away, and after going up to London to get Dr Barlow's opinion, to take Nellie abroad for seven months; to go to the Italian Lakes next month, and spend the winter and spring until June in either Egypt or Algeria.

Alfred didn't delay but went straight to London, in the first place to explain to Lord Rosebery why he must now withdraw from the offer made to him. Rosebery received him at his house in Berkeley Square:

> "He spent 20 minutes with me chatting & making it very easy for me, telling me that Houghton would have liked me at Dublin as R. put it 'You have a charming wife & are fond of sport & would be useful to him, but I told him I wanted to keep you for myself.' He said, 'However, when you come back, you have only to come back to me & I will make a place. Just come to the receipt of custom!'"

Alfred had made arrangements for Dr Barlow of Wimpole Street to see Nellie. Barlow could find no active disease but didn't like the condition of the apex of her right lung. He agreed to their going to Algeria and not returning until next May. He was against the children going with them which added to the trial of exile. Travel arrangements were immediately put in hand.

26th Sept, 1892. Pinchinthorpe. "Although I went to bed rather late, it being the last evening before leaving home, I did not sleep well. I rose at 5.30, and thought I would go and see hounds at Yearby Bank where I expected to find them. It was a lovely September morning, still, soft and fresh and I got my grey horse Norah whilst:-
'the dapple gray coursers of the morn
Beat up the light with their bright silver hoofs,
And chase it through the sky.'
As I passed the farms and cantered over the field by Holbeck Mill and George Sayers' to Dunsdale Bridge in the first sunshine of the day, and saw the farm horses being taken out, and heard the pleasant sounds of preparation for a harvest day, and cast my eye over fields to the blue wooded heights of Guisborough Banks, I felt it hard to be leaving it all, to lose a whole season of England's autumn, with its beautiful October and soft grey November days.
At Yearby I did not find the hounds, but saw the keeper walking homewards and overtook him. He told me he had made the same mistake that I had, that the hounds did not meet till eight. So I turned homewards again, riding by Wilton Woods, Court Green and Guisborough Park, and after shaking hands and saying goodbye and getting a God Bless you from old Dicky Moon, I returned in time to dress for breakfast, whilst Christopher and Lavender chatted away to me. I finished off my last arrangements, gave my last orders, said goodbye to the little ones sitting at breakfast in their pinafores in the nursery and hurried off to the 9 train for Darlington, leaving Nellie and Sophie (her maid) to join me there ..."

The children, following their parents' departure, went to their grandfather at Hutton Hall, and Pinchinthorpe House was shut down, dust sheets covering the furniture.

Arriving at Algiers on 29th September, Alfred and Nellie took rooms at the Kirsch Hotel. They remained there until 9th November when Dr Stephann, who was monitoring Nellie's progress, felt dissatisfied, and who urged them to move to a dry desert area. They moved on about 280 miles south east to Biskra. Having decided to make the most of exile, Alfred spent the six weeks at Algiers finding out all he could about the country, and especially about its potential for sport.

During this time, a friendship was struck up between the new arrivals and the Maxses. Ernest George Berkeley Maxse was British Vice-Consul. Little was known about the interior at this time, and in answer to Alfred's question as to what lay beyond Ouargla in the Sahara, Maxse said that the Arabs reported a land full of pasture and a big town of wonders:

"That there is a fine pasturage is known from good cattle and splendid horses having been brought through by the Arabs. Those who have tried to penetrate have either been driven back or have never returned."

Upon arrival at Biskra, Alfred found comfortable quarters at the Hotel Victoria. During their first evening there, an Arab, by name Chaban, introduced himself. Satisfied with Chaban, Alfred engaged him, and with him went to Batna (about 75 miles north of Biskra) to buy horses, there being nothing to take his fancy in Biskra.

Out of three hundred horses at the market, he picked half a dozen to follow, and found a white mare for Nellie that looked gentle enough, and he also liked the look of a grey mare with black points, but which the owner had not brought to sell. With the intention of returning to attempt to make a purchase of the grey mare, Alfred went off to the vegetable market and a neighbouring caravanserai.

"Whilst walking through the dirty yard, and looking up at two camels' heads under which I had to pass, I caught my foot in an iron frame and fell very heavily on some iron bars and flat in the filth. I was bruised and in a filthy state, and when I got over the first pain of a bad bruise on my stomach, side and hip, I realised my position was an awkward one, as I had not brought any other clothes to Batna. Chaban helped me to the trough, and there I washed my coat and scraped my nether garments with my knife, and then sat down to rest on the floor of a dirty little Arab cafe, where I drank a cup for two sous, and smoked a cigarette."

The following day he went back to the market to try to purchase the grey mare that was not for sale, and after being refused at different times, but now and again adding a little more to his previous offer, Alfred obtained the owner's capitulation, and the mare was bought for 800 Francs. An expensive purchase it may have been, but he was satisfied he had made a good one.

He then returned to Biskra leaving Chaban to bring the horses on by rail next day. When the train arrived at Biskra,

"I had great difficulty in getting the station master to allow me to take the mares off the train, but he gave way at last, and we had to shunt two trains by hand ourselves, Chaban, Spedding (an acquaintance made here, an Englishman from Ireland) and two negroes and an Arab. We made a rare shuffle of the two trains before we could get the horse truck into the siding."

Now at last fully equipped, and having enlisted Spedding as a companion, Alfred made several two or three days sorties into the desert, and on one such, on 18th December, heavy rain fell during the night, the deluge continuing the next day:

"... the river, formerly dry, was a roaring flood from bank to bank. Palm trees and other things came floating by - the desert looked like a sea. The telegraph went yesterday and the railway it is said, has been swept away. My horses are standing in six inches of water and mud. Twenty six tents and belongings, including the families have been swept away at Saâda, 12 houses have melted in le Vieux Biskra - and all this in a country where it never rains!"

At the same time, coming out to Algeria for Christmas, was Joseph in the company of a daughter (Maud) and Alfred's three children. Fortunately, by the time they arrived at Constantine, the railway track, washed out in the flood, had been repaired.

Whilst Alfred waited for the happy reunion with his children and his father at the station at El Kantara near Biskra,

"I had déjeuner at the buffet there, a pig being killed and dissected on a table by my side, and poultry and dogs living in the room, whilst an old turkey cock gobble-gobbled under the table. The meal was uneatable. I walked about El Kantara until the train arrived, and then saw Father's and Christopher's heads looking out of the window."

How different a Christmas was this was from other years, but the best was made of it, and Joseph reflected:

"My children have been most devoted to me - Alfred's loss of his election would, at other times have been a sore trouble to me, but my own loss occupied my thoughts. I was anxious about his sweet wife's health, and here I am out with them in Africa, trusting I am doing something to cheer their banishment - She does seem better, but I should like to know that the cough has gone. Albert's *(Jack's)* entrance to Parliament has no doubt been a gratification to me - but still, life seems so altered that its interests flag. I dare say I may feel different some day - but so ends 1892."

1893

To make his father's stay as enjoyable as possible, Alfred had bought a horse for him, but the planned expedition was delayed. Alfred had sustained a leg injury, so it was not until mid-January that the party was able to set out on a two day expedition to Aïn Naga, making the return trip in a sandstorm.

After a happy interlude of a month, Joseph, Maud and Alfred's son, Edward, returned home, Edward to school and Joseph to his many cares.

The two younger children remained with their parents at Biskra.

On 30th January, Alfred, Spedding and Chaban set out again for Aïn Naga for a four-day expedition, together with a mule loaded with five days' rations and sleeping blankets. They took up their accommodation in a doorless Arab house where the party had stayed on the last trip with Joseph. At that time, the first thing that Alfred had done was to remove the goats and the manure so that they could make the place more or less habitable, and had given Joseph a "bed" on a shelf just above the floor. On this occasion, after their arrival,

> "We turned into our blankets on the ground and had a fair good night, though much disturbed by the dog outside, and a mad marabout woman up a palm tree, both howling all night at the full moon or at us."

On the third day of the trip,

> "Another perfect day, after a perfect moonlight night. I got up early, cooked, saw to the horses, and then got off at 8 - as we turned out of the village in the light of the sunrise, we passed the mad marabout woman. She was a weird sight. A woman perhaps thirty years of age, in fairly good condition, but dark skinned, was standing half way up a crooked palm tree, dressed in a dark blue sort of chemise, holding herself by two palm branches, one in either hand, and continuing the loud and dismal song she had howled all night. I don't know if she cursed the Roumis, but we had a bad day of it somehow or other.

In the early afternoon a solitary gazelle buck was spied. Alfred, under the directions of Slieman, (the landlord of the Arab house they had made their lodge) got behind a thorn bush 60 yards distant, whilst Slieman started to drive the buck towards the gap separating Alfred from Spedding:

> "Slieman manoeuvred successfully, and the buck came straight for us ... To my horror, when he was just half way between us, I saw Spedding put up his gun and fire. In this fraction of a second I knew I should be shot, but before I could shout, I caught his first barrel of No. 1 right in the face and head, and was in a moment covered in blood. A second barrel of buck shot immediately followed, but just cleared me, and then two barrels quite clear of me with the ·500 Express and expanding bullets! One shot entered my head through four folds and the peak of my cap, and gave me great pain, the other under my left eye, glancing over my cheek bone, buried itself in the upper region near my jaw joint in the meat. I cannot think how he did this, as he is generally very careful. He was very kind after and did all he could for me, and said he knew where I was, but for the moment quite forgot my existence.
> I lost a good deal of blood, but feeling quite strong, I insisted on going straight for

Biskra, as we were two hours from Aïn Naga and, when there, 50 kilometres from Biskra. It was a serious undertaking in my condition, after being in the saddle since 8 in the morning, however, we got into Aïn Naga at dark, getting a drink of water at an Arab tent on the way ... When the moon rose at 7.30, I mounted my good mare and we started for Biskra. It was a perfect night and we crossed all the obstacles on the route safely. Before reaching Sidi Okba at midnight, we sent Chaban on to see if he could get a trap of any kind for the rest of the journey, as it seemed unlikely our horses could go on from there to Biskra (23 more kilometres)

The heavy wooden gates of Sidi Okba opened for us at 12, and Chaban had hired the daily diligence between Sidi Okba and Biskra for twelve and a half francs. We loaded the diligence, unloaded the mule, left Chaban to feed the horses and get them into Biskra, and the gates of Sidi Okba swung open and let us pursue our night's journey.

At last at 3 a.m. we reached Biskra. I walked upstairs to Nellie's room in the dark, chatted for a minute and got a warm welcome. I then told her I had got hit in the head, and had come home sooner than I intended. The garrison surgeon was here in ten minutes, and then I had a horrible hour and a half during which he, assisted by Spedding, cut and probed and failed a dozen or twenty times, to get the ball which was quite flattened into the bone of my head. When at last he got hold of it, and pulled it out, he shook me by the hand and seemed quite nervous and done. It was an immediate relief. He could not find the ball in my face and said, to my intense relief, that it must not be cut out, at any rate until next day."

At Hutton, on the same day, and at about the same time as Alfred was shot in the head, Joseph was just starting out on his roan cob to go to see his brother Arthur, at Cliff House, Marske-by-the-Sea. This house was Arthur's second residence more usually occupied by him during the summer, but where now he was laid up, lame in bed from a riding accident.

Joseph, had just mounted his cob at the front door of Hutton Hall, when the animal turned suddenly wild and bucked him off as he was attempting to dismount. Very shaken, and cut about the head from his fall on the gravel, he in consequence had a quiet day at home and noted:

"It is curious that both he *(Arthur)* and I should be lame (as I am very stiff) with horse accidents."

How much more curious he might have observed, had he known the fate befallen Alfred at much the same time.

During the few days since Joseph's return from Algeria, he had learnt that his son, Jack, had been offered the post of Private Secretary to John Morley, and when on the 3rd February, Joseph went to Marske,

93

(this time in a trap) to see Arthur he found

> "Arthur not very well pleased at Albert's getting John Morley's secretaryship, and in so much leaving business. I told him that I wished things otherwise, but at 33 they were their own masters."

The following day, Joseph at Darlington had a chat with David Dale and

> "... told him what Arthur had said about Albert - he did not complain, though he has most right to do so."

This was perfectly true. Dale was the man constantly at the helm in the choppy business waters.

Back at Biskra, on 4th February, Alfred emerged from a bad night,

> "... but the doctor said all was going well, and I got up and wrote three letters, but had very bad pain which got worse and my head swelled."

Dr Diquemar expressed surprise at the size of the hole in Alfred's head from which suppuration had started. The second slug was removed a few days later after which the healing process began.

Just after this, Vincent Hamlyn arrived in Biskra. Alfred was keen to take his brother-in-law out into the desert to camp, and did so. During the trip, Vincent declared himself quite ill with the heat. This was quite likely. Vincent Hamlyn, mildly eccentric, was

> "... wearing a puggaree and two hats, one on top of the other, and a pair of great blue goggles - he looked simply awful, and I have no doubt the natives took him for a marabout! Although he is a bit of a Jeremiah, I am glad of his company and enjoy his talk, some of which is wise, some clever and some neither of these things, so that his conversation has the pleasing quality of variety.
> After lunch, Vincent said he would sit under the cliff and sleep, and we were to call for him in the evening. I proposed that he should find his way back to the tents, but Ali (a guide from the Saharoui tribe) would not hear of this as he said the Arabs were 'Makesh Meleh' and would shoot him if they saw him. I thought this great nonsense, and offered him my little rifle.
> After a debate it was decided to take Vincent on to some Arab tents and commend him to their hospitality until evening. This we did, and after eating some dirty dates there, and drinking some thick water from a goatskin, Ali and I went off again ... and then we had a long journey at sundown to recover Vincent who complained much of a headache. But he seemed better after dinner. Vincent decided to return to Biskra the next day. Ali and Chaban thought the country unsafe till El Outaia, so I arranged for Chaban and the owner of the tent to go as escort ..."

12. Alfred and Iarrowi at Goleeah.

Two days later Alfred was back in Biskra,

"... glad to be rid of a week's dirt, and the clothes, not one of which had been off my back since I left. Found all well - a lot of letters. Loder[3] wants me to join him for a week, but I cannot go again so soon, or afford sport at his rate of expenditure."

This encounter with Sir Edmund Loder was the beginning of a lifelong friendship. For the moment however, he had a further three day expedition to Aïn Naga with Nellie, after which Alfred felt able to declare her wonderfully well. It was getting close to their time to depart from Algeria.

The main event at home in England during this time, that is from January to the end of April, 1893, had been the winding up of the *Yorkshire Chronicle* as a dismal failure. During the short life of this newspaper over which Lord Ripon had presided, the first editor, Marchmont had been succeeded by a man called Goadby who had moved over from the *York Herald* to the *Chronicle* at the time the new newspaper had been set up. Alfred said that every crank in the city had wanted to use the paper as an instrument for his own ends, but he took the credit for putting in Goadby as Editor; a position where he could make a reputation for himself. The cost of the venture to Alfred and his father was what the former termed "a fortune," and with its collapse, Goadby laid the blame with Alfred as the one person responsible for the ruination of his career in journalism.

Other events were, that in February, Joseph had called on his cousin William Whitwell, an ironmaster, whose rolling mills were at Thornaby-on-Tees - a satellite business interest to Joseph and Arthur - and to which they had given, with some reluctance, an overdraft guarantee and

> "... where I was astonished to find that pressed by the Bank, he had additionally overdrawn his a/c by £6,000 making it £24,000 in all. Asked to *(be)* supplied with all particulars ..."

And in mid-February, Joseph had been to dinner at the Portsmouth's London home where

> "... he and Beatrice discussed at great length their idea for a realisation of B's fortune. They always seem to think that someone will buy when there is no income. Left them at 10.30 promising to look into it."

He did, and for several days wrestled with Beatrice's affairs, and when she came to Grosvenor Gardens for tea he was still no nearer finding any solution, but he sat and listened

> "... to her everlasting complaints about her want of income, which did not come up when there was a good coal trade."

This was a reference to the isolated good year, 1890-91 coming up in oceanic years of trade depression. It was useless to complain - everyone was hard up - and things were not getting better.

In the colliery and ironstone trades,

> "... contracts and prices tumbling down, quantities loss & pits on short time, a poor look out."

The district in March was producing 30,000 tons a month surplus to demand and serious consideration was being given to blowing out furnaces.

The same month, March, the N.E. Railway was drawing heavily on J & J.W. Pease's banking operations, and the Consett Iron Company, which held its account at the Counting House, was overdrawn, and on

96

9th March Joseph was troubled by a letter from Walker, the manager at Stephensons,

"... wondering if he can meet his bills on Monday,"

and two days later,

"... bothered in my head about £.s.d. and Stephensons ... saw C.R. Fry at D'ton. He not very happy about £.s.d."
- after which Joseph made haste to London,

"... trying to put my trust in Him to clothe the grass of the field - but it is teaching to one's pride. Jack has been hunting in Hertfordshire - knew no one!"

At Algiers, just at the point of departure, Nellie, who had seemed wonderfully well, suddenly became very seriously ill, and medical advice was to get her away from the warm moist air of Algiers as quickly as ever possible.

Alfred made hasty arrangements for the shipment of his horses home and on to Pinchinthorpe, and booked revised passages for Nellie, himself and the two youngest children through to Geneva.

The sea crossing to Marseilles was a nightmare, the ship's doctor in constant attendance on Nellie who was running a raging temperature of 105°. Immediately Marseilles was reached, Alfred sought the best medical opinion, calling up Dr Isaak, a malaria specialist, who was in doubt about the nature of Nellie's illness, whether malaria, typhoid, tuberculosis, or as the Algiers doctor thought, blood poisoning, emanating from the right lung. Dr Isaak urged them on full speed to Switzerland, where once arrived, Nellie started a fearful battle for life.

Notes:
1. Elections and Recollections, by Sir Alfred E. Pease. p120. Published by John Murray, 1932.
2. Afyon Kara Hissar translates as Opium Black Rock - so named because it was the great emporium for the drug, and where, so it was said, many people drank it without evil effects.
3. Sir Edmund Giles Loder from Leonardslee, near Horsham, Sussex, a great traveller, sportsman and an outstanding botanist whose garden at Leonardslee is famous for its rhododendrons. Alfred many years later wrote Loder's biography.

CHAPTER FIVE

Switzerland, Algeria & Financial Cares

1893 continued
The crisis in Nellie's life lasted one and a half months, during which time
at Geneva, Alfred never left her side except at night for a walk and fresh
air, and then only after she had been settled by the nurse.

At no time was any doctor able to inform Alfred of the exact nature
of the illness for which Nellie was being treated, though the tubercular
condition was the one uppermost in his mind. Whatever it was, a
Professor Veulliet who had retired from practice was induced to interest
himself in the case:

> "I have never witnessed such devotion; he gave his whole time for weeks to
> it ..."

The immediate treatment ordered by the professor for the uncertain
condition for the first twenty-one days was

> "... about a bottle of brandy & 1 bottle of champagne per diem, *(a sip of)* one or
> other every 20 minutes - also some injections - no medicine - open air, cold
> bathing of the body - quinine rubbed into the armpits & massage of limbs to *(the)*
> heart to keep up the heart's action. She was an absolute skeleton.
> The day came when she could not keep down either brandy or champagne, & he
> told me there is only one chance left -
> He kept her 24 hours without anything, & then said 'get the best bottle of Château
> Lafitte you can find.' He gradually got her from a bottle of this a day to squeezed
> raw beef juice by teaspoonfuls, and from this to scraped raw beef into wafers of
> 'bran bread,' & then on to milk."

13. Helen (Nellie) Ann (Lady) Pease
née Fowler as a young woman.

Her condition on arrival at Geneva had been absolutely desperate, and Alfred entertaining the worst, had telegraphed his fears to his father.

Joseph and a daughter (Lottie) arrived in Geneva within the first few days of the crisis. Before setting out however, he called on Dr Barlow in London who, from what he was being told, considered the blood poisoning theory unlikely, and said that the condition seemed more likely to be malarial fever.

By 1st June Nellie showed some very slight improvement, and was taking milk and half a bottle of brandy a day. During the daytime, Alfred lay beside her on the bed and they talked quietly to each other. She told him that their weeks alone at Algiers and at Biskra had been the happiest in her life; that she retained the will to live because of him. She also told him that he was never to go near York again, that he had been treated shamefully especially by the upper ten of the party there.

On 14th June,

"At 2.0 a.m. I was called up and spent an hour sponging her face as she felt very sick. This passed off & she had some nice sleep till morning & woke feeling better, but looked very ill in her face, drawn and white & her eyes very bright & large & sunk. Dr V. ordered the same treatment to be continued & two injections during the day of Saunder's peptone & egg - the day passed with less, much less nausea than the previous day, but she took very little nourishment indeed besides the bordeaux and champagne."

By 20th June the doctor declared he was satisfied with her progress, and a day later he considered that she might be moved from Geneva to Les Avants for a long convalescence at 5,000 ft. Alfred left by the earliest train to prospect for a doctor and rooms, and was relieved to find upon his return that all had gone well during the day.

They transferred to Les Avants on 29th June, Alfred's thirty-sixth birthday and the battle for life looked won. That morning, despite what she had been through she had not forgotten his birthday, giving him good wishes, and with loving expressions, a gold and sapphire stock pin.

With her weight at just over six stone, she had a lot of ground to recover, but the days at Les Avants were bright and sunny, and now that one of Nellie's sisters had arrived, Alfred felt it safe enough to go to England at the end of July to collect the children, Edward from school, and the two younger ones whom Joseph had taken back with him to London after the initial crisis point had passed.

Whilst Alfred was back in England, he broke off one day only to call in at Pinchinthorpe, and throw back the dust sheets from his writing table to catch up with some correspondence. His last few days were spent with Frank Lockwood, from whom he learnt:

"They want me to stand at York again ... I don't intend to commit myself."

He returned with the children to Switzerland in early August, where, by the middle of the month, Nellie was starting to take short walks and gaining weight, and in September Alfred returned to England to set Edward off to school, and have a brief stay at Hutton.

Joseph, since his return to London at the beginning of June, came under renewed pressure from Beatrice, for an interview 'on our affairs'. He made arrangements for a meeting, together with his brother and co-trustee Arthur, to meet Beatrice on 23rd June, but due to forced attendance at the House, he had to abandon until the following day:

"Arthur would not tackle her without me."

At this meeting with Portsmouth and Beatrice:

"... after a few preliminaries they enunciated their scheme that Arthur & I were to take all and pay them a joint and several annuity of £10,000 a year. This requires much consideration and a good deal of working out."

By mid-July, being back in the north, he discussed the Portsmouth proposal 'backwards and forwards' with David Dale. Even if Joseph wished to bring to an end all the interminable bickering, and he surely did, it must be presumed that the annuity option was unacceptable to him for we hear no more of this scheme. Equally it was impossible to accede to the Portsmouths alternative demand for a buy-out. Until there was an upturn in business confidence, playing for time was the only possible option open.

There was now a strike in the Yorkshire coalfields, and this proved beneficial for demand from the Durham collieries, and Pease & Partners sold 15,000 tons of coal in five weeks during August and September to the West Riding, which as well as improving Pease & Partners' results, helped liquidity at the Counting House, though profiting from the plight of others was an unsure foundation for the future.

At Les Avants at the beginning of October, Alfred started to make preparations for a second winter in exile in Algeria. During his walks with Nellie as her progress improved, he often reflected about his strangely altered life; of everything going on in England, and of,

"... the H of C still sitting, debating Employer's Liability, massacres at Matabele, the strike in the midlands and Parish Councils Bill - of the hunting at home, and all things appertaining to my former existence."

During his walks with Nellie, they were frequently accompanied by Mlles Jeanne and Laure Sugnet, who though living at Vevey, were regular visitors at Les Avants, and were part of a bright young international set there.

On 20th Nov. 1893, preparing for Algeria,

"More snow - packed up - wrote letters - took a few last photographs of Caux in the snow. After déjeuner said farewell to all our friends and drove down to Glion ..."
(Mlle Jeanne Sugnet was at the station at Terrilet)
"to bid us bon voyage, which she did with many pretty speeches & gave Nellie a nosegay of roses and flowers, & me a pink carnation for my buttonhole from Mademoiselle Laure - who sent us her parting wishes and excuses."

A week later Alfred and Nellie and the two youngest children were back in their old quarters in Biskra and warmly welcomed by their old Arab friends:

"We feel no longer visitors, but have a sense of possession in Biskra, and our

101

children are as much at home running among the Arabs and negroes, making their little purchases of dates and oranges, and giving their coppers to the blind beggars, as if they had never seen England."

The two youngest children were by now thinking and conversing more in French than English.

Henceforth, Nellie was able to join Alfred's expeditions on a more regular basis, and when Christmas came the only sadness was that they didn't have Edward with them, but he was coming out again with his grandfather at the start of the new year.

Since the Portsmouths' proposition that Joseph and Arthur should "take all in exchange for a joint and several annuity" had foundered, the Portsmouths became thoroughly fed up. Beatrice told her 'father' in a letter that she was placing all her business matters in the hands of a London solicitor, Sir Richard Nicholson. She wanted no more correspondence on the subject whatsoever, and in future he must deal with Nicholson. To this, Joseph replied that it pained him that an outsider was being brought in, and he found the whole thing and the Portsmouths' attitude thoroughly disagreeable.

In November, Pease & Partners were invited to interest themselves in buying Ushaw Colliery from the Chaytor family for £80,000. Following some brisk negotiation, a deal was struck at £72,500 on deferred payment terms. This deal serves to indicate Joseph's long-, if not short-term confidence in the collieries, and if he, as head of Pease & Partners had so much confidence, then it was not unreasonable to expect a little of the same from the Portsmouths.

Towards the end of November, 1893, Joseph had a meeting in London with Sir Richard Nicholson and

"I think I cleared his mind on some points. Left it that he was to send me some points for further information, and then he would like to see Lucas and Fry, then me, before he goes to France and I go to Africa! Say Dec 18 to 21st. He seemed a pleasant gentleman,"

and on 11th December 1893,

"Then set down with Lucas and Fry on Sir R. Nicholson's requisitions into the administration of Edward's estate from the beginning. It is too bad, and makes it often difficult to remember the why and the wherefore of arrangements made 13 years ago. There seemed a good answer to all his questions which were a good deal confused."

and a week later,

"He" *(Nicholson)* "seems about beaten with his quest but wants further information on Middlesbro',"

and in his New Year's Eve annual summary:

"My main bother and trouble (which I have felt exceedingly) has been Beatrice Portsmouth's treatment, after I have done all I could for her, to throw all her papers into the hands of a new lawyer, Sir R. Nicholson, hurt me much. I asked for time as Arthur and Alfred were away (no, not a minute) and I was not to write to her on business. I have spent most of my leisure time on her affairs this year, I have done nothing political."

1894

Joseph set out for Algeria and refuge in a warm climate for a few weeks. This didn't last long. Alfred received a letter from C.R. Fry on 12th January, 1894 about the state of *"the banking account."* Though the letter from Fry was to Alfred and not to Joseph, there is nothing to suggest that Fry's concern related to Alfred's account, but rather to the general state of things.

This letter gave Joseph

"A bad night thinking about Fry's letter and had to read the 34th Psalm before I got much sleep. Studied Fry's figures, found £10,000 wrong cast in his asset side!! Wrote fully to Albert for Fry."

This intrusion so unnerved Joseph, that he cut short his holiday to get home to make arrangements for further temporary borrowing of £46,000.

Following his departure, Alfred was joined at Biskra by Sir Edmund Loder. It had been decided that Loder and Alfred would go in search of rhime[1], a species of gazelle found only in a remote and then little known part of the Sahara.

"Loder and I had long known of the existence of this species, but all my endeavours to obtain information as to the nearest place where it could be found were not very successful. One Arab would tell me they swarmed in the Oued Souf, another that it was to be found at Chegga two days from Biskra. Others, to please me said to my question 'is it at this place - or that?' 'yessur, yessur' (a great many). I knew well by this time that the 'yessur' of the local liar meant 'probably there are none' or its nearest approach to veracity 'one has been seen,' but at last I wrote to Loder that I really did believe it was to be found somewhere beyond Saâda or Chegga."

14. *Sir Edmund Giles Loder and
Alfred Edward Pease at Biskra, Algeria.*

Alfred, Nellie and Loder set out in search of the rhime on 8th February, 1894. In addition to themselves they took six Arabs, two camels and four mules:

"We also had an old hunter, in future referred to as the 'Hungry Man,' supplied to me by the Bureau Arabe as an infallible guide to the rhime country. This one turned out to be an impostor with a capacious stomach. He was old, lean, gentle and plausible.

At sundown we camped under the Bordj Saâda (Taha Raçou), a dreary fortified caravanserai, the first stage on the government route to Tougourt. The water here is quite undrinkable, and even the horses and mules would not touch it."

The next day took them beyond Chegga where they left the Tougourt track and struck E. of SE. for the Chotts.

"There is an artesian well at Chegga, but in spite of the Hungry Man's promise of rhime here, we found not one of the half dozen inhabitants of this dirty station had ever heard of it.

I had wandered wide of the caravan a part of the day with the 'Hungry Man', who fell in my estimation as he pointed out dorcas tracks as rhime footings, and his friendliness began to charm me less as he kept plaguing me for food, sitting down at times and repeating all day plaintive 'mackash mange, mackash imshee' which was his Franco-Arabic gibberish for 'No food, cannot walk.' Hunks of bread and pounds of dates did nothing to lessen his pangs of hunger."

104

10th Feb. "We passed south with the Chotts in sight on our left, and made the lonely Bordj of Aïn Ghebra at 1 *(o'clock).* Beyond, sand appeared, and here all declared we should find the rhime. So we pitched our camp amongst the sand hills beyond Aïn Ghebra, and left our camels, horses and mules to revel amongst the halfa grass, and off we went to see the rhime. Again we were disappointed, and we came into camp after dark.

11th Feb. "Off again, east for Ham Raier, where the 'Hungry Man' swears by God the rhime are. A very hot day this, and we are glad of a midday halt by the sweet water well of Bir Bel, by one of the Ghimeras that mark this bewildering route to the Oued Souf. A weird place of sandy hillocks and earthy cliffs, with those vast false lakes all round, quaking and sparkling under the white hot sky - a strange and silent country.

In the afternoon we reached the great plateau of harder earth, with sage green plants known as the Stah Hamraier. For hours the only object on the horizon was the distant Bordj, which seemed to keep its distance, and loomed in the quivering atmosphere like a great feudal fortress. At 4 we got up to it, disturbing gazelles from time to time. Ham Raier consists of the usual block house, and the more than usually nasty warm medicinal well. 'Hungry Man' more hungry than ever."

12th Feb. "Loder and Ali took one direction, and 'Hungry Man' and I another, full of hope that the rhime was here - but he was not. There were plenty of dorcas and, when at last my hungry fraud pointed out a minute print of a dorcas little one, and swore it was 'el rhime' I turned back to camp.

Nellie made good use of this day, for she had, with Ahmeda's help, secured a negro, who had come on his bi-weekly errand of watering the herd of female camels he had charge of in the desert. This man was a wonder. His name was Ibrahim, and for seven years he had lived without a tent in the desert on the camel's milk and dates. He knew where the rhime were - two days further to the east.

All Ibrahim's worldly goods were on his back and in his hands. His outfit, a shirt and burnouse, and a pair of woollen Soufi sandals. His whole furniture a big stick, a reed flute and a bundle of charms."

13th Feb. "Ibrahim was formally engaged and left his camels for us. The 'Hungry Man' was paid off, getting the best of us who shelled out rather than listen - it is better to be robbed than driven mad. He started on his long walk to Biskra with ample food for two men for a week, but probably had eaten it all by noon.

After a hot walk across the Chotts and hillocks, we arrived at Sef el Menadi at 3.30 - here is another block house with its solitary guardian and a most horrible well of water, hot and fouled by camels. It was a disgusting thing to do, but here we had to fill our barrels and skins with mud, camel's urine and hot bitter water - we then pushed on to the north east - Ibrahim our guide - into a sand dune country, but sprinkled thickly with genista monosperma and other desert shrubs. At 6, in one of the myriad sand hollows we dressed our camp."

14th Feb. "Breakfast 4.50 - then started ... It was a very hot day, and our ride of three hours brought us late onto the ground for hunting. Leaving the horses and mule with Baub, Loder and Ibrahim made for one lot of high sand hills, and Ali and I for another. The deep sand and hot sun soon takes the steam out of you.

Ibrahim discovered a well for us - a most curious one, and no one could find it except those who knew of it; about ten feet deep in a sand hill, carefully hidden, and its sides made of plaited halfa grass. Ibrahim simply disappeared into it and, with his feet in the water offered drink to us from his dusky palms. Towards evening I saw some rhime, and all day long their unmistakable tracks.

Spent three hours plunging back to camp through the sand. We could never have found our way without Ibrahim. We skirted a thousand hollows in any one of which our camp might be.

16th Feb. "We are tired out, but must make one more good bid before we give up this most arduous chase. A very hot day - seven hours in the saddle - riding home by moonlight, after seven hours trudging in the heavy sand. We had some difficulty in finding our trail back to camp at night, and had to ride at a certain angle to catch it by the light of the moon. I walked most of the way bare foot, and sometimes in slippers.

Ibrahim is an excellent hunter. Both he and Ali, by the lightest touch of a print in the sand with the finger, can tell the age of it to an hour or two, Ibrahim just touching the track with his big toe."

During the expedition, Loder bagged the only specimen of rhime. This species was at the time known only to the French colonialists, and indigenous Arabs, and unknown to naturalists. Loder had the distinction of having the rhime gazelle named after him *"gazella Loderi"* by the Zoological Society.

Then followed the three-day journey as they headed for Biskra. On the morning of the third day,

"Nellie, Loder and I started at 6.30 alone, intent on reaching Biskra by daylight. We made Taha Raçou (Bordj Saâda) at 8, then a storm of wind came on, and it was soon dark with dust and sand. In a few minutes we were all in the horrors of a sand storm in the desert. We managed to keep our bearings by the wind and instinct, but it was a most disgusting journey - our faces wrapped up - our eyes crying mud - our nostrils though covered, choked - our horses' mouths and eyes bunged up.

Nellie's horse, young and faint-hearted, gave up the battle, so I changed horses with her, leaving her to get on to Biskra with Loder, and boasting I would get him in. I never had such a job. When flogging and spurring would do no more, I dragged and pushed him in turn, and more than once was on the point of leaving him for the hyaenas and jackals, but I made up my mind not to abandon him as long as he could stand up, and eventually I got in.

Our caravan arrived the same night, also in the pitiable plight from the sand storm."

The following day, Mandell Creighton (now Bishop of Peterborough) and Mrs Creighton arrived - and left again after one day, disgusted with Biskra.

15. Alfred and his horse, 'Tiffin Time' , in the desert.

By 20th April, Alfred and Nellie and the two children were in Tunis and making back to England by way of Geneva. Alfred was also taking home with him a jackal, found when a day or two old. 'Jackie' was bottle fed by Alfred and properly cosseted and travelled in his hatbox. All arrived in Geneva on 27th April.

Nellie was seen by Professor Veulliet who expressed satisfaction with her progress, but declared there was still some mischief existing in her lung, and advised a three-week delay before she returned to England. So Alfred went ahead with Lavender and 'Jackie' and arrived at Pinchinthorpe on 19th May.

"Got home at 6.00 p.m.. Lavender remembers little, did not recognise the house or know her way to the nursery, but knew where to find her toys. It is strange to be once more here. It was Sept. 1892 when I said good bye to the children at breakfast in the nursery & wondered when we should all be home again, & if I should ever bring Nell back again. I hope she will be here in a few days. It is cold & a bitter wind, but everything looking very pretty and comfortable - the lilac at its best & *(the)* may half out."

Walking over to Hutton village the next day, Alfred met the head gamekeeper, Cockfield, who

> "... simply greeted me by putting his hands on his knees & exclaiming 'Baa George!! Well! Well!!' - Visited Spite Hall *(Alfred's farm)* in the afternoon and found all trim."

The next two or three days were spent in getting the house back in order after such a long absence. He was assisted in this by

> "... Pearey - who in the present servantless condition of the establishment is housekeeper, window-cleaner, parlourmaid, housemaid, valet & decorator. Saw all my horses & rode Zena over my farm - old 'Twig' is still living & delighted to see me as is 'Richa,' 'Bess,' 'Ben' and 'Wasp'."

"Richa" was one of two greyhounds Alfred had bought in Biskra on the first visit there.

He went up to London to meet Nellie from Switzerland, and a few days later took her to Dr Barlow. He gave a favourable report, and considered her lung healed, but felt great care was still needed and gave leave for them to stay at home until September.

During the time since January and now (May) when Joseph had returned to England from Algeria worried sick about finance, he had had a dust-up with the Portsmouths. On 26th February he wrote:

> "... to Darlington to dine with Dale and meet Lucas on the Portsmouths' affairs. Conference with Fry and Lucas. The latter has heard nothing from Nicholson - I had a telegram from Portsmouth wanting an answer - to his impudent letter to Fry - Lucas quite approved of my letter to Portsmouth telling him he must either have confidence in us - or let everything go through solicitors; that Fry kept our books, not his - and owed no responsibility to them."

It hardly needs saying that Charles Fry, who kept the trust accounts, had responsibility for keeping proper records of everything taking place, and this he did most scrupulously. But this was a responsibility to the Trustees, Joseph and Arthur, who in turn owed the responsibility and were answerable to Beatrice. Joseph most strongly objected to Portsmouth taking a hectoring attitude with Fry.

In March Joseph had a session with Sir Richard Nicholson,

> "... and had a long chat with him, most friendly in its character - he pressed me to make some scheme for supplying the Portsmouths' needs - I showed him the difficulties whichever way we turned."

The other principal event to have taken place in Alfred's absence was a disastrous fire at the Priestage Mills, which once more forced serious consideration to be given to their future, and Alfred records the outcome of what was considered at a meeting held at 44 Grosvenor Gardens.

> "Decided to rebuild the Mills, contrary to my way of thinking but I was not listened to & did not speak very strongly when I saw the seniors had their minds made up - Just the same with Stephensons - Father will not see the folly of trying to bolster up a badly arranged, antiquated, losing concern."

Stephensons had three months earlier recorded a loss for the half year of £10,000, but Joseph's view expressed at that time was:

> "What we want now is more shipyard orders. We want more money to work it with!"

The day following the meeting about the Mills, Alfred dined alone with Lord Battersea at Surrey House. Lord Battersea had, as Cyril Flower, been Liberal Chief Whip and had been sent recently to the Upper House.

> "Cyril said to me that my father had only to give the hint if he wished to have a peerage - did he want one? - I said I did not know - he asked me to sound him, for I said he will never ask for one if he did."
>
> *1st June.* "I asked him, (Father) - he said 'No, I do not think in the present condition of trade I could. Sometimes I have thought I would take one, but at my age it is more a question for you than for me -' I replied 'As far as I am concerned, I have no ambition that way, but do not let me stand in the way, as I am quite indifferent if you would like it'."

The matter of a peerage introduced in this way was promptly dropped, and Alfred set out for the House of Commons to hear the Uganda debate in which Jack was to speak.

> "Very curious being there as a stranger & being told 'you sit on that corner by that bald man' by the pampered menial in charge of the gallery."

He was again pressed this month to allow his name to go forward for York, but he continued to remain uncommitted. He was busy in the north attending, in Joseph's absence, to Stephensons' affairs, the Counting House and overseeing his farm, and in general carrying out duties of one sort or another as though there had been no (almost) two-year absence.

During August, Joseph in the course of business met Arthur to whom he again expressed his dislike of Arthur's intention of fighting (the recently created baronet) Sir Theodore Fry at Darlington. Arthur replied that 'the Duke of Devonshire and others made him feel it to be a duty.'

"I could not add to this," was all Joseph could say, holding that avoidance of family conflict came before politics, and quite puzzled that Arthur thought nothing of kinsmanship with Fry.

Despite the political differences between Joseph and Arthur, there was still a great bond between them. Arthur's fairly casual attitude to business left Joseph doing all the work. When in August the two brothers were involved in discussion with a solicitor over the drawing up of a Trust Deed and

> "... there were a great many points to discuss which took us a considerable time, to my amusement, Arthur, who staid *(sic)* for 3/4 of an hour left me to finish, in fact to do all, and went to visit the lunatics at Over Dinsdale Asylum! He told me about Stephensons," *(where Arthur had been the previous day)* "and that as the balance sheet was not audited he did not trouble to look at it!!"

Stephensons had lost £12,000 in the second half-year (making £22,000 loss for the year) and in September it was decided to close the shipyard as soon as possible and pull everything into the profitable parts of the business. It would seem that this decision was shortly afterwards put on 'hold' for we hear more about the shipyard later.

1895

Three days before Christmas, 1894, the Chairman of the North Eastern Railway, John Dent, died. In the first days of the new year, at a dinner following the monthly North Eastern Railway traffic committee meeting in York, held always on the day before a board-meeting, Sir Isaac Lowthian Bell suggested that the traffic committee directors discuss the question of the succession, and said that he understood that Joseph would be prepared to take it on.

Joseph for his part, after a number of kind things had been said by his fellow directors, said that in his altered domestic circumstances (a reference to the loss of his wife), much of his ambition had gone out of him, but that he was prepared to do his best. The following day, 4th January, Joseph was appointed Chairman.

This was an honour of which he was deeply conscious, but he was also conscious of the trials facing him in other directions.

He had financial cares at the Counting House, there was dullness in the colliery trade, a bad year at Wilson Pease's, (Ironmasters in Middlesbrough), and there was always the carousel of impossibility surrounding the Portsmouths' wishes, compounded by a bombardment of letters from Sir Richard Nicholson, which Joseph, exasperated, considered *"too bad"* and *"absurd,"* but which culminated in his receiving a final letter from Nicholson which he interpreted as meaning

"War!"

With the threat of war, Joseph consulted Arthur Lucas who

"... suggested our taking over collieries &c at ¹/₂ price and trying to end the Executorship."

Acting on Lucas's suggestion, he set about framing a scheme to meet Nicholson's demands, and at the same time stalling Nicholson until a face-to-face meeting in London could be arranged. One of the points raised by Nicholson was the question of *ultra vires* regarding the taking up of shares by the trustees at the time that the collieries became incorporated as Pease & Partners, when at the time of his death, Edward Pease's interest in the collieries was in the form of partnership capital. Joseph took Counsel's opinion which, when it came on 26th March, 1895 Joseph declared

".. generally greatly in our favour."

He began to suspect that Nicholson's tactics, in firing salvo after salvo of questions, demands, requisitions and threats of war was done with the sole aim of worrying him, and wearing him down into submission to the Portsmouths' demands. Worrying it certainly was, and the demands made on him meant less time could be devoted to other things where attention was vital.

The only bit of good news on the business front came in March when the sale of the Mills Combing Department was confirmed:

"... good riddance at a great loss."

During November the previous year (1894) Alfred and Nellie had once more set out for Algeria, this being the third visit and the second period in exile.

Safely arrived at Phillipeville they moved on to Batna, - 60 or so miles to the south west from where they set out to explore the Aures and by way of Chelia (40 or 50 miles south-east of Batna) and made their way, without incident to Biskra, arriving there just before Christmas.

In January, before setting out with Sir Edmund Loder on a two-month expedition to the Souf, Alfred had received invitations to stand at Stockton and at Scarborough, both of which he declined.

The expedition into the Souf country had as its main object this time to find addax antelope. It commenced on 12th February, and in addition to themselves, Alfred took a retinue of Arabs, ten camels, two horses and two mules.

There is no intention to give here a detailed account of this largely abortive expedition. It is sufficient to say that they marched to the great French fort at El Oued (approximately 125 miles south-east of Biskra). There they were told that it was extremely dangerous to go beyond Berresouf (90 miles or so further to the south-east) and that the French there would wash their hands completely of any responsibility if the party left that district, the desert beyond being Touareg[2] country. The Touaregs were a marauding people, resentful of foreign influence, and had attacked and murdered past adventurers and explorers. Whilst at El Oued awaiting clearance south, news came through that because of trouble in the Sahara, Alfred and Loder were expressly forbidden to go south of El Oued, but if they cared to wait a month, they could proceed under an armed escort which would be leaving for the south.

Instead of waiting, they travelled over the desert into Tunisia to Touzer about 90 miles north-east of El Oued, El Hamma, Chott Rharsa, and Zeribet El Oued and were back at Biskra by 4th April.

On the expedition, Alfred adopted a wild boar (a few days old) which rapidly became very attached to him, and which upon leaving Algeria went with them on a tour about the south of France until their eventual return to London on 13th May.

Seeing Dr Barlow the following day, he reported that Nellie had done no more than hold her own - he could not say more:

> "We left with tears in our eyes, for we thought our three years' battle was over & we are not done with the struggle."

Later that month, Alfred attended the annual meeting of the Royal Agricultural Society and was elected onto the Council. He also, in response to a letter from Lord Rosebery (now Prime Minister), called at 10 Downing Street. Rosebery told him he was putting him on the Royal Commission on Horsebreeding.

"I found him looking older than when I last met him. He has had a hard time & has felt I am sure the disloyalty of Harcourt & the misrepresentation of those who ought to have backed him ... He asked me to the Durdans for Sunday & Epsom - I accepted (though I want to get home) as I felt very much his kindness in wishing to have me for Sunday & the Derby Day."

26th May. "I went down to the Durdans at 10 with Lockwood, had a delightful summer's day on the lawn with Rosebery - saw his yearlings & stallions - no one else there but his 2 girls ...
Ld. R gave me a pin with 'Ladas' on it 'as a token of affection in memory of 1894'."

29th May. "... then to the Durdans - spent half an hour in Rosebery's room & strolling about with him - & then drove with Lockwood & Ld. Gerard to the course - & had a fine view from Rosebery's Private Box - he came in soon after & said he had shouted for me all over the place as he wanted me to walk up with him from the Durdans. The race was a very good one & 'Sir Visto,' Rosebery's horse won easily by 3/4 of a length."

In June, Alfred paid a short visit to Edward North Buxton where they talked out their thoughts for making trips to the Caucasus, Abyssinia & Somaliland,

"... but I do not quite see how to do it."

By July the dissolution of Parliament had taken place and Alfred was once more invited to stand for York. He declined. A deputation of York Liberals headed by Joseph Rowntree came to see him, and he declined to give an affirmative to their very pressing and complimentary invitation.

"I do not wish to stand anywhere & had refused to take H.F. Pease's place in Cleveland, *(or fight)* Stockton & *(or)* Scarborough."

Following this, a few days later, York Liberals, together with Joseph and David Dale put heavy pressure on him, and Alfred wobbled under the weight of it:

"I went to York having decided after all not to stand, but so many representations were made to me by Wood, Bellerby, E.T. Wilding & others that I relented at 6 p.m. and let myself in for it."

113

Four days later on 8th July, he opened his fourth election campaign in the city - a very short one - with the result that he came bottom of the poll for the second time, with 95 fewer votes than Lockwood.

"Nellie who has been a sweet companion & great help nearly fainted at the count when it was known I was beaten - they have had their fight & (I believe most sincerely) thank me for uniting & encouraging the Liberal Party in the city."

The day following Alfred's defeat, he learnt that his Uncle Arthur had finally wrenched Darlington from Sir Theodore Fry, drawing the comment from him,

"I am sick at the thought of a Pease being the first Tory M.P. for Darlington."

And when Joseph learnt of the Darlington result,

"A tremendous victory for them - the first Tory Pease elected! What a come down. It disturbs me much these two bad beginnings."

Alfred then set about helping his father hold on to Barnard Castle, which he once more won, but with a reduced majority. Alfred was further in demand to assist Henry Fell Pease in Cleveland, and Jack appealed for him to come to Tyneside to help there. Jack held Tyneside with a 435 majority, and after all this sudden, sharp, strenuous political activity Alfred comments:

"I am very worn out, cross & in low spirits - & find that this like last summer is anything but rest & a pleasant life at home."

Except for mention of his election victory, what about Joseph since we left him in March? He had managed to get away from the pesterings of Sir Richard Nicholson, and had been on holiday in Italy during April. Shortly after his return, Joseph met Nicholson who now wanted to have the Edward Pease Trust Accounts audited.

A pleasant diversion from this troublesome business took place in June when Joseph, Jack and Elsie went to the opening by the Kaiser of the Kiel Canal, going as guests of Sir Donald Currie on one of his Castle Line vessels.

In July, just as the General Election was getting under way, Joseph's sister Emma had died at the old family home Southend, Darlington. When, following the funeral Beatrice came up to Joseph she

"... kissed me, so I could not show my temper at her worryings."

This August, Joseph took his seat for his eighth Parliament amid self-questioning, which centred around business problems and his age, now 67, whether he ought to have stood again.

In the middle of the month he went up to Sir Donald Currie's place at Garth, near Perth, for the shooting. He had gone there with unrelenting financial troubles on his mind and during his stay, a letter received from C.R. Fry disturbed him greatly. So much so that

"Fry's appeals making me get up at 1.30 a.m. & look quietly through finance."

The following morning Joseph informed his host that he thought he had better return home, that his knee which he had sprained some time before was playing up, and letters from home were troublesome. Sir Donald asked Joseph the nature of his troubles at home, to which he replied: low profitability; having to advance money to Stephensons and they were working with too little margin; that the Counting House was over its borrowing limit with London.

"He offered to lend £25,000 for 12 months to be renewed 6 months after if I wanted. Anything more generous I never knew, it nearly knocked the wind out of me."

At Darlington a few days later the loan came through.

At the end of August, Pease & Partners were in no position to declare a dividend at their General Meeting. On the other hand, business was showing some signs of stirring both there and at the Mills - in fact the latter had never been so busy for years past.

The *Northern Echo* newspaper was sold about this time for a price sufficient to cover its liabilities, and this cleared Joseph and Alfred of all further involvement in that area of activity.

Through September things went very well, and at the end of that month the fiftieth anniversary of Joseph's first day at the Counting House in 1845 came about, which he celebrated by inviting heads of departments of all the concerns to Hutton. There was a colliery band from Wooley, Co. Durham, and another band from Marske-by-the-Sea, the day was fine and warm and everyone had a good time of it.

Portsmouth started on a new tack at the end of September, by inviting Joseph and Arthur to take over the Edward Pease Trust for the sum of £200,000 to rid Beatrice of something from which she derived neither "pleasure nor profit." The offer, after short reflection, was declined, and in his reply Joseph pointed out that

"Since your marriage, the 'profitless investment' *(to the end of 1894)* has yielded the Trust Estate £64,000, or putting these figures together £8,000 a year."

Being curious about the £200,000 offer-price, Joseph asked Portsmouth to explain the basis on which he arrived at such a figure.

Portsmouth, to justify his offer-price referred back to figures quoted by Joseph in 1893. At that time Joseph had arrived at a figure clear of all liabilities, of £220,000 as the net book value of the Trust Estate which, in addition to the commercial assets, included estates in Worcestershire and Shropshire together with sundry other small properties in Co. Durham and Yorkshire. From the figure of £220,000, Portsmouth had simply lopped off £20,000 as bait, and this formed the basis of his offer. Portsmouth added to this by suggesting that *"you can mortgage your collieries to buy Beatrice out"*. But this was ridiculous, impossible and wrong was Joseph's retort. The collieries were not his to mortgage, they belonged to the company, Pease & Partners Ltd., and the revolving argument between them started all over again, paralleled by correspondence between Joseph and Nicholson, and Nicholson and Lucas. Joseph explodes in his diary with

"What a ------ he is!"

Joseph and Arthur were being invited (i.e. pressured) into doing precisely that which Beatrice's father in his carefully framed will had been at strenuous pains to avoid, namely, as the surviving brothers having to buy out their deceased brother's shares.

Silence descended again when at the start of November, Beatrice in a short letter to Joseph said 'this correspondence should cease' and only be conducted through their respective legal representatives.

At the commencement of this furious phase of exchanges, Alfred and Nellie went off to more pleasant surroundings at Schwarzen See, Styria, in search of chamois in the company of Sir Edmund and Lady Loder.

The autumn proved calm and Alfred and Joseph both found time to engage in their country pursuits. Trade, though wobbly, was overall showing a marked improvement.

At Hutton that Christmas there was a parade of the new generation when ten of the twenty-two who sat down to dinner were Joseph's grandchildren.

By 31st December, Alfred and Nellie, trying a new experiment for her health and his interest, were travelling on the Nice Express to Marseilles, and then on by boat to Aden, thence to Bulhar, a point just up coast from Berbera in the British Protectorate of Somaliland.

At parting from Alfred, Joseph wrote,

"I do wish he was more at home, he is everyone's favourite and very precious to me."

Notes:
1. Sometimes spelt 'reem' or 'rime,' or otherwise known as sand gazelle.
2. Touareg being the Arab name given to the inhabitants of that part and meaning 'abandoned by God'.

CHAPTER SIX

Olive Branches & Swords
Somaliland & Free Will

Alfred, Nellie and Ted Leatham[1] left London bound for Marseilles on New Year's Eve 1895, and calling at Brindisi, were joined there by Edward North Buxton.

At Aden, from where the Somaliland Protectorate was administered under the India Office, they obtained shooting permits and then crossed the Gulf to Bulhar. At that time, with the exception of the Residency, Bulhar was nothing more than a collection of mat huts, but was one of three principal points of disembarkation, lying about 80 miles up coast from Berbera.

1896

Advance arrangements had been made for their caravan and escort, and on 13th January, 1896, as they approached to disembark, they caught sight of their fifty camels, eight ponies, and some sheep and goats stringing along the coastline.

In addition to themselves, the Somali escort numbering thirty-seven men, was made up of headmen, shikaris, camelmen, cooks, syces and bearers.

They set out just as soon as their equipment and stores had been checked off and loaded, the camels being tied in strings of five or more, head to tail, the caravan marching west from Bulhar. The provisions were sufficient for an expedition lasting nine weeks, and for the escort there were 35 Snider rifles and 1,000 rounds of ammunition.

Their journey took them through the Gadabursi country via Aliman, the Harrowa valley, Jerrie, the Marar prairie, Jifa Madeer, the Northern Haud, Hargaisa, Argan and the Jerato Pass and finishing up at Berbera.

The country varied from thorn jungle and elephant grass, to stony or shale plateau and mountains, and there were often days when they would pass without sight of the native population.

They were advised very strongly against going anywhere near the Abyssinian border as the Italians and Abyssinians were at war, and the latter were highly suspicious of any Europeans, who were liable to be shot on sight if found in that vicinity.

Buxton was laid up with fever for some days, but with this exception there were no mishaps, and with the further exception of only minor irritations between them over small matters, the expedition was counted a success. The climate, which was profiting Nellie, was ideal, the country lovely, the wildlife varied and numerous.

When Berbera was reached on 18th March, 1896 the game bag for each was as follows:-

Buxton	Leatham	Pease
39 head	40 head	55 head
(including 1 hyaena)	(including 1 lion)	(including 1 cheetah and 4 hyaenas)

Alfred and Nellie returned to England in May, 1896.

During Alfred's absence, Joseph continued weighed down with problems. His cousin and neighbour, Isaac Wilson, living at Nunthorpe Hall was, in Joseph's words, in a *"queer way"* financially, but he felt unable to find means *"to aid him further in his old age."* Over many years Isaac Wilson had been heavily propped up by Joseph in the defunct (since 1890) Middlesbrough Potteries business. But Joseph indicates in an entry on 24th March, having a discussion with his solicitor, Lucas, on *"Nunthorpe mortgage."* Whether Isaac Wilson initiated or increased a mortgage with Joseph at this time, and to what extent we cannot tell, but one or other seems certain, and to some extent Isaac Wilson seems to have been further aided.

At the same time as Joseph was labouring with Isaac Wilson's financial difficulties, he faced a completely new problem; litigation brought by James Taylor of Middlesbrough over an agreement made in 1881. This concerned the Tees Union Shipping Company which plied trade between the Tees and the Thames.

In 1875, Taylor, a shipowner, metal broker and manager of the Middlesbrough and London Steam Shipping Company, went bankrupt

119

when disaster stalked him with a ship lost at sea and a further ship wrecked, and at the point when he went bankrupt, he had only one vessel remaining in commission. Four years later in 1879, Joseph and two associates took over the Middlesbrough and London Steam Shipping Company renaming it the Tees Union Shipping Company, and in which Joseph's stake was one of £26,000 in shares. In November 1881, James Taylor was brought back into the business as manager of the company, and entered into an agreement with Joseph that after seven years he, Taylor, would redeem Joseph's shares at par. When the redemption date (1888) came round, Taylor was unable to fulfil the agreement, and was now (1896), claiming that the agreement of 1881 had been forced upon him; that he had been afraid to complain because he might thereby lose his position as manager.

The case came up in the High Court in February, 1896, judgement being given against Taylor who then went on to appeal. He lost, and against all advice, appealed to the House of Lords who pitched it out with costs against him, leaving Taylor in a fearful plight once more.

Additionally of course, Joseph continued to be harassed by Sir Richard Nicholson and an accountant (C.W. Jackson) acting for the Portsmouths. Jackson, though pleasant enough, wanted to examine balance sheets and inspect everything appertaining to Edward Pease's Executor's accounts, and he was afforded every possible facility to do so. When Jackson came to examine Robert Stephenson & Co Ltd accounts, he did rather express astonishment at the size of the accumulated losses. Joseph swept this observation aside by pointing out that the Stephenson family had the majority shareholding in that company, and the day-to-day management was in their hands.

Joseph spent part of July and August with Sir Donald Currie on his new steam yacht all about the Norwegian Fiords. Immediately upon his return, the Portsmouths, finding they were getting nowhere, and in exasperation, brought matters to a head by serving the Trustees with a writ to have the Edward Pease Trust administered through the Court.

To have the regular conduct of business fettered by the court's administration of the Trust was something Joseph wanted to avoid. He talked the matter over with his solicitor, Lucas, on 24th August, and was advised that a suit of this kind could very well drag on for five years. So, going home, he swept up the whole of his correspondence with Nicholson, Beatrice and Portsmouth from the beginning, and handed it all over to his lawyer, and as the Portsmouths meant business, made arrangements about the appointment of Counsel.

"What a world of trial have these people been to me!"

He went contentedly about the grouse moors at home, and enjoyed his sport this last week in August. After one such day, Alfred made the proposal that they should seriously consider exploring ways to make an offer to buy out Beatrice's colliery interests, the greater part of the trust commercial investments being in Pease & Partners. As we know, Joseph had never seen it as being either timely or possible to do this before, but now, feeling absolutely cornered and driven to it, he started to turn the idea over in his mind, and on 31st August,

"Then worked at Alfred's proposal, can we buy out the Portsmouths from the collieries? It is difficult to find them a permanent income."

A Capital reconstruction of Pease & Partners may be necessary to solve the problem, and nine days later, he had sketched out a line of approach which he discussed with Arthur Lucas at Darlington. The starting point was to attack the Debentures; to redeem the 5% Debentures and make a new issue at 4%, and then tackle the larger problem of share capital, possibly introducing a new class of share, and he started work around this rough line of approach.

On 25th September Sir David Dale, (created a baronet the previous year), Arthur Lucas, and Edwin Waterhouse (the accountant partner in Price Waterhouse) came to stay overnight at Hutton and a full discussion took place over the week-end. Lucas reported having received a conciliatory letter from Sir Richard Nicholson now that some proposal looked forthcoming, and on the morning of 26th September, Sir David Dale drafted a letter to Nicholson offering that Lucas and Waterhouse should meet Nicholson and Jackson in London.

On 17th October, following a meeting with his counsel (Arthur R. Ingpen) on the matter of the writ, Joseph records:

"Ingpen's Chambers 10.30 consultation until 12 on Portsmouth's actions. Ingpen thinks he can make but little of it as Herschell's Act of 1888 and a newer Act of 1896 both protect trustees, but he thinks we need no protection. He thinks Portsmouth's plaint is over not realising assets at the right time for he can make but little really ... off north at 2.20, found quite a party at dinner, Alfred's party, Gerald Buxton &c &c – glad of my bed and quiet."

Armed with Counsel's Opinion, the pressure for an early solution to a complex problem was reduced to some extent, and more time could be given to finding a satisfactory way to meet the Portsmouths' demands, and there for the moment we can leave Joseph with this particular predicament, in which not a circumstance had changed to make a solution any easier than before.

At a colliery meeting on 19th November, there was produced the best monthly statement for three years. Business by the third quarter of the year, with some fluctuations, was generally beginning to pick up. Iron prices were firmer, coke sold well, the Mills were full of orders and Stephensons landed a contract with the Spanish Government for a pontoon dock for the Philippines at a cost of £175,000. The engine works and foundry were full of work with 21 engines on order and 10 in for repair.

Nellie had been unwell since August, her cough having returned, and she spent some time confined to the house if not in bed. September had been wet, the corn standing stooked in the fields waiting for a few dry days to get it into the stackyards.

With the approach of winter, Alfred and Nellie prepared for another period in exile, again in Somaliland, and this time being joined by Sir Edmund Loder. As they set sail for Somaliland on 19th of November, it is with regret that we must remain behind with Joseph – at least for the time being.

During the first days of December, a totally unexpected event took place. On the morning of 7th December, Joseph being back at Hutton Hall, he was awakened early by his butler, Oliver, with a letter from Lloyd Pease, with news that Lloyd's half-brother, Henry Fell Pease, had died very suddenly the previous day. Henry Fell Pease was Cleveland's M.P., and in business his principal sphere of responsibility had been, (since succeeding his father, Henry Pease) at Pease's Mills. He had been at Hutton only a fortnight ago shooting, on which occasion Joseph had remarked how thin he was looking, though he seemed well enough.

His death was arresting to Joseph for two reasons. His mind raced firstly to his own position as H.F. Pease's Executor, and the concern he felt over the financial affairs of the deceased which he knew to be decidedly rocky. He felt that his cousin had inherited a trait for speculative investment from his father, but which in H. F. Pease's case had proved infertile. This rockiness was reflected in his bank overdraft at the Counting House, which stood at £181,843, and though the bank held certain securities against part of these borrowings, there was a large unsecured gap of £70,476.[2] Here the question arose, not as one might suppose, how would the bank recover such a large sum, (still less how the account had got into this mess in the first place) but rather, how would Lizzie, H.F. Pease's widow, be provided for? The second arresting thing was Cleveland politics. Who was to run at the by-election?

Directly following the funeral, Joseph discussed Henry F. Pease's affairs with John William Pease[3], his brother-in-law and co-executor, and concluded that there would not be *"much balance"* in his estate after *"meeting his engagements."*

> "John took a very low view of it. I wanted a little more careful treatment, but if we pressed our claims there would be little."

A few days later when the picture became more clear, it seemed that the estate would amount to no more than about £9,000, but with suggestions from Joseph for allowing interest on his liquidation account, by foregoing claims and by a bit of tinkering here and there, the estate could probably be jacked up to £25,000 – £30,000. This was the patriarchal (and sacrificial) side of Joseph's nature showing at its very best; to find ways to help any member of the family in need. As head of the family, Joseph saw this as a duty to be placed in front of every other consideration.

Two days after the funeral, and after discussing with David Dale the question of Cleveland politics, Joseph concluded that Alfred seemed

> "... by far the strongest candidate we could put up."

This was now taken a step further:

> "Had an hour's chat with O'Connell Jones *(Liberal Agent, Cleveland)* abt. the prospects of the Cleveland election – It seems to be Alfred absent v. Jos. Walton present – I gathered from Hugh Bell that if Alfred stood he would not be opposed – also from Dorman & Swan, but one can never rely on these reports and on individual sentiment."

On 13th December, Joseph Walton communicated an offer to Joseph to nominate Alfred as candidate, and two days later followed this up by calling at Hutton Hall.

> "Walton came at one o'clock, had a long chat with him. He behaved very well; he

was determined to propose Alfred, but wishes to run himself and retire. Of course I could not oppose him as he thought that would do him good in the Doncaster division."

Doncaster was another constituency upon which Walton had set his sights. That evening there was a Liberal meeting to consider the question of the candidate:

"When we came to the meeting, the Walton men were there in numbers. Walton proposed and Belerbee seconded Alfred – I explained Alfred's position – when Trow held up the *Gazette* with a paragraph showing that Alfred had been *(already)* fixed upon, (a most unwise paragraph) they wanted to take a vote, but as there was no choice, Walton having retired, I declined to put it – I think it would have been very even, but the agricultural element was not represented. It was a cold night and although all the Walton men said they were going for Alfred it left a cloud."

Alfred of course was in total ignorance of even the death of his M.P. cousin, let alone that he was about to become the absentee Liberal candidate for Cleveland. There was at this time, no statutory requirement for a candidate to declare his willingness to accept nomination – so that any views Alfred may have had in the matter were of no consequence whatever. Like it or lump it, he was to be the candidate. There was, after all, to be a contest, the Conservatives putting up Colonel Ropner.

Far away on the African continent, Alfred had already set out, in fact had started out on the day following H.F.P.'s death. Marching happily on his way, somewhere in a thorn jungle going in the direction of the Ogaden, he was taking at the head of the caravan a sheep which he had bought as a mascot, thereby saving it from ending up as dinner for the Aden garrison, and which because of its fine black head and black legs he had named 'Muther Hamadou' (Black Head).

Joseph now had his hands full, and worked with a will. He prepared a speech for a meeting at Skelton for the night of 19th December, and set out in the dog-cart on a dark night, well wrapped up as he records, against driving rain, sleet and snow for the 5-mile journey there, where he found

"There was an undercurrent of Walton's men in the meeting, but I think it was washed out – but Walton's vanity has done a lot of harm, but I think we can live it and speak it down. Toyn behaved badly as he knew that Walton had resolved not to stand at ten o'clock on the morning of Tuesday *(15th)* and he set all the men's backs up by complaining of a surprise – still the Skelton meeting was hearty and enthusiastic, the 2 men who proposed and seconded Walton (not in order) declaring themselves satisfied."

The day following the Skelton meeting, Walton appeared again at Hutton, at lunch time – and he was absolutely livid,

"... because I had said at Skelton that he had urged Alfred's candidature. I had two uncomfortable hours – At last he would say that that if he had known how strong the feeling was, that he would have submitted his name to the meeting – that he regretted not having done so, but having withdrawn, he now fought for Alfred. I had to remind him that he had signed and amended Alfred's address – then off to Redcar with Harry Paulton and we had a capital meeting – Walton talked about himself, and I called my Skelton language too strong as regards sentiments abt. standing, and all went off well. They had a good meeting at Marske."

Hutton Hall, filling up for Christmas, was full of activity. Everything stopped for Nanny Wilson's traditional Christmas Eve tea party, and on Christmas Day there was the bran tub ceremony in the cooling room of the Turkish baths, with a present for everyone. Sylvia and Christopher had to deliver presents from the pony-cart calling at the village houses – then out to the more distant farms and cottages. It took Sylvia a week beforehand to wrap up and tie those parcels, and all morning to deliver.

Joseph used the Christmas holiday period to organise a full programme of meetings, settle committee rooms, polling districts, agents, taking the lead in all the arrangements, doing much canvassing himself, finding supporting speakers, marshalling and directing Jack, David Dale, Theodore Fry and a posse of Liberal M.P.s, and doing more than his fair share of the platform speaking himself. Had he been the candidate he could not have worked harder. But Alfred was pushing on in the heat of the African jungle, still in absolute and total ignorance of what was going on at home in his name.

Alfred's and Loder's caravan was slightly larger than that of the expedition in January, eleven months ago. They marched by Kaldigo, Jerato, Oossbhor, Horlakhudut (where they had been previously) and were at Adadleh at Christmas, where they had joined up for a few days with Lord Delamere at his invitation, and they acceded to this diversion in their intended itinerary for a few days before going on.

125

1897

On 10th January, two days before polling in Cleveland, Alfred received news by running camel of Henry Fell Pease's death more than a month earlier, and a suggestion, no more, that he, Alfred, would be the best man to fill the vacancy. Halting in his tracks, he wrote immediately to his father saying,

"I am alarmed at the idea that I may possibly have to take H.F.P.'s seat for Cleveland and as soon as I can reach you with a wire will telegraph I cannot stand ... what with winter absences and full summers I could neither satisfy myself nor my constituents."

The letter continued with expressions of disgust at the present state of the Liberal Party, and enumerated his many differences of view over important issues of the day. Thus unburdened, he turned the running camel and rider round facing the direction of Berbera, despatched his letter with 'God speed', and returned to the pleasant business in hand.

It was on the day that the count was taking place at Guisborough, 13th January, 1897 that Alfred bagged his first lion, not in spectacular fashion but

"About 9.30 news came in that a lion had killed two camels last night, at the village two hours off. Off I started at once, being told that I should find him still at the camel, and that Somalis were watching him. When at last I got there he had been three times during the morning to the camel. After a fruitless attempt to start tracking, we built a zariba over the camel, and at 5, dinnerless, Hassan, Ali Mugan and I were built in.

It was a long thirteen hours – the earlier part of the night, and till 2.30 there was a half moon, and we had great difficulty keeping the hyaenas away – they returned a hundred times after being frightened off. About 12 I saw the lion – a monster – walk across an open space a hundred yards off, but till the moon set and it was quite dark he never came near the camel.

As he was moving round and round the zariba, we were kept on the stretch till 3.30 a.m. when he came on. It was now very dark indeed, and all but impossible to see anything against the dark bush. Hassan, while I was peering to make the head end of him, was frantic, whispering 'kill him, dackso! dackso!' I was as anxious to kill him as Hassan, but was not going to fire until I got him head on. He came once breaking the camel's ribs two yards from me and I got his head against the sky or high ground as he pulled and snorted – and pulling under his chin I fired. He gave a roar and pelted off.

Till daybreak at 6 we listened in suspense. We then examined the ground and found no blood, and when it was light we continued our search with rifles full cock. To our great delight we found the big lion dead – a hundred and fifty yards from where I had shot. His heart was riddled. He measured, without moving him or pulling him out, 112 inches in length from nose to tip of hairs on tail."

With Sir Frank Lockwood's Compliments,
and begging your kind support for an old and valued colleague.

16. Sketch of Alfred distributed to all the electors in the Cleveland constituency by Sir Frank Lockwood Q.C. Roseberry Topping, a landmark close to Alfred's home, is in the background.

While Alfred was oblivious to everything but thorn jungle and lions, his victory in Cleveland with a 1,425 majority was being celebrated at home. Joseph was absolutely jubilant:

> "Splendid victory. I lunched all the Agents I could lay my hands on. It was a great pleasure to have them, they have worked well."

At this celebration lunch, with Alfred's elder son Edward absent, Christopher aged ten returned the vote of thanks for his father's health. Before this, Joseph sent off a telegram to acquaint his son with the news.

Since Alfred received mail only after a running camel had returned from the despatch of outgoing letters, it was not until three weeks later, on 8th February at Gohowaine in Abyssinia, that the stunning news that he was again an M.P. came to his notice. It was a fearful blow to his peace of mind and his longing for domestic quiet, and an honour quite uncoveted. Writing to Joseph he said,

> "You could not guess with what astonishment I opened and read the telegram informing me of my election for Cleveland – this is one of the events in one's life, which seem to knock on the head any doctrine of free will – To think of all the labour and worry that you and my friends have undergone for the cause and for myself in my absence, makes me feel unworthy of so much kindness and support – You know that this is not at all what I would have chosen for myself – you and my neighbours have chosen it for me, and much as I dread the added responsibility and destruction of my home life, the only return I can make is to accept and try to justify the choice of those amongst whom I have lived and amongst whom I hope to end my days."

By the same post came a telegram from Col. Ferris[4] warning Alfred and Loder to give the Abyssinians a wide berth as Ras Makonnen[5], (Abyssinian Ras of Harrar district) was behaving badly. But he and Loder were already in Abyssinia, and surrounded by Abyssinians, and within four days' march of Harrar.

> "The Pol. Agent Consul desires that you should avoid the Ogaden & Hargaisa, returning eastwards as soon as possible," was a further message.
> "We called Adan and Mohammed Ali into my tent, and told them not to breath a word to the men, but we had to go back to Berbera and not by Hargaisa; this leaves only one way of getting to the coast, viz. the way we came, but Darror pool is long since dry, so we must march quickly by Milmil to Aware, take water there, and strike across to Adadleh. What it all means we cannot tell, but we must get quietly and quickly to Milmil. After getting to Aware, all risk must be at an end unless the Abyssinians are coming to Berbera:-
>
> > 'That worse than Tantalus was *our* annoy
> > to clip Elysium and to miss *our* joy.'
>
> Loder was quite nervous and ill with the news and disgust at leaving the elephants and rhinoceros. Fancy our disgust, just as we started to get news of a lion sitting on a horse the night before. Nellie, always plucky and cheerful, is an example to us, but she has not the distress of feeling that it is goodbye *for ever* to the wild African elephant."

On the eighth day of the eastwards retreat,

> "We are in a perplexity about our plans ... Awkward rumours are brought that the Court is closed at Berbera, that the 'Egyptians' are at Bulhar and Berbera. Hundreds of Ogaden Rer Ali, with thousands of camels and sheep are pouring in from Aware district, as the water is giving out. As we are bound for Aware, we ask if there is any water there, but one says 'yes, enough for you,' others say 'none.' Tomorrow we send Hassan Mohammed & Ismael Oualli to Aware to see if there is water, and to return to us at Hagal, where we go today."

128

After two and a half hours' march they reached Hagal. Just as they pitched their camp, a native camel corps from Berbera arrived, camels and men looking done in:

"It was pleasant when feeling isolated from the coast, and perplexed as to what was up, to see the British uniform and receive a salute. He had come across the Haud from Hargaisa via Ful-ful, about a hundred and thirty miles in two days!"

They received orders afresh to avoid Hargaisa and to keep to the north side of the Haud, forbidding any stay on the Haud. The messenger said all was quiet at Berbera, but rumour was rife including one that Lord Delamere had been taken by the Abyssinians, and that 200 cavalry had been despatched in pursuit. Compounding uncertainties, Alfred's and Loder's provisions were running low with only seven days' supplies remaining.

The caravan moved on and crossed the Haud in seven days reaching Berbera on 14th March, and at the point where 'Muther Hamadou' had started his march with the caravan, they stopped to toast his health, and his great achievement in having marched more than 1,000 miles. Alfred had become so attached to his mascot that he could not leave him behind to an uncertain fate, so took him on board for the return to England on 18th March. He also took with him his Somali servant Mohammed Ali and arrived home at the end of April, 1897.

Events at home during Alfred's five-month absence, extra to Joseph fighting his election for him included, Lottie (Alfred's sister) getting married in February to Howard Hodgkin, a barrister, but not before a morning when Howard would *"argue and argue"* over Lottie's settlement matters, until Joseph was both weary and cross. Some years earlier Lottie had refused Howard, at which time Joseph, unsurprised at this claimed, *"I could not live with so argumentative a mind."* Whatever Joseph thought, Alfred was very fond of Howard Hodgkin.

Business was better during this five-month period, (Dec. 1896 to Apl. 1897) and at Stephensons the order book was standing at £350,000. Pease & Partners had been able to declare a dividend of 3 per cent[6] for the half year ending December, 1896. Then one day in April, Arthur telegraphed to Joseph that it was imperative that he came up to London immediately.

More bother. More family affairs, this time concerning William Fowler, Joseph's brother-in-law,[7] who was £70,000 adrift with his petroleum company. Joseph went straight up to London, and with Arthur at a meeting with Fowler's solicitors, they both agreed to aid Fowler by £10,000 apiece,

> "... but what a mess for such a man."

After a short holiday he returned to wrestle again with William Fowler's affairs which in the interim had shaped up a bit:

> *6th May.* "£35,000 more wanting to pull William Fowler's affairs through. Agreed at last against my better judgement to go to Dimsdale and try to raise £25,000 on Arthur's and my own guarantee & £45,000 on W.F's securities. Went into the city. Prescotts let me have £25,000 ... this is I hope the end of this affair, but it all depends on oil wells and ships!!"

Alfred's return from Somaliland in April had been marked by a tremendous reception. As he stepped from the train at Pinchinthorpe Station, which was decorated with flags and bunting, a silver band struck up to mark his victorious return as an M.P., and at Hutton Hall the next day there was a celebration party attended by 3,000 people, at which

> "Alfred made an excellent speech, especially about foreign policy – I never saw so many folks at Hutton. The hearty welcome Alfred received was splendid and such pleasant hearty people everywhere."

We can now return to where we left Joseph last autumn tackling the twin problems of finding a fair and full settlement acceptable to the Portsmouths, and the means by which it could be brought about. A satisfactory proposal from Joseph and Arthur was a precondition to the withdrawal of the writ. From Joseph's viewpoint, an out of court settlement was preferable to the risk, however great or small, of the trust being administered by the Court and the directors of Pease and Partners thereby being hampered in the conduct of business.

Joseph was struggling with his plan to rearrange Pease and Partners share capital and debentures. Negotiations with the Portsmouths and their advisers dragged on until late spring when by 1st June, nine months after the service of the writ,

> "We settled subject to Portsmouth's approval, all the points of payment."

What now appeared settled verbally, was the price to be paid by a purchasing syndicate for the trust commercial assets only. The agreed figure was £273,555. The verbal agreement also provided for the discharge by the trustees of all the trust liabilities. These amounted to £222,833 and included a £65,000 mortgage on the Bewdley Estate in Worcestershire, though the property itself was not part of the assets to be purchased under the agreement.

Accordingly, a syndicate would buy the shares in the trust from the trustees who would apply the funds in the discharge of the liabilities and pay the Portsmouths the balance (£50,722). This of course, even after obtaining the Portsmouths' approval, was still subject to sanction by the Court, and that was yet a long way off.

Further elucidation is rather important to any clear understanding when we come to consider what followed.

Firstly, the reader is aware that Joseph and Arthur were the executors of Beatrices' father's estate, and they were also Beatrice's settlement trustees.

Secondly, Alfred and Jack and one other, Sir George Wyndham Herbert, were the trustees in Beatrice's marriage settlement. The last named trustee must be allowed to fade from view since he played no part in what followed.

Thirdly, the purchasing syndicate was made up of Joseph, Arthur, Alfred, and Jack. So that Joseph and Arthur each wore one hat as settlement trustees, and another as part of the syndicate. Alfred and Jack similarly in their role as trustees of the marriage settlement, wore the other hat as the other half of the purchasing syndicate.

Fourthly, in arriving at the offer price, Joseph had naturally given consideration to the valuation of each block of shares in the separate businesses, and these were (perhaps inadvisably) later shown in the schedule to the agreement. Joseph wanted the separate valuations shown so as to make it perfectly clear how the total valuation was made up. The separate values when aggregated formed the offer price. But the offer being made was one 'for the whole,' and irrespective of any weight given or not given to particular blocks of shares, was accepted as such by the Portsmouths and their advisers. Alfred, Jack, and Lucas the solicitor, all thought £273,555 far too high and too generous a price. Alfred and Jack had joined the purchasing syndicate under protest, and only to aid Joseph and Arthur in ridding themselves of a trust that had become too onerous to administer. Furthermore Sir David Dale and Arthur Francis Pease had been invited to join the purchasing syndicate but Sir David Dale refused, and Arthur Francis Pease withdrew, but both did so on the grounds that £273,555 was far too high a price to pay.

Even the accountant Jackson, acting for the Portsmouths, stated in an interim report dated 26th February, 1897, that having regard to the contingent liability for calls on unpaid capital amounting to £83,099, from which liability the Portsmouths would be released by a sale to the syndicate,

"The price offered for these shares is higher, we think, than their present value *even were the market open* instead of being, as it is, extremely narrow." *(Author's italics)*

Jackson didn't need to be an expert in anything but accountancy to determine that this was a generous price. He was perfectly capable of forming a view on his own by comparing yield with market price in other mining concerns. In any case he had been furnished with all the information he had asked for.

By mid-July, 1897, Portsmouth's acceptance was still awaited, and Nicholson appeared even then to repudiate the verbal agreement reached at the meeting on 1st June (mentioned above) when everything appeared settled. Joseph met his solicitor Lucas, on 28th and again on 30th July, Lucas being very annoyed with Nicholson calling him *"an ignorant bully."* A week later, Lucas had a letter from Nicholson stating that correspondence must cease until, as Joseph records,

"... he knows the colliery dividend for 1896 – which he has had since Feb, 10th – and that for *(six months ending 30th June)* 1897 which he has nothing to do with."

As Joseph saw it, a line had been drawn under 31st December, 1896, and everything germane to the agreement related to the period before that date. Anything subsequent to that date he regarded as being none of Nicholson's business. Nevertheless, if the dividend for the first half of 1897 was going to be a sticking point, Nicholson could have that additional information also.

On 7th September, 1897, Joseph and Lucas were in Darlington, to meet with Nicholson, and Freeman (Nicholson's partner).

"After a great deal of sparring, we got the question confined to the accrued income paid in the first half of 1897, this came after the apportionment, according to our scheme, to a sum of about £7,000, this at last I divided *(between)* Beatrice and ourselves. It just takes away the profit on the first half year of £3,490 odd that we had, but it was better to settle the affair and we settled the agreement."

The agreement was not finally sanctioned by the Court until ten months later, 7th July, 1898.

In the midst of the final period of wrestling, on 2nd September, Sylvia Hamlyn telegraphed from Devon where she had been staying with her father, saying that he had collapsed and died while giving chase to some poachers on his land that day. He was only forty-three years old, and Sylvia now at the age of sixteen had lost both her parents. As for Beatrice before her, Hutton Hall became Sylvia's only home for the remainder of her upbringing.

Alfred and a Devonshire solicitor were Vincent Hamlyn's executors, and having commenced the winding up of his affairs, the former went off with Sir Edmund Loder for a fortnight to Schwarzen See in Austria.

Upon his return, in October 1897, some discussion between Alfred and his father took place on how to meet all the conditions of the settlement with the Portsmouths, once it had been sanctioned by the Court. Of this Joseph writes:

"We had a long chat over my Pease & Partners reconstruction papers. Alfred agrees with Albert *(Jack)* and myself that the alternatives are to sell out or buy in £400,000 ordinary shares. The sell out scheme wants very careful digesting and the particulars trying out in detail."

As the terms of the compromise agreement provided for the early discharge of the trust liabilities as soon as Court sanction had been obtained, it was imperative to direct urgent attention towards establishing the means by which a corresponding amount of cash could be raised by the syndicate.

But no settled plan had yet evolved. So far as any thought had been given to a reconstruction of the capital of Pease & Partners, it had been along the lines that Joseph had worked upon since the autumn of last year. The idea was as already stated, to repay the old and issue new debentures and to raise a class or classes of share. The term 'sell out,' though capable of wider interpretation was, in the absence of share buyers within the family, at this time weighted in favour of a scheme for bringing in a limited number of friends and allies, and maintaining Pease & Partners as a private company. The last thing Joseph wanted was the general public being brought in. This was apparent even to Portsmouth's accountant, Jackson, who had prepared and dated a report as early as 7th May, 1895 part of which reads,

17. The Counting House Partners'. From left to right: Alfred Edward Pease M.P.: Sir Joseph Whitwell Pease Bt., M.P.; Joseph (Jack) Albert Pease M.P.; Arthur Pease M.P.

"Throughout the original Articles of Partnership, the wills of Charles and Edward Pease, Articles of Association of the company and the Marriage Settlement, there is one common idea and intention to be traced, viz. *the absolute retention so far as could possibly be achieved, of the money in the Pease family." (Author's italics).*

If the syndicate, after acquiring the trust securities, could not off-load some or all of them onto the Pease family (which they found they could not, but call it Scheme One), the next best thing would be to include friends and allies, (Scheme Two). These two alternatives up to now had formed the main thrust of Joseph's approach. A sale to the general public, (Scheme Three), was an impossible option at the present time having regard to the general state of the coal trade, and not viewed with any favour by Joseph for the very good reason stated above by Jackson. It was very necessarily a rising background thought nevertheless; a solution of last resort to be considered only after all other avenues had been exhausted. But even giving background thought to Scheme Three, however much he disliked the idea, one seemingly insurmountable problem appeared, at first sight, to block the way forward.

For the half year ending December, 1896, and again at the year end in June, 1897, it had been possible to pay an actual dividend of 3% each time. There were signs of improving trade, but not yet enough to reduce the balance of risk of a failed public issue of shares. A return of eight or ten per cent at a minimum, was Joseph's view of the kind of yield sufficient to induce an investor to buy shares in a mining concern.

Pease & Partners Ltd.,
Record of dividends paid in each year ending 30th June.

1883.	5%	1890.	7%	1897.	6%
1884.	1.25	1891.	5.5%		
1885.	Nil	1892.	0.9375%		
1886.	Nil	1893.	Nil	Average for:-	
1887.	Nil	1894.	2%	last 2 years	4.06%
1888.	Nil	1895.	Nil	last 3 years	2.71%
1889.	Nil	1896.	2.125	last 4 years	2.53%
				last 5 years	2.02%

Quite clearly, by the criteria considered necessary for a successful public issue, this past performance was not good enough. So therefore Scheme Three remained in the background for a solution.

In the mining industry, Joseph may have been viewed as a "Prophet in Israel", (Sylvia Hamlyn's term for him) but no one could say *when* the depression would end – it just obviously would one day.

As we move on to November, 1897, we might here briefly update some extraneous matters aside from the Portsmouth saga. This month, Joseph made arrangements to acquire the Nunthorpe Estate from Isaac Wilson by May Day, 1898. The Estate adjoined that of Pinchinthorpe, and included Nunthorpe Hall and 197 acres. There is nothing to indicate prior negotiation with Isaac Wilson, and absolutely no mention of the amount or nature of the consideration passing in the transaction. This being rather unusual in such matters where Joseph's diary is concerned, it may possibly be, but without certainty, that Joseph accepted the Nunthorpe Estate in satisfaction for sums owed to him at different times by Isaac Wilson.[8] That, as we move towards winter, was one thing.

Among other events at this time, Nellie was urged to try the experiment of a winter in Switzerland. Alfred's York ex-colleague Sir Frank Lockwood died in December, and Arthur Pease had gone to Egypt for his health, and on 31st December news reached home that Elsie's valiant father of renowned erratic behaviour, General Sir Henry Havelock-Allan, had been found with his horse – both dead – on the north-west frontier with Afghanistan. Of this news Joseph wrote:

> "It seems he had left his escort to ride on to some fort ahead of them – and was missed, and his horse and himself soon after both found dead. It is a tragic ending to a soldier's life. Latterly he had been very wild. I fear drink occasioned it – he was a brave and clever man no doubt – but alas! entirely wanted ballast – how far his hardships & sun strokes accounted for his many eccentricities I know not."

1898.

At the end of January, Pease and Partners' profit for the half year ending 31st December, 1897 was £81,000, on which a 3% (actual) dividend was paid.

Alfred in Switzerland with Nellie was leading a life not much to his liking, and in February he returned home, troubled with the recurrence of heart palpitations, which perhaps a few days hunting would put right. This made Joseph anxious:

> *6th Feb. 1898.* "I not easy about him – his old complaint of heart palpitations troubles him. A Dr declined to pass him for life insurance, he wants a much quieter life – they tell him it is the nerves of his heart, and that now there is valvulation disease, but it is not pleasant hearing."

In March Alfred was told by a London doctor that no evidence of disease could be found, but that his heart was never likely to be normal. With this news he decided that instead of anticipating imminent death, he might just as well get on with the business of living.

Beatrice by this time was just about beside herself, hard up and frantic to get the agreement with her 'father' settled, and wrote to him urging him to get on with it. Joseph replied that it was not he who was holding things up but Beatrice's lawyers, and at the end of March, nineteen months after the service of the writ on the trustees, all the parties thereto

> "... signed agreement with the Portsmouths kept going for $4^1/2$ years by Sir R. Nicholson their solicitor."

Joseph felt that everyone now was contractually committed, though with the sanction of the Court still to come. This at long last looked like the end of the affair. As we prepare to draw what we believe to be the final curtain on the Portsmouth saga, we can happily state that on 18th April, 1898, Joseph and Arthur resigned their trusteeship of the Settlement Trust, Alfred and Jack at the same time resigning their trusteeship in the Marriage Settlement. They might reasonably be excused for believing therefore, that as from that date, their responsibilities in the whole business had finally come to an end. If they did believe that, then they were very much mistaken.

Now trouble at Robert Stephensons rears up.

In April, 1898, war broke out between Spain and America. Stephensons had contracted with the Spanish government to build a pontoon dock at a cost of £175,000 for the Philippines, (then Spanish) but the Spanish government was a long time making payment for work in progress. In early May, the Americans attacked and wrecked the Spanish fleet in the Philippines. During the delay by the Spanish in making payment for work in progress, Joseph had to find money himself to pay wages and meet creditors' bills. Transparently, Stephensons business could not be conducted for long on an ad hoc basis such as this, and the company looked to have a very short future.

Doubly pressing was the need to settle the form the restructuring of Pease and Partners capital might take. In conjunction with this, there was a Pease & Partners meeting on 6th May attended by Edwin Waterhouse, where a proposal for a new arrangement of capital was discussed. Joseph's Scheme Two share capital solution was now produced. This was simply to find buyers for an issue of preference shares, and reduce the number of ordinary shares in issue to the extent of those to be acquired by the syndicate from the Portsmouths.

Edwin Waterhouse advised taking counsel with Mr Wimpole Greenwell the London share-broker. In consequence, a meeting was arranged with Greenwell for 12th May. No figures, papers or plans were produced at this meeting which took the form of a very general discussion, with Greenwell asking a lot of searching questions.

When Joseph advanced his idea for an issue of preference shares, Greenwell pointed out, that of about eleven coal and iron companies with market-quoted preference shares, nine were trading at a discount of between thirty and eighty per cent, while only two were at a premium.

Therefore Joseph's scheme was no solution. Greenwell, from what he was being told, felt that the need in this case was for a wholesale reconstruction of capital, and for a sale of Pease & Partners to a new public company. Joseph interrupted him saying they did not want a new company, but wanted changes brought about within the existing Pease & Partners, maintaining it as a private company. But there was no alternative, and Greenwell's advice, with whatever reluctance, would have to be followed. Greenwell suggested as a model, a capital structure taking the form of an issue of about £300,000 Debentures, 4-700,000 Ordinary shares and 2-300,000 Deferred shares. The meeting broke up to digest the advice given, and a further meeting with Greenwell was arranged for the 24th May.

As things now stand, Joseph, by his 'too generous an offer' to the Portsmouths, has prevented any possible resale of the ordinary shares in Pease & Partners without loss to the syndicate, and with his preference share solution scrapped, he is now absolutely forced to turn to Scheme Three for his solution.

The dire consequences following from this point on, bring us to a shuddering halt. We already stand on the edge of a legal minefield, which two years later it took eight eminent barristers ten days in the High Court to cross. Though it is impossible to avoid this most tiresome obstacle to progress, there is no intention here to dwell at length upon all the complexities of argument, but to get to the other side as rapidly as possible, without being blown up.

In a letter Joseph wrote to Edwin Waterhouse on the day following the first interview with Greenwell, that is on 13th May, he said,

> "... desirable that you should ask Mr Greenwell and his solicitor to sketch out the kind of prospectus we should issue."

This is the first time there is any mention of a prospectus. But at the second meeting arranged for 24th May, Greenwell made it perfectly clear, that he would not entertain issuing a prospectus and bringing out a new company, without the management of the old Pease & Partners agreeing to tie themselves to a set period of years of service to a new Pease & Partners, and further to that, the management had also to agree to lock up for a period of years, the Deferred shares, which as management shares were not to be made available to the public. Joseph strongly objected to both these conditions. Joseph and Pease & Partners' other directors did not capitulate on Greenwell's conditions until 29th

August. Nevertheless, Joseph continued to work upon other aspects of the reconstruction.

To Jack was delegated the task of supplying information and suggesting outlines for a prospectus. His production of outlines, which was prolific, he fired off at short intervals to Greenwell's solicitor (H.S. Brenton) who filed them. During the following weeks, a cascade of different draft prospectus outlines, sent by Jack, were put on file. Brenton came to regard the mounting heap of paper as a joke. Jack later conceded that the most attractive features of his output were those he had culled from bits and scraps of other company prospectuses found when he scrabbled amongst rubbish in his waste paper basket. These he 'worked up' in the train before despatching them to Brenton. Even so, there was absolutely nothing that could conceivably be considered a properly defined prospectus.

After 24th May, Greenwell dropped all further consideration for bringing out a new company, until he had knowledge of the profits for the year ending 30th June, 1898, and those figures would not be available until mid-July at the very earliest. Until then, any outline draft prospectus would have to remain a skeleton with terms and figures missing.

At this time during May, Joseph would have unaudited figures only up to the end of April – two more months of trading figures wanted. Of course he had a forecast of the likely outcome at the year end, and this was estimated to show profits of about £115,000. As to the question of timing of the issue of any prospectus, Greenwell pencilled in 'after the holidays', meaning, about the end of September. This it is presumed was not a target date, but another way of saying that, 'all other considerations being straight and correct' there could be no issue to the public before September because of holidays.

On 24th May, Joseph wrote:

"Letters and then to Greenwell in the city about colliery reconstruction ... we had a long chat resulting in Waterhouse agreeing to take out figures as to the real net income for the three years to end June 30, 1898. The capital to be £1,350,000. 350,000 4 p.cent Debentures, 700,000 Ordinaries and 300,000 Deferred. The a/cs we think would show £115,000 net."

So, although the capital structure appears settled, yet the conditions upon which Greenwell would entertain bringing out the company remain unfulfilled. However, with a conjectured loan and share capital of £1,350,000 and assumed profits of £115,000, the following might be anticipated for profit allocation in a reconstructed Pease & Partners:-

350,000	4% Debentures	14,000
700,000	Ordinary Shares (% say 8%)	56,000
300,000	Deferred (say 8%)	24,000
1,350,000		94,000
	Depreciation	18,000
		112,000
	Surplus	3,000
		115,000

On 27th May, Joseph having first glanced over the Portsmouths' affidavit, made in preparation for the Court hearing, to see what it contained, he then made his affirmation on his own statement. The Portsmouths in their affidavit stated that they wanted the compromise agreement, *"whether or not the securities proposed to be sold* (to the syndicate) *are or are not likely to increase in value"*. There could be no more conclusive evidence of the Portsmouths' wishes. The agreement gave the Portsmouths what *they* wanted. This appears to give the all clear to Joseph to concentrate on his own problem of raising funds to meet the Trustees' obligations under the agreement.

His diary entry on 4th June, when he went to Ted Backhouse at Barclays (formerly Backhouses) Bank in Darlington to arrange for a £40,000 loan for four months reads:

"Had a very interesting chat with Ted who strongly urged our going public and securing our capital, never minding loss of revenue – There is a great deal of good sense in this – and meets our views, but I merely said it was often in my mind."

Scheme Three now becomes the main thrust for a solution to finding ways and means. But it is no more than making a start at building a framework. It is so far only taking initial and prudent steps to having in outline a possible scheme in preparation ready to spring it at the first opportunity. The only thing in place is the agreement with the Portsmouths, with the sanction of the Court awaited.

The forty-four day period from 24th May until 7th July, proved absolutely critical when the time came, and attempts were made to show what had been in Joseph's mind at the time, and what had not been disclosed beforehand to the Portsmouths or the Court about the Trustees' intentions. But the course being followed by Joseph was the only one open. Arthur does not appear to have involved himself greatly in any of the various stages of discussion.

On 15th June, 1898, Joseph

"Then spent a long time over draft prospectus for the public of Pease & Partners; recorded our views & then left it with Greenwell, Albert & Dale to canvass again."

This was not a 'draft prospectus' at all, but a draft for a prospectus which needed to be worked up into a proper form. It was the contention of both Joseph and Greenwell, that no defined prospectus was prepared until 29th August, 1898. In fact, in Joseph's words, *"between 19th June and 29th August"* there was nothing but a state of *"chaos and confusion."*

On 27th June, word was received that the Court had heard the Portsmouth case and approved the settlement subject to

"... a little declaration about the money paid to them out of capital."
6th July. "Then a good deal of discussion about the prospectus in which we propose to open the concern to the public ... At 4.30, had a full meeting of Pease & Ptns. Arthur, Alfred, Albert, Lloyd, Arthur F., Dale & self meeting Greenwell & Renton *(sic) (Brenton)* and Meek. We went through the P. & P. prospectus carefully – lasting from 4.30 until nearly 7."

There was no decision made at this meeting to bring out a new company. This fact was later stated by H.S. Brenton, Greenwell's independent solicitor who was present throughout the meeting.

The next day, 7th July, the full sanction of the Court for the compromise agreement was given, and the obligation of the Trustees to discharge the Trust liabilities of £222,833 was, in accordance with the terms of the agreement, duly carried out.

Joseph did not attend the hearing before Mr Justice Stirling – he saw no need to attend what was a mere formality.

Pease & Partners' results for the year ended 30th June, 1898, enabled the directors to recommend a final dividend of (actual) 3% which, with an interim paid in January of the same amount, made 6% for the year.

Joseph went away to Scotland for some fishing with Sir Donald Currie returning on 19th July, and the following day at a meeting with

Jack and Sir David Dale, Joseph reveals that the last three years' average profits of Pease & Partners to be £123,600.

On 31st July, Joseph, in a letter he wrote to Sir David Dale, about the reconstruction of Pease & Partners, said:

> "... looking at the great cost of the proceedings, *and the present condition of the coal trade,* it is one of those things that makes me consider whether we ought to go on with the company at all." *(Author's italics)*

To which Sir David replied,

> "... but we must not give up reconstruction or defer it. Let us amend but proceed."

At this time, Arthur, who had gone to Cornwall on a political engagement, took ill. He was detained there and seemed to have completely broken down in health.

During early August, Joseph's attention was diverted towards trying to get a sale of Robert Stephenson & Co. Ltd. or otherwise winding it up. He wrote on 9th August,

> "Worked all morning on Stephensons a/cs and pondering how it was to be wound up, as if he *(G. R. Stephenson)* adheres to his £ *(sic)* of flesh he has a great pull over us who have advanced monies without debentures to cover us."

But he was simultaneously engaged on the Pease & Partners proposals and records on

> *22nd Aug.* "Then colliery meeting, and Meek *(the solicitor partner in the firm Lucas, Hutchinson & Meek)* on Greenwell's wants; he is inattentive and absurd in some of his proposals."

Almost seven weeks after the compromise agreement had been sanctioned by the Court, the draft prospectus looked far from being cut and dried.

Throughout the first three weeks of August, Joseph was kept closely informed – almost daily – of his brother Arthur's increasing weakness. It had been clear to him from the beginning of the month that the inevitable could not be long delayed. He wrote on 6th August,

> "Feel very sad at parting with him. His change in political views – so warmly held, has had its effect in parting us, but not in the bottom of our hearts' affection."

Expecting bad news at any time, and on 24th August, whilst shooting on Westerdale Moor, he noted,

"Drove grouse on the outside beats to the north over the road leading to West House &c and on that side ... was quite alarmed at seeing Robinson on a grey mare coming to me, I was sure it was bad news of Arthur, but it was only the old thing – Stephensons out of money for their pay, £10,000 coming from Spain and £9,400 next week from their Australian contract. It is most annoying."

The expected telegram announcing Arthur's death came on on 28th August:

"He was a kind, affectionate loveable brother, of an excellent judgement in all business matters, but he disliked detail & never consequently worked at business."

Joseph had a quiet talk with Arthur's widow, May, after the funeral:

"She said Arthur's last message to me was 'tell Joseph, he knows how I have loved him, but I have never thanked him for the way he has worked for me.'"

Joseph Whitwell Pease, in his 71st year, was now on his own, the sole survivor of seven brothers and three sisters.

Arthur's death brought about a vacancy in the Darlington constituency and within five days his son Herbert Pike Pease was put forward as the Unionist candidate. This was a very short snap election with polling taking place only sixteen days after Arthur's funeral. Joseph did not interfere in the campaign, or try to persuade Herbert against it, and was roundly castigated by Lady Milbank over lunch at the Dales' home at Darlington for

"... forsaking my own party and letting Herbert stand for Darlington without attacking him or joining in the fight."

Herbert Pike Pease – popularly known as 'Pike Pease' – held Darlington for the Unionists with a slender majority.

Returning to the Pease & Partners reconstruction developments, on 10th September, 1898, Joseph's diary entry includes the following:

"Dale, A(rthur) Francis (Pease) and I went through the draft prospectus of our new company and practically settled it. The only serious thing was a proposal to lower the amount of the Ordinary shares and raise the Deferred by 100,000. I put in a strong caveat and it was abandoned." (Author's italics)

In a separate note, Joseph states that on this day, he expressed himself strongly *"as to chucking up* (the whole thing) *if Greenwell was so nervous."*

On the 14th September, three days before Darlington polled, there was a meeting at the share-brokers, Greenwells', in London attended by Joseph, Alfred, Jack, Sir David Dale, Arthur Francis Pease and Lloyd Pease, where

> "We had a good many discussions on wordings and, *I suppose, finally settled the document."* *(Author's italics)*

Between March and September 1898, the price of coal in Co. Durham had risen 12.3%. The contract price for coke to Barrow Haematite Steel Co. Ltd. from Pease & Partners rose 10% between June, 1897 and November, 1898 (seventeen months) of which rise almost 7% came between June and November, 1898. Well founded optimism was suddenly back in place. From the point of view of the timing for the issue of the Pease & Partners prospectus on 17th October as the boom continued, it proved at one and the same time fortuitous, superb and disastrous.

On 18th October, Joseph went to Darlington for

> " ... a very exciting day, a regular run for our shares, telegraphs coming and going all day. Jack as busy as a bee – by 4 o'clock we had applications for 349,200 stock including our own, and for 34,005 shares £340,050 – Dale telegraphed me that 1,250,000 in Debentures had been applied for, 100,000 to allot and 2,500,000 shares, 300,000 to allot – an exciting day -
> 1,250,000
> 2,500,000
> —————
> 3,750,000 for 400,000"

Within ten days, Portsmouth (who, probably for reasons of courtesy, had been sent a prospectus) his attention arrested by the breathtaking success of the issue, was making enquiries through Sir Richard Nicholson for some kind of explanation. How could a flotation have been possible in so short a time since the Court had sanctioned the compromise agreement, unless the whole thing was in preparation *before* and there had been non-disclosure of material facts?

Of course Nicholson, in writing to Lucas allowed that a perfectly reasonable explanation was possible – he was not suggesting fraud, but he would like to know how this had been achieved, because clearly the terms of the settlement were considerably less than would have been obtained had Beatrice shared in the sale to the public.

Lucas was firmly of the view that Sir Richard Nicholson, by restarting a flow of questioning letters, was simply trying to *"fish up a case by correspondence,"* as he had done between 1893 and 1896.

Joseph went further. Stung by imputations of deceit if not fraud, he said there could be no correspondence between the two sides until the imputations were withdrawn, but if not, then they could please themselves whether or not to serve due process, and if they did, any subsequent case would be most vigorously defended. For eighteen years since 1880 he had administered this onerous Trust – an absolute plague to him – pledging his own credit to assist it at a cost borne by himself, devoting endless and endless hours of labour to it, receiving neither recompense, reward nor thanks and was totally and utterly pig sick of it.

Jack had written to Beatrice saying,

"After the matter had been finally disposed of in Court, it is annoying to find lawyers again commencing a correspondence and I want you to stop it."

And,

"In going to the public we took, of course, the risk, and we were advised it was not an inconsiderable one, that the shares would not be subscribed for."

To this, and other points made by Jack, Beatrice replied,

"You say that in going to the public you took the risk that the shares would not be subscribed for. What I feel on this point, very strongly, is this: that, inasmuch as my Trustees were simultaneously with the long pending negotiations which preceded the compromise, preparing to launch the new company, I ought not to have been kept in ignorance of a fact which so nearly affected my interests."
She concluded by saying,
"I should be extremely sorry to cause father *(sic)* any unnecessary worry – I made no inconsiderable sacrifices when I accepted the terms of the compromise for this very reason – and I am sure he will do me the justice to say that I was especially anxious and careful (and so I think were my advisers) to avoid everything that could reasonably give rise to 'domestic antipathies'."

A threat to open the whole thing up again, if carried out, would torpedo all that had taken place during the last four years. To Joseph this looked like blackmail.

He sought Counsel's opinion which he received on 8th November, 1898, and which expressed the view that the Portsmouths could not get relief, or upset the compromise agreement simply because par value had been obtained for shares bought in by the syndicate at a 33 per cent discount. Not only that, but the Portsmouths had provided evidence in their affidavits that they were content, and desired to make the settlement without regard to the future value of the shares being more or less than the sum at which they were sold to the syndicate.

After a further sharp flurry of correspondence, the Portsmouths instituted legal proceedings, principally upon grounds of non- disclosure to either themselves or to the Court in July, 1898, of the intention to float Pease & Partners as a public company. It is rather important now, to anticipate and summarise some of the main defence arguments advanced two years later when the case came up in the High Court. When in due course we come to the High Court action, and having dispensed with some of the argument, it will simply be to record Joseph's daily diary entries.

The defence rested mainly on the following contentions:-

1. That during the fourteen years of Beatrice's marriage, there had been, with the exception of two good trading years, a great trade depression. The Portsmouths disliked the speculative nature of the colliery investment, and had constantly urged for it to be realised, and the proceeds reinvested to provide for them a known and stated income. The Trustees had throughout urged patience on them, to await an upturn in trade for a sale of these shares. The pleas for patience made by the Trustees had been rejected, and with each rejection, the Portsmouths had turned the screw of pressure to force an agreement out of them. When the Portsmouths failed by persuasion, they appointed an outside solicitor and an accountant to do the bidding for them. When that failed to produce a solution, they issued a writ to have the Trust administered by the Court, and thereby forced the compromise agreement out of the Trustees.

2. That the forced compromise agreement provided for the sale to a purchasing syndicate of shares in four separate companies (Pease & Partners Ltd., Robert Stephenson & Company Ltd., The Owners of the Middlesbrough Estate Ltd., and William Whitwell Ltd). The agreement was for the Trust shareholdings in these companies to be taken and paid for "as a whole," admitting of no breakdown of

146

separate valuations. This condition was understood and fully agreed to by the Portsmouths themselves and by their advisers.

3. That in their affidavit, the Portsmouths stated that they wanted the Compromise Agreement "whether or not the securities proposed to be sold (to the syndicate) are or are not likely to increase in value".

4. That on 7th July, 1898, there was nothing to place before the Court as clear evidence of intention by the Trustees (in their capacity as company directors) to reconstruct Pease & Partners by a sale of shares to the public. That there was no prepared prospectus; that there was no contract with the share-broker Greenwell. There were preconditions, as yet unfulfilled, set by Greenwell before he would entertain proceeding with a public flotation, and there was no Pease & Partners (old company) resolution to reconstruct. That the resolution to reconstruct was not even considered by Pease & Partners Board until 12th September and not confirmed until 5th October. Between the end of June and end of August a state of chaos and confusion reigned. Were the Trustees therefore, expected to express to the Court the hypothesis of an intention to sell to the public, before anything but a framework for a scheme was in place? – one that was being explored for at most two months before the compromise agreement had come before the Court, and which in so short a time, could not possibly have had any precise shape or form.

5. Greenwell the broker had postponed all further consideration of bringing out a company until figures to the end of June were available (mid-July at the earliest possible). There was therefore uncertainty about the proposal. Additionally there was still argument with Greenwell during September about the contents of the prospectus. If there was argument in September, how could a precise plan have been expressed two months earlier in July? Any thought of proceeding with the issue was just as likely to be reversed and indeed, was almost reversed in September 1898.

6. That Joseph had been advised that any advance public knowledge of a possible sale of shares – and more particularly, a sale to a new company that had assumed no definite shape at 7th July – would put at peril any chance of success. This was not a reason advanced for non-disclosure, but simply a statement of the probable consequences of an upset sale following from a premature disclosure.

147

7.   That at 7th July, 1898, when the Compromise Agreement was before the Court, market conditions were such that even the vaguest consideration of any time-scale for a sale of shares to the public was impossible; that the profits made by Pease and Partners during the five months to the end of May, 1898, averaged £2,331 per month less than during the half year when the agreement had been settled between the parties to it in September, 1897. This being so, if it was not an advantageous time to find a buyer for the colliery shares in September, 1897, it could not possibly be an advantageous time in July, 1898. No one could tell in advance when a time to sell to the public would present itself; that the groundwork, such as had been done, was neither more nor less than that which any prudent business man would initiate – the framework for a plan of action ready to spring at an opportune future date when circumstances were favourable.

8.   That by September 1898, a quite unexpected boom was getting into full swing. It was this that was the deciding factor in the timing of the issue of the prospectus. If the boom hadn't come when it did, or had the public share issue flopped with the discredited shares left on the hands of the syndicate, the Portsmouths would have made no complaint.

9.   It was argued by plaintiff's counsel, that the 'prophet' (Joseph), with the great foresight they attributed to him, had known in July, 1898, with his 'expert knowledge' that a great boom was coming, and that was the reason for not declaring his intention to float Pease & Partners as a public company. But this was nonsense. It was idiotic to suggest that he had power to look into the future. Had Joseph been able to anticipate a coming boom, and the likely extent and length of it, then he and the purchasing syndicate would, in every probability, have held onto the shares bought under the agreement, and had they done so, then they would have enjoyed almost the whole of the vast profits made for themselves, instead of sharing them with the public. The general improvement in trade (though not profits) in early 1898 was widely known, and it had been with the Portsmouths' full knowledge of this improvement that the conditional agreement had been signed by them in March of that year. Additionally, accounts up to the end of 1897 – the last practical date for furnishing half-year accounts before the Court hearing – had been produced to the Portsmouths' advisers, even

148

though under the compromise agreement, the price for the sale of "the whole" was based upon a valuation made and agreed as at 31st December, 1896. With the knowledge of some improvement in trade made known to the Portsmouths through their advisers, they could have declined to proceed with the agreement, and the Trustees and the Syndicate would have been pleased had they done so.

10. That it was the Portsmouths who wanted the agreement and not – but very definitely and most emphatically not Joseph, or any other member of the purchasing syndicate. No inducement whatever had been offered to the Portsmouths to enter into the compromise agreement; that the price was more than fair to the Portsmouths, was evidenced by their own accountant (Jackson) in his affidavit; that no one other than the syndicate could be found to buy the investments; that A.F. Pease and Sir David Dale had refused to join the syndicate because the price offered was too generous; that Alfred and Jack joined only after heavy pressure had been brought to bear upon them, and then only under protest and to aid their father rid himself of a trust too onerous to administer.

11. Further to that Joseph argued, the difference between the price paid to the Portsmouths and that obtained from the public was easily accounted for by the following factors:
   (a) by the sudden boom in the price of coal;
   (b) the inclusion in the prospectus of a management clause which gave a guarantee of ten years service to the new company by a management held in high public esteem, thereby giving added value to the shares;
   (c) the attractiveness of the Ordinary Shares, further boosted by the creation of Deferred (i.e. management) Shares ranking for dividend only after the Ordinary had received theirs at the rate of 8 per cent;
   (d) the earning power on the new Ordinary Share capital of £700,000 which at a rate of 9.5 per cent, was virtually the same as on the old shares at 6 per cent on an ordinary share capital of £1,100,000.

All in all, the animal sold to the public was one quite different to that bought of the Portsmouths.

Meanwhile, on 30th October, the day after Nicholson had asked for an explanation on the speed of the issue of the prospectus, Alfred and

Nellie had left home for London en route to Marseilles and the Sahara. Whilst very briefly in London and walking back to 44, Grosvenor Gardens, Alfred met 'Harry' Paulton, who told him that *"friends in the know"* considered it rash to go to Algeria in the present condition of things, as war between France and England was likely – a consequence of the Fashoda affair, Dreyfus and other unsettling factors. Just the same, they went.

Notes:

1. Vide supra p.
2. At a later date, this loss to the bank was shaved down to £48,579.
3. John William Pease of Pendower, Newcastle had married Helen Fox who was Minnie's sister. John William Pease, a partner in the banking firm of Hodgkin, Barnett, Pease, Spence & Co at Newcastle was a a descendant of Joseph Pease of Feethams, Darlington, who was a brother of Edward Pease (Alfred's great grandfather).
4. Political Agent Consul, Aden.
5. Alfred renders the spelling of the name Makonnen as "Makounen" in his early journals. At a much later date he and others adopted the former rendering, and for the sake of consistency and to avoid confusion "Makonnen" is that adopted throughout the book.
6. Expressed as 'at an annual rate of 6%.'
7. Rachel Pease, Joseph's sister married firstly Charles Albert Leatham (d.1858) and secondly William Fowler. William Fowler was a first cousin of Sir Robert Nicholas Fowler.
8. As a possibility, this may be examined in slightly more detail.
   The two business interests of Isaac Wilson which at different times, became satellite interests to Joseph, were:
   1. Isaac Wilson & Co.,
      This was a potteries business, one of the first to become established in Middlesbrough in the 1820s, and had been started up by Sir Joseph Whitwell Pease's father, Joseph Pease senior. The works, managed by Isaac Wilson over several years, closed in 1890 after a long-loss making run. All the losses in this concern were met by the partners in the Pease Bank. How these losses were apportioned between the Counting House partners is not known, but as senior partner, Joseph would bear the heaviest load.
   2. Wilson Pease & Co., Ironmasters.
      This business was managed by Isaac Wilson and his son Robert Theodore Wilson and Isaac's nephew John Frederick Wilson. It was not a spectacular performer. In the 1880s the firm had a partnership share capital of £118,000. The company was later reconstructed and formed into a limited company at which time it had an overdraft at the Counting House of £155,435.
      There are three key diary entries made by Joseph with reference to Isaac Wilson and the acquisition of the Nunthorpe property. The first of these entries comes on –
      25th Jan. 1897. "Isaac Wilson retires, we paying out his capital to those who lent him money at 10/- in £."
      The second on –
      25th Sept. 1897. "Lucas on Isaac Wilson's affairs, transfer of Nunthorpe &c.")
      The third on –
      8th Nov. 1897. "At 11.30 rode over to Nunthorpe ... to see Isaac Wilson about arrangements for taking over the farm stock and Nunthorpe properties generally – May Day 1898 – he seemed very well, but seemed in haste to have them completed feeling how uncertain life is."

CHAPTER SEVEN

The Sahara, & the Stephensons Wreck

1898 continued

Algiers, Alfred found, was a very changed place since he was last there five years ago. Trams drawn by horses had taken the place of the camel caravans between 1883 and 1893, and now in 1898 the tramways had been electrified. The whole place seemed more untidy and less picturesque than before.

Alfred sent a telegram to Chaban who had been his Arabic interpreter when in Biskra, asking him to join up with himself and Nellie at Bordj Bou Arreredj (approximately 140m SE. of Algiers). There were very few English in Algeria this year because there had been Jewish riots, and the fear of war between France and England had kept people away.

The purpose of coming again to Algeria, where they arrived on 6th November, 1898, was to venture some way into the Sahara, to obtain specimens of rhime, dorcas and addax antelope, an itinerary involving a loop march of 7-800 miles, starting from Bordj Bou Arreredj and finishing up at Biskra.

For two reasons, they could not proceed as intended immediately. First, the three reliable Somalis, who had been on the Somaliland expedition, hadn't arrived as arranged, and secondly, the Chef du Bureau Arabe at Djelfa, (Capitaine Rodet, who had been so helpful on previous Algerian visits), had wired that the expedition was not to proceed until he, Rodet, had given clearance.

After a week at Algiers, just kicking their heels while awaiting clearance, they set out on 14th November by rail from the Agha Station to meet up with Chaban, and found him

"... looking the same as ever. Bordj Bou Arreredj is a dismal bastioned town in a desolate plain - we made our way to the Hotel des Voyageurs, dirty & squalid, though the landlord did his best to make us comfortable & the beds were clean, dinner bad, wine good, bread good, some other things indescribable - we went to bed at 9.30 & rose at 5.30 after getting as much sleep as the dogs & cocks would allow."

On the journey across the desert plain to Bou Saâda, (about 65 miles further to the SSW.), the prearranged caravan assembly point,

"One incident during the day amused me. Scene - a great plain, broken only by swamps of mud and the outlets of the great Shott El Hodna. I asked an Arab in French 'is there any game here?' He exclaimed with whistles and gyrations of his hand and outstretched forefinger that there was a great deal at Baniou, 'yessur - wheu - bezeuf perdeaux-wheuu-flamandes, wheu-u-u.' -
'Des gazelles?' I inquired
'Oui, Oui,' - a most unlikely country for them so I added sarcastically 'Et moufflons?'
'Wheu, wheu, oui, oui, yessur à Baniou,'
Nellie here remarked 'C'est curieux cela; perdrix, flamandes, gazelles et moufflons tous ensemble!' which tickled Chaban immensely, and we all laughed except the local liar, who asked us in an indignant whine what amused us. Chaban doubled up with laughing, with his one eye and odd teeth making him a study said, 'Vous savez, mon ami, qu'on ne trouve pas les moufflons dans les lacs.' The Arab's disgust was what tickled us most."

Upon arrival at Bou Saâda, nine days were spent in engaging men, buying camels and mules, and on 28th November the three Somalis, whose arrival had been awaited, turned up. The caravan now consisted of Alfred, Nellie, and Chaban the caravan manager and interpreter, a hunter, tent boys, five camel men and a cook, making up a total of thirteen in the party.

The eleven camels were very fresh and frisky, and Chaban and the camel men were sent into the desert for two days to get their excitability worked off.

On 30th November they were able to make a start, Alfred and Nellie following a little while after the caravan had started out.

"When we got about a mile out of Bou Saâda (at 2.30p.m.) we found our caravan all over the place; some of the camels in the ravine, some in the mountains, some lying with their loads under their bellies, and Chaban and all the Arabs demoralised, our three Somalis alone keeping their heads. With the help of the three Somali boys, Nellie and I got all the camels together at last, save one which went off full gallop with Nellie's bath and other luggage - I rode it down several times after it had got rid of its load, but could not hold it up until the cavalier and

Ben Backai came to my aid."

1st Dec. "Marched till 3.30 through barren mountains at first, then through thick
scrub and then into thuia (sic) coniferous trees or shrubs and pine forest."

That night they camped at Djebel M'saad among thick pines, ilex
and halfa;

"The men kept strict watch as it is a brigand haunted place"

On the 2nd December, the caravan camped at Lem Haïgen where it
was very cold and with very little shelter and here,

"When trying to get something out of my saddle-bag, my mare, who is a demon,
turned on me and kicked me over on my back, cutting and bruising me on the
elbow. Two bad fingers, a bruised arm, a bad shoulder, an ulcer on my leg and a
bad cold are among the present ailments I have to put up with, but I prefer this to
the worry & cares of public and business life and the ceaseless rush of
engagements at home."

Continuing on their way, and after fifteen days' journeying:

17th Dec. "Off from a rather nice camp at 8.15. Our route today absolutely
monotonous like all the previous days - all stones and sheir. Nothing seen but

some clouds of Kangar[1]. The event of the morning was that we lost our track which often disappears, but after a long storm of words and recriminations, we recovered it and marched to Dthaia Khriebar. We are now in the region of the dthaias[2]. This dthaia is very extensive being nearly a kilo*(metre)* in length and 300 metres wide with many big trees, gommier, jujub and thorns ('wait-a-bit', sedraia), with grass and mud and pools amongst them. Very windy, and the wind cold but the night warmer."

All the time that Alfred had known Chaban, he had had an irksome cough, but this night he started to cough more than usual.

After all had turned in, Alfred and Nellie being asleep, and at about midnight, Mohammed Ali roused them saying that Chaban's cough was very bad and that he wanted something. Nellie got up and took him some of her cough mixture, and by the time Alfred arrived at the tent, he was in the last stages of exhaustion. He gave him a further dose of mixture, whilst

"... the men unscrewed my brandy case with the key. The cork stuck and before we got the corkscrew he was in his death agony, calling 'Ia Rhabi, sidi Mohammed!' and staring at me saying, 'Mot, mot (death, death) Monsieur Pease!' His head fell, and with a single struggle he breathed his last in the arms of my two Arabs, with his hand in mine. The rest of the night was terrible with the men's prayers, chants and ejaculations. I felt in rather a hole, all the Arabs being new men, and a wild lot, all unaccustomed to Europeans, with no interpreter but my Somali, Mohammed Ali who spoke Arabic, though not the Algerian form and the local variety of it here."

At daybreak, Alfred appointed Ben Backai as caravan manager, and preparations were made to bury Chaban in his sewn up brown burnous, about a mile out in the desert,

"... and leaving three to guard the camp, Nellie and I and the rest of us set out with the burial chant, 'La lillah ella ellah wa, Mohammed rasoul elaha!' which was kept up all the way. The service was very quickly over, shoes taken off, sand ablutions (there being no water) the men standing in a row, their faces towards Mecca and between intervals of silence saying 'Allah Akbhar.'
He was very well yesterday and very content at reaching Dthaia Khriebar saying to me, 'Quel joli campement.' I said 'Nous allons reposer un jour ici' and he replied 'Vous avez raison, Monsieur, Il serait bon de se reposer ici un jour.'
I do not know how I shall get on without Chaban; he always consulted my interests, was absolutely honest, and an excellent interpreter and buyer. He leaves a wife and two children at Biskra. We spent a melancholy Sunday. All felt the awful suddenness of Chaban's death; to be happy and laughing at 8, to be dead before morning and buried at sunrise! All of us were very fond of Chaban who was a cheerful manager of our little society."

19th Dec. "A cold night with frost and dew. I got up long before dawn to warm myself. We started with sad thoughts from this camp, which probably none of us will ever revisit, on this almost unknown way across the dreariest of deserts. In every way this desert differs from the others I have crossed, and there is not the litter of camel skeletons that marks the more frequented roads."

20th Dec. "We believe ourselves to be within a few miles of Guerrara, but there is no change in the desert to proclaim it."

During the early afternoon of the next day, a noticeable change was discerned; in place of stones, there was sand and soil, and slight signs of vegetation. After three weeks' march across absolute waste, without sight of trees, (except at the dthaia where Chaban had died), or towns or gardens, their excitement grew as they came upon the city of Guerrara.

Two men were sent on ahead of the caravan to arrange for accommodation, and returned with the news that the Khalifa would be delighted if they would accept his hospitality. This was gratefully accepted.

"Our arrival excited great interest among the people and much terror among the children. Directly after our arrival, Nellie strolled into the school. She found it clean, with about forty little Mozabi and negro boys sitting on benches with tables attached. One class was learning to write French, one to read; some learning Fontaine's fables by heart, &c. Quite unconsciously she took up one of the lesson books and began to read out loud. The schoolmaster said 'the children are astonished, because they did not know any woman could read.' As soon as school was over, the boys flew home and said, 'Here is a white woman who sings our songs and can write and read'."

The Khalifa was most attentive to his guests, and following a great banquet in their honour - a banquet of a whole sheep, eaten with fingers, kous-kous, cold eggs, fried eggs, dessert, tea and coffee, he offered to give Alfred the house he was staying in plus a Mozabite wife, a slave, and a garden if he would stay among them.

The following day, 23rd December, was spent in exploring the desert city, and in the evening,

"At sunset a pair of travel stained men with their guns came in bearing us letters sent from Djelfa to Messaad by Rodet. The Kaid had sent these two men on here with a letter dated December 15th. This budget included an account of my sister Claudia's wedding[3]. The Khalifa came in at this time and drank tea with me offering all I could ask for - houses, servants, a wife and negresses - if we would live here. I told him I could make no such change in my life without consulting my family in England!"

26th Dec. "Passed through the gates and bade adieu for ever to this pretty place at 9.30, and out into the desert once again. It was a dull grey morning, but as we halted a mile or so beyond in the oasis, to take a farewell look at Guerrara, a gleam of sunshine pierced the clouds and fell on the city, lighting up the one spot in the vast landscape."

After a three day march, and on 28th December, 1898,

"Entered Ghardaia and looked for quarters .. and sought for an Arab house; found one and took five rooms, a kitchen and a large yard for 3 francs a day. Here I could stow all I had - camels, goats, selves, baggage, men &c."

1899

The stay at Ghardaia was one of a week, leaving on 4th January, and after a days march camped that night at

"Oglat Zelfana - a harder day than was good for Nellie, but the men spoilt yesterday by dawdling at Ghardaia and El Ateuf, and everybody had to pay for it today."
6th Jan. "Left Zelfana 7.45. Camped at 2.45 in the absolute desert; no wood, no vegetation except very scanty gethem - small bits twenty feet apart."
7th Jan. "Marched on the Treg Carossa from 8 till 3.10 - At Ober-raht we found the soldiers (discipline) who left Ghardaia two days before us. It was an odd sight and sad after travelling across barren stony land, to suddenly come upon these poor exiles busy washing their clothes in a large fountain built for the purpose. Even there the guard was standing with his loaded pistol in his belt keeping watch, though where a poor creature could run to in that waterless country I don't know. Poor fellows! they are bound for Ouargla where many will lie in soon forgotten graves. The mortality is dreadful among the troops there."

On 9th January, after camping at Melala, they left at 7.30 a.m. where three and half hours earlier, at 4.00 a.m. the caravan in camp was joined by one Ali Ben Aziz, sent on to Alfred by Captain Rodet as a new headman in place of Chaban. He spoke fluent French and soon proved to be a most capable addition to the party. Ali Ben Aziz had marched night and day all the way from Ghardaia, about 100 miles!

"After about 2 hours or less, we came in view of the great flat below the higher desert which breaks into the lower ones in nabs like Huntcliffe[4], and in isolated hills and hillocks. In the distance we could see the palms of Negousa. About an hour and a half after discovering the palms of Negousa in the distance, we came in view of the Shott and the palms of Ouargla."

One can see at once that Ouargla is an unhealthy place. On our road this morning, we met the 'compagnie' of soldiers who have done their year at Ouargla. The sergeant, a very pleasant nice fellow told us that this summer, but principally in October, the death rate from dysentery and fever was terrible - twenty seven out of eighty soldiers having died. The heat in the town under the great arcade had been 137 Fahr. in the shade."

After going through his stores with the new headman, and having a wash, Alfred went to report his arrival.

"I reported to the acting Chef du Bureau Arabe, Lieutenant Dinaux. He received me most courteously, and to my surprise informed me that he had received instructions to allow me to travel where I liked. I was therefore in a position that never before would have been permitted, to go as far south as I felt inclined if I wanted to hunt addax. This has set me thinking."

Whilst in Ouargla, Alfred got into conversation with some Chamba hunters about the availability of game in the vicinity. The Chambas supplied gazelle meat to the market, and they said that addax gazelle could be obtained by hunting within two or four days south of Aïn Taiba this year.

12th Jan. "I have provisioned my camp for some three weeks and all but finished my money - I have only 80 Francs left."

After great difficulty, he secured the services as guides of two Chamba hunters:

"Our headman, Ali Ben Aziz is quite terrified by my projected tour. He says what is true, that they" *(the Chambas)* "come with their Mehara[5], and if they choose they can leave us in the unknown and disappear or betray us, that he will never get an hour's sleep the whole time till we get to Tougourt, and that if anything goes wrong he will shoot all the Chambas with us. I say I hope he won't as I don't know the road. We shall be fairly strong; four guns, three rifles and other small arms. My men show a tendency to mutiny against the sterner regime of Ali ..."
13th Jan. "We did not get off today. Our Chamba hunters have hooked it so I spent a good deal of time finding another who had a camel."

Lt. Dinaux considered the replacement Chamba safe enough, and as extra insurance, offered Alfred the services of a Chamba cavalier who knew where good water could be found. This was a rather important addition to the caravan since the desert sands were shifting all the time, and in such circumstances a man could be lost only a hundred yards from his starting point.

19. *Ali ben Aziz, who succeeded Chaban as Alfred's Caravan Manager and Interpreter.*

"This is the first day of Ramadan ... What nasty tempers the men will have! Sherief is already sick tonight after his first day. May God bless my three Somalis for giving up Ramadan. Tonight the first row of Ramadan - mutiny of Abd el Kadr of Djelfa. I discharged him."

14th Jan. "Marched at 7.45 but did not start well as we tried to buy goats (but failed). Marched till 2.15 and camped at the well near Hassi Tafaya. I reckon we did about 27 kilometres. My Chamba hunters turned up at sunset with their two camels and two old guns - one a very long flintlock."

Alfred found that getting rhime was most difficult as they were *'kittle'* (nervous) and prone to move away, even when at a great distance, upon sight or wind of humans. Thus far, and since November, Alfred had fired his rifle three times only.

18th Jan "I feel pretty much convinced that I might spend a long time here without ever getting what I call a good chance *(of game)* and I fix to march tomorrow. We are so far from civilization and the distance to Biskra is so great that we both wish to knock off some days of marching and get to Tougourt. I reckon a week's steady marching should land us there at longest."

19th Jan. "Saw rhime and dorcas today but never got within 1,000 yards of either."

22nd Jan. "At 2 we camped just beyond the well at Mat-mat. The Touaregs often raid up here after March - but not further."

158

20. Alfred with baby camel.

23rd Jan. "We have not seen anything like a regular track yet since Ouargla"
24th Jan. "We came in sight of Tougourt palms which practically are coterminous with those of Temacin to the south.
Sat up late explaining the universe to the Arabs over the camp fire! the formation of the globe, and the fact of its being the shape of the pomegranate I held in my hand caused much debate and excitement. The moon was full, and the light of it on the pomegranate facilitated my exposition of the tropical and arctic areas and the explanation of the climatic differences. I think I convinced them that the earth was not balanced on a cow's horn, but I am not sure."
26th Jan. "I have at last extracted from the Somalis what our nicknames were when we were in their country. The Somali always nicknames everyone. Edward Buxton was 'Othigie' (the old chap), Ted Leatham was 'Biddar' (Bald head) and I was 'Wal' (the restless man)."

Two days later the caravan started out on the return march to Biskra.

30th Jan. "In the night, one of the many robbers of whom our men have talked so much, and who are the constant terror of Ali Ben Aziz, stalked our naga. Khrouider and Ali pursued, but he was too quick for them, and they never got a shot at him. It is a pity as these robbers infest the caravan routes, and the poorer and weaker the party, the more likely they are to be robbed, and a solitary wayfarer runs a great risk of being murdered. My men have orders to challenge twice and then to shoot with buckshot."
31st Jan. "No robbers in the night."

1st Feb. "Our fifth day's march from Tougourt. Nellie and I intend to ride in the remaining 54 Kilometres to Biskra before déjeuner tomorrow. We have had no meat since Tougourt, no game to be shot and no chickens to be bought on the road. We have eaten potted meat and salt tongue but lived chiefly on kous-kous, dates, porridge and camel's milk."

2nd Feb. "Last night there was an attempt to loot the horses. The guard and Ali were not sure for a moment if it was not some of our caravan so fired on the miscreant rather late, and only with my revolver and missed him. Horses are very good night guards, and if a man or wild beast is about and it is pitch dark outside the light of the camp fires, you can get a very fair direction for your aim by noting which way your horse points."

Alfred and Nellie made an early start, and as anticipated, arrived in Biskra at lunch time.

3rd Feb. "Visited Chaban's family, paid them 50 francs and promised another 110. Late in the evening a note was brought me addressed 'Milord Capitaine Pease' stating, in good writing, that the writer had a message of the most important nature concerning myself, that he desired to see me alone and where no one could observe us. I went out and found a soldier in uniform at the hotel door. We stepped into the dark outside and he said, 'C'est vous Monsieur, qui êtes arrivé hier soir?'

'Oui, c'est moi, M. Pease,'

'Je suis venu vous dire que vous êtes signalé devant le Commandant Supérieur pour ayant reçu des lettres ou dépêches chiffrées, et comme espion Anglais vous serez arrêté.'

'Moi! Je n'ai jamais reçu une lettre ni une dépêche chiffrée dans ma vie.'

He then repeated what he had said and I asked him -

'Alors donc, faut-il que je vous accompagne chez M. le Colonel Commandant?' then he mumbled something that I could not catch about 'moi je ne suis pas trop patriot,' and I think he was about to blackmail me when a party of tourists arriving, we separated. I shall report the man to the Commandant in the morning ...."

The following morning Alfred called upon the Commandant, Colonel Freyedel.

"I handed him the letter, explained what had happened, gave him a note of the conversation and said I could identify the man, that if I was an English spy the man was a traitor, and if not, he was a blackmailer; that I wished to have all my letters arriving here opened by the authorities, that I was well known, and that after all the kindness I had received I could not bear the idea that there should be any doubt on my honour.

He was very indignant and said he would make the man pay for it. Later in the morning I found that Ali had been at the Bureau to have his 'permis vised' and that the authorities were surprised to find that he, a cavalier of Djelfa, was in my service.

160

I went later to the Bureau and saw Captain Massoutier, Chef du Bureau Arabe and told him all about my caravan and journey. He then said that he had been deputed to go to the bottom of my story about the soldier ... he will parade the whole garrison for his identification. I feel sure that the porter and I can pick him out.*

6th Feb. "In the afternoon ... I rode out alone at 1.30 over the old hunting grounds of Chicha, which awakened memories of long days spent with Nellie, with Spedding, with Vincent Hamlyn, with my brother Jack, and with Edward and my father pursuing gazelle and bustard.

Now there is not a track of gazelle and they have almost been exterminated there. After dinner I went with Ahmeda *(an Arab tourist guide)* to the marabout whom Chaban patronised, and gave him 170 francs to be distributed for the benefit of Chaban's children. He told me he had warned Chaban that he was too ill to go, but Chaban had said that he would go anywhere when I called him. He also said that Chaban had gone to pray in the mosque with him before he started, and prayed that he might die where he could be buried out of reach of his mother who had been a trouble to the family here, and trying to scratch open the grave of her other son who had died here."

During the evening of the following day, a garrison lieutenant called to take Alfred to identify the man whom he had reported. When he picked out the soldier responsible,

"He refused to recognise me, but I was certain of my man. I feel sorry for the poor wretch who I expect will be severely dealt with. The Bataillon Afrique to which he belongs is recruited from ex-convicts and gaol birds."

15th Feb. "Ali Ben Aziz wept today because Ahmeda derided him, asking him to look at the beautiful clothes he wore, and remarking with contempt that Ali only wore cotton gandora that cost 1.50 at Biskra. Ali is much hurt at the treatment he receives here, and the superior splendour and ill-gotten gains of the guides of Biskra. He swore by the head of his father that he cared only for my interests - if I was pleased it was all that he wanted - and that it was the soul of man and not a man's dress that was important, but that I should console him very much if he might ride about the town on one of the mares this afternoon. I indulged him in this, to his immense comfort."

On 20th February, Alfred's brother Jack together with Howard and Ella Pease[6] arrived in Biskra for a months expedition around the old hunting ground of Aïn Naga. Two days later they all set out for the mountains.

"Ali Ben Aziz too ill with fever to do anything. He wept and gave me dying messages to his family, and asked me to have his clothes and things sold, and the proceeds given to the poor. I persuaded him to get on a horse and start with us, and cured him the same night with a dose of phenacetin, followed by fifteen grains of quinine."

On the 8th of March, when the party were up in the mountains,

"After we were all in bed and asleep, we were roused at 10.30 by the arrival of an Englishman - named Barker, I think - who had accomplished the feat of reaching us over dangerous paths in the dark in one day from Biskra; he came direct from England to interview Jack! I think to urge him to join some Board of Directors. Jack did not give him exactly a warm welcome, but I heard him offer a glass of water and a place on the stones by the camp fire to his guest. In the early hours I got up and shared my porridge with the visitor. He was stiff and sore, and no wonder, as he really performed an almost incredible feat in reaching our mountain eyrie in the dark, after a long day over the desert. I wonder he did not break his neck. He left again at daybreak ..."

Ten days after this extraordinary, though commendable test of enterprise and endurance of questionable urgency, they all arrived back in Biskra and there found

"... the most ridiculous articles in the paper about me."

The newspaper references were of the suspicions surrounding Alfred's spying activities:

"The General of Division has had an inquiry made into my case, proceedings and antecedents. Luckily the Commandant Supérieur (Freyedel) said he knew me personally and testified to my harmless character."

During the next few days, Alfred started to wind up his affairs in Biskra; sold all his kit and livestock in the market, except for five mares which he was shipping back to England; saw Jack, Howard and Ella off to Tunis and arranged to meet up with them at Marseilles.

"Though I have been worried by the spy mania, I leave Biskra with my sentiment of affection for the place and my acquaintances unimpaired."

At Algiers,

"After a touching farewell from Ali Ben Aziz, who kissed my hands and said he would go anywhere, and serve me in any capacity, he shed genuine tears again, and more when I gave him the ring Nellie had bought him."

They sailed for Marseilles, from where they continued by rail to Calais and once more home.

During the five months that he had been in Algeria, he had made no mention about events at home, of which at regular intervals he was updated by his father. Doubtless the latest bother over Beatrice and her affairs had been a talking point between Alfred and Jack in the desert during March.

Meanwhile at home, Joseph seemed at no time to betray the slightest evidence of being troubled by the impending High Court action while he attended to other matters. He saw no reason to be other than perfectly confident about the eventual outcome of the case. There were however other sources of irritation giving rise to a few nights when he retired to bed with

"... a little too much in my head."

One diversion from the Portsmouths' affairs came with William Fowler's Petroleum Company which had resurfaced like the monster. A man named Pollock, whom in April, 1897, Joseph saw as the right person to pull that company out of the morass into which it had sunk, wrote making a strong plea for more financial backing. By now, Joseph was running short on patience, and told Pollock to find it himself out of profits.

This, when it reached Fowler's ears, must have come as an awful shock. Anyone in the family who in the past had made a great mess of things, could have relied with total confidence upon Joseph to bail them out - those halcyon days seemed about over.

Then Joseph's nephew, Arthur Francis Pease, started to interest himself in the Fowler business, and produced a paper for a new scheme which he put to Joseph,

"... for getting up a company to take up William Fowler's Petroleum things - it half sickened me to think of such a thing."

If Fowler's 'petroleum things' was a peripheral irritant, another and much more serious one lay in trying to find a way out of long standing difficulties with Robert Stephenson & Co. Ltd.

Stephensons, a secondary but important business interest to Joseph, was originally established in 1823 as a partnership principally between George Stephenson, his son Robert and Edward Pease, (Joseph's grandfather). Edward Pease had put up 40 per cent of the initial partnership capital. Over the next sixty-three years there followed partnerships between succeeding generations of Stephensons and Peases. The Deed of Management gave the running of the business exclusively to the Stephensons. The locomotive building works at Forth Street, Newcastle, had been sited curiously, at a place where there were no railway lines. The transportation of the finished locomotives to a track must, to say the least, have been very inconvenient. Since the 1870s, Stephensons, under increasing competition from other railway locomotive manufacturers, had turned from being highly profitable into an uncompetitive and loss-making concern. Joseph concluded that Stephensons management had fallen fast asleep, and he had so far failed to rouse them from their slumbers.

In 1886, at his instigation, the partnership in the concern had been converted into a private limited company. The reason behind this change was to put a definite ceiling upon the liability for calls on capital. This had been especially necessary in the case of Beatrice's trust holding of shares, when only six years after her father's death, the Trust Estate was in need of protection from calls on shares.

At incorporation in 1886 the capital was:-

(a) The Stephenson family interest, and (b), the Pease family interest.

(a) held 1,436 shares of £100 ea. £83 paid £119,188 [57.9%]
(b) held 1,044 shares of £100 ea. £83 paid £ 86,652 [42.1%]

2,480   £205,840

Each share therefore carried a contingent liability for calls of up to £17. Sometime between 1886 and 1895, two classes of Debenture Stock had been created. These purported to pay interest at 5 per cent, but in fact paid out nothing whatever.

At incorporation, Beatrice's trustees had converted her late father's financial interest in the partnership into 312 shares of £100 each (£83 credited as paid up, nominal value £25,896 with liability for calls amounting to £5,304) and they later added a disproportionate mix of both classes of Debenture Stock, which last mentioned in total amounted to £15,686.

In the compromise agreement with the Portsmouths the previous year (1898), the purchasing syndicate had taken the Debentures and the 312 shares, together with the attaching liability for calls on the latter. The Trust's total interest in Stephensons, was shown (by way of illustration) in the schedule appended to the agreement, at a grand net valuation total of "nothing." It will be appreciated when we shortly glance at the balance sheet of Stephensons as it stood even in 1895, that the share capital was totally, absolutely and irrevocably lost. In point of fact, in view of the liability for calls, if there was a valuation point below zero, Stephensons shares were showing it.

Five years ago, in May 1894 it will be remembered, Alfred had seen the folly of, and expressed anxiety at his father's attempt to bolster up a badly arranged, antiquated losing concern. Alfred and his brother Jack had themselves no financial stake in Stephensons, but of course had been interested as Trustees in Beatrice's Marriage Settlement. Furthermore, as partners in the family banking firm, they had reason to be concerned about the level of Stephensons borrowings. Under Joseph's direction, the Counting House had conducted a very liberal and open ended lending policy to that company, and during the latter period of the last twenty years or so, this had enabled Stephensons to continue to enjoy the almost uninterrupted luxury of steadily losing money.

In 1895, it may also be recalled, when Portsmouth's accountant, C.W. Jackson, drew up a report on all the trust investments, he expressed great astonishment at the accumulated losses shown in Stephensons Balance Sheet. In his report, Jackson summarised the rough position at 31st December, 1895 as being:-

Liabilities			Assets	
Share Capital		205,000	Land, Buildings,	
			Machinery &c	264,000
'A' Debentures	40,000			
'B' Debentures	98,000			
		138,000	Balance being agg. loss	
Ordinary Creditors		187,000	or admitted deficit	266,000
		530,000		530,000

If this was the state in 1895, we have heard of nothing sufficiently dramatic during the last four years, to suggest that it was any less of a facer now. Why nothing had been done at an earlier date to correct the relentless drift towards insolvency is a mystery. Either the time for grappling with the problem was unpropitious, or there was some other concealed reason for inaction.

Certainly while Beatrice's Trustees had been holding shares for her in the company, had a call been made on the shares, the shouting would have been heard in Yorkshire coming from Portsmouth's Hampshire home. The sum involved (£5,304) as concerned the Portsmouths, was quite large at a time when, as they viewed it, they derived "neither pleasure nor profit" from her investments.

Now though, with the compromise agreement out of the way, the coast was clear to face the problem head on, without the slightest risk of further complaint from the Portsmouths. Joseph as the company's banker, as well as a Stephensons director, was having to face at almost the fifty-ninth minute of the eleventh hour, the awesome alternatives presented by this shambles. The time for doing so was made more opportune with the improving and continuing signals of an end to the long depression.

Of the alternative courses open to the company, the first was to wind up voluntarily and close. Hardship for employees, and the undermining of business confidence, spreading and percolating through associated industries may have been inhibiting factors against following this course at a much earlier date. The second option was try to sell the business with a full order book (if possible) as a 'going concern' (!!). This had not been attempted until the previous year, (1898) when Joseph made an approach to Sir Christopher Furness with an asking price of £220-£230,000. Furness, though interested, was only prepared to pay a figure based upon his own valuation which didn't come anywhere near the asking price.

In April, 1899, at the point when Alfred had just returned from Algeria, Stephensons were getting towards completion of the Spanish pontoon dock contract and several others.

Alfred joined his father now in considering alternatives. As Joseph records,

> "... had a long and grave talk with Walker *(Manager, Robert Stephenson & Co., Ltd., Forth Street Works, Newcastle)* who is offered some Chatham & Dover engines on which he could begin at once, at almost his own price. He thinks we should book the order and then try and reconstruct the company. He thinks it would *go*. Alfred & I felt carrying on so serious a responsibility that we arranged to call a meeting at York on Friday (21st April) after the N.E. Board to consider whether it was best to book such an order & try to reconstruct, or simply work out our orders & close."

On Saturday, 22nd April, 1899, at the arranged meeting in York, put back a day, he noted:

> "At 3 o'clock a regular meeting - Dale, Albert, *(and)* Arthur Francis who came up on purpose on Stephensons affairs. I made out the list which I showed when we

166

could close. All engine contracts will be completed by Decr. - All shipbuilding ones by August - we have got the Spanish Dock contract to complete at Cadiz in lieu of the Philippine Islands - this looks as if it might be a profitable one - agreed to close unless we could reconstruct the company."

A fortnight later, he had a meeting with Sir Christopher Furness,

"... about purchasing R.S. & Co works at Newcastle - he seemed inclined to go into it, if Whithy" *(sic)* *(Henry Withy)* "of Hartlepool would join him - he would telegraph for Withy."

The next day:

"Then with Alfred and Albert to meet Sir C. Furness & Withy about a joint stock Co. for their purchase of Stephensons - we seemed to make some progress, but all seemed to depend upon Withy's decision to act as manager. I think we could get a good Board."

Joseph now paused for breath and went off to his Falmouth home for a fortnight's fishing.

He returned to London on 1st June:

"Making ready for meeting Dixon[7], Furness, Herbert Pike *(Pease),* Alfred, Albert, self and Crump[8]. After some chat it was agreed; syndicate to purchase R.S. & Co. for £110,000. Furness, Dixon & Pease, *(i.e. the syndicate),* to sell to new company for £200,000 - but to pay interest - say, for two years during rebuilding &c ..."

The first directors of the new company were to be Sir Christopher Furness, Sir Raylton Dixon, Henry Withy, Joseph and his younger son Jack. Withy was to be allowed £3,000 for the reconstruction with a suitable staff. Although Alfred was in on much of the discussion, he was not included as one of the new directors. Perhaps the now established need for Nellie's sake, for long winter absences abroad, and in no small measure, the rather jaundiced view Alfred held of the old company, carrying over to a lack of enthusiasm for the new, these may all have been factors behind his exclusion.

In preparation for the winding up of the old company, Joseph started by doing everything possible to protect everyone except himself from financial loss.

Garbing himself in a hair shirt, he bought up the old company for himself to sort out the mess, before selling it on to the syndicate, paying at any rate G.R. Stephenson £15,000 for his interest in the company, adding this heap of rubbish shares, plus Stephensons debentures to his

167

own, and when a call was made, paying that - also the calls on what had been Beatrice's Trust shares. His late brother Arthur's shares he took together with a £35,000 donation from Arthur's Executors; a hand-out on the basis of *"take all, pay all"* i.e. calls, losses &c, which he did. Then he secured for himself the whole of the remaining Debenture Stock (and on the way, refusing for himself his legal right to prior repayment in the winding up) and chucked them to the top of the rising stack of junk.

Joseph's reason for doing this was to protect the company's creditors from loss, and to ensure that they were paid 20/- in the pound. Notwithstanding great financial sacrifice to himself, he wanted the good name of the old company - which it did enjoy - to carry over to the new. The personal cost to himself of this exercise was put at £108,848. He recovered absolutely nothing for himself when he sold the company to the syndicate of which he was himself a member.

Though the syndicate sold the old shell to the new company for £200,000, after making provision for paying interest on the preference and new debentures during the anticipated two year period for reconstruction, and after further provision for paying the underwriting fee in the public issue of shares, stamp duty &c and leaving a margin for contingencies, the £200,000 was effectively brought back to the price at which Joseph had sold the wreck to the syndicate.

It was on 23rd June, 1899, which was also Joseph's 71st birthday, that the call of £17 per share mentioned in the foregoing was made:

"A curious way to spend my 71st birthday!!"

Curious indeed. In another age and context, what he had done might be likened to buying the *Titanic* after its $2^1/_2$ mile plunge to the ocean floor.

The prospectus for the new company came out at the end of July, 1899, and with the issue successfully underwritten, £750,000 of new share capital and debentures was raised by public subscription, the issue being more than three times oversubscribed. A new site for the company's locomotive manufacturing base was found off North Road in Darlington (next to the mainline railway track), and work commenced upon building the largest dry dock in the north-east at Hebburn.

Though it is to digress, it is interesting to note, that in the negotiations for setting up the new company, John Walker, the manager of the old, had had an interview with a Colonel Watts, about building for Stephensons a graving dock to which Armstrongs, (warship and armaments manufacturers) were to be offered pre-entry. Whether or not Joseph winced at this conflict with Quaker conscience cannot be said, but on 28th July his entry reads:

> "... bothered in my mind by Thos. Pumphrey *(a leading North East Quaker)* attacking me about Stephensons new concerns; arrangements with Armstrongs, and my position as President of the Peace Society, and Chairman of docking war vessels! Wrote him in reply."

Alas, no record exists of how he squared the circle of Quaker conscience.

Joseph now went off to London suffering from hay fever, and at the same time, Alfred went off to Bad Nauheim in north Germany for treatment for his heart condition under the care of Prof. Schott, who considered his case a most serious one.

At the beginning of July, Joseph had obtained agreement from his London bankers[9], to liberate the executors of his late brother Arthur's estate from liability in the banking firm of J. & J.W. Pease. This when acceded to, left Joseph, Alfred and Jack as the remaining partners in the Counting House.

Early in June, Joseph had had a touching interview with Charles Fry the accountant manager at the Counting House who, suffering from heart trouble, had been ordered by his doctor to take a long and complete rest. Joseph tried to cheer him up, he who had served the family most faithfully for almost half a century, and arranged that during his absence Charles Dickinson should take his place.

At about the time of the Stephensons public issue of shares, Pease & Partners declared a dividend of 10% for the eight month period between flotation as a public company and 30th June, 1899. Things were really beginning to go straight at last, but prosperity had been a very long time coming.

Alfred returned from Bad Nauheim at the end of August, and seemed certainly better than when he had gone away, and though he tired easily, he was able to enjoy some shooting, and within two weeks felt sufficiently fit to rise at 5.30 to go cub hunting. He was keen to get back to work, business and political, though if he took the advice of Dr Ghee and Dr Barlow whom in London he saw in October and November respectively, he was to do no work of any kind either bodily or mentally, no hunting, no shooting - and no smoking, and in time he might come right. He had not the slightest intention of spending months in

169

restraining chains, and quietly went his own way, doing what he wanted as long as he felt able.

At Nunthorpe Hall this September, Joseph's cousin and colleague on the N.E. Railway Board, and at one time associate in business and politics too, Isaac Wilson, died. His death meant that Joseph would shortly have to decide what to do with that place - but what he hardly knew.

At the end of December, he and his two sons went to look over the house.

"Alfred, Albert & I went down to Nunthorpe, Elsie joined us there and looked over the whole place; no paint, paper or repairs have been done I should think for 20 years! and much is required. It is a good but not well arranged house. Alfred and Elsie most amusing, he arguing every point with her."

In fact the house was in a state of disorder, with the roof leaking in several places, damp walls and decay and heading fast for dilapidation. Jack, a visionary, saw its potential and quite made up his mind that he wanted to live there. Elsie, viewing dangling ceiling papers, the buckets placed to catch the drips, the mouldy walls and crumbling plaster was not at one with Jack in this. She said that to live there would mean banishment; a prospect altogether too frightful to contemplate. She was either overruled (unlikely) or won round.

After consultation with an architect, and suggestions and counter-suggestions had been thoroughly raked over, a general outline plan for the total renovation of the house was put in hand for an estimate.

As they moved towards 1900, Charles Dickinson, so recently appointed as accountant at the Counting House in place of Charles Fry who was visibly failing, announced that his own health was such that he felt it necessary to retire. His place was filled by promoting Cory Badcock who, Alfred felt, would make an excellent head; a man whom he liked and who would swiftly take up his responsibilities with the same degree of loyal efficiency as Charles Fry and Charles Dickinson before him.

Three months before the year's end, the Boer War had started in South Africa. Between Christmas and New Year Edward, Alfred's elder son, now just turned nineteen, suddenly went missing from home. With a tendency toward quiet rebelliousness, he was found to be next day at York, where he had enlisted in the army. In a Quaker household this caused a considerable furore, and Alfred swiftly disentangled him from this commitment, and he was brought home under a cloud of severe disapproval - probably in Alfred's eyes, more because the boy had brains, and if he worked at it, had a brilliant future ahead of him. Edward doubtless had caught a whiff of the war fever which was sweeping the country. In Joseph's pacifist view, his grandson's behaviour was an indication that within Edward's head, the awful seed of unreliability was sown.

Sylvia Hamlyn, Edward's cousin and one of his earliest childhood companions, might have been the one showing the greatest sympathy with him in this rash display of independent mindedness. She could recall a day when she was aged about fourteen, and driving up Pall Mall with her Aunt Lottie who, apropos nothing, blurted out that she had something 'very terrible' to say concerning Sylvia's father, Vincent Hamlyn. Sylvia, wondering what was coming gasped in horror, and listened electrified as Lottie said,

"He has joined the North Devon Yeomanry ········ !!!"

And so he had.

Alfred and Nellie had not made arrangements to be out of the country this winter. The old lung mischief had shown itself up again at the end of the old year, so that extra care was very necessary when the worst of the winter was still to come.

1900.

With Pease and Partners showing a half year profit of £151,000 to the end of December, 1899, a dividend of (actual) 2.5 per cent was declared at the end of the January.

In preparation for the Portsmouths' pending High Court action, the Court required the defendants[10] to exhibit what Beatrice's position would have been had there been no compromise agreement. Alfred and Arthur Lucas declared it impossible to fulfil this request. Too much had happened subsequent to the Court sanctioning the agreement in July, 1898. The request from the Court for this information had come on 15th February, 1900.

The day prior to this, Charles Fry had died, and the funeral was to take place on 17th February. On the 15th however, at Darlington, the day was winter wild, which soon turned to a heavy hypnotising relentless blizzard. Alfred at the Counting House was watching the snow falling and swirling about as he discussed with his father the predicament and difficulty of complying with the Court's requirement, and at 2.00 p.m. he decided to bolt fast for home to Pinchinthorpe,

"... fearing I might with difficulty get home if I went later, as I know what a high wind with snow can do in Cleveland - When I got to M'bro', I had lost my connection & Byers, the stationmaster, gave me a special at once, the 3 o'clock train having gone on with 2 engines ... I had an awful walk up from the station *(Pinchinthorpe)*, up to my waist in snow & the most awful blizzard in my face - The special ran on to Hutton where ... the train ran into a drift beyond Hutton station cottage (about half a mile on) where the 3.0 train & 2 engines were buried. No more trains ran except the 5.0 train which struggled on with 2 engines & ran smash into my special, telescoping the van & 3rd class compartment ... The fireman (Hayton) of the special was down behind the engine & was killed. The two men in the 3rd class compartment" *(who had taken advantage at Middlesbrough of Alfred's "special")* "were badly hurt. Father who intended to come home by a later special got stuck at Nunthorpe, but got back to the Cleveland Club at Middlesbrough for the night."

Nellie went off with one of her sisters to the south of France in mid-March, and Alfred took advantage of a trip to Falmouth with his father who was taking his annual fishing holiday a month or so earlier this year. It was 1892 that Alfred had last been there, and his time was spent in nostalgic ponderings about all the changes from days now long past.

"I walked to where Uncle Joshua's *(Joshua Fox)* house stood, no vestige of it left, save an ivy covered stump that was the left hand door post of his rustic dwelling - the paths where he stood with his shirt outside his clothes hanging down to his knees, with the birds feeding from his hands & mouth, & where his great dogs challenged the rare visitor, are all lost & overgrown with the great laurels, underwood & weeds. His three daughters who played strange musical instruments & sang, & lived curious lives buried in this tanglewood, are all dead too.
We then went past Buddock Water, but the water is no longer there, and then went by Bereppa where Capt Bull & Josephine *(one of Joshua Fox's daughters)* lived out their last years, but the Banksia roses which buried the house are all pulled down & the old place pulled down ... All reminds me of the old days, which have given way to the hard handed work of our rushing age -

Lie softly leisure doubtless you
With too severe a conscience drew
Your easy breath & slumbered through
The gravest issue

But we to whom our age allows
Scarce space to wipe our weary brows
Look down down upon your narrow house
Old friend, I miss you."

Notes:
1. Sand grouse of the Algerian desert.
2. A desert depression where water is often found just below the surface.
3. Agnes Claudia Fox Pease married Alfred Wilson of Birmingham.
4. Huntcliffe Nab, a cliff near Saltburn-by-the-Sea.
5. Running camels.
6. Howard and Ella Pease of Pendower, Newcastle, son and daughter of Alfred's uncle by marriage, John William Pease.
7. Sir Raylton Dixon Bt.
8. William J. Crump, a London solicitor.
9. Prescott, Dimsdale, Cave, Tugwell & Co., London, which provided extra funds to the Counting House, especially at times of large drawings for dividend payments by the North Eastern Railway, Consett Iron Company, Pease & Partners &c.
10. (1) Joseph, as surviving Executor and Trustee, (2) Arthur Francis Pease and (3) Herbert Pike Pease, as their father's (Arthur Pease) Executors - though in themselves, the last two named A.F.P. and H.P.P. had nothing to answer for. (4) Alfred, (5) Jack and (6) Sir George Wyndham Herbert, as Marriage Settlement Trustees, (Sir George W. Herbert equally having nothing to answer for).

CHAPTER EIGHT

Abyssinia & a Law Suit

1900 continued

Nellie returned from France while Alfred was still at Falmouth. Joining him there, she showed no great improvement from her stay in a warmer climate, which was a very bitter disappointment.

At the beginning of May, the estimate for the repairs and alterations at Nunthorpe Hall fell into Joseph's lap, and the cost was put at £9-10,000.

"Too much!!"

In his view it should be £3,000 less. Perhaps the cost could be paired down as the job progressed. At any rate, work started in the late spring.

At the end of May, William Fowler's company, now styled as the European Petroleum Company Limited, issued a prospectus, and its flotation went off badly. At this, and since Alfred expressed utter dismay in his journal, it is fair to assume that he had bought some of the "flopped" shares.

During this same month, Nellie accompanied Alfred to Bad Nauheim for his further course of treatment at the hands of Prof. Schott. Their elder son Edward was in Germany at this time, at Dresden, studying music between leaving Winchester and going to Cambridge. He had won a senior seven years' scholarship to Trinity College to study for an Oriental and Classical degree.

Alfred hated and was frustrated by his inactive six weeks or so at Nauheim. There was nothing to do. He read a few books - *"mostly rubbish"*, there being nothing much else to do except write letters and *"loaf about"*.

As he prepared to leave Nauheim, he saw Prof. Schott,

"... who said my heart is not normal (wh. I knew) but that it was better than last year (wh. I knew) & that I must come back here next year (wh. I don't know)."

At his departure, Prof. Schott after advising him to lead a quiet life, asked him in relation to the fulfilment of this advice, what he planned to do. Alfred replied, that he proposed to go on an expedition to Abyssinia and the Sudan.

"Vell!" *he was told,* "You - are - med!!
YOU - ARE - EBSOLUTELY - MED!!"

Nellie went off to see Edward at Dresden and Alfred arrived home at Pinchinthorpe on 15th June on a

"... lovely summer evening - laburnum, guelder roses, may, lilac, azaleas all out and everything very sweet and fresh outside - 3 Arab & 1 thoroughbred mare, all with foals standing up to their knees in grass. Indoors, all upside down."

Soon after this, when Nellie had returned from Dresden, they rode over to Nunthorpe Hall to see how work was progressing and as Alfred records:

"The solid old house is practically destroyed - roof off & a good deal pulled down."

A day or two earlier, Joseph had been there in the dog cart, but as he had injured his foot which was in plaster, and because the trees were all in leaf, he couldn't see from the road what was going on. He did however take a look when out of plaster a month later.

"After lunch drove ... to Nunthorpe where we got out and saw the ruins of Rome and the building of Caesar's Palace."

Everyone went to have a look. Even through Sylvia Hamlyn's young eyes, what she beheld in her amused gaze, she considered to be a Palace arising set to rival Blenheim.

Whatever the Jacobean Nunthorpe Hall had been before the renovations got under way, it looked like finishing as a delightful mansion, with 27 bed and dressing rooms, 2 halls, 4 reception rooms and stabling for 17 horses.

Perhaps there was no alarm at the scale of the alterations going on, as during July, Pease & Partners' excellent year end figures were revealed. Of these, Alfred says,

> "We have had our best year by far since I went into business in 1880. Father always said it would come again, but I never expected to see it."

Profit for the year		386,218
Debenture interest 4%	16,000	
Special Exp. to Reserve	15,600	
Depreciation	14,494	
		46,094
Remaining Balance		340,124
Balance brought forward from 1899		10,120
		350,244
20% Dividend	165,000	
Reserve: Bad Debts	10,000	
Against shorts	10,000	
Fire Insurance	5,000	
Investment Reserve	100,000	
		290,000
		60,244
5% dividend already paid		35,000
Carried Forward		25,244

Joseph alone, throughout the worrying long years of depression had urged patience upon the pessimists; that good times would one day return was as certain as the sun's rising, and here they were. Not least, this oft repeated appeal for patience and confidence had been pleaded of the Portsmouths. Now, at this great good turnabout in fortune, Joseph declared,

> "No wonder that P(ortsmouth)'s are sore!"

Yes, without doubt. The price of Pease and Partners' £10 ordinary shares was now £23.10.0d. - and went higher. The Portsmouths had missed out on this - but so had the purchasing syndicate through having to sell out to the public.

During the summer of 1900, Alfred was busy making preparations for the expedition to Abyssinia. He was going out with Colonel S.L. Harrington, (British Consul-General at Addis Ababa) who was to join en route, and also Arthur Keyser, (British Consul at Zaila), and some others, including he hoped, J.L. Harwood, a naturalist, who was not personally known to him.

6th Sept. "A busy day - 2 hours at the stores, then an interview with Grant at the S.K. Natural History Museum & obtained his promise to fit out Harwood, who I want to take with me as a naturalist with his collecting outfit, & to pay his fare out & back, & to buy specimens that they want - Harwood came at 2.0. I was favourably impressed with him, & engaged him for £5 a week & arranged for what he required."

Also this September, Parliament was dissolved which Alfred considered

"... a dirty trick - to forestall the new register wh. would give the franchise to more than a million electors in a few months' time. Hostilities are not yet concluded (in South Africa) the country is fast feeling sick of the war, heavy taxation must be imposed; the Liberal Party is coming together, trade is waning, prices rising, securities falling - Dorman[1] kindly said he hoped there would be no opposition to me - Jim Lowther & Hugh Bell are the same way of thinking."

And on 22nd September whilst Joseph was at Bishop Auckland being re-selected for the Barnard Castle constituency, Alfred met the Cleveland Liberal Association at Hutton Hall.

"Everyone most kind - I told them if I was their candidate they must understand that my health was not resolved, that I was leaving for the winter; that I was of the same opinion as ever on S. Africa & still a Home Ruler, and that if the Conservatives gave me a w. over I shd. have no meetings - I was much touched by the unfeigned kindness & confidence shown to me.
I am not well - the worry of the election & having to stand again has upset my heart action again."

He was returned unopposed for Cleveland. Joseph aged seventy-two, had a contest but won with a good majority. Herbert Pike Pease held Darlington for the Tories, but Jack was the family casualty this time, at Tyneside. He knew he had a hard fight on his hands, and had anticipated defeat.

Leaving home for Abyssinia this October was a great pull for Alfred, most especially leaving the two younger children behind - Edward was going with his parents on this adventure, Christopher was at school at Winchester, and Lavender, aged eleven, was going to her grandfather at Hutton.

At breakfast time on 15th October, 1900,

"I left home with a heavy heart after a heartbreaking good-bye from my dear little girl who left her porridge untasted, & sobbed with her head turned away."

This scene, as he departed from home, with the feeling that his own life was uncertain, that he might never return, haunted him throughout his months away in Abyssinia.

For Joseph the summer and autumn, (except for the election period) was spent in routine business, and with most problems of the past straightened out, he was now able to give more time to his pleasures. He shot the moors, clumps and woods around Hutton and Pinchinthorpe regularly, and enjoyed it all with his retriever 'Jenny,' and in the autumn rode to hounds.

On 20th November, he had house visitors for the shooting, including the Bonham Carters from Petersfield, a few others as well as family, in all a party of six or seven guns.

"Shot Bousdale and Roseberry road; into the house at darkening. Bag 192 pheasants, 11 rabbits, 1 hare, 1 woodcock. In the evening, got the unwelcome letter that Albert & I must be in London as soon as possible tomorrow - had quite a melancholy evening, but the Portsmouth matter has to be settled one way or another."

21st Nov. "Off at 7.40 with Albert to London. Had a quiet journey up with John Walker of Stephensons for a companion. Went straight to the Law Courts & to *(Mr Justice)* Farwell's Court. Sir Edward Clarke *(Plaintiff's Counsel)* was opening Portsmouth's case - by reading my brother Edward's will. This lasted until 4 o'clock. Albert & I went to Brooks's for dinner."

22nd Nov. "To consultation with Swinfen Eady and Messrs Ingpen and Russell *(Defence Counsel)* then to Court where we were astonished to hear that Sir E. Clarke had thrown up his brief - it afterwards appeared on good evidence that he would not charge *me* with fraud, and so relieved, we had a long weary day with Warmington reading letters and correspondence. Again dined at Brooks's and home early."

23rd Nov. "Warmington again at letters and correspondence trying to pin us to all sorts of things - trying to deceive the poor Portsmouths. This went on again all day - The Judge seems to have got their side well into his head. Home. Dressed and dined with Lottie and Howard, pleasant evening but glad to get to bed."

24th Nov. "To consultation at Swinfen Eady's 9.45. - as usual a great deal of scramble. The main subject was the creation of the deferred shares. Then to Court where Warmington ended and examined Nicholson, who was ably X examined by Swinfen Eady, I was quite tired out by 2 o'clock and gave up going to see Claudia at Birmingham - Lunch at Reform. Worked slowly and badly till tea & almost to dinner time."

The Court retired until Tuesday, 27th November.

27th Nov. "To consultation at Eady's, then to Court where Portsmouths ended their case calling Beatrice who gave her evidence beautifully and really sweetly.

178

21. *Lavender Mary Pease on 'Zacchaeus',*
from a painting by Heywwood Hardy.

The*(n)* Portsmouth and then Jackson. Swinfen Eady examined them all well and then opened our case which he did well! I think the judge has got it into his head that we concealed from them improved coal trade, which is after all mythical at the time of June 1898. He seemed strong in his views about the liability of a Trustee to disclose (when buying) all he knows - This point Eady laboured well, heartily tired dined quietly at Brooks's."

28th Nov. "To Consultation at Eady's. He began the end of his speech and then I was called. I was examined in chief, not at length, by Ingpen and then *(cross examined)* at great length and in detail by Warmington until 4 o'clock. Tea at Brooks's - but not so bad as Tuesday *(27th)*."

29th Nov. "Warmington began his cross examination again which was not quite so obnoxious as yesterday - Then Dale followed me, he did fairly well but was a bit more caustic than Farwell liked; he lasted the day out. Brooks's, tea; Lottie dined with us."

30th Nov. "To consultation and then to Court. Dale under cross examination - Then good evidence from Albert who did it well. Then his cross examination which lasted till closing time. To 44 G. Gardens; packed up and to the Great Northern Dining Car train 6.15 - a really good dinner, few stops. Home about 12.30, Maud to welcome me and glad to be in my own bed once more."

Joseph spent a quiet restful week-end at home.

Sunday, 1st Dec. "Gardens. Mac Indoe (Head gardener) and others of our men, seemed to think from what they had read, that we had made out our case against Portsmouth. I fear Farwell's Law will override his Justice and common sense. After lunch to the village and saw Nannie (nurse) who seems very well, then went

179

to see old Charlton, our odd man; he seems very weak, but looked very clean &
nice, quite himself. It is quite touching how these old retainers appreciate a call
from me."

3rd Dec. "To London by 3.45 train with Maud. Chat with Badcock and on
probable adverse decision in the Portsmouth case. A capital dinner in the train,
Maud, Albert & I."

Joseph is now quite prepared for the worst, and in his transition
from confidence in his own case, to coming quietly to prepare his mind
for defeat, he shows no rancour or spite, or self-reproach, just taking
calmly to that which he had not been expecting. There is even a very
strong trace of family pride and affection for Beatrice in his comments
on the way she gave her evidence. There was of course no exchange of
words between them as they faced each other in the courtroom.

4th Dec. "To consultation. Albert to continue his cross examination. He did very
well indeed. He was followed by Edwin Waterhouse and then Arthur Lucas - all
did well. The(n) Ingpen followed with his closing speech on our side, Farwell
interrupting him a good deal and evidently of the view that more information, or
rather, information about our plans should have been given to the Court of June,
1898."

5th Dec. "To consultation and then into Court once more. Ingpen concluded his
summing up of our evidence, Farwell interrupting him a good deal. He evidently
has got into his mind that our plan for making a comp'y ought to have been
revealed to the Court - he does not see the bearing that no confirmation of the
Agreement - no company - and if the Portsmouths did not want to go on, they need
not do so. Warmington concluded in quite a mild way and we were up about 12.30
- Farwell saying Judgement reserved, the papers are numerous. Lunched at home
and then down to the House and took my 9th Parliamentary affidavit *(sic)*
(affirmation) I was real(*ly*) tired and glad of my bed."

The following day, and after a N.E. Railway Board meeting in
London, Joseph returned north to await the Farwell Judgement which
came on 11th December. He made no comment whatever when what he
anticipated arrived, but simply turned his back on the whole business.
He attended for many days afterwards to the wave of letters of sympathy,
and then just got on with what he was doing, only reserving for himself
the comment he had made once before:

"What a trial that match has been to me!"

In his very long Judgement summing up, Mr Justice Farwell
stated,

180

"I do not say a Trustee *desiring* to buy is bound to disclose his intended mode of using the property if he gets it."

The distinguishing feature in this case was that the Trustee's *did not desire to buy,* and for years had resisted doing so.

Mr Justice Farwell continues,

"But the non-disclosure here is of a fact, that is the advice given by the experts, and although it is true that the Company might have been a failure, or might never have been brought out, yet those considerations do not affect the duty to disclose; they only affect the weight that might have been attached by the Judge to the fact when disclosed."

An appeal against the judgement was kept under consideration for some considerable time. The decision when reached by Joseph, after consultation with Alfred and Jack, was simply to leave things as decided, and carry out the Court's directive.

We must leave the final comment to Alfred, who reserved his view on the whole affair until he came back from Abyssinia:

"In my journals so far, I have not alluded to the Portsmouth v Pease case, the judgement in which was a source of infinite worry to me while in Abyssinia, but it is not for myself and my share, in what I regard as the equally unjust & scandalous finding of the Judge, but that anyone so much the soul of honour, integrity, & kindly generosity as my father, should have been so cruelly slandered from the Bench - Conscious of his moral rectitude, he has borne this with great patience & without bitterness -
The Judge seems to have been absolutely blind to the history of the Trust, to the conditions under which we were bullied into an agreement we none of us desired to make ... If my father had wound up Beatrice's estate within a few years of Edward Pease's death, there would have been nothing left, but by his industry, ability, & with his own money & credit, he pulled the things through, & was always ready to make great sacrifices, & spare himself no pains to make her happy & comfortable."

The outcome was that the 1898 Agreement was set aside, and that Joseph must transfer to the Portsmouths 5,257 Ordinary shares and 6,760 deferred shares in Pease & Partners (together valued at £241,000), plus a cash payment of £61,000 and the costs of the action.

This Christmas of 1900, was for Joseph just as much as in the years that had gone, a happy occasion. Though Alfred, Nellie and Edward were in Abyssinia, Christopher and Lavender were at Hutton, and there was a great gathering of most of the remaining family and grandchildren. Surrounded and supported as he was, Joseph was able to conclude that day as follows:

> "In the evening we had *(the)* great Bran Tub in the cooling room of the Turkish Bath, and we all came away much richer in *love* and gifts."

1901

A studied calmness in all affairs descended upon Joseph's life, and the decision of the Court was in due course executed, and that phase of things concluded. Referring to this final act when it came in the autumn of this year Alfred says,

> "We have now paid off the Portsmouth gang - I wish them joy in their dishonest gain."

Joseph, with slightly less éclat, says much the same thing:

> "Yesterday *(15th Oct)* we paid £61,000 odd, the amount actually stolen from us by course of the law, by Lord and Lady Portsmouth."

So we can now leave Hutton, and turn to the Abyssinian adventure.

Alfred, Nellie and Edward had arrived at Aden in the previous autumn, on 28th October, 1900.

> *29th Oct.* "I engaged all the Somalis I intended to take with me. I have got a fair lot of men. I judge rather quickly of what I want and what I like; and now I know the ropes, what formerly took me days now takes me minutes. Of Deria the cook who 'speak Inglish werry well,' I asked if he could bake bread with baking powder? He said 'Of course I know. No bake hims, no make hims.' I dare say this is so."

Six days later the party were at Zaila on the Somali coast where they stayed to organise things with Colonel Harrington and Arthur Keyser. Here was gathered in preparation, a huge caravan estimated by Alfred at 150 camels, and an indeterminate number of mules, donkeys and ponies.

On 9th November the great caravan got under way from Zaila. The party consisted of:-
1. Lt. Col. J.L. Harrington - H.B.M. Agent & Consul-General at the Court of Emperor Menelik II.
2. Arthur Keyser - H.B.M. Consul at Zaila.
3. Mr Huskinson (Keyser's guest)

4.   Maj. C.W. Gwynn, R.E., D.S.O.
5.   Capt. Arthur A. Duff - Vice-Consul Addis Ababa.
6.   Nellie.
7.   Edward Pease.
8.   J.L Harwood - Naturalist and
9.   Alfred, and
     Mohammed Ali as Head Somali, cooks, shikaris, syces, goat boys
and tent boys &c.
     Colonel Harrington was leading the expedition as far as Addis
Ababa where he was to take up his duties:

> *10th Nov.* "Our manner of marching and camping is a novelty to me. No one has
> any idea how many men or camels are in the caravan, and there is no order in
> camping, beyond that everyone dumps down his kit wherever his section's flag is
> placed. We have no sentries, no zariba, no camp fire &c but this is because we are
> on a regular track. Got to Manda at 11.30 p.m."

Five days later they were on to the higher ground of Abyssinian
territory and had seen a lot of game; wart-hog, geranuk, hyaena,
porcupine, and Alfred had got specimens of warblers, bee-eaters, owl,
sun-birds, and red-faced finches, for the Natural History Museum, South
Kensington.

They received news that the 'mad mullah' (Hadji Mohammed
Abdullah) was marauding about Milmil; though this was not in their
path, it was as well to take account of his whereabouts.

When on 19th November the caravan arrived at Gildessa,

> "We were received by the Acting Abyssinian Governor, who turned out the
> garrison in our honour - about a hundred and fifty soldiers - we pitched our camp
> on the west side of the river in the usual happy-go-lucky way ... After tents were
> up I went to sleep and was woken up by a shot or two and the Aysa[2] war-cry from
> the top of the hill just above Nellie's tent. I rose and asked Mohammed Ali what
> was up. He said 'it is the Aysa calling to fight the Habasha *(Abyssinians)* who have
> shot and killed two of our camel men.' I got my glasses and awoke Harrington,
> and in a minute we saw the Abyssinian soldiers, about eighty or a hundred of them
> retreating in a disorderly mass towards the town opposite us, followed by the
> Aysa, screaming and throwing a spear now and again. When the Abyssinians got
> near the town, they wheeled round and opened fire on the Aysa, the bullets coming
> high over us, who were about 200 yards or more distant. I got Nellie under cover,
> and began to arrange my defences. Harrington put Gwynn in charge of the camp,
> and arming himself with a Mauser pistol, he and Keyser went to see if they could
> prevent further fighting.
> The Abyssinians, after firing into the Aysa ... ran as hard as they could up to their

183

The British Agent Colonel John Harrington & one of his escort.

Jan 18 1901 Addis Abeba

22. *Lt.-Col. J.L. Harrington, H.B.M. Agent & Consul-General at the Court of Emperor Menelik II. (Sketch by Alfred Edward Pease.)*

fort. The Aysa gathered in numbers till about three hundred spearmen were massed in the river bed. Keyser very promptly sent some of the local Aysa Chief men and elders who had come to see him, to stop the Aysa coming in and attacking. Harrington was successful in keeping them in check till things had been talked over, and Gwynn and I made dispositions in case we were mixed up in the row.

We selected the place to zariba in, then lunch being ready, we fell out. After lunch, the wounded Aysa were brought into our trees, and Gwynn and I were told off to see to their wounds. One was mortally wounded, shot through both thighs, one being pounded to pulp; two others shot through the thigh; the others less seriously hurt. These wounds are as big as those made by snider bullets.

Harrington sent across for the Governor, to show him what his soldiers had done, and the old boy came out with a big escort. Immediately he appeared in sight, the Aysa began to clamour to attack, but by dint of our efforts, and Harrington sending Beru *(interpreter)* to ask the big man to leave his escort, what threatened to be a worse fight was stopped. Harrington eventually got the Governor to put two of his soldiers who had fired into the two men most dangerously wounded, under arrest.

184

The cause of the row is briefly this. For some time there has been a tax levied here on Aysa caravans, to pay compensation to the Abyssinians for past Aysa raids. Our men had been told that they need not expect to pay this as coming with Harrington. They however, instead of waiting, as they should have, thought it safer, after depositing their loads, to bolt. Harrington had not told them what he was going to do about the tax when he paid them off; when they tried to bolt, the soldiers followed, and the sequel is as I have briefly put it.

Gwynn and I spent the whole of *(a)* very hot afternoon removing the wounded into Gildessa, and dressing the two worst cases; the one with the pulverised thigh was really past doing very much for, but for two hours we did our best. We nearly undertook to cut the leg off, but it must have been so high up we thought we should kill him. A first class surgeon would perhaps have saved his life, but I do not think anything else could."

That night, for the first time, sentries were mounted round the camp, and there being no further trouble, the following morning, they moved on. Led by Col. Harrington, they separated from the main caravan body, which they arranged to meet up with on the desert route at Errer Gota, whilst they themselves marched on to Harrar.

"We marched all day, up into the mountains, through pretty gorges with very beautiful trees, at times some very enormous ones.

The jowari (Holchus Sorghum) being harvested. A severe climb up to Balawa (5,679 feet altitude), about 3,000 ft. rise - very hot. Edward saw plenty of baboons; I saw nothing but a few new birds of which I got one. A pretty camp under hasaaden trees (Candelabra euphorbia)."

21st Nov. "Left Balawa at 6.30 and got to Dega Dalali at 12.15. A lovely road up to the top, through a jungle of euphorbia, wild olives, wild fig, firs, and flowering bushes and trees; a great deal of jowari grown and being harvested. Edward reports that Gwynn makes our ascent today to be 1,700 feet and the top of the pass 7,430 feet above sea-level. The Gallas very industrious, busy with the crops and watering their cattle, donkeys, horses, sheep and goats. I collected more than a dozen new birds; a lark, two kinds of redstart, two finches, one black chat, a seven sisters bird (thrush), a warbler, a wagtail &c. I saw an emerald green parrot but I did not get him."

Having camped but a short distance from the city of Harrar, the following morning, early, Harrington took Nellie ahead of the rest, and they were immediately shown into the presence of the provincial governor, Ras Makonnen, with whom they drank coffee and talked for some time.

When Alfred and the others arrived, they found

"The place was crammed with soldiers, every available man evidently turned out to impress us. The fort fired a salute of 13 guns under eight (green, yellow and red)

Abyssinian flags. I had my men in uniform for the first time - khaki turbans, and long tunics, scarlet kummerbunds, red white and blue lunghis and bandoliers over the kummerbunds. Quite nice with their black skins. Gwynn's boys had a similar uniform but different lunghis."

"We did not know quite where to go when we rode through, under the gate, followed by Keyser's camel corps and our boys, so I asked to be conducted to Gerolimato's[3]. On the way there, we were told that the Ras wanted us to go to his Palace. So we went there; were shown through a dense block of black shankallas (slave soldiers) with their rifles, into a roasting oven of a yard, and here we waited till our tempers grew as hot as our bodies, and as we demanded to be taken out of the sun or allowed to go back, we were refused either, and were forcing our way out and trying to mount, when we were told we might come in ... I never will be kept waiting indefinitely if I suspect it is deliberately done. I resent it at home, but I take it as an insult in Africa.

The Ras was very gentle and polite, and after a short interchange of compliments, we went to Gerolimato's."

At night, they camped outside the city on the western side.

"Though the immediate neighbourhood of Harrar is beautiful, luxuriant and attractive, the city is indescribably horrid. It is, of all the filthy towns I ever saw, the dirtiest. Its rock-strewn gutters and open sewers choked with manure heaps, and decaying carcases, where mangy sore-covered curs pass their disgusting lives, are the only roadways. The town population (40,000) is, for the most part, miserable and unwholesome to look on, but the crowds of Gallas, Somalis, and Abyssinians, and others who enter for the purpose of trade, mitigate a little the impression of squalor in the streets."

23rd Nov. "I have had threatening of dysentery for some days, and this morning, after a griping night, I took opium and then a large dose of ipecacuanha, and after two hours was very sick."

During their stay, Alfred and Nellie had an audience with Ras Makonnen in his Palace, and had an amiable conversation about each other's countries. On 27th November, and following a thirteen course breakfast with Ras Makonnen, they broke up their camp and left Harrar. Arthur Keyser's party remained behind and was returning to the coast.

29th Nov. "Haramaier to Dengago. Gwynn, Nellie & I climbed the mountain opposite our camp, and on the top found villages of Gallas among the juniper and large jowari fields, while sheep and goats climbed the precipices below. It is a rich populous country, the natural wealth of its soil must be enormous, and I believe anything could grow; the climate is one for a white man."

From Dengago to Anjerra they descended through jungle and after diversions to look at ruined buildings on their way, followed by a confusion, because the main caravan body had missed its way to the

186

appointed meeting place; it was early evening before the caravan came together again.

> *5th Dec. Hoorsa to Fulfull.* "It was a lovely camp last night, and a hyaena came and put his ugly mug into our tent; he went off double quick before I could lay hold of my gun. Edward bore the march well. His temperature is normal."

Some days earlier, Edward had been running a very high temperature with fever. He had been wrapped in blankets and dosed with quinine and sweated his fever out, but this had delayed the march for a few days. On 6th December the party were back onto the caravan route.

> "Timbacho ... the terror of this country, 'Chief' or 'King' of the Oderali Danakils has come in to see about camels and how he can blackmail us."
> *7th Dec.* "Timbacho has sent in a lot of his savages and some camels; they are a wild looking set of men; they have mostly ill-conditioned faces, and the under lip is generally distorted and bulging from the practice of this tribe of wearing a quid of tobacco there ... both sexes cover their heads with ghee which glistens and drops ... The putting of great quantities of ghee on their heads is to diminish the effect of the sun, and is efficacious, but if the mutton fat they often employ has not melted, it sticks like particles of rice to the hair.
> I asked my syce why they put rice pudding on their hair like Somalis? He said seriously, it was not 'bereece,' and was quite huffy about it."
> *8th Dec.* "Errer Gota to Tula River. From 6.30 to 1.30 Timbacho and his braves wandered amongst our loads, and each warrior stuck his spear or shield on the load he selected for his own camel. Anyone who moves a Danakil spear declares war on its owner. We waited patiently under the trees all this time."

Discretion being the better part of valour, it was settled to pay Timbacho a fee to accompany the caravan, and his men to load and unload the camels at the start and finish of each of sixteen days' march henceforward.

> "The Danakils have always been a terror to strangers and neighbours; they are wild, savage, independent and often insolent, but as far as I have learnt or heard, they are not treacherous."
> *10th Dec.* "Tula to Daira Aila. Our Danakil savages took from 5.30 to 7 to load our 150 camels and we had a hot march over rolling stony ground, grass covered and sparsly sprinkled with trees."
> *11th Dec.* "Another ridiculous performance. The Danakil camel men did not get their camels loaded till 10.15."
> *12th Dec* "Markoto to Dalato or Daladi. We are now in the Itou Galla country. The people in these countries seem all at peace and quiet - the frogs are very noisy here."

23. Timbacho's Oderali Danakil warriors, Abyssinia. (Photograph by Alfred Edward Pease.)

All went on fairly smoothly during the following week's marches, except that Alfred's old ·256 Mannlicher rifle came to pieces, the screws falling out with the heat, but by filing down ordinary screws, a temporary repair was effected. He had in any case a new Mannlicher as a spare.

19th Dec. "Katyanwaha to the Hawash - The Danakils having spent hours fighting with their camels over the bridge instead of fording the river, all struck against going on after reaching the west side of the river ... My men came to blows with the Danakil this morning. A Danakil had thrown Edward's oryx and geranuk skins off his camel. Liban (E's shikari) had protested and they rushed at each other. The Danakil got a big stone to beautify Liban's sufficiently ugly features with, and another Danakil joined in. I came up and brayed them apart with the barrel of my gun."

Christmas Day, 1900. "Choba to Mallabella, 5 hours.
Christmas dinner.... in my tent...

188

MENU
Oxtail Soup
Sardines
Chicken cutlets and petits pois
Roast Bustard, bread sauce
Sausages
Plum pudding
Champagne & green Chartreuse"

26th Dec. "Our last day with our Danakils and their camels. They have been difficult, noisy, impudent, but as I sat on the cliffs of Balchi overlooking the steep road down, I felt it sad to see the last of these wild brutes, for if they are bad to bide, they are men, whilst the Abyssinians are unspeakable - I mean the common classes. We passed through and were well jostled by a rabble army going down to the Hawash to bring up rifles. Among them were insolent ruffians who shouted 'Ali' at us as we went by."

It had been the Italians, who during the recent war had called all Abyssinians 'Ali,' in derisory fashion - now the Abyssinians were turning the tables on any European they met with shouts of 'Ali' to purport the same thing.

27th Dec. "McKelvie (one of the British captives released by the British expedition in 1868) turned up today; He speaks English quite well, but in other ways is Abyssinian - swollen red bare legs and feet, Abyssinian dress, sore eyes, orange and brown teeth, unkempt scraggy beard; a disgrace to have a creature of this type loafing over the country and known to be English; at the same time he is to be pitied. He is a good interpreter and has some good qualities."
28th Dec. "Shankara to Jiffi Dunsa - four hours and a quarter. Our two hundred and seventy one mules got away in good time, We had a dull march over hideously ugly country."
30th Dec. "As you approach the capital you see the King's enclosures and the Gibbi (Royal Residence) with many surrounding huts and tents, standing on a small rise in the midst of an amphitheatre of mountains, barren for the most part ... single huts here, bunches of huts there, white tents pitched in groups. Here a whitewashed foreign residency, a mile or so beyond another, with satellite huts and farms hard by, and all these hamlets and detached habitations linked by no roads, nor are there any definite bounds to the town."

The Emperor had gone to supervise the building of a new capital some two days' journey away, but Harrington was able to convey to Alfred the intelligence that the Emperor would take no responsibility for his intended journey on from here, through from Kaffa to Gora. Fighting between Waldo Gorgis's people (Kaffa) and the people of Goreh (Ras Tassamanado's) meant safety could not be guaranteed.

For this reason, and also because a German expedition of Baron

Erlanger's had forestalled Alfred's intention to go to Kaffa and Sobat, some revision of plans was necessary. After a restless night, he decided to try to march to Tsana, thence to the Bar Es Salaam and Takaze Rivers, and to Tomat, and thence to the Blue Nile and Khartoum. Harrington thought he might get the Emperor's leave for this route, and Harwood thought it would yield as good ornithological results as Kaffa &c.

1901

By 12th January, still in Addis Ababa, Alfred was feeling the effects of altitude, and was frightened of becoming ill, which in this place would be dreadful. Edward had sores on his legs which had been bread-poulticed and scalded, which, bringing the skin off, made things worse. A few days later, the Doctor who had advised this treatment said that Edward would be able to start the following morning. When the next morning came, the Doctor said that one of his legs was so bad he might have to have it amputated!

Attention was diverted from Edward's condition, when on 18th January, the Emperor Menelik returned to his capital for the Feast of the Baptism the following day. A further reason for his return was that the following week, Ras Makonnen, a widower, was to marry the Queen's niece, a girl of eleven years of age, by which event he might lay some claim to the succession.

Alfred was granted an audience of the Emperor on 18th January, after the Feast of the Baptism.

> "The entrance to his Palace was through a series of yards, the outer ones filled with soldiers lying about on guard! You then get to a door round which is a dense crowd waiting for the chance of entering; they are flogged aside with hippo kibokos, and a porter asks through a hole for the door to be opened. At last the door is opened, and about a dozen blacks fly out with their sjamboks, and flog as hard as they can till the way is clear, and so you progress forward from one yard to another."

The Emperor received him, sitting cross-legged among cushions upon a four-poster bedstead, over which was draped the Abyssinian flag. He was surrounded by *"Rases, officers, fly whiskers, high chamberlains and other functionaries."*

> "He has a very kindly agreeable face; he has a pleasant smile and the gentler expression of the darker races ... After shaking hands, and a welcoming word to

each guest, everyone sat down at the only table in the room. Food was brought, wheat and teff bread, rice soup, stew, salad, kebab, omelette for us; but the others ate chiefly raw meat (brando) from great quivering slabs that hang from the arms of attendants; they drank their tedj and araki out of decanters."

On 20th January, the Doctor attending Edward, declared that he could on no account be moved for a week or two. Alfred was totally bowled over by this news:

"This bolt has panic stricken everyone; here I am in a fix; I cannot stay at this altitude - Edward must ... Harrington has suggested his going with Kouri (French Vice-Consul) to Djibouti in six weeks' time, but I cannot bring myself to leave him in spite of having to abandon a trip planned with such elaborate trouble and great expense. I have, I think, fixed to go down to the Hawash and wait for Edward's complete recovery, and then if it is too late to go to Nasser, to go to Rosaires."

Alfred received word the following day that the Emperor would see him at 4.00 p.m. Off he went, riding Harrington's white charger, and wearing a cocked hat. After he had been shown in, the Emperor entered the reception room, whereupon all but Ras Makonnen and three other Rases retired. After some conversation, Alfred made a presentation to Menelik of a new Mannlicher Rifle:

"He asked about the ammunition, took sights and fingered it often during our long talk. I liked him instinctively and feel quite a warm admiration for him in his troublesome life."

After asking Alfred about his travels and plans, Menelik said,

"You may travel where you like - you shall be handed from one officer to another, from this Ras (pointing to Waldo Gorgis) to this (pointing to Tassamanado) the Rases governing Limnou and the Goreh districts respectively."

At the conclusion of his audience, and having expressed his appreciation to the Emperor for all the kindness shown to him, he returned to Nellie with an invitation for her to breakfast the following day with the Empress Taitou.

Nellie found the Empress Taitou too proud to show much interest about things outside her own country, but they had some conversation about cooking, and especially how to make the hotly spiced and peppered bread they were eating, served with the soup for breakfast.

The following day, 23rd January, leaving Edward with five or six mules to follow on when he had recovered, Alfred, Nellie and Harwood departed from Addis Ababa, bound for the Hawash.

> "My men have taken a tremendous number of mules loaded with their kit, and I went off with seventy, and two donkeys loaded, two riding mules mounted, three led, one horse led, Mohammed Ali's horse, Hailo Mariam's two mules and Nellie's horse."

Alfred's seventy Abyssinian followers had been engaged at Addis Ababa by Beru, the Emperor's interpreter.

> *26th Jan.* "The officer of the district came, and I gave him tea and whisky. They will not eat with us as they regard us as pagans. He liked the tea, and the whisky more; I gave him a bottle of it as a present."
> *27th Jan.* "The officer appeared at 6.30, just as we were finishing our breakfast out of doors. He seemed grateful for the whisky and was especially struck by our not wanting the bottle back. It is tiresome that these Christian people do not care for anything but firearms and strong drink. Saw no hippopotamus but tracks of him and many birds."

On 1st February a batch of letters arrived by runner from Addis Ababa. It seemed that Edward was going on well and leaving on 5th February. News in letters from home included the deaths of Queen Victoria and the Bishop of London (Mandell Creighton), both of which came as a great shock. Alfred delayed moving on until he had written to Mrs Creighton - and to Edward, to arrange to meet up with him at Gifoorsa on 8th February.

The night of 1/2nd February had been pouring wet. Nellie was coughing a lot and Alfred made immediate plans to split the caravan, himself, Nellie and Harwood going with a light section to make a flying visit to Lake Zwai, the others going on to Gifoorsa. The headman, Hailo Mariam, was very frightened at being left with the main caravan, and pleaded for Alfred to take him and leave the Somalis with the main body. This was irritating, but Alfred insisted on his orders being carried out, heartily wishing he had never engaged Hailo Mariam.

Since leaving Addis Ababa, the Abyssinians in the party had had no meat until today, when Alfred had shot a Swayne's Hartebeest. This became a source of annoyance as the Abyssinians would not eat meat cooked by Somalis, and if the meat had been hallaled[4] by a Mohammedan, this too made the meat unclean.

> "They have been particularly stupid today."

After shooting the hartebeest to provide meet for them,

192

"My Abyssinians would not eat the beef, because they said I ate beef that Somalis had cooked, and I had shot the beef."

They reached Lake Zwai on 4th February. Most of them had colds or fever with the incessant damp.

6th Feb. "Marched from Harra, Zwai towards Guerague range of mountains, four hours through the forest and bush; We crossed the Meki river three hours and a half from Zwai. For an hour and a half we marched through extraordinary quantities of locusts; every tree for five miles long being one dense mass of dark red locusts - all the leaf and green entirely gone ... I saw the locusts come up yesterday, and now the whole country is eaten up."

7th Feb. "We found Hailo Mariam and my main camp alright. I saw the skeleton of an elephant today and asked when the last was killed here? Thirteen years ago was the reply."

8th Feb. "I am better today *(Alfred was suffering from a badly infected throat)* but got the most disappointing letter from Harrington, who says Edward will not be fit to travel for a *month*. This is awful. I have to give up my trip altogether. I have written to him to say that I abandon my expedition. I gave the Ashaifi Chief, Atto Shiffou, a revolver and 36 rounds in return for all his gifts and visits. He said he hoped to see me at the Hawash bridge once more. I said in English, I hoped not. I am worried to death by these visits."

9th Feb. "A very bad night with my throat and much pain. At 10 we marched down out of the everlasting clouds that affect this plateau. The local Chief arrived as usual ... he appointed a guide to take us up again into the clouds, and a day round about; so I told him to take us *my* way, and he was very insolent and said we had only permission to go the way he chose, and he would compel us to go that way. I told him he could go any way he liked. I was going *down* to the Hawash; he .... galloped off to his Chief to report us, and told a crowd of Gueragues to watch us and stop us. We treated them with absolute indifference, formed up and marched four hours and forty minutes down to Kora or Korada. On the way the guide picked us up and we told him we had no need of him. I am tired of being interfered with and shall go my own way until I am stopped by a bigger man ..."

Their march this day was over rolling grass hills with thin scrub, and trees in places, and past picturesque Guerague houses. The Guerague people were very shy, never having seen Europeans before.

"They have a language entirely of their own, and are distinct in race. They are Christian, as Christians are counted here, about as near, I suppose, as people at home."

After halting for a day for Alfred to try to shake off his bad throat condition,

12th Feb. "I had a bad day of it; constant quarrels to be settled; the bone of

193

contention being a Galla guide, Oda, whom the Abyssinians demanded to have dismissed and I refused. In the evening, fifty came and demanded that I send Fyeesa away. I refused. They said none of them would stay. I said 'then you can all go' &c and paid them their wages after dinner. They were astonished and said no more."

13th Feb. "... another big row all the afternoon over Fyeesa and his things."

In the evening Alfred saw a large number of Hippopotamus in the waters of the Hawash and firing at them killed one, afterwards much regretting what he had done.

"It is a poor sport; I felt rather sick with myself and shall have no more of it."

His remorse was intensified the following morning when coming to the river he found that he had shot three dead, and he had wanted but one.

"We launched our Douglas folding boat to fasten ropes on with ... one Hippopotamus towed right across the pool."

After taking what he wanted, he gave the Hippo meat to his Abyssinians and Gallas. Whether from inducement or hunger, the Abyssinians appeared now prepared to eat the meat he had provided for them.

18th Feb. "I shot another reedbuck early in the day and saw about fifteen. At lunch we had a great fright as our camp caught fire; the grass was in flames and all hands turned out and just got it stopped within two yards of Harwood's tent, and about ten yards from ours."

22nd Feb. "Our Abyssinian men made night hideous with their cries and our camp looked like an inferno, as they fired the trees, and became terrified of the hyaenas. Hailo Mariam woke me requesting that the Abyssinian soldiers, as he calls them, might fire on the hyaenas. I flatly refused foreseeing a general massacre of my mules."

This day whilst hunting, he saw crocodiles basking on the river bank and claimed one.

After another day of trouble with his Abyssinians, he was overtaken on the march by letters from Addis Ababa, and one from Edward to inform his father that he was starting the next day for Tadejemelna where he hoped to meet up on or about 5th March.

3rd Mar. "When I got into camp at 2.30 I found Edward, fourteen mules, thirteen men and two donkeys had arrived at last, well and cheerful ... During my absence (and Harwood's) there was a dangerous row. The Abyssinians led by Hailo

Mariam setting on the Gallas and Fyeesa. Hailo Mariam and others got Fyeesa down, and Hailo, loving raw meat ... bit a piece out of Fyeesa's arm. Nellie had caught one of the Abyssinians masked and stalking Fyeesa with his rifle, so she very pluckily disarmed all the Abyssinians herself and collected all the rifles into the tent. When I came in, I found all the rifles stacked on her bed. I ... sacked Hailo Mariam and made him leave camp at once."

8th Mar. "It is now breeding time for birds and animals ... many birds are building and laying. The weavers are changing their feathers with extraordinary rapidity, the plain grey and brown ones are now becoming scarlet and black."

24th Mar. "I was called by the Abyssinians to judge a prisoner they had tied up with machanyas, Walda Sadik, one of our men ... *(who)* was caught in the act taking things out of Edward's luggage. The men wanted him to be sent to Ras Makonnen to be punished. I never intended to do this as the Abyssinian punishments are quite merciless.

After hearing what he had to say, which was only 'It was an incident and misfortune which has happened to me,' I gave him a choice of being punished by me or sent to Harrar. He chose at once to receive his punishment at my hands. I ordered him twenty strokes at once ... with a hippo koboko. They said it wasn't enough. I then said to the men that he was not to be ill-treated, and all was to be forgotten and I paid him off in full, including the baksheesh allowed to his comrades.

The men said they felt his conduct very much, as I had been a father and not a master, and the dishonesty of one of many might cause me to give a bad name to Abyssinians."

After this incident, and as Alfred rode away, he was very much moved by many of his men running after him, and kissing his hand:

"No one can persuade me that you are worse served for being kind and liberal to your men."

Notes:
1. Arthur Dorman, (later Sir Arthur Dorman) of Dorman Long Ltd.
2. The Esa Somalis generally call themselves Aysa, but the word is spelt Esa, Eesa, Isa according to fancy. *(Alfred's Journal footnote)*
3. J. Gerolimato, British-Vice Consul at Harrar.
4. After killing, bleeding from the neck.

CHAPTER NINE

'The Ruins of Rome' & the Ruined

The previous November, Alfred had set out for Abyssinia before taking his seat in the new Parliament. Now being back in London, he made his affirmation, and signed the roll at the table of the House on 29th April, 1901.

He and Nellie were at Falmouth with Joseph towards the end of May, and during this time, Jack was busy fighting to get elected for the Saffron Walden division of Essex:

> "Father very much excited & restless about Jack's election; he is longing to be there, & talks and worries about it as if it was a matter of life and death - I do not understand these paroxysms of excitement. I do not think there are any grounds for anxiety about the result - it has always been a very Liberal seat under the most adverse conditions, & Jack is a good respectable candidate - I do not know why he goes carpet bagging down there - but that is his look out ... I am not very enthusiastic about Jack's politics - he is now posing as favourable to the Agricultural Rates Act, and only objecting to it because it didn't give Essex a fair share - He opposed the Bill tooth & nail before - He told the Newcastle people that the coal tax necessitated Pease & Partners sacking 200 men - he now resents the quotation against him as a lie! What I do not like at all is his wobbly attitude to the war - it is not respectable to run any risk of being called a pro-Boer, & it might not pay - However, he has my hearty good wishes ..."

There appears a note of mild irritation in this quote; irritation with his father, as with Jack. The reason for this is not immediately apparent, but at this point Alfred knows something he has not yet revealed.

Joseph had been helping Jack in his election before coming down to Falmouth. The result came on 1st June; Jack was elected with a 700 majority, and when on 6th June, 1901, he took his seat, his signature on the roll came immediately after Alfred's of two months before.

A week later, there was a meeting at 44 Grosvenor Gardens to

196

consider the reconstruction of Wilson Pease & Co. (Ironmasters). Alfred's account reads:

> "The new board is to be:- E.K. Fox[1], J.F. Wilson[2], Theodore[3], Jack and myself - they fixed to make Jack chairman at £150, Theodore managing director at £600, J.F. Wilson & Edwin advising directors at £250 each - and me nothing.
>
> I try to cultivate a meek spirit, but find it sometimes hard to put up with the constant favouritism shown by my father for Jack - I was ten years in business before he would give me any salary at all, & then I got £200 a year, & have never had anything since in addition; he would not let me go into the colliery office, and put Jack there, & gave him a big screw at once. He has now beside ordinary fees I believe, £1,200 or £1,500 as a Managing Director; practically a sinecure for most of the year when he is in London, in Scotland, abroad, shooting, cricketing, hunting & golfing; he gave him I think £250 a year for going occasionally to Stephensons, he put him on the Stephenson board; he spends thousands over him at Snow Hall & Nunthorpe, puts him in a position to own his house in town, makes him many presents of hunters & carriage horses, new guns &c &c.
>
> It puts me in a very false & awkward position - I am a mere vagabond in London; live in an attic, in a cabin of clothes, boots, papers & books - while Jack lives in Mayfair with men servants, carriages, secretaries paid for by Pease & Partners - yet my father never sees the injustice of it all - He did me a bad turn when I was in Algeria & debited my account with £3,000 taking a heap of shares in the flour mills[4] when I said I would not have more than £400 in them - he says it was the only way to float them ..."

This is quite an outburst. But Alfred still hasn't revealed the larger reason for the irritation with his father. We must wait some while longer for this.

As the war in South Africa dragged on, Alfred gave expression to his views, recording something of a long chat he had with "Harry" Paulton, the M.P. for Bishop Auckland:

> "... he takes the *(Lord)* Milner & London Club view of politics in South Africa - necessity of harsher methods to ensure peace &c. My view is unshaken, that as long as Milner is in South Africa & Chamberlain here, all these windy threats will have no effect, but further exasperate the Dutch - but that a change in the personnel - say, Rosebery here & Edward Grey (in South Africa, or vice versa would give the Boers some hope that fair terms would follow surrender - But at present, the threats of enforcing *unconditional* surrender & leaving *no shred* of independence on top of farm burnings, war on private property, concentration camps, arming the blacks, proclamations of confiscations & transportations, hangings &c will have no other effect than 1st. the prolongation of the fight, by every self respecting Dutchman. 2nd. the making of reconciliation impossible and therefore 3rd. the impossible grant of political power to the Dutch & 4th. probable ultimate loss of South Africa."

He remains unshaken in his unpopularly held views, returning to this theme in September, 1901:

> "The curious thing to me is that John Bull cannot understand that the Boer is fighting for his independence, just as we should, and doing it wonderfully well - It is all very well to call them bandits & threaten all kinds of severities by proclamation - today *(15th Sept)* is their last day for coming in - I do not believe any but skunks will surrender & the others will fight on with greater determination."

A week later,

> "I thank God I lifted up my voice against the brutality of Milner and Chamberlain's policy & pleaded for prudence and just dealing. But now that we have done all this wickedness & folly, I cannot bring myself to believe that we can afford to sit down & say we are licked."

At the beginning of October, General Sir Ian Hamilton came to stay with Alfred presenting a further opportunity to discuss the war:

> "It is interesting to find how different a view Hamilton takes to Bertie Philips on the South African situation - Hamilton who has military seniority at the War Office and long experience of the Boers ought to know, thinks the Boers will soon give in and settle down quietly - I judge only from my own views of human nature & exasperation & cannot see it; or how all these desperate men who are now our prisoners will come back reconciled to passing under the yoke - however, Hamilton said, asking me not to quote him, that he considered the Boers & Dutch the most law abiding section of the population, & ultimately more likely to be on our side assisting us against the Uitlander &c lot, who would probably be our worst opponents in the long term. I think the war will go on for months ..."

Alfred, knowing his views were wholly unpopular, did nothing to keep close counsel. In October, whilst staying in Norfolk and being one of a number of guests at the home of Hugh Barclay,

> "Mrs Hy. Buxton had a bad night owing to what I had said about the war last evening - I did not start it & I did not intend to upset her convictions or distress her ... but I could not hide my convictions when challenged."

The war in South Africa ranked uppermost in his mind this November:

> "The war goes on - 10,000 Boers keep 250,000 British on the defensive, & Milner has managed at last to raise the Dutch rebellion in the Cape Colony as I always foretold he would."
>
> *26th Nov.* "Last evening, I presided at the annual Missionary Meeting at the

Pinchinthorpe Chapel. I told them my views which I think appalled them - what with missionaries looting in China, & preaching violence & race hatred in South Africa & telling lies, deceiving people at home and displaying bigotry & ignorance, instead of charity & sympathy, they do as much to discredit the religion of Christ as the example of 'Christian' soldiery & moneymakers."

While all this was going on, the Earl and Countess of Portsmouth were trying to get rid of the colliery shares they had won in the judgement:

> *10th Dec. (London)* "I joined Father at Greenwell's in Finch Lane & discussed a suggestion he made as to our making an offer for 3,400 P & Partners shares that Portsmouths want to sell; the present price is a trifle over £16 & if we cd. buy them at £15 I think it might be worthwhile, but there is no telling what the future may bring forth, & if we are buyers, it is more likely that we can buy them cheaper when the market falls, as it should do if all these are placed on it."

Edward, now at Cambridge, reached the age of twenty-one this December, but the celebration was delayed until New Year's Eve, at Pinchinthorpe House. Alfred was keen to mark his son's majority in the accustomed manner. There was a dance and a feast for 180, which went on until 3.30 a.m. and repeated the following night, for 120 servants and tenants over whose land Alfred went shooting.

Joseph went to the first night's supper and dance but seems somewhat muted in his enthusiasm, saying nothing about pride in his grandson, or his academic progress to date, or how the future was opening out for Edward, but simply recording:

> "... all provided and *well provided* & done by the Army & Navy Stores, and all went off as well as possible."

1902.

This winter, Alfred was invited to visit India and stay with Colonel Ferris, formerly Political Agent at Aden, now Political Resident at Kolhapur. He and Nellie set out and arrived at Bombay on 22nd February. Unlike previous trips abroad, this was much more a personal visit to a friend, about which it is not proposed to say much, except that in the course of a five or six weeks' stay, he met the Maharaja of Kolhapur who was planning to come over for the Coronation of King Edward VII. The Maharaja asked Alfred to use his offices to persuade Lord Curzon to allow Col. Ferris to accompany him as friend and advisor. He was very concerned that whilst in England, he was correct in his behaviour, eating habits, and things of that kind; Alfred saw no occasion for giving advice on this score since his manners were impeccable, such as would carry him in any society without embarrassment.

Soon after returning to England, Alfred received a telegram that Nellie's only brother, Sir Thomas Fowler had been killed in action in South Africa. He had joined his Regiment, 1st Battalion of the Wiltshires in 1899 when the war had started.

> "Poor Tom. His time has soon got over; he was fond of his home & life in the country, and there seemed such a good place for him & happy years ahead, and when we are gone, there is no one that will care much who he was or what he was, only one more counter lost in Milner & Chamberlain's bloody game."

The spring this year was cold and wet. It continued the same into the summer. This, combined with the news of her brother's death, it was supposed, caused a recurrence in Nellie's lung weakness, and her health looked once again precarious.

It was just a few weeks after Tom's death that peace was declared on 1st June in South Africa.

On 2nd June, Alfred went to meet the Maharaja of Kolhapur, now in London for the Coronation, which was postponed because of a decision suddenly made, that King Edward VII must undergo an operation. The Maharaja was invited to come to Hutton at the end of the month.

Also in London was Ras Makonnen. The postponement of the Coronation set London wondering what to do; all the flags and bunting were in place, streets everywhere decorated and nothing to celebrate. Alfred was

> "... bored by the incessant & useless questioning of what is to be done & the education debate at the House, & went to see Ras Makonnen at the Westminster Palace Hotel where he has been given very wretched accommodation. He was really pleased to see me & said, you don't know how pleasant it is to see one face I know - Beru was there to interpret, otherwise we were alone and had quite a good chat. He is much impressed by the immensity of London, & spent, he told me, the greater part of the day looking into the street (Victoria Street)."

The Maharaja came to Hutton as arranged at the end of June. Alfred took him to stay two nights at the Johnson Fergusons at Spring Kell, Carlisle, for the Royal Show. From there they returned by special train to Hutton and for a few days Alfred entertained him, taking him everywhere about the place. In particular,

> "... he desired to see where the rabbits live & he is very excited about them, & waded thro' nettles & wet grass to the burrows to see if the holes were large enough for foxes and cats in India to kill them, if he had any."

On 11th July there was a Pease & Partners Board meeting.

> "A full attendance ... We appointed Parker the Secretary to the company in place of Jobson who is retiring from the service of the firm after 63 years in the office. There was some discussion as to how we were to recognise his long connection, & on my suggestion, he was elected to the Board - Lloyd objected strongly, but gave way to the rest of us - Herbert coming over - I feel it is not a bad thing to secure the use of his long experience & familiarity with every detail of our present & past circumstances, nor to show to those of our staff that have long been with us, that we are ready to make them equal with us when their service has been so long & so loyal."

A few days after this,

> "All morning at Hutton with Father over finance. The necessity of doing something to relieve ourselves & especially Father of the biennial crush & difficulties has been very apparent - & Jack, Dale & I have got him to face it, & he has worked very hard to put the affairs in a shape that we can deal with it - the way has opened to putting our position before Barclays who have intimated a desire to take over our J. & J.W.P. Banking business - my father's position is the crux.
> The taking over in the family concerns & interests, the shares held by his brothers, Gurney & Charles in business at their death; the wiping up of old concerns of his father's *(Joseph Pease, senior, 1799-1872)* that had gone to the bad, or been kept on to find employment for others (e.g. Isaac Wilson & Co, (Potteries), M'bro); the bolstering up in the bad years of the seventies, many of his personal friends & their businesses, & loans unrepaid to relatives (e.g. Howard (&) Theodore Fox, Butler, Dodds, Bolckow Vaughan & Co &c &c) and a series of unprecedented and disastrous years for the coal trade, not to mention the great loss involved in the ironstone department, owing to long contracts foolishly made by Gurney Pease & Cockburn *(Hutton mines manager)*, & the failures of Hutton, Tocketts & Windlestone & other mines - all brought about the heavy overdrafts on my father's accounts, so large that the whole of his income did not suffice to meet interest.
> All these led to the present state of things - whilst without being able to do more than he was doing to economise, without injuring his credit - all this never shook his courage or faith, that good times would reinstate his financial position - & he would have put everything right in 1899-1901 had we not been driven by the Portsmouths to make the arrangement with them which led to, & necessitated our going to the public with Pease & Partners -
> The decision of the Portsmouth case, robbed us of the advantage that the

agreement would have given us, & we lost through them $^2/_3$rds of the profits in the subsequent good years to our selling our concerns - Had this profit come to us, my father's financial position would have been secure."

It might at this stage be helpful to an understanding of the above history, to realise the full extent of these overdrafts in Joseph's name at the Counting House which were revealed a month or so after Alfred made the above entry.

Sir J.W. Pease private account	£456,937	
Sir J.W. Pease revenue account	1,298	
Sir J.W. Pease No 2 account	93,073	
Maud M. Pease House a/c Hutton Hall	2,132	
Maud M. Pease Stables a/c	583	
		554,023

Other overdrafts that may be identified and grouped with all the foregoing narrative included:-

Alfred Edward Pease	12,951	
Alfred Edward Pease Farm a/c	1,788	
Helen Ann Pease	845	
Alfred Edward & Sir J.W. Pease	4,170	
		19,754

Joseph Albert Pease	9,729	
Ethel (Elsie) Pease	404	
Nunthorpe Hall, Building a/c	12,407	
		22,540
		£596,317

There were other very substantial overdrafts but these were chiefly company borrowings, including Stephensons, the Mills, and Wilson Pease & Co Ltd.

At the end of July, Alfred was adamant about resigning his seat in the House and cast around for a successor, but he could find no one to commit himself.

"So I suppose I go on again. I seem fated not to get out."

During the first week of August, 1902,

"At my accounts all day except for a ride & a walk - I find my total liabilities amt. to about £17,000 - & my assets apart from settlements & insurances ... to about 50,000, taking things at a fairly low figure & at the present bad prices.

8th Aug. "At Hutton discussing the Barclays negotiation re J. & J.W.P. - went with Father by the 1 train to Darlington & had a long interview with Dale, Hutchinson & Meek - a very disagreeable one; Dale saying things likely to spoil the negotiations, & crab the value of J. & J.W.P. - Of course we know that my father's position is not what it should be for the easy & smooth working of our Bank, but it is solvent if properly taken in hand - but the unliquid nature of his assets makes Barclays shy of taking us over - and they suggest his friends taking shares in his estate, and substitute more realistic securities acceptable to Barclays to the amount of £200,000. Arthur and Herbert have most generously offered to take £25,000 between them.

Another question was their insisting on knowing how we proposed to meet the dividend time this year. We had not been prepared for this, but were able to put before them our scheme, which included extra overdraws from Prescotts &c, but I said that we would not like to do this & then immediately after receiving these accommodations, chuck Prescotts & give ourselves up to Barclays, & asked if Barclays would, in the event of Consett, N.E. Railway &c drawing all out, ease our finance by giving us what we required.

Eventually Ted *(Backhouse)* agreed to let us have 150(,000) on securities of M'bro' Estate Shares & P. & P. Deferred - a harassing day - & I returned late & tired."

It was eight days later on Saturday, 16th August, 1902 that we have Alfred's next important entry:

"Near the end of this awful week of worry & anxiety -
I really cannot recollect the incidents of each day - I have nothing to remember but masses of figures & puzzles and the reams of paper consumed in working out financial problems at Darlington & Hutton - There is nothing to affect our characters and integrity, but with things at their present prices, the problem of finding cover for all our accounts is terribly difficult to solve - and if the negotiations with Barclays fail we shall have to call our Bankers together & do the best we can.

In any case, we lose nearly all hope of having anything but our settlements to live on - and I cannot see what the outcome will be if our credit is lost - I have got out full statements of everything for Harry Birkbeck and intend that everything is shown as it is - Poverty does not alarm me, but the process of reaching it is the hard part."

It is now worth noting, that at this most critical stage, Joseph has stepped back to let Alfred take over the top position - for the first time in his life.

It was only during the following week-end that he had time to set down the course of events and consequences:

"What a week to have to record -
On Mon. *(18th August)* I went to Darlington by the early train & took all my

203

papers & figures & reports on each individual account & on the value of the Hutton Estates to Hutchinson's office after a preliminary interview with Father who, though very brave, knew that my interview with Harry Birkbeck & Hutchinson would probably save the position or bring about the deluge.
In Hutchinson's room I found Hutchinson & Harry Birkbeck - Harry was exceedingly kind - I submitted sheets 'A' & 'B' with schedules."

On the calculations submitted by Alfred, he showed that the cover required from Barclays was £271,000.

"We put down 120,000 as the value of our business, leaving 151,000 & I think by putting in everything Jack & I & Father possess in the way of securities not pledged already, we just did it -
Eventually I agreed to secure my father & Jack's assent to placing everything in J. & J.W.P. for examination, & to give instructions to Badcock to supply all balance sheets & information - I first tried to get H.B. to say that Barclays would, if this were done, see the thing through - He could not do this, but said having once taken it up, he would work at it & was sure that there must be some way out of it & straightening my father's affairs - that his father wd. have done it & he did not say why it was impossible - One of them asked if I would agree to Peat *(the accountant)* being called in & I said I did not like it at the present moment.
In the end, H.B. said nothing much can be done till after September; in the meanwhile we have given you all the money you require & you can begin drawing when you want & you are all right for the present. This referred to the 150,000 they agreed to give us on 110,000 P. & P. Def. Shares & 50 or 60,000 Middlesbro' Estate Shares; we had made the transfers & all signed the guarantee - He said now all is fixed up for the present, tell your father to go away to Scotland & do not make any alteration in your plans.
I then went back to our office & sent father's & my authority in writing for Hutchinson to have access to all our affairs *(in)* J. & J.W.P."
Tues. 19th Aug. "All being in order at Darlington, I started with Christopher for Scotland to see Gerald & Ethel & have a week's shooting & holiday after all this turmoil - I wired to Jack to meet me on Perth Station (he was at Glenarthy & had been out of all this trouble) - I explained to him all that had occurred. Father went to Arthur's near Oban the same day."

Glenarthy was Sir Christopher Furness's shooting lodge. Arthur was of course Arthur Francis Pease to whose shoot, near Oban, Joseph had gone. Alfred continues:

Wed. 20th Aug. "A delightful day on the hill, we got about 20 grouse, 20 rabbits & a few snipe & coming in at 4.30 - I picked up a telegram - 'Hutchinson wishes you to return at once' - What could this mean? I telegraphed to Jack *(that)* I was off again - "
Thurs. 21st Aug. "I left at 4.30 a.m. and got to Darlington at 2.0 p.m. & to my horror found that the 50,000 M'bro' shares were not available as security owing to

an article in the Article*(s)* of Assocn. - that Peat had been called in & apparently had advised Barclays not to proceed with arrangements - Dale had had a heated meeting with Ted Backhouse & Hutchinson declaring they were honour bound to see us through as the N.E.R. dividend was due on 23rd - 160,000 for which we required the money - nothing however would they take in substitution in the way of good securities we offered - (e.g. Jack's & my P. & P. shares, N.E.R, Consols &c, Ayton farms) I was alone at Darlington, Jack & Father had not arrived, & I got home at night in a great state of anxiety as to what would occur - Ted & Hutchinson went to London this night or next morning."

Fri. 22nd Aug. "BLACK FRIDAY came - I returned to Darlington, Father & Arthur had arrived last night - Arthur being a real brick - the night had been partly spent in concocting schemes. During the morning, the best terms we could get after meetings with Peat, were the following, subject to B's Board's confirmation - and we were to wire our acceptance to Lombard Street - they are dreadful, but if our fortunes are sacrificed & our credit saved we have not lost everything. The terms are these:-

1. B & Co.- to purchase J. & J.W.P.'s assets at fair values wh. shd. be as near as possible realizable values.
2. Subject to Clause 7, goodwill to be paid for in addition, at a sum agreed on (Arthur told me he had secured a minimum of £60,000)
3. Proceeds of 1 & 2 to be utilised for payment to the creditors pro rata, of J. & J.W.P.
4. All current Bankg. a/cs of J.&.J.W.P. to be closed & reopened with B & Co who will allow credit to approved customers as required for their immediate current requirements.
5. The assets of J.&.J.W.P. to include the private estates of Partners other than furniture, horses & carriages.
6. Any difference of opinion as to the value of assets to be settled by arbitration at the cost of J.&.J.W.P.
7. Any surplus over valuation on realizing the assets to be in addition to the sum to be agreed for Goodwill, any deficit to come off that sum.
8. B & Co. to take over the staff of J.&.J.W.P. on terms of their existing engagements.
9. A maximum of 2 years to be allowed for realising assets - interest on the value till realisation to be charged by B & Co.

All this time, the remembrance that the N.E.R. dividend was due in 24 hours weighed on me - Father struggled to show other ways out of it, but Peat showed B & Co wd. do nothing else - I wanted Jack to be there, but he had not arrived & a decision was of immediate importance - I felt, knowing as we did, that Peat would not say that we were solvent, & feeling that if we did not fail today, we could not continue properly as Bankers with the knowledge of our condition now before us; & even if we are solvent, as I think we are, I pressed Father to assent - he at last said, if Dale & Peat both tell me it is the best thing I can do, & you wish it, I will do it - & the fateful message was sent.

Jack turned up at 1.15 & found this awful state of things."

Now Alfred reflects on everything that has happened:

205

"It is hard on him *(Jack)* and me who are far more than solvent and had but a fractional interest in the Bank. We returned to our homes at night having made over all we possess and knowing that the places we had tended & made, the savings of all our lives were all gone from us - I went to bed in a very anxious frame as no confirmation had come from Barclays."

Sylvia Hamlyn who had celebrated her twenty-first birthday just a fortnight before, was at Hutton Hall where all had been as normal as possible. This "Black Friday" however, she received a telegram sent by her grandfather from Darlington which read

"Returning home - meet the train at the station - ask no questions."
Joseph and Sylvia walked back to the Hall in silence and once there, he disappeared into his study, leaving Sylvia wondering what had happened.

The next day, Saturday, 23rd August, returning to Darlington, Alfred found that

"... the terms of our surrender were confirmed ... I came home. There were my yearlings in the grass & my brood mares opposite the house - all have to go, - there are the woods & hills I have wandered amongst all my days no longer ours; there is my little garden that Nellie & I have wandered around for 22 years & tended and loved passed to others & on top of all this, the thought of Father's long life of hard work given to the family & the district yielding no other fruit than this ... Then there are all the people who have had their money with us, who will be anxious till we are sold up & can pay them in full - I feel little responsibility in this matter as I have done all I could to discourage private people banking with us ...
Nellie has been the greatest comfort to me & been most sweet & helping thro' this dreadful week."

Another fortnight passed before Alfred's next entry.

7th Sept. "I do not know how to record what has occupied me from 7 every morning till late at night each day - but we are now nearing the hour when we shall know exactly where we are, & whether we are to be bankrupts or voluntarily wound up - There are no figures yet as to the gap between our liabilities & assets"

adding,

"I cannot believe our liabilities exceed 600,000."

Joseph's entries throughout the period of crisis, though much more brief are very much to the point. He felt the whole débacle involved *"much humiliation."*

At the end of August, Sir Christopher Furness put down a sum of

£40,000 to prevent bankruptcy proceedings, and this staggering generosity Joseph felt to be, which it was, *"overpowering."*

With such an embarrassingly generous start, Joseph sat down to write to others who he felt might help save them. Over many years Joseph had been the recipient of such pleas from others which had not gone unanswered; now the roles were reversed. Joseph's entry continues,

> "He placed down £40,000 for Peat to use to keep us out of bankruptcy provided other friends came forward, and friends enough for the purpose were raised ... Saw Ted Backhouse who added £10,000 to £40,000 of Furness."

Arthur Francis Pease added £20,000 and thus a guarantee fund began to get underway, many friends outside the family adding most generously and reaching in total, a sum of about £160,000.

A month later, as preparations at Pinchinthorpe commenced for the first stage of disposals for sale, of horses, farm stock and game trophies to enable him to settle his private debts, Alfred writes,

> *21st Sept.* "It is a curious experience having no money. I have only in 14 days spent ¹/₂d over a newspaper & was glad to have 2/- I had lent repaid me - We are living on my farm - I killed a sheep this week - & my oats & hay will just keep my horses till they are sold next Thursday.
> Servants being a first charge on our estates, their wages are provided by Barclays till notices expire - but they have not given one of us a 6d to provide us with common necessities - a pack of mean hounds who have broken faith with us at every turn & have treated us most shamefully ..."
> *23rd Sept.* "With Jack & Arthur to London - arr. 7.15. at 44 Grosvenor Gardens, found Father had had two of his giddy attacks & looked ill. We helped him upstairs and put him to bed - he was soon asleep."

On 25th September, Alfred went to York to see his horses sold,

> "... a sad job seeing the results of my many years breeding thrown away ... then home - to my empty stalls & fields round which I went with Lavender whose tears rolled down as she saw the vacant places of her pets - for she knew not only the breeding names *(and)* ages of everything on the place, but all their individual characters, tempers, & dispositions."

By mid-October Alfred was calculating what, in his new circumstances, he might expect to have as an income. If, as seemed certain, through having to make arrangements with creditors, he lost all his directorships, all he would have would be about £500 a year from his settlements. His estimated outgoings he calculated at £780 a year.

"I am beginning to break down & have bad headaches, a thing I have never had before."

At this time, in the middle of October, he turns to his journal for another great outpouring which explains a lot about his earlier expressions of irritation with his father as with Jack.

"I wish to put on record, two or three facts which my children ought to know someday - & which explain the inferior position my father has placed me in during many years in respect to financial arrangements ..."

Referring to Jack:

"When he married, my father agreed with Lady Alice *(Havelock- Allan),* unknown to me, that I was not to be made an eldest son ... When I went to Abyssinia in 1900, Father informed me that as he did not consider my life a good one with my weak heart, he intended to alter his Will & leave Hutton to Jack, as he did not consider it a good thing to leave Hutton to go to Edward - & this, without altering his existing will in respect of his leaving Nunthorpe, Morton farms & Ayton to Jack - I felt this keenly - Today I asked Jack if he had been told this & he admitted it, and also said that he considered Father had not carried out what he called 'the honourable understanding' with Lady Alice to show me no consideration as an eldest son in dealing with his property & fortune, & this was his reason for letting Father into £14,000 expenditure over Nunthorpe the last year or so -
I have never protested about these underhand proceedings preferring peace & injustice to myself to family troubles over money - and have had too much pride to care to stand up for my own interests - & now that all has gone from us, the whole thing is a matter of comparative indifference to me - but I hope no child of mine will care enough for riches, to try ever to best a brother or sister in a struggle for wealth & social position - I would rather be a penniless man as I am today all my life than feel I owed a single pound to scheming against one of my own blood ...
I find now that Jack & Elsie & Lady Alice are scheming to hold on to Nunthorpe & to let Hutton be sold if possible to Spencer! *(Havelock Allan - Elsie's brother)* - Father & I & my sons are to be cuckoed out of our homes. These things hurt my feelings; it is not the thing itself, but the thought of what a brother & a scheming wife can bring themselves to do, in order to keep their feet on the political & social ladder -"

Following this great outpouring, he added -

"(This was written in an hour of irritation that passed)".

Though Black Friday had changed everyone's circumstances, Alfred fully believed until now, that he had been disadvantaged under his father's Will, which he presumed to have been altered during his absence in Abyssinia. Following Jack's admissions and revelations, but at a later date, Joseph told Alfred that he had in fact not altered his old will in any way; that his intentions expressed in 1900 had been made because of his annoyance at Edward enlisting for the Boer War.

At the end of September, Joseph, as Chairman of the N.E. Railway, but with his financial plight now public knowledge, had gone to attend the monthly Board Meeting in York. He felt extremely awkward about whether he was any longer wanted, and whether or not he would be granted a hearing, and there is something pathetic but courageous about him as he sits quite alone outside the Director's Meeting, waiting for some kind of guidance from his colleagues on the Board.

"Chat with Dale & Sir I.L. Bell on mode of procedure. Meeting began at 12.15 - 20 minutes past one had heard nothing. I should not like to depart this way, but there are two sides to being on a great Railway Board at 74 years of age! Dale came up and told me (about 2 o'clock) that the Board thought that it would be too painful to see me, though I should have much preferred it. So I got some lunch and went home ..."

The following day in response to a telegram from Sir David Dale, Joseph went through to Darlington. Dale gave Joseph an account of the N.E.R. board meeting in York:

"It seems at the Board they elected Lord Ridley Chairman without having had my resignation. Dale told them he had no authority from me to hand it in, so they asked him to get it. This unpleasant duty (to him) he did with kindness and tact, but of course I was quite ready and drew it out so that they might telegraph to insert the paragraph in the papers as arranged. I got home to dinner at 8.40. Dale said nothing was said about my seat."

In October Joseph wrote to Sir Christopher Furness,

"... about sending my pictures to his house, as after the munificent way he has treated us, I don't like that he should lose by us, and our furniture is not pledged."

Doubtless this most generous man swept Joseph's offer aside, for on this subject we hear no more.

Alfred was now forced by his own financial position to resign his seat as the M.P. for Cleveland, and on 22nd October,

"I received today my appointment to the Stewardship of the Manor of Northstead & am no longer an M.P. Thus ends all my parliamentary life & I bury finally the ambitions & hopes & anticipations with which I entered Parliament 17 years ago."

25th Oct. "Received a cheque from Elfreda[5] for £600 & one from Lotta[5] for £500. I am overwhelmed by this kindness & generosity - I destroyed Elfreda's cheque & returned Lotta's - I am determined to have no help from anyone till I need it for bare necessities or some articles I may wish to save from the wreck ... though I will take help from my relations to save my wife & children from hardships."

The sale of all his farm stock at Spite Hall - cows, sheep, implements, everything - came at the end of October, and, he later learnt, fetched reasonably good prices.

While this was taking place, he went up to London:

"I went to 8, Hertford St. to Jack & Elsie's ... Jack arrived with me. We were met with a storm of curses & ravings by Elsie - I cleared out ... & then dined with Bertie & returned to 8, Hertford St. for a sleepless night."

31st Oct. "Elsie at it again - Paulton called after Harrison *(Solicitor)* had been with Jack & me, then to the city &c - then to Brooks's for letters - met Gerald & he gave me the chance of coming to Birch Hall. I greedily accepted it glad to fly from 8 Hertford St - Got to Birch Hall late."

Elsie, at times capable of paroxysms of rage, was wont to throw missiles - vases and such like - full or empty - at the object of her abuse. Sometimes her luckless French maid bore the brunt of the verbal assaults, but it was more usually Jack, who by way of a bonus of flowers, received the missiles - *"Jack! - you fool!!"* But Jack - he adored her - would just smile, say nothing, and await the passing of each storm. On this occasion, her rage was obviously a consequence of seeing all social ambition in ruins - the Social & Personal columns would never more refer to events attended by "the smart and delightful Mrs Jack Pease."

By the 5th November, Alfred was back at Pinchinthorpe.

16th Nov. "Father has authorised the sale of Hutton. It is heartbreaking - but I think it is quite right and has my full approval."

A few weeks before now - *"when all known conditions vanished,"* - Sylvia Hamlyn had left Hutton for Bridestowe in Devon, to carve out a new life. Though she loved Hutton dearly and all Cleveland too, she never again returned north to recapture and savour there once more *"the smell of hot heather - and the night air a riot of pine"*. In time, she managed to establish herself, becoming a most successful breeder of Dartmoor and Exmoor ponies until her death in 1962.

Joseph was now temporarily at Pinchinthorpe. He was really

24. *Ethel (Elsie) Pease née Havelock- Allan.*

pathetically shunting about between his sons' and married daughters' homes as preparations for the sale of all the estates got under way. Alfred records that he and his father went shooting for their food:

22nd Nov. "Shot Bousdale - bitterly cold & frosty. We got about 235 pheasants, 10 hares & a few rabbits."

28th Nov. "I had a long letter from Harrison explaining that Cooper & Butterworth for the creditors had been difficult to settle with about our private liabilities, being very indignant at Jack & Elsie's extravagance over Nunthorpe & 8 Hertford Street - this had prevented his being able to obtain for us more satisfactory terms - We have secured for our creditors from our family & friends over £150,000 - Barclays guaranteed us our furniture & live stock - yet we are now to give up everything except £2,000 worth of furniture apiece - I do not mind if they will take everything I have got if only they will be done with it & cease worrying us to death week after week - Hutton is advertised for sale."

3rd Dec. "Father has *got leave* to stay at Hutton for a fortnight or so! - We are spared no humiliation that the 3 lawyers can inflict ... Father left us & Maud arrived at Hutton fr. Birch Hall - they live in the old dining room & eat in the schoolroom -"

12th Dec. "Went with Nellie to Ayton Banks & looked for a site for a cottage to live in as soon as we are turned out of here - selected the one I have thought of in the corner of the plantation - walked home - Edward came home."

211

17th Dec. "Darlington. P. & P. Board. Present. Sir J.W. Pease, J.A. Pease & A.E. Pease, & Lloyd came in late and we are those *(except Lloyd Pease)* that are to go off the Board on the assignment of our estates!"

The Deed of Assignment was signed the following day:

"Harrison has secured for me better terms than I could have hoped for - viz. all my furniture & personal effects, the amounts Nellie & I have in the Bank £788, & £40., shares in P. & Partners & also half of my Post Nuptial Settlement of 2,000 P. & P. shares wh. will leave 1,000 in the Trust with the income to me for life."
Christmas Day 1902. "I spent all day at my writing table - I had some kind letters & 3 turkeys & a case of champagne sent me and we made the best of the day we could; a little complete party and all well - but what a change from last year and other Christmas's at Hutton - Hutton and Nunthorpe are empty - & soon I suppose it will be our turn to go,"

Joseph spent his Christmas at Birch Hall, Theydon Bois, with his daughter Ethel and son-in-law Gerald Buxton.

Before the end of December, the liquidators set out the final position of Joseph and his two sons. The gross liabilities amounted to £1,268,031 and the gross assets were estimated at £1,017,816. These figures represented the position *after* the condition of the three partners in the Counting House had become public knowledge, and *not* when the Counting House was a going concern with its credit unimpaired.

1903

There were kind friends and neighbours, mindful that the Pinchinthorpe House stables were empty, who were ready to provide Alfred with a mount to hunt that winter. He gratefully accepted such offers, and in the first days of the new year let his troubles take second place for a while.

7th Jan. "Went to London at 12.9 to 44 Grosvenor Gardens - to Brooks's to dinner. Sat at a table next to Portsmouth. We did not exchange so much as a look, but he made the room resound with smacking his chops -"
9th Jan. "... to bed 1.0 a.m. My last night at 44 Grosvenor Gardens."
10th Jan. "Bid farewell to this place where I have spent so many weeks of so many years & which is full of memories of labours happy days & of my sweet Mother - Went before leaving into the rooms that were hers, her bedroom where when she was on the sofa I used to come and hold her hand & talk during her last illness - then to her sitting room with her things still there on the walls - Home at Pinchinthorpe at 5.30 in low spirits - I had a letter yesterday from Meek who evidently is going to attack the 250 shares I gave to Edward after he came of age ..."

212

25. *Elephant tusks, Hutton Hall.*

He also got a letter from the new Secretary of Pease & Partners, J.A. Parker - bald and formal, simply recording the resolution which removed Joseph, Alfred and Jack from the Board of the company.

"I was most hurt with its want of kindness, & absence of any expression of regret, or thanks for past services than with anything that has occurred of this sort.
I also got a notice that my name wd. be taken off the Cleveland Club[6] - this is a dirty trick as I wanted to resign a few years ago & they begged me to stay on, & I have paid them some 70 guineas for about 3 lunches & two teas in 23 years! - If I am good enough for Brooks's I shd. have thought my company wd. not have hurt the habitués of this pot house - Snowing all night."
20th Jan. "Father seems rather feeble on his legs - & walks with difficulty."

Alfred had now to think about his future. A Residency job in Lower Siam was being considered by him carrying a salary of £1,000 a year.

"I should take the job like a shot but dread the long exile from my children - still beggars cannot be choosers ... My once happy home, soon to be ours no more has got on my nerves, & I long to shake England & its petty narrow life off - the people among whom one would have to toil here for a living have no souls for the most part above dividends and dinners; are quite content to call a dirty grey day with a biting wind a fine one, & are oblivious to smoke buzzas, charabancs, motor cars and all the new sounds of 20th century country life."

213

He did not get the Siamese Inspectorate appointment.

"I left home on Sat 31 Jan & returned on Feb 9th - after being in London, Birch Hall, Sussex & Birmingham - I took £5 with me and spent £4. 8. 0.d. in the whole time ... I must say I loathe travelling 3rd class - it is the thing I bring myself with the greatest difficulty to do - If you get into a smoking 3rd, the men *spit* on the floor & make disgusting noises & keep the windows up - if you get into another, dirty children stand about and suck oranges & make patterns on the breath steamed windows, & the parents do all sorts of funny things - suckle babies and sweetmeats - I suppose one would not mind if one had been brought up to it - but at 45 one changes one's habits with an effort."

25th Feb. "The pictures all went from Hutton today. I think Father feels parting with his pictures and the gradual dispersal of all his belongings."

27th Feb. "I got a letter from Count Glenchen offering from the Sirdar an Assist. Inspectorship for Edward in the Sudan - I cabled acceptance - he is to join on May 1st - £420 a year - I wired Edward."

6th Mar. 1903. "Got a horrible letter from Harrison, who at the instance of Meek & Co. asked us to leave my house *'at once'* as our presence was detrimental to the sale ... he asked me to see that my father turned out at once too - I rode over to Hutton & gave the insolent message. Ethel was furious, Maud's eyes full of tears - Father indignant but quiet -"

7th Mar. "I had a letter today from Paulton asking me to see Lord Onslow 12.30 on Monday & Tuesday."

8th Mar. "In low spirits packing up. I leave my once happy home tonight and take refuge in Bertie Philips rooms in Jermyn St - Nellie & Lavender clear out tomorrow by the 7.30 a.m. train at the bidding of these damned swine who now hustle us about - they go to Sister Mary's *(Nellie's sister)* Cottage at Farnham - Went to Hutton for lunch - our last little family gathering in the old home - Drove to Middlesbro' at night with a sore heart & got to London 3.30 a.m."

9th Mar. "To the Colonial Office at 12.30 - Where Onslow said Milner & Joe Lawley wished him to offer me a Resident Magistracy in the Transvaal - and £1,000 a year - I asked him what my duties would be. He answered 'Oh you will have an easy billet, no office work, just riding about the Veldt and being a father to the people.'

I reminded him that I had been politically hostile to his government and to Milner's pre-war policy; he replied 'so much the better'; that I should be free from any prejudice that existed against the more aggressive people, and in a position to administer impartial justice and be a conciliating influence. I asked for some days to decide in.

I have always loathed the idea of So. Africa & its sordid population & barren landscape. I don't know what to do - they say that you cannot get a house under £250 a year & living is most terribly expensive - but it is a good offer - & they want me they say, as they find it difficult to get men who have some knowledge of the world who are gentlemen & likely to conciliate the conflicting interests and animosities caused by the war."

He brooded over this offer, had many consultations, including one with Albert, Earl Grey, who confided that it was he who had suggested his name to Joe Lawley and Lord Milner. Grey urged him to take the job; Lord Milner was very ready to accept him. This was really a most curious and unexpected turn of events; being offered a job by Lord Milner against whom Alfred had raged. He concluded that he appeared to owe more to his political enemies than to his political friends.

On 16th March, Alfred and his father met up, and had lunch at Brooks's where they discussed the Lord Onslow offer.

"He does not want me to go to the Transvaal, but is not strong about it, and is rather supine & hazy about what I am to do if I don't go."

18th Mar. "After agonising debate in my mind I have decided to accept the appointment in the Transvaal ... & must now leave it to providence to direct my path - Wrote to Lord Onslow accepting. This day terminates the 3 mos. period in respect of our assignment."

19th Mar. "Heard there was an attempt to make us bankrupt yesterday at the last moment - the brutality of some people is incomprehensible, deliberately waiting for 3 months to let us think it was safe - however somehow the thing was saved - We were told on the 18th of Mar. we were absolutely safe & on that day, dividends would be sent to our creditors - now there is fresh deception & no dividends are yet issued & we are told that any creditor who refuses a dividend can at any time, if he is vindictively inclined, put us in the bankruptcy court - The lawyers are absolutely shameless in the way they have spun this thing out & deceived us."

20th Mar. "Edward arrived from Cambridge in good spirits, though he must feel as I do intensely the cruelty of having to abandon 6 years of his senior seven years' scholarship, his Oriental & Classical degree & a most promising career ..."

The following morning, a letter arrived from Peat saying that he would, on 30th March, ask leave of the Creditors Committee for Alfred to return to Pinchinthorpe to pack up there.

"It is sickening - someday please God we will get even over this business."

Alfred with Edward spent a few hours at the Army & Navy Stores fitting the latter out for the Sudan. That day Alfred got a wire to say that Hutton, Pinchinthorpe and Nunthorpe were unsold at auction, failing to reach their reserves. This news immediately set his mind racing and he

(27th Mar.) "Discussed with Father the possibility of bidding for Pinchinthorpe. Wrote many letters."

In the face of financial ruin, to even entertain an attempt to salvage Pinchinthorpe from the wreckage was a wonderful and characteristic display of boldness from Alfred. Seeing hope in even this, the blackest of crises, alone, he left London and at full speed raced back to Pinchinthorpe House where,

Sun. 29th Mar. "Once more here in the familiar quarters - still hoping."

After eleven days of the most feverish activity,

Fri. 10th April. "Edward today signed the contract for the purchase of Pinchinthorpe ... for £14,000 - I have worked hard to get this done - & to raise the £1,400 deposit. I found £200 myself (& Nellie) Maud, £300, & Elfreda Fowler £900 - I hope to raise £8,000 on it. Elfreda Fund £4,000, Maud £2,000, and what is required for exes &c."

What he had got back, putting the property in Edward's name, and mortgaged to the hilt, was Pinchinthorpe House, two farms and seven small cottages; in all, 278 acres including woodland.

The intention behind salvaging Pinchinthorpe was that there would be a home in the old country for Joseph to live out his remaining years, while Alfred started his new life in the Transvaal. For the time being, he calculated, with income from rents, settlements and Transvaal salary he could just about live and pay the mortgage interest.

Edward left for the Sudan on 14th April.

Joseph, a refugee, spending most of his time with his daughter Ethel Buxton in Essex, was, when up north, occupying himself in sifting and sorting through his masses of papers and re-reading old letters, his mind drifting back down through all the years, and reflecting upon his once busy life:

"How many irons I had in the fire in the 1860s & 70s."

His 1903 diary now tends to trail off into sporadic, gappy entries, sometimes with an air of unreality surrounding everything; seeing life through a haze, giving at times an indication of only numbed awareness of what has really happened. Then at other times, there he is, the same old Joseph, still in charge of everything.

In February, he indicated to the Liberal Council at Bishop Auckland that he would not seek re-election at the end of this Parliament. His loyal supporters showed him the greatest kindness and understanding when he went to meet them.

Alfred found it hard work saying goodbye to his father at the end of May.

> "He has been hanging about me the last day or two, wanting to help me and evidently feeling our coming separation, but keeping sentiment down as is his wont. He seems cheerful and brave and he went off with Lottie by an earlier train to Falmouth. It was a hot day and he had on a thick Harris tweed suit and white spats."

Joseph, after their separation in London, wrote,

> *30th May.* "Not a very good night - parting with Alfred for Africa is a terrible break up of one's feelings. Resolved not to go to Southampton. Lottie most sweetly went to Paddington with me and saw me off for Falmouth 10.40. A warm fine day, travelled alone; pretty punctually at Falmouth 7 o'clock. Delighted to see a quiet night and a smooth sea for my travellers - but it is sad work at my time of life. God in his goodness, bless them and me."

He had come home to Kerris Vean, the Falmouth house he had some years before given to his unmarried daughter, Maud. And next day,

> *Sun. 31st May* "A cool day, but a quiet sea - thought much about our voyagers in Meeting and out of it."
>
> *11th June* "Worked steadily at letters to gamekeepers - Mills[7] leaves me and I make Parker head at Pinchinthorpe - Letters from Alfred & Nellie from Madeira."

And three days later,

> *14th June.* "Drafted a letter to Gerald in reply to one he wrote to me about peace with Beatrice Portsmouth."

Beatrice had written to Gerald Buxton asking him to mediate in an effort to bring about peace with Joseph.

On 17th June, not feeling well and rather drowsy, almost falling asleep over his tea, Joseph intimated to his daughter Maud that he felt that he was, as he put it, coming to *"the wind up."*

His entries cease four days later at 21st June - in a very shaky hand.

On 22nd June, he was anxious to get his new, short and very simple will signed and sent back to his solicitor. Oliver, his most faithful butler who had refused to desert him, and Dr Owen attending him, witnessed his signature.

23rd June was Joseph's 75th birthday. In the afternoon, up and dressed, he wrote a long cheery letter to his grandson Christopher whose birthday was next day, then feeling unwell at 4.00 p.m., went to bed and quietly died two hours later.

Notes:
1. Edwin Fox was Joseph's nephew who lived at Pinchinthorpe Hall.
2. & 3. respectively son and nephew of Isaac Wilson late of Nunthorpe Hall.
4. This is a reference to the Cleveland Flour Mills in which Alfred had had some passing interest.
5. Elfreda Fowler and Lotta Barbour were Nellie's sisters.
6. A Middlesbrough businessman's Club.
7. Peter Mills had succeeded Cockfield as head gamekeeper at Hutton some time before now.

CHAPTER TEN

South Africa & a New Start

1903 continued

As Alfred, Nellie and Lavender set out for South Africa, Edward was starting his career at Suakin in the Sudan, and Christopher was back at school at Winchester, the fees for which, Alfred hoped, he might just manage to scrape together.

The voyage out in most respects was nothing special, but

> "I saw things on this boat I never saw on any other liner, including a free fight in the first class saloon, a foreign Consul, well smashed up and all but lynched for an indecent assault on a woman; two first class 'ladies' pulling each other's hair out on the deck, and pouring volleys of the most filthy language into each other. One of these Jo'burg ladies had pulled back a child of the other's, in order to view better some sports which were going on, whereon the outraged mother went for the 'lydye' - 'I'll teach yer to touch my ------- kid.'"

They arrived at Capetown on 16th June where they booked in at the Royal Hotel - the name belying the style it might suggest for the third rate expensive accommodation there.

The next day, the three of them set out by rail from Capetown, bound for Pretoria, where they arrived after a journey of 51 hours on 19th June. They booked in at the Grand Hotel - more third rate and expensive accommodation.

> "It is clear we cannot live in any hotel here at less than £30 a week. If it had not been for a most generous present to Nellie from Sir Edmund Loder when we left England, I should have been 'dead beat' in a week - as it is, it made me perspire to look forward."

The Governor was Sir Arthur Lawley, known as "Joe" Lawley, a friend and contemporary of Alfred's at Cambridge, upon whom he now went to call.

"He was most kind to me, but had not expected me - the Colonial Office which had instructed me not to communicate direct, having forgotten to advise him they were sending me out."

It was soon established that he had indeed arrived in the right country, and that he had an appointment to take up somewhere, and Lawley took him round to meet various Government officials.

The following day, Alfred had his first meeting with the High Commissioner, Lord Milner. Milner could only have known of him from passing him on the stairs at a time when they had rooms in the same house in Bury Street, St James's, when Alfred was a young and new M.P.

"He is certainly a charming man. In the afternoon I took Nellie to a garden party at ... ZASM[1] House. We there met the Lyttletons (General Neville L. being Commander-in-Chief), Gen. Clements, Smith, Director of Agriculture *(and)* Louis Botha (whom I liked, and with whom I had a pleasant little conversation). It is singular that having been seen in close conversation at Governt. House with Botha - Joe Lawley & one other informed me not to be 'too friendly' with him - but I never thought him anything but absolutely honest & trustworthy."

On 23rd June, he went to the Law Courts, where he was to spend some time familiarising himself with Dutch and Roman-Dutch Law, ordinances, proclamations and statutes.

"This is my father's birthday and the anniversary of my sister Effie's death."

This same day, and already finding his money diminishing alarmingly, he went off to the Standard Bank to see what interest terms he could get on his little remaining funds.

"'Interest!' said the man 'what do you mean by interest?'
I explained.
'Well' he said, 'we don't allow any interest; we charge you for taking care of your money.'
'Well!' I said, 'that sounds a funny sort of Banking!'
'Why?' he asked.
'Because it strikes me as curious, that you should undertake to take charge of my money, use it as you like, and then take so much of it every year,' and, I added, 'I suppose if I leave it here long enough, and come here one day and ask for it, you will tell me it has all gone.'
He replied 'That is so, and *that* is the way we do business *here.*'
I went away more than ever impressed with the horrible nature of the country, but I had to 'stick it' like every one else around me."

The following day, 24th June,

"In the evening, on coming in from the Law Courts, I had a cable in 'unicode' from Jack which, deciphered read, 'Father died yesterday - particulars by letter - taken ill suddenly - funeral takes place Darlington.'
This dreadfully sudden blow coming on top of so many others is hard. I regret intensely having left him, but never guessed that the end of his hard fought and bravely lived life, was at all near ...'"

The following day, Lord Milner sent for Alfred to meet him at Johannesburg, and he left Pretoria that afternoon, for a longer talk than at their introductory meeting.

"I enjoyed it very much; I found him kind and sympathetic, and went to bed encouraged about the task before me, but I cannot keep my thoughts off my father lying dead at Kerris Vean, and the closing of another chapter of my life; he was associated with all the greater happinesses of my life, and was a most affectionate and sympathetic father."

Alfred had now to bury the hope he held when he had come out to South Africa, that his father would at some time be able to live at Pinchinthorpe. That house was now full of Hutton Hall furniture for Joseph, Alfred having sold his own to settle debts.

After a further talk with Milner on 26th June, he returned from Johannesburg to Pretoria where he found that in his absence, Nellie had suffered a lung haemorrhage. This made him very anxious to get her away from there as soon as possible, and whilst at lunch with 'Joe' Lawley, his drifting thoughts were really in England and about Nellie, their future together, and of how everything would be affected by his father's death.

By 19th July, still in Pretoria, where, because of a mix-up over vacancies, he had not yet been allocated a District,

"This is a constant worry to me for many reasons, but acutely so from the financial aspect, as though I have hinted that it would be a convenience if I might draw some of the pay due to me, there seems no way of getting a shilling of it, and in this country, out you go into the street if your hotel bill is not paid to the minute."

A few days later, given the choice of several districts, he settled upon Barberton. He made this choice, a perverse one in Lawley's view, because it was suggested that

"... you would never want to go to such an outlandish district, with fever country to visit and wild low Veldt. I said that sounds like suiting me if Barberton itself is a warm climate. They were surprised at my taste, but my chief idea was to escape from everything that was like Pretoria, with its cold and dust and loathsome hotels and hideous country."

With his instructions in his pocket, having already seen plans for Barberton's new municipal buildings, his new Law Courts and offices on all of which, he understood, work was to start at once under his supervision, they set out at 10.00 that night and

"... shook the red dust of Pretoria off our feet ... The following morning, we were rushing down from the bitter cold of the High Veldt into my new district and the hot country. The railway throughout the length of my district follows the Crocodile River till, beyond Kaap Muiden, the valley is really a deep gorge, with towering mountains and forest and bush-clad Kopjes[2] of the grandest kind. Beyond Kaap Muiden, the northern wall of the valley opens out into an immense Low Veldt bush country, and is practically uninhabited, forming part of the great Transvaal Game Reserve. The railway main line continues east to the frontier at Komati Poort, and enters Portugese territory through the gap in the frontier range of mountains called the Lebombo Hills.
Our spirits rose as we entered this beautiful country and revivifying heat ... At Kaap Muiden, we changed onto the Barberton branch line, and our journey then was a slow drag up the De Kaap valley, through forest and scrub-covered mountains ... It was late in the afternoon when we drew into the station."

At Barberton Station to meet them was the acting Resident Magistrate, Alfred's future assistant, Oscar Staten, from whom Nellie and he received a particularly nice and warm welcome.
Alfred's first impression of the town itself, was one of

"... a most untidy ramshackle collection of shanties and tin houses. We are at the Phoenix Hotel, which is clean and much more to our liking than the filthy hotels of Pretoria, and if only I have health, I can take an interest in this place, and I think make something of my job."

The district he was to administer measured at its extremities roughly 80 miles by 80 miles. He had three courts for civil and criminal jurisdiction namely, Barberton Headquarters, Komati Poort and Kaapsche Hoop.

"I find I am not only a magistrate and county court judge, but governor of the largest convict prison outside Jo'burg and Pretoria; manager of the civil hospital; at the head of the constabulary and frontier guards; coroner without jury; I am also in the place of mayor and manage the streets and sanitation of the towns; I issue all licences for arms and ammunition; have to look after education; take charge of orphans, intestate estates, lepers and lunatics. I am also collector of all revenues;

registrar of lands; receiver of gold claims &c revenues; registrar of diamonds; issue residential, municipal, domestic and travelling permits for natives; contract for prison labour and at least a score of other duties besides."

He was to start his duties on 1st August, and as it was now 31st July, he had one day in which to acclimatise. He made a start by inspecting the gaol and hospital. Next he made a list of things he had been asked to attend to at once, and others needing prompt attention in his war-shattered district.

"Among them are:- to get what office records and archives that have survived the war put into order. Most have been destroyed, and all have been looted and overhauled for postage stamps by the British tommies and others. One cellar under the Court House, contains heaps of records, registers, deeds, judgements - all torn up, muddled up, covered with mud and dust; just a mountain of scraps and loose sheets of paper. These are the archives of the court, town and district!

The philatelists appear to have arranged a nice programme for me in the task I am set, of recovering the titles to land and rights out of this torn up mess which is only a fraction of the original records.

I have to take charge of the confidential code; get the Gazette circulated through the district; see to the issue of notices under the liquor ordinances; make myself familiar with the whole file of prison circulars, hospital circulars and rules; the same for forestry, field cornets, traders' licences, arms &c. See to the insurance of government property; see to the powder magazines; arrange for the hearing of war compensation claims by myself; look after the markets, pounds, cattle disease, branding, brothel, *(and)* gambling regulations. I have to find men to fill the posts of J.P. and one of two resident J.P.s and help to get the Repatriation Camp wound up and the Agricultural Society onto its legs.

It is difficult for anyone to realise at home, the absolute chaos made in a district like this by the war, with nearly every farmhouse in ruins, land derelict, whole towns wiped out, the old residents dependent on their return on public aid to restart life, every civilian almost, overhead in debt, tradesmen unpaid, and no one to do the work on the roads."

On 1st August, 1903, he moved into his house on the outskirts of the town.

"There is no road yet up to our house save a faint kaffir track through the long yellow grass; there is no garden, nor even fence, nor any kind of enclosure. As for the house, it consists of simply four rooms of equal size, all opening onto the stoep,[3] which runs round three sides of the house ... under the eaves at the back of the house are two tiny little places in which cooking can be done, and stores kept. There is no outbuilding, no sanitary convenience of any kind. Inside there is not a fixture, nor a peg, nor any mortal thing. The floors are thick with dust and the walls too, and the windows quite opaque with dirt."

For two days Nellie and Lavender set about scrubbing floors and washing windows and walls. They furnished the house with their camp beds and camp chairs; their trunks served as sofas, and the packing cases doubled as sideboards, dressing tables and bedroom furniture. Nellie, with *"an old campaigner's foresight"* had brought Indian, Algerian and other silks and made the place sufficiently comfortable for their own tastes. Next, Alfred bought an old French cooking stove, which he set up behind the house. There was a tap outside and good water. The problem of sanitation was solved when a day or two later, attending a sale of the Repatriation Camp stock, he bought two sentry boxes for ten shillings. After removing the back panels of one box, they were fixed together, front to back, and a door made at the remaining open end. A packing case made a seat, and he installed a pan closet. A tin roofed hut, bought at the same time became an outside room. For this house he paid a rent of £120 per year.

The Commandant of the S.A. Constabulary in the district was Captain Shewan D.S.O., who had about 100 white mounted men under him. The S.A.C. posts throughout the district consisted chiefly of one white constable and one or two native police, mostly Zulus. There was another force, more or less coming under Alfred's authority. This was a body of men called the "Eastern Frontier Guards" that had been formed from a disbanded outfit after the war, then known as "Steinaeker's Horse." So far as Alfred could judge, the "Eastern Frontier Guards" were an awful crowd, and had been sent to the Portuguese border at Nomahasha, well out of the way of things, where, it was suspected, their principal occupation now was poaching and smuggling.

Before leaving England, he had engaged a groom who had followed out on another boat, bringing with him one horse. This was to save the greater expense of buying a horse upon arrival. Horse and groom had now arrived.

Alfred's day started at 5.30, when for an hour or so he did homework on frequently complicated compensation claim cases. After breakfast, either he or Oscar Staten would hear any criminal cases and pass sentence. After this he went on a tour of the gaol and hospital, or considered plans for improvements; then mounting his horse, galloped home for lunch, galloping back to work till evening when he was home by about seven o'clock, had his dinner, then back to considering compensation claims again.

224

In the first weeks, this routine was varied by visits to Komati Poort, the fever lands, and from there, in connection with immense compensation claims, he sometimes went on the disused Selati Railway the eighty kilometres up to Sabi River. This railway was being constructed when the war started. Now only the track remained. Bridges and stations had been destroyed, rolling stock, warehouses, and stores together with contractors' materials had been either commandeered or looted. The only means of getting up to Sabi River fairly quickly was by trolley, which had to be pushed along the grass covered track by a relay of natives, some resting on the trolley while the others pushed.

On arrival at Komati Poort for the first time, he found it to be nothing more than

> "... a straggling lot of shanties and tin stores with two decent buildings, as far as I could make out viz. the railway station and the customs clerk's residence. I was most hospitably put up by the customs clerk, W. Hutton. The Director of Customs, Honey, happened to be there ... *(and)* one Hotchkiss, a storekeeper ... I began by a tour of what is called the town, saw my Court House, a little red hot tin room, inspected the charge office, and constabulary quarters.
> Komati Poort is now considered a pestiferous and awful hole, where men linger for a year or two and then peg out with fever, but I do not think it will remain so if I get my way. The worst form of fever is 'Whisky fever'. The white population is ... with a few marked exceptions, a dreadful lot. One of my objects is to find someone fit to exercise judicial powers as a resident J.P.. Hutton has other work to do. Hotchkiss is a possible man, but he has strong prejudices, and is a German hater, he might be rough with natives too."

The man who thought himself best fitted to be resident J.P., was "Colonel Baron von Steinaeker". This man had been a German adventurer, in appearance a curiosity, very tall and slim-built with a moustache eighteen inches long, a foot of which was waxed, and complemented by a neatly trimmed beard. Such oddballs as Steinaeker interested Alfred enormously, and while coaxing whisky down the "Baron's" neck for two hours, he attempted to elicit from him the story of his life.

If there was truth in what he said of himself, he had had a strange career. He had been kicked out of the German army; claimed to have been a General in the Bulgarian army; obtained from Kitchener with his plausible tongue, a full Colonel's commission in the British army, was given a D.S.O., then sent to England to grace King Edward VII's Coronation procession. Despite Steinaeker's seemingly considerable

Colonel "Baron" "von" Steinaecker D.S.O.

26. *Colonel 'Baron' 'von' Steinaeker, D.S.O.*
(Sketch by Alfred Edward Pease.)

qualifications for being made a resident J.P., Alfred found sufficient excuse to avoid giving him this appointment.

After a few weeks' work, preparing plans for improvements at Komati Poort; for planting an avenue of pepper trees and other nice things, and trying to get the local population, as at Barberton, to take an interest in improving their own surroundings while he was acting as "a father to the people," Alfred realised the extent of this uphill task.

10th Sept. "I passed some heavy sentences today. Komati Poort is a sink of wickedness, and a refuge for rogues of all nationalities who have been too long allowed to do as they like. I am doing all I can to make the place healthier and pleasanter to live in, and I will do all in my power to help them, but brutality and such drunkenness as is prevalent here, must be severely checked.

I gave a locomotive fireman 3 months for being drunk on his engine, (the Mail from Pretoria to Lorenço Marques). It is impossible to describe the drunkenness and want of discipline on this railway. Some trains lately, have not been able to proceed after Komati Poort, as the driver, fireman, and guards were all helplessly drunk, and when we hunted up other railway employees for the emergency, they were in a similar state. I also fined a railway man £20, and a storekeeper £25, for brutality to natives. The first cut open a native's head with a fearful blow with a sprag, because he refused to procure him a black woman; and as a sample of the standard of morality here, the defendant gave the refusal of this demand as in his opinion, justifying the punishment inflicted on the kaffir. I am not one of those,

226

who do not realise the necessity of remembering the possible effect on the native mind of too suddenly changing custom."

It came as a sudden and nasty surprise to the white men, that they ran the risk of being punished for unmercifully sjamboking the natives.

While Alfred spent his days administering justice, Nellie's were spent in receiving visitors, entertaining them in their "house", and when not so occupied, she was giving Lavender lessons.

In mid-September, though suffering from fever, Alfred set out to visit certain parts of his district. He went to Wit River where the Government proposed making a great Land Settlement and where there was a large scattered population of poverty-stricken squatters.

It was difficult to know what to do with these scattered families. The scene was a most depressing one. Of those visited by Alfred the parents were dirty and the children shoeless, half naked and even dirtier than their parents. The men had been offered work at brickmaking, but the only work they were doing was scratching at a few square yards of mealie patches:

> "It is shocking that children should never be washed, nor taught anything. If I get a school here, as I shall do, how is one to get the children to the school over these distances without establishing a 'boarding house' - besides, they want washing and feeding and a Doctor within reach ... "

Being at pains to make friends with the people, he had to drink

> "... what they called coffee at nearly every place and I had not been able to face a meal for several days, yet I swallowed these nauseating drinks, made with sugar, dirty water and something else which may have been roasted mealies. I think one sample of what I went through will do. A filthy cup was produced and wiped out with the dirtiest rag produced from a dirty pocket in the dirtiest dress of a dirty woman and a still more filthy spoon found, which the woman licked out before stirring the sugar into the mess. But I drank it without flinching, and with a smile and a heaving stomach."

At lunch time and feeling ill with fever (if nothing else), Alfred went to lie down on the floor of a farmhouse belonging to a man named Lawrence.

> "I then rose *(from the floor)* for my afternoon duties which included the marriage of several of these Boer couples whose union depended on the occasional visit of the 'Magistraat'. All the couples were Bothas; they turned up with their parents and friends and sat round a long table in stolid silence, heavy ungainly creatures

mostly, who made a weird procession across the veldt as I watched their approach.

I was about to issue my certificate for one couple when I noticed that the girl was crying, so I told her not to be afraid and to tell me if anything was wrong. She said she did not want to marry this Botha. To her parents' indignation I told her she need not, and that unless she was sure ... I would not marry them. The mother was furious with her daughter, the father mildly expostulated, the bridegroom never moved nor spoke nor did any expression of any sort show on his face. The old lady finished up by saying that it was dishonourable for the girl not to marry a man who had given her so much 'finery'. I asked what he had given her. The mother replied 'a pair of boots, a pair of stockings and a pair of gloves.'

I took the girl with Lawrence as interpreter into Lawrence's room, and told her that she must tell me exactly what she wanted, that I would not repeat what she said ... the result being that it was clearly a wicked thing for her parents to force her. Then I sent for her father and the old lady insisted that she should be present too, but I kept her out of the way till I had dealt with the old Boer, who ... at heart took his daughter's side but who was terrified of his 'missis'. Then I sent for the 'missis' and told her what I had decided, and warned her that if she was not kind, and did not ... treat her daughter with a mother's affection and understanding heart, I should hear of it &c.

I asked the bridegroom if he had anything to say. He grunted out 'Nay', the girl dried her eyes and departed cheerful and the whole party ... filed away across the sunny veldt slowly, the old dame with set mouth followed by her husband followed by the girl followed by the bridegroom's parents, friends, bridegroom, one behind the other in most solemn Indian file."

Alfred found in due course that he, and other government officials, but especially himself, had become the target for abusive articles in the local press. These he traced as coming from his Health Board Secretary, writing under a nom de plume.

"I do not despair of turning him to better uses, but as he is a government servant and my subordinate, I sent for him ..."

After asking the man if he was the author of the offending articles, and receiving neither admission nor denial, Alfred delivered him a lecture saying,

"If a man takes service under a firm, under a government or under a private individual, as long as he takes pay and service under him or them, he is morally obliged to be loyal, and as soon as his conscience does not allow his actions to be loyal, he has no other choice if he is an honest man, but to resign his position. I left him to think over the matter, and do not intend to take any further action at present, as he would glory in being made a 'martyr' for conscience sake."

From this time on, the scurrilous articles in the paper ceased.

27. *The Rupture of the Betrothal. (Sketch by Alfred Edward Pease.)*

He had settled into a strenuous routine, and the challenging aspect of his work was to his liking. He was far too occupied with the present, to think where his long-term future lay. He felt that as far as Nellie was concerned, if in the climate of Barberton her health didn't mend completely - she was still subject to occasional lung haemorrhages - then a cure seemed depressingly unlikely. She never lacked for spirit, was utterly stoical, a great support, and uncomplaining of every demand of time and energy made upon her. Nevertheless, she hated the separation from her sons, and forced family dispersal.

Now that the worst of the last twelve months was over, she was quite determined to see Edward, and arranged to meet him in Cairo, from where they would both go on to Geneva to meet up with Christopher. She also wanted, during this time, to make advance arrangements for Lavender's further education in England. For Alfred, the prospect of Nellie setting out alone on this trip was unnerving. As the time for her departure approached, it was arranged that Alfred's sister, Maud, would come out to South Africa to be with Lavender during the day.

1904

The summer of December, 1903, and January, this year, was a bad one for malaria and horse sickness. This latter was a fearful scourge, with the animals often showing no symptoms at all until perhaps two or three hours from death, and often much less than that. The symptoms were a white discharge from the nostrils and "blowing".

> "None of the preventatives seems of much use, but I think there are few cases among stabled animals. This supports my own theory, which I believe some vets begin to hold, that it comes from *(the)* mosquito fly, or tick bite, and it must, (if this is so) be an insect that is developed, or whose bite becomes fatal, during the rains .and summer season; but how strange that no one has found the 'beast' that inflicts this shocking malady.
>
> The Portuguese at Lorenço Marques are dying like flies - 60 to 70 a day it is said - it is bad enough here - I brought back a man with fever from Komati Poort with me, intending to have him at the Barberton hospital as Boistock has his hands full at Komati Poort; he was raving mad, and on the journey 3 S.A.C. had to hold him down in the train - on arriving I could not put him in the hospital under the nurses, so I put him in the gaol hospital and asked Dr Worral to attend to him."

One of the curious things about young children he observed, was that they lost their teeth and hair very rapidly:

> "I should think there is not a single European girl without false teeth. Whether the result of water, or climate, or absence of milk, fresh butter, fresh meat or what I do not know."

During January, 1904, Nellie put all her affairs in order, and made preparations for her three months' absence from Barberton. As her time to leave drew near,

> *10th Feb.* "My heart sinks at the prospect of her leaving me out here at the end of the week, and I tremble when I look at her thin little frame and tired face, and at times I rebel at the partings and trials which are forced on us. The hope that the peace of the voyage homewards, the meeting with our boys, and a few months of civilised life may do much for her alone helps me to bear the thought of the separation, and my anxiety about her health."

He now, with Nellie gone, buries himself more in his work, and gives an indication of his open-to-all-comers office life, while he tries to cope with his daily correspondence.

"A man comes into my office with an old gun, and asks permission to retain the stock, *(and)* hand*(s)* over the old barrels; he holds a licence and wants to know if he may put his licensed barrel onto his unlicensed stock - next man wants to move stock onto another farm and asks for a permit. I send him to the District Vet. on whose opinion I act - A couple appear before me to marry them. I summon two witnesses from my staff - I put the necessary questions - in this case the woman is a divorcee, and produces no re-marriage certificate - I decline to proceed with the marriage till I have wired the Master of the Supreme Court - he sanctions it, but his reply comes after 4 00 p.m. when the law does not allow the wedding to take place - ceremony postponed till 8.45 tomorrow - next a man applying to be naturalised, and I take his application and administer the oath - but he is a Jew and has to go for his hat - Button comes in and asks if anyone may shoot on Sundays - I tell him the Law says 'No' but I have been directed that persons are not to be prosecuted under that section - Wilhelm comes to consult about the Voters Roll - then an old American comes in, indignant that after 17 years' residence he has no right to be on it - I tell *(him)* he can be naturalised but he won't have that ... and so the day goes on to 6.00 p.m. or sometimes to 8.00.

I sometimes get homesick and fed up, but I suppose I must go on, and that the future will shape itself for me - what has upset me most is a proposal to move Staten and leave me alone here - it will be several years before this District is reorganised sufficiently for one man to carry on - why, the court work at Barberton alone and hospital take up the whole of Staten's time."

Back in October the previous year, Alfred had arranged a public meeting, at which the people of Barberton were invited to express their views about trying to obtain municipal status for the town. He used his endeavours to get them to support it, believing that taking up some responsibility for themselves would tame them, and help bring to an end abuse of the government's local administration. The outcome of the meeting was support for the change, and in March, 1904, the Municipal Council was elected. Alfred having made all the preparations, acted as the Returning Officer. His assistant, Staten, was out of action, having gone down with fever. In April, Alfred also went down with fever, and was nursed day and night by his sister, Maud, who had arrived in March.

"As I recovered, I was depressed, and longed to escape from this fever country. Every time one of us goes to Komati Poort we are laid out with fever ... things that in ordinary health would not worry me were torments during this time; the thought that they might take Staten away, and leave me to battle with three men's work, and fever, alone."

With the coming of May, he was looking forward to Nellie's return. She had met Edward in Cairo on the outward journey. They had been to the pyramids, and travelled on to Geneva, where they met up with Christopher out from England. They arrived at Southampton on 14th April, then to Melksham in Wiltshire to see her sisters, on to London, then Birch Hall in Essex to see Gerald and Ethel Buxton, back to London, then Darlington, and to Hurworth Moor, Lloyd and Blanche Pease's home, and on 22nd April, to Pinchinthorpe where she found the house very clean, straight, and comfortable, and the garden beautifully neat. Harry Long who had been Joseph's coachman at Hutton was looking after the house and gardens wonderfully well.

During the time that Alfred was in the Transvaal, it was arranged that Herbert Samuel, Alfred's successor as M.P. for Cleveland, would occupy Pinchinthorpe House as his constituency home, at any rate for the time being.

After attending to things in the north, Nellie parted once more with Christopher for Winchester, and travelled back with Edward, leaving him in the Sudan, and sailed on to Delagoa Bay and Lorenço Marques where she and Alfred were reunited.

With Nellie's return to the Transvaal, Alfred's sister departed taking Lavender back with her to school in England. This was another great family wrench, but was made slightly less painful by the knowledge that proper schooling and the acquisition of some social refinements, of which there were few in Barberton, would be best for her.

Alfred and Nellie were now on their own. To make up for the expense of three months' peregrination, they let their four- roomed house, by now properly and adequately furnished, at £5 per week, themselves moving into even more modest accommodation.

Jack kept Alfred informed of news from home; that Edwin Fox, late of Pinchinthorpe Hall, had bought the "Palace", at Nunthorpe, on which so much money had been expended. Of Jack himself, he had been to Mexico in connection with some Pease & Partners business, and shortly after his return, had won back his seat as a director on the Board of that company.

In July, by which time Alfred had become Head of Native Affairs in the Barberton district, he went out to Jeppe's Concession, for an indaba with the Chief Metama. To get there meant leaving the railway at Hector Spruit, followed by a twenty-mile ride through the bush. Chief Metama was

"... a fine old Chief with 37 wives, which bevy of beauty were the source of one of his trials and grievances, on which we had a long discourse, and in which the old man had my sympathy.

There is now a £2 per head levy on wives; 'Wife Tax,' and the burden of paying £74 appalled him, and as he argued fairly, it was unjust to make it retrospective - nearly all his grievances were genuine; he had the usual and very reasonable desire to know, in face of the grabbing of all good native territory and 'farms' by the Land Department, where he might live without fear of being turned out. I sympathise very much with my Chiefs on this subject, as it is the practice of the Land Department to sell a farm (thousands of acres) to a settler, without making the slightest provision for the natives - This is one of the things I mean to get put right, but oh, what struggles, and correspondence it requires, to get anything done which common sense dictates.

The policy of ourselves, in the Native Department, is to protect the natives in their unsophisticated state, to maintain the tribal discipline, all useful and moral native customs, and their code of rules, and to prevent them becoming contaminated by the vices, and degraded into insolent apes by the whites. If you argue with a Land Department official, he is for breaking up the tribal organisations, and forcing the wretched native into the ghastly mess we call 'civilization,' according to Joe Chamberlain's ideal proclaimed here, to create 'wants,' (Brummagem products), and want money, and want work in order to satisfy his new created desires; it will be good for the Empire (Birmingham), and damn the kaffir; why shouldn't he work for the white man!"

Upon his return to Barberton, Alfred found a letter informing him that a cousin had left him a legacy of £1,000:

"It is by far the biggest legacy I have ever touched, and comes at a time when I have been worried about the mortgage on Pinchinthorpe which the Bank requires me to pay off. The whole of the fortune I received from my father was £1,000, and this I employed to reduce the mortgage, and I had to find another by December, & could not think how I was to raise it - and here it is."

On 12th August,

"What a host of memories of faces and of moorland does this date call up - I spent a busy day in Court and in my office, but my mind often turned to the hundreds now on the hills, and to the shooting lodges in the Highlands, where others are now enjoying what I used to revel in. The 12th was also Tom Fowler's birthday, he lies now in the cemetery at Ficksburg; the 13th 'Uncle John's' birthday, and the 22nd, the day in which nearly all material possessions were taken from me - & I can thank God, and believe it is best so."

Jack keeps Alfred fed with news from England:

"Till matters are settled at home *(further litigation and other problems)* I have to live out here, serving under men who have had very little experience of the world, and know about a tithe of what I know - it is sometimes humiliating, but I enjoy a great deal of my work, being a worker from love of it. Jack tells me that Pease & Partners *(£10)* shares are at only £7¹/₄!! "

At the end of the summer term in England, Alfred gave Christopher the choice of having one more term at Winchester or coming out to Barberton. Christopher opted for Barberton, and set out in August, 1904. In correspondence with Arthur Francis Pease, Alfred found Christopher a starting place at Pease and Partners to take up in the New Year. In early October,

"I had a very nice letter from Joe Lawley, written on the *Kenilworth Castle* on his way home - anxious about my repeated doses of fever, begging me to take Zeerust (District) instead of Barberton, and alluding to the good work I am doing - I told him I am old after the last two years, and would prefer going home if I cannot stick it - Nellie often begs me to get away from the fever here, but I do not feel inclined to - she likes it - and yesterday I put in an application for a perpetual lease with option of purchase, in case of deproclamation, (you cannot buy proclaimed land in a mining district), of some 13,000 acres near Louws Creek. It is a magnificent block of scenery, plenty of natives, and timber, with grazing and one or two well watered valleys. The rent would be about £30, and if deproclaimed the price about £1,500 - the place is full of game, kudu, bushbuck, impala, zebra, rhoi and vaal rhebok &c - and if I get this, I might quietly finish my days here."

8th Oct. "After a very tough week, I had to force myself to go to inspect my post at Sabi Bridge, and was very keen to show Kit *(Christopher)* something of my country, so taking my Mombasa boy, Salim, with us to cook, we went to Komati Poort, and took the trolley, and boys to work it as far as kilometre 29 on the abandoned Selati Railway that night; slept in the bush, in a deserted gangers' hut till 3.30 a.m., when we made tea and started with first signs of dawn for Sabi Bridge - I did this to let Kit see the Reserve. We reached the camp at Sabi Bridge at 12.30. On the way (81 kilometre) through the bush, we saw 9 steinbok, 3 duikers, 1 rietbuck, 1 hyaena, 2 wildebeest, 12 impala, 5 great ground hornbills, 6 quail, 11 partridges, 2 paw, 3 koran - It was extremely hot all the way. I found everything right, and not much to do except look at the records and sign things."

23rd Oct. "Col. S... (S.A.C.) has written me a rude letter about Lt. Bailie - I suppose they are mad with me for trying to put down scandalous irregularities in the Frontier Guard, and at my reporting that it can, without risking anything, and with a great saving of expense be disbanded, and any good men in it be drafted into the regular constabulary. I have written to him at length, and I hope civilly and to the point."

6th Nov. "One day, when one of the new warders was in charge of one of my convict gangs, I was giving him some instructions of how I wanted the road making, when he replied with a pure Cleveland accent. I could hardly believe my ears. I said 'Jones - you come from Cleveland.' 'Aye' he answered 'Ah cooms frae aside Redcar - I ken you Sir well eneaf.' I seemed to know his face, but couldn't think where I had seen him. He reminded me that he had once been 'Charlie' the whipper in - Another day, one of my convicts, having completed his sentence and being discharged, came to see me to get some advice as to his journey. He said to me - 'I know Hutton and Pinchinthorpe, and all about you and your family,' and told me he belonged to Whitby, and his father had been one of my Uncle Arthur Pease's supporters when he was an M.P. This man's name was Stanley; I gave him a little help after testing his local knowledge."

At the end of November, Alfred, writing in respect of his affairs at home, sees the prospect of £500 a year added to his income. He doesn't explain where he expects it to come from, but,

"I feel I can return home at any time, and possibly manage to live at Pinchinthorpe ere long."

The yearning to be back at Pinchinthorpe rapidly crystalised.

4th Dec. 1904 "I have pretty well made up my mind to wind up here with the financial year June next year, and to return home to my own country and my own people. I have done all I could here, and worked hard, and will during the next seven months, do all I can to put things on the best footing possible, and if spared, look to sailing next July. I shall have learnt much, and God knows if I shall have accomplished much - chaos has been restored to order, and if people here have, (apart from the devoted work of my staff), done little to help things, they certainly do much more than at the beginning."

Contemplating the future of South Africa,

"The speedy reconciliation of races in South Africa, is only to be brought about by leaving the country to run itself, and being content with nominal sovereignty, with bonds of mutual good will and respect. Undoubtedly this would be the best policy for the people who are here now, but if left to work out its own salvation, the Dutch will be the most numerous, and must be the preponderating element. Still, the admixture of British and other races will leaven the lump, and our own energy may keep a place for us till the races fuse."

On an overdue visit to the school which had been built at Wit River during the previous twelve months:

"I was very pleased with the school; they were Boers of the poor class (mostly) whom I had seen a year ago running dirty, almost naked and quite wild; some of them were bare foot, but many now can read and write."

Alfred was in Pretoria in December discussing with the Secretary to the Law Department, the best time to retire from his post, and it was decided mutually to make it 31st March, 1905.

In a letter Nellie sent to Alfred while he was in Pretoria, and in answer to his questioning her about the next phase in their lives, she gives a hint that she doesn't care what happens, as long as they are together:

> "... as for our own lives, I feel the days and the weeks and the years fly - just as our old library clock has so often told me" *(four pictures on the clock face, Spring; a shepherd and lambs. Summer; a gardener mowing and roses. Autumn; a harvester raking in a corn field. Winter; an old man by the fire)* "and yet I do not find any expression of what I should like, either to you or to my children ... I cannot show you somehow, that I have never in my life seen any man I would care for a moment to set beside you."

1905.

On 3rd January, Alfred went with Christopher to see him off for England from Lorenço Marques. Now the one thing in his mind is the happy anticipation of getting home, to seeing his daughter and being once more free.

> *2nd Feb.* "Staten has been away - he came back yesterday, so I took a run down the line to Tenbosch, to see the Komati Coal Field and stopped the train at the ganger's hut there. The ganger has died this morning in hospital at Waterval Onder, having been found here at his last gasp with fever - he has had to live here quite alone in this desolate fever bush. It almost gives you fever to look at this country with its 'Fever Trees' and their nasty ominous mustard yellow stems and trunks. Hotchkiss from Komati Poort met me, and we went on into the bush, where J. Moore is sinking the first shaft on the newly pegged claims - The Mines Department have by proclaiming it, given an assurance that it is a coal field - I spent a long afternoon and evening at this queer spot, looking at the coal indications in the measures, visible in the cliffs of a spruit beyond the shaft. From a study of the map, I think the best coal is probably beyond the Komati River; all the pegging is this side.
> I went down the shaft 53 feet deep and 6x4ft wide, all in rock, and had a nasty experience coming up. Hotchkiss and Moore were winding me up with a rope with a foot loop in it; when I was half way up, the rope was twisting and swinging and my foot slipped out. I did not know if I could hang on till they got me to the top, but I got my foot in before I got to the top.
> After dark, and a meal, Moore told me some yarns, like many I have heard from these old prospectors and diggers. He has lost faith in gold in this district."
> *10th Feb.* "OUR SILVER WEDDING DAY. It is 5.30 a.m. We have as usual slept on the stoep. It has been wet in the night, and the rain has kept up a constant rattle on the iron roof over our two camp beds - the mountain tops are in the mists, and they hang along the rivers down below in the valley - our Swahili boys are chattering and cleaning up behind, and the poultry are running about. I have just taken Nellie her tea and grapes, wished her many happy returns of the day and

received a sweet greeting ... I have often wondered whether we should see this day together, and where it would find us. It has found us together, far from home, with Edward at Khartum, Christopher beginning life at Darlington, and Lavender at Birch Hall - our little family, though scattered is complete.

I was at this hour 25 years ago, lying awake at the Methuen Arms, at Corsham, in a very cold room, and feeling very young, with a heart full of anticipation and confidence. Now I am battered and scarred, with hair turned grey and wearing spectacles - Nellie's hair is also turning slightly grey, but she still has the energy of character and that sweet courage that has kept us going ... I suppose if I pictured where we should be in 1905, it was amongst the festivities at home, surrounded by children, brother and sisters, with no guess that my heritage had passed away, and of all of us apart. But there remains to me, all that is best, and a quieter spirit dwells in me than in those far off days - And now to work at my office and in the gaol."

26th Mar. "There are but five days left for me of office - If the stress of work makes it easier to give up work, the expressions of regret, and the kindness of people make it seem difficult. This week, very poor people, as well as farmers and officials have said very nice things to me. Perhaps if I had guessed their feeling, I might not have given up. The one thing that seems to have pleased them most, is that no matter at what hour, nor how busy, I have always been accessible, always seen everyone, heard everything they had to say."

1st April. "Last night I finished my career as an R.M. - I saw a great number of people, paraded and inspected the gaol, held gaol court; took requests and complaints as usual - gave testimonials to the gaoler - also Native Affairs to Wheelwright - sent Slatter my thanks to the S.A.C. - saw Slatter - welcomed Staten and Cowie back - took the key off my bunch, handed it to Staten, left my office, *(and)* hauled down the flag for the last time.

Today is the sale of our household things, furniture and stock. I am going to exercise my first day's freedom in taking out licences to peg coal."

He had in fact one more duty to perform. Lord Milner was ending his term as High Commissioner, and being replaced by Lord Selborne. Alfred's last duty, was to go down with Capt. Slatter and a small constabulary escort, to see Milner safely out of the Transvaal.

3rd April. "We had the S.A.C. 'guard of honour' posted under the Union Jack at 11.00 a.m. on the station platform, and then awaited the departing High Commissioner who, when he arrived in his special train, stopped for 25 minutes at Komati Poort Station. I got into his carriage, and had a chat with him and with Joe Lawley, who was seeing him away too. They both said nice things to me about what I had accomplished, and then they steamed out and we beheld the last of the man who has made history here ... as he passed through the Lebombo and over the frontier, and out of the Transvaal for ever."

Notes:
1. ZASM House was Government House, Pretoria.   2.   Low hills.   3.   Verandah.

CHAPTER ELEVEN

Coal Mines & Gold Mines
Capri, Transylvania & the Sudan

Arriving back in England on 5th June, 1905, but being homeless as Pinchinthorpe House was occupied by Herbert Samuel, Alfred settled into a flat at 97, Cadogan Gardens for two months doing nothing in particular - seeing relatives and political friends - and lawyers, who were still, three years after the smash, raking about in the rubble.

At the beginning of August, Alfred went to Gerald Buxton's Essex home to collect Lavender:

> "... her eyes filled with tears as she left what has been for her, 'home' for a year, & those who had done everything they could to make it that for her - It is impossible to describe what Gerald & Ethel have done for me & mine for 3 years - the amount of trouble Gerald has taken to help us through the storm is amazing, and no one could have done more. His tact and sound judgement have been invaluable, and with it all, they have lavished their affection on us."

Nellie being with her sister Jean Fowler in Wiltshire, Alfred went to Darlington, where Christopher gave him a bed at the rooms he occupied. From there,

> "Kit and I to Pinchinthorpe where we spent the day rummaging in the boxes in the Museum[1] looking for things - It is stacked with Hutton boxes & my boxes & So. African cases - What a change all round!"

The next day, the 12th August,

> "Kit and I joined Jack at 10.00, & went to Ayton & shot the bit of moor I have from Proctor's Trustees. We started to shoot at 12.15. We had no dog, no keeper, Jack's man carried the lunch & I hired Campion to carry the bag - rather different from the old days - but we had a happy day together on the familiar ground & among the

views of moor & hill and bagged before 4.30 19 brace of grouse - We all went on to Headlam to spend Sunday there."

Headlam Hall, Gainford, Co. Durham was Jack and Elsie's new home in the north country. After a week-end stay there, Alfred went a round of visits to friends and relatives. On 21st August, he went to Horsley, Eastgate, to shoot with Col. W.H.A. Wharton of Skelton Castle, and Claud Pease,

"I am the only one without a dog for the first time in my life - & I am rather lost without one - I have not a house, a room or a servant & I am sick of the sight of my kit bags & trunk which I lug about from place to place ... I was not satisfied with my shooting. I shot for the first time with my father's Purdeys; they did not fit and one went wrong - & I have not shot for 3 years at driven grouse."

A week later, now joined by Nellie and Lavender, Alfred went to Pendower to stay with his Aunt Helen Pease, where he was

"... much struck with the luxury of life. It is curious how when you had all & everything & lived in luxury, you do not notice these things, & take all as a matter of course. Now that I have been without men & anything but necessities for three years, it seems strange to be in it all again - but I must say, I feel on the whole happier & freer for loosing all this, & have always been able to accept the change, & believe in its discipline & blessings - and were I ever rich again, I might have a few servants & horses, but should try to keep life simple - my idea if I get to Pinchinthorpe is to have my own personal surroundings quite simple & practical."

Whilst at Pendower,

"I went to Meeting for the first time for nearly three years with Nellie, Christopher & Lavender - I knew no one there - I liked the time for reflection & became more satisfied that all religion is within, & that for myself outward forms of conformity to religious habits & customs *(mean)* nothing to me - to me, prayer is more a self examining & trying to get right with one's soul & a submitting to what we call the Will of God. From custom & childhood's training, I appeal to God with my wants & for help, but I cannot truthfully say that I am conscious of any direct response, except that which comes from within."

From Pendower, on the wander, and still lugging his baggage, he next went up to Orgill Lodge on Orkney for a week with the Arthur Francis Peases and their four young children.

On again from there to George Albright's at Drumochter for a week's shooting, and then to a temporary base at Shull, near Hamsterley, South Durham. Leaving Nellie at Shull after a couple of days, he went up

239

to London to attend to one or two matters, but particularly to see one Taylor Hallett *"about our coal venture."*

Just before leaving the Transvaal, in May, 1905, Alfred had pegged 2,400 claims in the Komati Poort coalfields and he had got Jack to join him in this venture, and went into partnership with a Mr Edward Dicey, a personal friend who was an experienced mining engineer, in a further 2,000 claims. Alfred and Dicey, shortly after this, entered into another partnership with A.G.Taylor Hallett, also an experienced mining engineer who had also pegged claims.

Government test borings had revealed two seams in the Komati Poort coal field. The upper seam, at a depth of about 114 ft., was found to be between 7 and 10ft. thick, and 30ft below this seam, another of some 33ft in thickness.

It was estimated that a sum of £2,000 would be required to prove the coalfield, and the discussion Alfred had with Taylor Hallett was in respect of this. Arising from the discussion, the Delagoa Eastern Transvaal Coal Syndicate Ltd. was formed.

Alfred, Jack and Taylor Hallett were the English advisory Board, and Edward Dicey was made Resident Manager to superintend the sinking and boring. The railway line from Johannesburg to Komati Poort continued on to the coast at Lorenço Marques, which was close to the claim. The coal, believed to be in quality equal to the best Welsh coal, looked to have an assured market. Johannesburg was consuming approximately 400,000 tons a year, and if the coal proved to be bunker steam coal then the outlet was there at Delagoa Bay, where needed bunkering facilities could be established. The venture was speculative but if coal lay beneath their claims, they were confident that they were on to a winner. Should good fortune smile upon them, they would float the small development operation with an issue of shares in a public company with a £500,000 share capital.

In early September, 1905, while Alfred was in London and the south, he attended at Tunbridge Wells, the funeral of his uncle, William Fowler of European Petroleum Company fame.

"He once was rich; if he had died rich, he would have had a large funeral - I saw half a dozen of my relations who did not recognise me - a proof that age has altered me."

At the end of September, Alfred went to stay at Nunthorpe Hall, to which his cousin Edwin Fox had recently moved from Pinchinthorpe Hall.

"The house most luxurious & good - I am sorry for Jack & Elsie, but I cannot understand how Father could have been got to spend so much over them when he would never do anything of the sort for me who was just scraping along - I suppose he thought someday I should get Hutton - It is a sad business but Edwin is very happy there."

Whilst staying at Nunthorpe, Alfred went over to Pinchinthorpe to pack up a few things for his next sortie.

In London during the first two weeks of October, he had a further talk with Taylor Hallett about the their South African coal operation. Then final packing, and off on 14th October from Liverpool, bound for Naples.

Arriving there, Alfred and Nellie, Lavender and her new German governess spent a day or two at the home of an old friend of Cambridge days, by name Freddy Meuricoffre, who lived at Palazzo Meuricoffre, Capo di Monte. After a couple of days, Nellie went with Mdme Carlotta Meuricoffre to Capri, to spy out the land.

30th Oct. "Lavender & I left at 8 & went in the boat to Capri - & with some trouble got our luggage and things up to the Hotel Elena, where Nellie has arranged for us to stay en pension at 7 francs *(sic)* a day. Nellie has seen a number of Villas - & we looked at 5 in the afternoon, & before dark selected the Villa Mercedes belonging to a Russian lady Mdme Ganboni - It is at the extreme east of Capri, clear of the filthy town & on the edge of fine cliffs, overlooking the sea with a beautiful view. - It is built on the site of the villa that Augustus built for his daughter Julia. I agreed to take it furnished for 6 months at 100 lira[2] a month."

Calculating that living comfortably on the island for six months could be achieved for less than £200, this would leave him

"... £100 for Egypt & our getting back to England - my a/c is just over £300 credit at Barclays."
4th Nov. "Began the day by cleaning Lavender's & my own boots! I find they know nothing about boot cleaning here - it is a bore - I hate not having my boots cleaned & shall have to do this as well as clean the lamps."

Three weeks later,

"I wrote to Edward this week telling him there were enquiries for the purchase of Pinchinthorpe - I don't want to sell, but Nellie does not much want to go back there; thinks Hutton will be on my nerves, and Edward dreads not being able to make ends meet, or having to do things badly - If we could get £25,000 I suppose we ought to sell, but this is not at all likely - I cannot bear losing the last bit of footing in Cleveland & of my lifelong home."

Looking around his island base, a new idea struck him, one that he thought worth further investigation, and which he discussed with Meuricoffre, and this was

"... my scheme for acquiring the Cerlosa Monastery & ground for an hotel; it is the best site on the island ... the price is I believe £4,000 - there being no really 1st class hotel here, & the site being the sunniest in winter & high up in summer, and in every way admirable & attractive. I am sure there is a good thing & useful in it - some of the antiquities, Roman & others would work in, building material on the spot & labour cheap.

He *(Meuricoffre)* agreed to go with me to Felsobanya[3] in Hungary next week - a bore, but may lead to something."

This was a further scheme to investigate. Gold was being mined at Felsobanya.

8th Dec. 1905. "We left by the night train (Fred M. & I) for Rome & got there at 8 - we walked about Rome till 11.30 spending most of the time at the Colosseum, Forum & Capitol ..."

9th Dec. "After a little meal, we left for Ancona, & passed till dark through pretty mountain scenery - After dark the mountains & villages were all lit up with bonfires & illuminations in honour of Our Lady of Loretto - At Ancona, we got on the dirty little Austrian boat; a fine moonlight night."

10th Dec. "Not much sleep & arrived at 6.30 a.m. Fiume[4] - had coffee at a little Swiss shop in the town at 7 & left at 8.25 - we passed through rather nice mountain scenery for an hour or two & then got on to the hideous flats of Croatia & Hungary - At Agram[5] a man got *(in)* who spoke English, & he gave us a number of useful hints; his name was Szitagyi Karoly & he was agent for the Standard Life Insce. Co., ...

We reached Buda Pest about 10 p.m.. The weather here is beastly cold & the trains horribly heated & stuffy; they are comfortable but dirty & no water supplied to wash with on the longest journey - In the restaurant car, when you go in to dine, you cannot see the length of the car for cigar smoke & the heat is stifling - the officials & all most attentive - German gets one along, but porters & most do not speak it - there is a great hatred between the Croats & the Hungarians - the bad terms on which all these nationalities, Austrians, Croats, Servians, Bulgarians *(co-exist)* is curious -

We put up at the Central Hotel & left at daybreak (11th Dec) by the 8 train for Felsobanya. We changed trains & had lunch at Satmar[6] *(sic)* & crawled on to Felsobanya, taking 3 hours - we got out of the horrible plains & into the hills with snow on them - At Felsobanya, we were met by J. Dowe, Hallet's man & put up in the inn dining room where we had our beds & meals."

12th Dec. "Walked up in the morning, 2¼ hours to the mine I had come to see, Sujor Hill. It was very cold & bright & a good cover of snow - the population here are Bulgarians, the language Romansh, the officials speak Magyar, the population work chiefly in the government mines & other mines - they are a very hardy simple people - men & women wear the great sheepskin cloaks, the men astrakhan caps & the women shawls on their heads - they bind up their legs in sort of putees & wear clogs & primitive shoes - their attitude is very polite - their houses, neat cottages, white or blue washed with wooden roofs - the churches & public buildings fine & substantial -

The Sujor mine was purchased some time ago by a Mr C. King - It had been worked in a sort of way by miners in 3 levels - Dowe is at work repairing No 2 level from which samples have been taken, 10 tons treated at the govmt. works & others sent to Engd. for analysis - Dowe is sinking in an old winze[7] to connect No 2 & No 1 (the bottom level) as No 1 had to be abandoned on account of foul air. We spent an hour or two in the No 2 level & took samples; the roof here is about 13 feet & looks good, full of iron pyrites & galena - The surface of this ground is 25 acres & the surrounding ground is secured by search rights - Everything has been very primitively done - irregular drifts into the hill up to 800 metres (No 1), planks laid along the floor & a little tub on 2 wheels drawn out by a dog! - I saw the tub in the log hut where the miners have poor quarters & where we lunched, & bruised our heads against the ceiling; it is not more than 4'6" high! - what with these bumps & ones in the mine, my head was so sore at night I could hardly brush my hair - We got back after a 6 mile tramp to our inn."

13th Dec. "Started again in the snow to Sujor & went over the surface, examined the outcrop which appears to be about 100 feet in width. It has been worked at for 200 years or so & stories are told of great results at times - we looked at sites for dams & mills. Last evening we tried in vain to puzzle out the result of the Govmt. analysis; it is done in such a curious way that we were beat with it. This evening, Fizely, the Govmt. Official in charge of the mine dined with us & explained it to us, but it does not convey the same meaning as the English process."

14th Dec. "We spent going over the Gov'mt Mills & Concentrate Works &c - Even here they use the old *wooden* stamps for crushing, & these are worked by water wheels - We also spent an hour or more at Fizely's looking at his beautiful collection of local mineral specimens; some of his things are quite extraordinary from gold nuggets & gold flecked ore from Veraspartak to curious masses of Galena & crystals &c &c - Spent the evening in making notes.

The Hungarians are pleasant people & seem sensible & go ahead in a certain way - they are apparently very immoral according to our notions - I had always heard that it was customary at private houses to offer you a choice of the maid servants, but it was quite new to me to find that the hotels are staffed with women & girls at the disposal of visitors, & that all chambermaids have to go through the police visit twice a week - the girls are often pretty, attractive & clean, but it is rather a dreadful state of things for anyone unaccustomed to it - An Hungarian thinks no more about having a woman than about spitting, & in a way I think it is less nauseating and rotten than our British immorality, which relegates the woman to an outcast clan - Nature being what it is, & man & woman made what they are, it is right that they should come together.

Our social system prevents it being done decently & forces it to be done in the most indecent & cruel way - to the ruin of women and the brutalisation of man whose natural passions are perverted to the most selfish ends - I think this question

243

is one of the most difficult & most important ones in the world. It has never affected me personally ... but one cannot go through life & not be convinced that man was intended, & woman too, to come together & to prevent it is to demoralise nearly all men & to preserve a class of pitiable women who lose all their womanhood."

15th Dec. "Left in the morning and got to Buda Pest at 9 p.m. - Central Hotel."

16th Dec. "Saw Horsly Pal after walking all about the gloomy cold town; he is a member of the Parliament, & much interested in the other mining propositions I have been asked to interest myself in at Veraspartak - he is a nice fellow I think, & after explaining the position at Veraspartak, & the proposal that the Hungarian Govmt., *(and)* the Hung. Bank should go in on equal shares with English capital, gave me a good deal of information on the state of politics ..."

Parting from Freddy Meuricoffre at Naples, Alfred returned to the Villa Mercedes on 19th December.

"The whole cost of my journey including hotel bills, meals, purchases, tips, postages, telegrams & entertaining &c was £18 - the zone system makes travelling a distance very cheap."

25th Dec. "Christmas Day - We all went to Church and had turkey & plum pudding for lunch & gave each other little presents when we came down this morning - the people here celebrated the anniversary of Our Lord's birth with bands & fireworks all night - perhaps not much less appropriate than the British method of doing it with surfeit & stomachaches, football matches & the like.

There is much that puzzles me in the conduct of those who profess orthodox Christianity - This morning, we had the Athanasian Creed & a sermon - the latter rather nice till the parson began congratulating us on our good fortune in not having come into the world before Christ, and dwelling on the love & mercy of God in sending his only son to save the world, that up till then was lost - It seems hard luck on all who came before him ... We are here with what we call souls, which know of right & wrong, & what is lovely & what is hateful, & they respond to the teaching of Christ, & man goes on saying Lo here is Christ or Lo there,- when the Kingdom is within us - Thus far I am a Quaker."

31st Dec. "I think another year living quietly in one place we can manage all right, & I hope that I may be able to earn something ... On Tues. 2nd Jan. I start for the Sudan - leaving them here - I hope no harm will come to them. Edward I hope to see after a long separation (3 years) at Suakin & Christopher seems well & content at Darlington."

1906

7th Jan. "Arrived Alexandria after a remarkably dull voyage, & glad to get out of the frightful noise made by the Italian passengers; they shout instead of talk, & scream imbecilities in a whirlwind of gesticulations all day; are filthy in their habits, spit at meals, pick their teeth, dirty linen, never have a bath & always wear

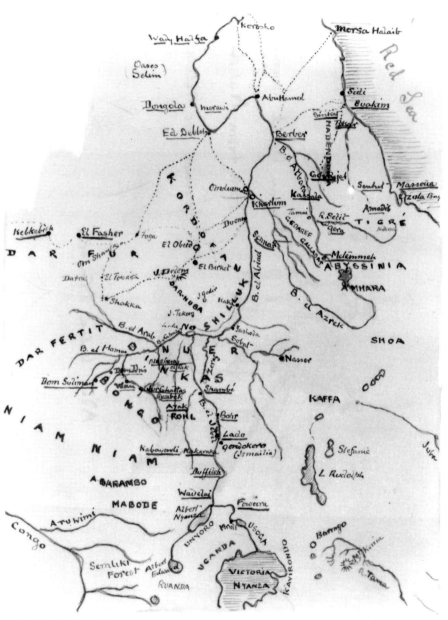

Wadi Halfa – Lake Victoria

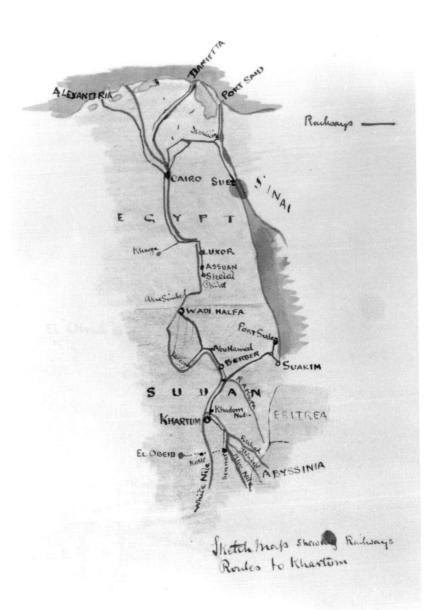

Railways ———

*Sketch Map shewing Railways
Routes to Khartum*

Alexandria – Khartoum

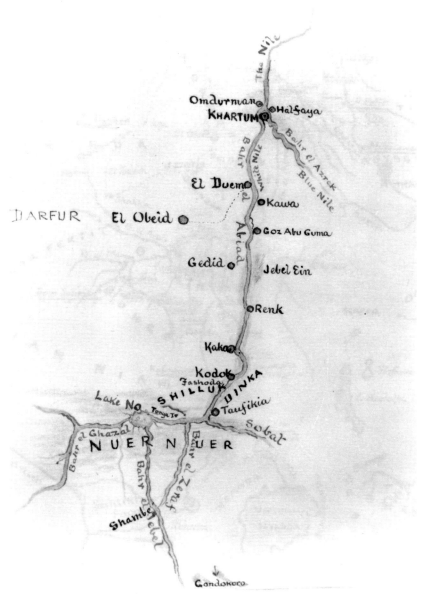

Khartoum – Shambé

new clothes - the women are fat & useless, & spend every minute arranging their appearance in front of looking glasses - the men cannot pass a mirror without looking at themselves in it - what they usually see there would make a dog sick."

9th Jan. (Alexandria) "To Cooks - Then to Sudan Agency. Saw Parker ... & Capt. Owen, the Chief - the latter particularly pleasant & explained that our desert trip would have been really dangerous, & that it could not in the present condition of that country be possibly allowed - he also gave me information that we are going at Lake No, on to ground where no white officer has yet been, & where the Nuers have not made their bow to British authority, & that they could not tell whether they would be pleased to see us or not - I am quite sure they will be - I have never yet found any wild natives who could not be conciliated with a little patience, & a few presents, if you see that your native following behave decently."

On 10th January, Edward North Buxton (then aged 65) arrived at Alexandria with Theresa, his youngest daughter. With Alfred, they called on Lord Cromer,

"... who gave E.N.B. a dreadful wigging for plaguing his officials - only partly deserved as they first sanctioned our addax trip beyond Tabari - then prohibited - then wired veto withdrawn - then imposed conditions, found on examination to be both inconsistent and equivalent to prohibition of reaching addax ... Cromer looks a very feeble bent old man, & was not particularly agreeable - tho' I like a chief who likes to protect his officials."

By way of Luxor, Aswan, and Shellal they reached Halfa on 13th January, 1906. Alfred was

"... interested in seeing a place where Edward was stationed some time, and where, for a period he was 'Acting-Governor' of the Province."

14th Jan. "Passed Atbara in the night, where I expected to meet Edward on his way to Khartum from Port Sudan as he is due there for Arabic and Law examinations - but he was not there ... dusty journey and hot - sand storm - reached Khartum North at 3 p.m., four hours late owing to the sand storm and there met Edward on the platform after more than 3 years' separation - he seemed a bit drawn & tired.

The Sirdar (Wingate) had most kindly sent his launch to bring us across the Blue Nile to Khartum - I spent from 4 - 7 with Edward, and we managed to get through some talking, but there is much to hear and say with regard to all that has happened since the dark days when we parted, he for the Sudan and I for a new life in the Transvaal, & most of the talking had to be done whilst rushing about with E.N.B. about our affairs ...

We all, including Edward dined at the Palace - Slatin Pasha[8] was there, a man I had wanted to meet; I enjoyed his company but was astounded to see a man who had lived through such appalling experiences so young, so gay, so fresh without a trace of his years of nakedness, torture, imprisonment and slavery - he was a very amusing and cheerful man to talk to, and gave me a thrilling account of his 12 years' slavery, and especially his escape, his flight across the desert and arrival at the British outpost[9]."

After parting from Edward who had work to do, Alfred and Buxton and Theresa went on to Omdurman by the Government steamer, and on down to El Duem. At Khartoum, they had called on *"Wild Beast Butler"*, the game warden who

"... pressed us to shoot all the hippo we saw - a nice thing for the Game Preservation Officer to do! But it is the official attitude here. It is senseless to exterminate the few at a place like this. There are not enough of them to do very serious damage to crops, and the natives, before our advent, were accustomed to swarms of them, and were never in such security as regards their crops and their markets as now ... the native is a better man for having to fight with hippo, and to make efforts for the protection of his crops ... but it is not for the sake of natives that we introduce civilization, but for the pockets of the commercial gentry ... Some people's ideal is to see the natives here transformed into a squalid mud-hoeing population like the Delta fellaheen."

At Renk, on 19th January, they took on board two shikaris, and two Selim Arabs.

20th Jan. "Passed Kaka about 10.40 a.m. and saw the first Shilluks with their curious head dress - the men are stark naked and carry spears and fish-spears - I also saw today on the East Bank a herd of about 200 buffalo, perhaps many more, all covered, and the ground round them, with white egrets. On the same side, which is the Game Reserve, I also saw white- eared cob in large herds for the first time."
21st Jan. "Made Kodok (Faschoda) about 3 a.m. - breakfasted at the Mudir's[10], Colonel Mathews and two other officers. Mathews was most kind in supplying us with information about the Nuers - he is only just getting into touch with them ... here I got a wire from Edward to say he was leaving Khartum for England; I am glad for him, but sorry to think he will no longer be at Khartum when I return. I fear he is about worn out with fever, dysentery, exams & work. At 11 a.m., Mathews found us a tame Nuer (Abd el Kheir) as an interpreter (can interpret out of Dervish Arabic into Nuer, and vice-versa). We boarded our Gyassa[11] and bid goodbye to the steamer, and with a stiff breeze were soon out of sight of the dreary place."
22nd Jan. "Passed Taufikia in the night - at dawn both banks were lined with villages, Dinkas on the East, Shilluks on the West. Here and there were patches of dhura[12], but I did not see much else in the way of cultivation ... today I saw several herons, lots of guineafowl and hippo - We ran into sudd[13], and stuck fast for 3½ hours ... The birds are wonderful, crowned cranes, herons, bitterns, night herons, great purple (rufous under wing) herons, a deliciously bright rufous coot, terns, fish eagles, waders, king-fishers in variety, myriads of weavers and clouds of

finches - Reached the mouth of the Zeraf, a narrow winding channel, difficult to sail up - saw gazelle and oribi from the boat - got up some seven miles and made fast, miles of sudd - millions of mosquitos bested us in spite of our mosquito protection. Before dark, I went on land and saw a lot of defassa waterbuck but did not disturb them; enjoyed seeing the tracks of much game including fresh giraffe and old elephant."

23rd Jan. "A lion roared at 4.30. Up at 4.50 - went out with Kheiralla and Abd el Kheir, and struck inland into a mixed grass and bush country, the grass partly burnt - saw gazelle, oribi, a herd of defassa amongst which was a nice bull. I got within 200 yds of his tail and got him - his horns were 25 inches. I saw 15 roan antelope; got within 400 yds of them but could not get up to 300 ... I went out again in the evening and saw lots of elephant and giraffe tracks & of course hippo tracks. Got near a Nuer village called Lil."

24th Jan. "Off at 5.30 a.m. with E.N.B. and Theresa to visit Lil in order to collect information about 'Mrs Gray'[14] which we cannot locate ...

Edward Buxton and Theresa went on to Lil, and I to look for the roan *(antelope)*.

While looking for a reedbuck I had shot in a labyrinth of high grass, I suddenly looked up and saw two gigantic Nuers, each with three spears and a club, stark naked and ashy corpse blue, wading straight for me through the 6 foot grass - when they suddenly caught sight of me, these two stood rooted to the spot, and I saw a third, far behind, stand for a moment, get a peep at me (I was on an open patch) and run like a hare. The other two waved their open hands forward - it is a sign of friendliness & not what I have seen described by Garstin as a deprecating sign - I did the same; they came and kissed my hand, and then Taleb's - adding a spit to Taleb's.

They stayed with me till I shot 2 Oribi for them, one being a nice male ... I left them dividing the meat with their spears. They were each of them at least 7 foot high, very long legged, covered with white wood ash and splendid young specimens ... I met E.N.B. and Theresa returning from Lil with a band of naked Nuers; a great friendship had been struck as Edward had agreed to take 25 Nuers across the Zeraf, men and women. This we did the same afternoon when they turned up where our boat was moored. Unlike the men, the women had a slight fringe of something round their middles, and some even a scanty skin petticoat."

26th Jan. "This day we tried to get in touch with Nuers in canoes, but all were frightened and paddled away as fast as they could ... We decided to push on to Lake No."

28th Jan. "At 11.30, we entered Lake No ... the lake is a queer place; you see no defined shores, only reeds as a rule all round the horizon, and floating islands, small & great, of Sudd. Where there is a bit of land between the khors[15], it is very flat, covered with rather thin coarse grass and innumerable low anthills. This puzzles me, and makes me wonder more than ever at these termites, which must survive when all this country is deep under water. Fish rise all over this lake, serpents swim on the surface - the fish jump high, and now and then a monster shows itself. Hippos grunted all night but though numerous do not show a great deal."

250

28. Our Gyassa.

29th Jan. "We set sail on this weird lake for the Bahr el Ghazal - beyond such boundaries of reeds and papyrus which form the horizon of Lake No, there are labyrinths of lagoons and khors, and there can be seen, only here & there, on a very different horizon, bushes & trees which give evidence of dry land.

Omar, who has navigated these waters before, either played us false at the helm, because he didn't want to go up the B. el Ghazal, or is incredibly stupid ... but he sailed us into a bay without an exit, with the wind pressing hard behind us, from which, only a very hard day's work wearing on cables attached to the reeds and poling extracted us. From the first I felt he was steering wrong and that even without a knowledge of navigation, a course along the northern shore would take us, sooner or later to the entrance of the river ... a fearful fuss all day - E.N.B. took the Berthon boat and reconnoitred for a channel through the reeds and sudd, and at sunset found a way through into the Ghazal."

30th Jan. "At dawn we sailed for three hours with a faint breeze; the river is extremely narrow, not more than 40 metres wide between banks, or rather walls of reeds & papyrus - on the true left bank, to the north, we could see the whereabouts of Nuer villages; at least the men said they were Nuer, though I understood up till now, that the Nuers were all south of the B. el Ghazal. But to the south, even when one climbed our mast, one could see nothing but endless swamp. Later in the day,

251

the land to the north also receded out of sight. After this, we sighted the solitary palm, mentioned by Junke'r, and here, just to the north of the palm, is the inflow from the Khor Delab. This khor looks as if it were, but is not, the main river. Today we have seen scores upon scores of Balaeniceps Rex, but up to today, only a few. I should think there hardly exists any bird on the face of the globe so protected by the inaccessibility of its habitat.

In the afternoon, as we continued our difficult progress up the river, we were overtaken by a government irrigation steamer ... We boarded their boat at their invitation, but had a very near escape of being hurt or drowned, or eaten by crocs. as our little Berthon boat got crushed between their boat and our Gyassa. They promised us, if we could get our 'Mrs Gray' in time, to give us a tow down when they returned from their inspection of the Bahr el Arab in 4 or 5 days' time. This made us easy in our minds about continuing up as we were hesitating about this, as we calculated that with the wind as it will be till March, that for every day we sailed up, we should require almost a week to wear & pole down, and if the wind was stiff and much sudd, perhaps 2 weeks for every day we went up. Tied up to the reeds for the night as usual."

31st Jan. "Sailed another hour up - I then got to land & did a long tramp through khors and got very hot, wet and dirty, but reached at last the woods which I have seen afar off from the boat, the foreground sprinkled with woods and absolutely teeming with cob, reedbuck and oribi and the ground covered with hundreds of quite fresh tracks of giraffe; saw only one in the distance. There was a fine forest on the horizon which I longed to explore - I shot 3 male white-eared cob and one reedbuck. On my return watched crocodiles crossing the river; they are often difficult to detect with their wood-like snouts just above the water and among the floating debris and sudd. The number of a particular kind of snake, dark green with a yellow throat and about 4 feet long which we see swimming is curious; they were very numerous in Lake No.

We made fast ... this evening and got in contact with some people from a village said to be only about a mile off, but evidently big khors intervene, and the country looks a sea of big reeds as far as one can see. It is easy at sundown to locate these villages, as at sunset, the natives burn wood and cow dung, and make a dense pall of smoke over every village for defence against mosquitoes, which here, are not simply in millions, but the air thick and dense with them, & of various sorts. Under this canopy of smoke, and lying in deep beds of wood ash, the Nuers sleep protected from an enemy which I believe, would kill almost any man left exposed at night in some three to four hours. The Nuer habit of covering their bodies with white wood ash, gives these giant men an awful deathly and weird appearance."

1st Feb. "We took today the most extraordinary 'road' to reach the village of the people who visited us last night which I have ever seen in years of travel. This is the dry season and the high road to the village was a sort of canal through a lagoon, walled with high strong reeds. We made our way with the help of a giant each, through the water, often up to the chest, and dirty smelling filthy water it was with the mud stirred up, but nice and warm, and after a struggle through deep black mud, reached the village. We were for at least a mile, up to or over the middle in water.

252

Jo This a bronze
or living Specimen
of Balaeniceps Rex

The Balaen Garden Khartum

29. *Balaeniceps Rex.*
(Sketch by Alfred Edward Pease.)

On landing at the village, it was early morning and the people just moving about and getting the cattle out ... We had an excellent reception and had a great indaba with the Chief and his population of giants ... Theresa & I were promised the sight of elephants nearby, and also of roan ... our guides were the Chief & 4 giants - we did not see the elephants, only plenty of fresh tracks, and though we saw plenty of hippo, the roan turned out to be defassa waterbuck & white-eared cob - I shot one of these (the waterbuck) a fine one with just under 30 inches of horn. The best horns I have ever seen, & then we waded back to our boat."

2nd Feb. "We sent the Berthon boat on overnight with carriers, to the khor beyond the village where Theresa & I had been, & then this morning, took outfit for a small camp by the khor, and after fixing the site, started for a place beyond the khor where three of the Nuers promised to show us 'Boag' as they call Mrs Gray's waterbuck.

We crossed the khor in our little boat in detachments, & while one lot crossed, one of us kept down the hippo with rifle fire, otherwise there seemed to be a fair chance of some of these very numerous beasts eating up or at least upsetting the little craft. Then we tramped across burnt plains, sprinkled or thick with scrub, and waded through six deep & awkward khors. After some 7 miles of this tramping and wading, we came on to the edge of another big khor with open water, where our guides said were the haunts of 'Mrs Gray'. But they scouted for her in vain while we rested under a 'Gob' tree. While we were sleeping there, some women from another village came to gather the Gob berries which had fallen & got a very nasty turn when they saw us.

253

It took us till sundown to make back to camp by the khor - a very hard day for Theresa - she had a small tent - E.N.B. & I tried to sleep on our camp beds under our mosquito nets, but we had a hell of a night, for culex fatigans and many other kinds poured into the nets through fissures & crevices in the ground, which was simply cracked mud ... to add to the infernal nature of this night, the hippo, not content with roaring, came ashore in great numbers and made the most frightful noise. The hippo became a nerve racking nuisance, so, muffling every bit of myself up, I seized my rifle and rushed amongst them determined to kill one, and I think did so as I fired into a great dark mass twice as he rushed past me into the water - this operation quietened the hippo ... and in spite of being muffled up, I was most cruelly punished by the mosquitoes."

3rd Feb. "Tramped 6 miles in the morning but saw nothing but hippo and unwanted things, so we all returned to our ship & sailed for an hour further up the river & tied up."

By 6th February, they had returned to Lake No, Buxton's efforts to get a male waterbuck had met with success, and they moved on to more pleasant ground. On 10th February, they moored up opposite one of the last of the long line of Shilluk villages fringing the northern bank before getting back to the Zeraf, and here, after a long stalk, at 150 yards,

"... seeing the great moment of my trip had arrived, I raised myself very slowly, got a bead on his chest and killed him stone dead, he having given me my favourite shot ... He had a fine head.

When we regained the boat, I had a nasty turn - the Gondokoro boat had passed and left us our first mail, a big one, with two letters from Nellie, the last of Jan. 17th, but with one from Lavender saying her mother was ill, and had been in bed & not allowed to speak for three days - I knew this meant a haemorrhage from the lungs. E.N.B. most kindly let our nugger *(sic)* start for Taufikia with a unicode cable from me."

12th Feb. "I had a strange & horrible experience in the night - at 3.30 a.m., I put out my hand after untucking the edge of my mosquito curtain from under my mattress to reach my canvas water bottle, and carefully and slowly drew it through it, and was immediately attacked by what I thought in the first moment were mosquitos, but they swarmed up my arm - I dropped the bottle on the floor of the cabin - In a minute, the creatures had hold of me all over - like a hundred tweezers - I leapt out of bed in the dark, only to find I was standing in deep moving masses - it was pitch dark - I tore off my pyjamas, and wrenched and swept the mounting myriads of what I now realised were ants of some dreadful kind - in a few seconds, my legs and body were columns of great ants holding on with nippers - nearly mad with pain & alarm, I yelled for Hassan who was sleeping on the roof above to come - & had the presence of mind to shout to Theresa in the next cabin on no account to move or touch her mosquito curtains.

E.N.B. was sleeping under his on the roof - Hassan hurried to me, but I was about to throw myself into the river to the crocs. or anything else when he shouted that there was water in the canvass bath in the bath cabin. I rushed there and stood in the water - Hassan arrived, luckily in his boots and stockings and day clothes, and kept sweeping them down off my body - reached in the dark for soap - found some - soaped hard while Hassan bailed in water from the river & kept throwing the buckets over me - he was immediately covered too, & the whole bath cabin was covered with them - they ceased to swarm up me, but many you had to tweak the bodies from their heads and claws as they hung on like bull dogs. Hassan was splendid as tho' covered himself, he rushed to my trunk through the seething mass and snatched a pair of trousers & a shirt & I put them on in the water, jumped on his shoulder & he carried me to the roof of the deck house.

Meanwhile, Theresa called to me that she was getting ammonia. I screamed to her not to move, but she had already just put her hand out and been attacked but warned in time made her net fast at once. Once on the roof, I took refuge under Buxton's net ... Hassan on reaching the roof tore off his clothes dancing and squealing while our two Arabs wrestled with the enemy clapping him all over and getting him clear.

When daylight came it revealed a most curious state of affairs. The whole boat, except the roof was one moving mass of ants & we saw them pouring on board, over reeds smothered with them that were in contact with the boat - some were fighting their way back to shore laden with loot (dhurra seeds &c) - when we looked to the shore, there was a great trough or road worn through the mud, all along the bank side, worn by these vast armies, and along this road more millions were pouring on -

Well, - by means of burning grass brought on board and boiling water and sweeping we cleared the ship of masses - and those which remained seemed to disappear gradually with the rising sun. I noticed that these ants were of different ranks for every ten to thirty of them, there was a big one with a great black head and lobster black nippers."

After this experience, they got the gyassa under tow from a passing boat to Taufikia, arriving there the following day. But during the night the ants re-appeared from the bilge and timbers. Alfred took refuge on the roof again. At Taufikia,

"... with tar & creosote and boiling water from the steamer we continued our campaign against the ants & then came down from the roof."

At daybreak on 14th February, he observed that the ants not slaughtered had transferred to the boat whose crew had aided them, but with a clear conscience, knowing that their helpers had better resources to fight the invaders, they cast off, drifted unnoticed, & then raised sail and watched, while all hands on the steamer were distractedly engaged in combat on their own account with the enemy.

When they got to Kodok, Alfred found a cable giving reassuring news of Nellie. From Kodok making slow progress, drifting down stream against a head wind, covering only about six or seven miles a day, making periodic stops and uneventful forays, they arrived at the point where the Khartoum steamer called on 1st March, and after paying off their crew, went on board the *SS Cairo.*

They arrived at Khartoum on 4th March, where Alfred took a large ground floor hotel room for two nights. On the journey, he had acquired a menagerie of two parrots and a monkey.

6th Mar. Khartoum. "I have much bother with my menagerie as it is composed of babies, and I have picked up another sort of baby to look after it -
Yesterday morning at dawn, I was lying in my bed, the windows wide open on to the verandah, when I saw a tiny little Arab boy who had been on the steamer from Goz Abu Guma, & who I had observed making himself very useful on board, come to my open window. He wore only a little white shirt; it was not yet 5 a.m.; he entered noiselessly, never looked at me, but tidied my room, folded my clothes, dusted my boots, emptied my wash basin, folded my towel - I then asked him who had sent him. He replied no one, that he knew no one at Khartum but was going to be my servant. He then untied a knot in the corner of his little shirt and put some 15 piastres in my hand & said that was all his money. I said what do you want me to do with it - he replied, when you go back to Egypt, I want you to take me back to my home at Abu Simbel.
I found that this little child, of perhaps 10 or 11 years of age, had been taken as a servant by an Egyptian officer into the Sudan and abandoned there; that he, with great resource, had managed to get on board steamers and work his way back to Khartum, and hit on me as a likely means of getting him over the next 1,000 miles.
I said, you know the journey in the trains & steamer will cost many, many more times than your 15 piastres; he simply said 'I am going with you, and will look after you, and the monkey, and the birds.' He kept his eyes fixed on my face and went on - 'I cannot go like this,' looking for a moment at his tattered but spotless shirt, 'I must have a new kamees, a tarbush, babug and a mahreme' - pointing to my pocket handkerchief. 'Give me the money and I will go to the souk and get these things.' I smiled, and gave him back his money and put a few more piastres to it, and off he went and was back, neatly outfitted in about an hour, with a little red tarbush, red slippers a new shirt and white socks and a little pocket handkerchief.
From that moment, he was always there night and day, anticipating everything, bringing me my tea at 5 a.m., cleaning my boots, washing my clothes, attending beautifully to my room and menagerie, or my cabin on board ship, carrying my parcels, understanding and carrying chits and messages.
This child is a wonder, and makes me think a good deal on one of my favourite questions, 'What really is education?' - This child knows more of the problem of how to live and how to travel, and is a better judge of human nature, has seen more, is more perfect in his carrying out of the job he has put himself to than any of our pedagogues and political lights in education matters."

Leaving by train from Khartoum to Halfa with his parrots, monkey and the little boy, they were in a sand storm for much of the journey, which slowed their progress.

8th Mar. "At Halfa we left the train and took the boat and passed Abu Simbel 1.30. Here at Abu Simbel, my little Arab boy regained his home and parents, and left his master with just a smile - which was quite eloquent enough for me."

Notes:
1. The Museum was an addition to Pinchinthorpe House and built in 1898. In dimensions 40ft x 25ft, it served Alfred as his big game trophy and writing room.
2. Approximately £10 at the then prevailing rate of exchange.
3. Now, following frontier changes, in Rumania and renamed Baia Sprie.
4. Renamed Rijeka.
5. Renamed Zagreb.
6. Now part of Rumania, the old Hungarian name Szathmar, changed to Satu-Mare.
7. Ventilation shaft.
8. Sir Rudolph Baron von Slatin was Inspector General.
9. Slatin wrote of his experiences in a book entitled *Fire & Sword in the Sudan.*
10. The local Governor.
11. A Nile dow with a deck cabin amidships, in all about 25 - 30ft in length.
12. Millet.
13. Floating vegetable matter.
14. Mrs Gray's Waterbuck, Cobus Maria Gray.
15. Dry watercourses.

CHAPTER TWELVE

British East Africa & the Pioneer

Upon his return to Capri on 17th March, 1906, Alfred found Nellie better than he had feared might be the case. Lavender now into long skirts, was looking radiant and had her hair done up. Edward had returned to England and was in a nursing home recovering from dysentery, but was cheered by the news that he had passed his exams in Law and Arabic with very high marks:

> "The Sirdar has singled his name out for mention particularly."

Of the three enterprise schemes that Alfred had in the boiling pot (in the Transvaal, in Hungary, and turning the Cerlosa Monastery into an hotel) the last, after further discussion and consideration, had now been abandoned.

On 8th April, Mt. Vesuvius erupted, pouring enormous quantities of lava down the mountainside and enveloping the whole of the Bay of Naples and Capri in a gigantic cloud of dust. Within a few days the streets of Naples were reported as lying three feet deep in ash, with many roofs collapsing under the weight of it. Many people died in the villages near the foot of the volcano.

Also this month, news of an explosion of a different kind reached Alfred. His cousin Edwin Fox at Nunthorpe Hall had failed for £60,000.

> "This is sad news - There seems to be a fatality about Cleveland. The last three owners of Nunthorpe have come to grief - Isaac Wilson - J.A.P. - E.K. Fox. Next door - Wm. Hopkins at Grey Towers. Just beyond, the Bolckows at Marton, Raylton Dixon at Gunnergate, & Swan at Upsall. Theo. Fox[1] hardly escaped & left Pinchinthorpe ruined as also I did in 1903."

258

Other news was that Sir David Dale had retired and he died not long afterwards. Arthur Francis Pease had become Managing Director of Pease & Partners.

"No hint that they would like me on the Board!"

Alfred, Nellie and daughter left Capri and arrived in London on 14th May. Alfred spent a day in the city talking over the Veraspartak and Felsobanya gold mining projects, and the Komati coal venture with Taylor Hallett before making north for Pinchinthorpe, the house having now been vacated by Herbert Samuel, and for a whole week, before Edward returned to Suakin, and with Christopher at home, they were all together as one complete and united family for the first time since 1903.

"I cannot put down what I feel at the goodness of providence, in allowing the cherished hope of three years, so full a realisation - to be complete in numbers & under our old roof it has been a happy homecoming.
Pinchinthorpe looks much the same, the garden gay with narcissus & polyanthus, the old peacock & hen in their usual haunts with 2 of a younger generation - the orchards in full bloom - I have heard once more the birds' songs in the early morning - my hair as well as Nellie's is turning grey, our children nearly all grown up - the house is full of Hutton things - the stables & fields are empty. Long, the old Hutton coachman is my gardener - we have three maidservants & intend to live as simply as possible. Lavender is busy with her new poultry and looking after the two dogs - Marvel & Bustle. The Wards, Moons & Welburns are on their farms without any change."
27th April "Today - wrote to ... Arthur who has asked me to join Wilson Pease's Board & asked me if I would like to join the Middlesbro' Owners Board - I have said yes."
3rd June "It is a lovely day, the lilac at its best, the laburnum just out, narcissus still blooming & the may bursting - The birds still singing in the early morning & trees in their fresh green - the weeks have been very busy. I have with my own hands, got through the stupendous work of unpacking & clearing over 100 cases & boxes - putting the Museum in order, filling the bookcases & hanging pictures throughout the house & putting up heads & skins."

This was getting Pinchinthorpe House back to what it had been before 1903 - replacing all the animal trophies, which at that time he had sold for £250 to Arthur Dorman for the Dorman Museum in Middlesbrough to help clear off his personal debts. Bit by bit, the place was coming together again.

15th July "Nothing of importance to record during the past week, beyond my having been re-elected without any opposition from the Portsmouths, to the board of the Middlesbro' Owners - My difficulty has been to qualify, but I have bought for £650 ex Divd. 100 shares from J.B. Dale & the Exors. of Sir David Dale by arranging with Barclays, an overdraft on 50 of the 53 shares I hold (& Nellie) in Pease & Partners."

25th July "I went for the first time to attend Wilson Pease & Co., Board at Darlington & re-entered after 3¹/₂ years Pease & Partners Board Room - where I was accustomed for 23 years to take my seat - I now come as a visitor!"

Pease & Partners had taken shares in Wilson, Pease & Co., Ltd, and the board meetings of this latter company were held at Pease & Partners, Northgate, Darlington offices.

25th Aug. "J. Cory Badcock, the old Manager of our Bank & now managing Stockton branch of Barclays, came & spent the afternoon & evening - I enjoyed seeing this loyal man - & picked up a good deal of news - He was, I think, as shocked as I was at the gross mismanagement of the liquidation & sacrifice of our securities & estates ... Badcock also told me that Ed. Hutchinson had told him that Peat, the liquidator, had said he intended to clear £10,000 for himself out of the liquidation - & what must have the lawyers done!"

Throughout the summer, when not diverted by other things, Alfred had spent his time in writing. He had in preparation a book on the life of Rachel Gurney, another on the Diaries of Edward Pease, and a paper on the Native Question in the Transvaal. In early September, while on the way to Drumochter to shoot, he called in to see his old friend Sir Edward Grey at Falloden who at this time was Secretary of State for Foreign Affairs in the Liberal Government. Grey's wife, Dorothy had died at the time Alfred was in the Sudan.

"Drove ... to Falloden to spend the day with Edward Grey who has been sending me messages that he wished to see me - he knows how I have felt for him, & our friendship is an old one - He was simple & natural & like his old self in most ways - certainly high office & honours have not spoilt him in the least - but the mark of his sorrow is on him. We had a walk for 2 hours round the grounds, familiar to me when I was young at Creighton's & where old Sir George & Lady Grey were kind to me. I pointed out to him, while he was feeding his ducks, where I first saw him coming across the Park with a keeper. I was then 19 & he 14 - We had a long & very intimate talk.

All pleasure & zest in life seems to have left him; his mind lives in the past, as much as his work will allow it - even his work awakes no enthusiasm. He said, 'I do my 5 hours a day at it, it is a great tie, but I do it mechanically & understand it so well that I can do it, but other politics fail to excite much interest' ...

I was much affected by my visit, & my heart rewarmed towards a man I have always loved & admired & trusted, tho' I studiously avoided mentioning myself, my future, or anything that might by any chance spoil the feeling wh. alone, I wish to exist between us. He, of his own kind thought said, would I like Edward (my son), to be transferred from the Sudan to the Egyptian Service. I told him I would like to consult Edward first."

Leaving Falloden, Alfred joined Gerald Buxton at the station at Alnmouth, and with their retrievers, went to the Albright's at Drumochter for a weeks grouse driving.

"The party there:- George & Margt. Albright, Toby Albright, young Churchill[2] - I was at Cambridge with his father, & often ran against him at Fenners, but he was too good for me, & I never got my blue for the quarter mile - Hankinson, Bonham Carter & Miss Bonham Carter, Lister Harrison, ... Gerald shot far the best of the party. I was not up to my best form, but I think came next."

At the end of September, while in Darlington at a Directors' meeting, he went, as he had on several occasions since his return in March, to call on his old Nanny, Sarah Wilson. After 1903, with increasing blindness, she had gone to live in the care of her niece in Darlington.

"Spent an hour with poor old Nanny who gets feebler, & is approaching her end I fear - It is curious to see how she, after her devout & pious life, & remembering how she used to tell me of the day she was Saved & gave herself to God, & the direct assurances she had of Salvation, to find her now distressed about the future, which she now declares is hid, & crying out to be saved, & weeping that she has no confidence or assurance - The hereafter thus remains a blank for the most religious."

This October, Alfred is at Hurworth Moor near Darlington for a rabbit shoot with Lloyd Pease:

"I only shoot now as a rule to see my friends. I have not the least keenness for it, & rather hate killing a lot of rabbits - The surroundings & grouse driving & shooting make the days delightful - but killing is no longer any pleasure, & my tenderness in this respect, which has often been a drawback, seems to grow on me - & I could lay aside my gun without any sacrifice - but not my rifle."

This same month, Alfred was in London for a meeting at 52, Queen Victoria Street, with Taylor Hallett about The Delagoa Coal Syndicate affairs:

" ... issued certificates for shares. Wired Dicey £100 - Agreed to the options he has taken over, but not to paying survey fees till coal to our liking has been proved - Agreed to make a Call - & to prove in one shaft - Our shaft is down 60' & shd. touch the coal, if it is there, very soon."

From such surviving scraps of information as there are, it would seem, that from the start of the venture to date, four shafts had been commenced in the claims area which was in extent some 15,000 acres. The location was about seven miles west of Komati Poort, and south and south west of Tenbosch.

What depth had been reached with two of the four shafts is not known. What is known is that there was bad luck with the main shaft when, having got down to 75ft, they came upon a rock fault which forced its abandonment, and necessitated retrying at No. 1 shaft. This it would seem, is the one that Alfred reports as having reached a depth of 60 feet.

During the previous year there had been some delay when the venture had run out of funds. The syndicate had started off with £2,000, a sum thought to be sufficient to prove the claim, and now in consequence, as Alfred said in a letter to his son Edward, *"We ... shall have to let others into our show."*

The share capital of the Delagoa Coal Syndicate had been enlarged to £10,000 of which £5,000 had been either subscribed for in partly paid shares, or otherwise credited to the promoters as partly paid up. Alfred, Jack, Taylor Hallett and Dicey's interests combined, was in 60 per cent of the share capital, whilst other subscribers included Arthur Francis Pease, Freddy Meuricoffre, Sir Christopher Furness, and a few others. Though the undertaking was very speculative, there seemed a convincing case for going on with it. Anyhow, there for the time being we must leave the prospectors to carry on with the digging, while we divert our gaze to the Hungarian business.

> *22nd Nov.* "Went to London - Had a most important conference with Hallett - Believing we have a really good list of really good Hungarian things. We decided to float if possible, a parent Co., to prove *(and)* develop ... Hallett reported good results of his interviews with the Hungarian Government Ministers - Went through a draft kind of prospectus."

The syndicate was to be floated and styled as The Hungarian Finance Company Ltd., for which a capital of £30,000 needed to be raised.

> *23rd Nov.* "Went to Richard Harrison *(Solicitor)* with Hallett re our prospectus - I am anxious to have everything strictly correct & to have no worries about it after - then home."

In December, laid up at home by a severe kick from a horse,

"My time has been fully occupied with a heavy correspondence with Hallett & others about our Hungarian ventures - It is more worry than I like, & though I believe in it, I sometimes think I would be happier free from all business cares, even when they promise interesting & profitable results - At any rate, I have no greed of gain, & place the pursuit of wealth as a very secondary kind of interest."

20th Dec. " ... then with Hallett over our prospectus till 1. Then looking for Ld. Milner in vain till 4.00 p.m. when I found him in - asked him to consider our prospectus & being our Chairman - had a good long chat with him & got as far as I could hope to, but I am not very sanguine. Then to Paulton's, after one or two tries to find him, & got him to join us."

At Falloden with Sir Edward Grey for three days' shooting between Christmas and New Year,

"It is wonderful how nice & simple Edward G. is - no one could be less spoilt by what is real greatness - One can hardly realise when spending days with him, that he holds perhaps the most responsible post in the world & does his work without a secretary or any fuss."

In his review of the year, 1906 he says,

"Started my Ostrich Farm in British East Africa near the Kamba Reserve & Machakos - & made a few small investments - & have £30 to my credit at the end of the year. I have done a good bit of work towards getting up a syndicate, to float certain promising undertakings in Hungary which, I hope, will be a success for all concerned, & give me some interesting work ... the past gets longer & the future shorter."

The British East Africa involvement is a new venture, of which this is the first recorded reference. The short history behind this scheme, is that Harold Hill, who had been in the Revenue Department at Barberton - a South African by birth - had followed his cousin Clifford Hill to Kenya the previous year, 1905, to start a new life. Clifford, the elder of the cousins, had worked in the Lands Department at Barberton. He was the taller of the two, a stronger man and very reliable with a cool head. Harold was keen and quick but had a red hot temper. They were both inexhaustible workers.

As pioneer settlers, Clifford and Harold Hill had taken up some land at Limouru near Nairobi. They shortly afterwards bought a long lease on some land at Wami on the Kapiti Plains. Their plan was to start ostrich farming by clearing the virgin land of scrub, ploughing out and sowing with lucerne as free range ostrich feed within a fenced boundary. As five-month-old chicks at Wami, the ostriches would be moved up country to Limouru. There was a good demand and ready market for ostrich feathers.

Harold Hill in correspondence with Alfred through 1906, wrote glowing reports about the country, the climate, the abundance of game around Wami, and the great prospects for the future. During this stage, Alfred enquired of the Colonial Office whether he could acquire land above the Kapiti Plains in the Mua Hills where there was better supply of water, and timber was available. He was told there was absolutely no chance of this, that the Mua Hills area was inalienably set apart as a native reserve.

After further investigation through the summer of 1906, he asked Harold Hill to purchase on his behalf, a 99-year lease on 4,998 acres (at $1/2$d per acre) of land adjoining Wami, at Kilima Theki. Alfred sent the funds to secure this virgin land. The Hills volunteered at an agreed salary to do all the preliminary work of land clearance, build a two-roomed "house" together with a couple of mat huts, some sheds, and set the whole thing up with an initial stock of ostrich chicks. The Hills would also do a certain amount of ploughing out, with Alfred paying for the capital outlay and remuneration, and he would follow out at the end of 1907.

The manner in which the ostrich chicks were initially procured, was for the Hills with native help, to go out into the wild and capture them. They became quite successful at this. If the capture of chicks was one thing, keeping them alive was another, and losses were considerable in the early stages. They improved on their early experience by taking ostrich eggs to incubate.

Alfred was motivated toward embarking upon this new enterprise in the first place because of his love of Africa, but spurred on by the despair he felt about things in England. He was thoroughly disaffected with Liberal politics, and the way in which the party was tilting to the left. Asquith and Lloyd George were competing with the Labour Party for votes, and the emergence of socialism as a force seemed to hold out the prospect, if not of revolution then at least the confiscation of capital. As the clouds gathered, and as Alfred read it, Africa offered a safe refuge from the coming storm. Even so, he wanted to retain Pinchinthorpe as an insurance against farming failure in British East Africa. But he is still in England.

1907

In January, Edwin Fox is again in trouble and

> "... pours letters on me begging for help to raise money - After his failure, he got squared up last year, & then went plunging on the iron market again, & is I fear in a dreadful mess. I have given him £10 to get to London to see some people."

To clear off this and another debt, Alfred agreed to accept from Edwin a cow in satisfaction. Shortly afterwards the cow calved. Edwin, hearing of this, rushed back to Pinchinthorpe to claim the calf saying, it was a most 'uncousinly' thing that Alfred should for a moment contemplate keeping them both, and the calf was yielded up.

During the first two months of 1907, his time was partly taken up with the Hungarian business which was making slow progress.

> *3rd Mar.* "I have neglected my diary for nearly a month & can not recall all my doings. We have been pretty quietly at home, Nellie visiting all the farms & cottages & seeming well, but finding the winter dull & long I fear - I have done a vast amount of reading of old letters & writing, & put aside for a while the too exacting & worrying work connected with the Hungarian prospectus - because the delays & ignorance & general dilatoriness of R.L. Harrison, the solicitor so irritated me, that I told him what I felt - that nothing in the world was worth all this bother & fuss & he withdrew, & got Price Waterhouse & Co., to do the same - a dirty bit of lawyer's nastiness - I know the thing is bona fide & honest & good business, but I have no desire to spoil the tranquillity of my life by being worried with it, as I have no desire to be rich & took it up because it interested me - whether I have any more to do with it or not I don't know, & don't care."

However, during the last week in March, 1907, Alfred sent out about eighty of the Hungarian Finance Company prospectuses to relatives, friends and acquaintances, but was not over-optimistic about getting the necessary funds for the launch. This was really just as well since, of the £30,000 wanted, only £5,000 in shares had been subscribed for by mid-April, and as this venture now fades totally from view, it joins ranks with the Cerlosa Monastery Hotel in the realms of moribund or ditched schemes.

> "We struck the worst year there has ever been in the city for starting anything in the way of mines abroad ..."

On 24th March, he got the news that his old Nanny, Sarah Wilson had died, and three days later, after her funeral he wrote,

> *27th Mar.* "We buried at Guisbro' Cemetery all that was left of our dear little

Nanny ... Maud, Blanche, Nellie, Kit & I joined the train that brought her coffin to Guisbro' ... I could not help a tear by the grave as all I remembered, all the intense love & solicitude the dead little old body held for me & mine - We brought Lily, her niece, who has devoted her young years to the often tiresome task for youth, of caring for her aunt, to Pinchinthorpe - where I read them her Will which made Maud & me her Executors, & left everything to us to dispose of as we think fit - Since Wednesday, Blanche has sent me the few little things she kept in her treasure box - she had wisely, as her sight failed, destroyed most, but 2 letters of mine & my curls as a child, & my mother's words in 1858, saying Sarah was so clever with Effie & me, & an inexpressible comfort to her.

She had arranged everything for her funeral. She had some 60 years ago had her little romance, but her betrothal was broken, the fault not with her, a subject on which she kept silence for ever, but when she died, there was the little store of sheets & linen she had prepared & worked at for her marriage untouched, save that she had taken out of it the night gown, the white cap and sheets in which to be buried, & in them she lies - The life & death of this humble sweet old nurse, is just as much & more *(moving)*, on account of its pure simplicity, than if she had been a Princess - & her religion, 'that in which the wayfaring man, though a fool, cannot err therein'."

23rd June "Tomorrow Christopher comes of age. It marks the flight of time; he was a charming child, & has been a dear good boy & has brains & great intelligence. His pride kicks against being in Pease & Partners, but he does not yet realise that he is not there on sufferance; that he earns every penny they give him, that he will only get what he deserves & no more at their hands ..."

During July, Alfred corrected the proofs of his books on Rachel Gurney, and also on Edward Pease:

"I ... feel horribly discouraged with my *(Diaries of)* Edward Pease which is not interesting or well done - being, like most of my work, done in haste - I have no sooner started a thing than I want to get it finished."

21st July "The last week my work has been rather interrupted by the arrival of the Slatter family, Capt. A.A. Slatter, who was in command of the S.A.C. in my district, his wife & baby. He poor fellow, has come back shattered with fever & worry & very depressed - he has given me a most gloomy account of the district I toiled in & of the Transvaal generally ... Komati Poort, where I tried to make the place nice, is not even what it was under me; my pepper tree avenue has grown, the Club has shut up ... the stores have gone bankrupt ... Furley has committed suicide, & his wife is drinking herself to death, many others are dead of whisky & fever - & only 40 whites or so left out of the 160 in my time ..."

30th July "The Slatters left. Slatter ill & depressed & I feel anxious about him that he may destroy himself, or become insane - have persuaded him to see a specialist in London."

Captain Slatter was a man of about six foot two inches in height, roundish-faced with a bushy moustache. He some years earlier had had an accident when partridge shooting and blown off his right hand, and the lower part of his arm had been amputated. Slatter reappears a little later in the story.

Through the late summer, Alfred was full of work; engagements, visits and visitors. In September his son Edward returned on leave from Port Sudan, and the hope was that with the decks cleared of work, November and December could be given over to hunting and shooting. The plan was upset when Edward received a telegram saying that his leave was cancelled and he was to return to the Sudan immediately, which he did, though Alfred was both indignant and disappointed.

> *6th Nov.* "Nellie & Lavender went to London - I am alone - Finished the last proofs of 'Edward Pease' & placed the illustrations - I do not know what to think of the production but however dull & dreary, it is a faithful bit of work - I have now completed my literary labours for the year."

Of his literary labours, in addition to the two books previously referred to - a four-hundred-page book on Edward Pease, a two-hundred-page book on Rachel Gurney - he had also produced a paper on the Transvaal Native Question and had in preparation a two-hundred-page Memoir of Sir Thomas Fowler; four quarto volumes of typed Records of the Gurneys of the Grove at Norwich running close to two thousand pages. He had also produced a number of genealogical tables and delivered several lectures during the year.

As the end of the year approached, Alfred received a progress report from Harold Hill on the Kilima Theki farming project. Hill made it clear that it was impossible to get on with farming properly at Theki, without access to an adequate supply of water, insufficient of which was to be found there. Alfred appealed to Lord Elgin, from whom he secured special permission to take up a thousand acres of land adjoining Theki, in the 'inalienable' Native Reserve in the Mua Hills. It was madly annoying that in his initial enquiries before ever buying the lease on Theki, he had been refused a similar request for land there. As it was, his limited development capital, which might have been put to better use, had been expended at Theki.

> *22nd Dec.* "Tomorrow we leave Pinchinthorpe for several months i.e. Nellie, Lavender & I ... I have been far too busy to write my journals lately ..."

1908

They arrived at Mombasa on 15th January, having been joined at

Aden by Sir Edmund Loder and Gerard Gurney who were taking off on safari. Alfred set out on the 288-mile rail journey to the Kapiti Plains, and to take a first look at his farm.

18th Jan. "At Kapiti Station was Harold Hill, with two Arab horses, very good ones which Edward had bought for me and sent from Port Said. Another horse Hill had borrowed for me, and a Boer wagon with a span of local native little oxen. Nellie & Lavender mounted the two Arabs and I the other horse, and about midday we started out for my 'farm', taking with us some of the boys to show us the way. I carried my Mannlicher as of old, and there is no part where it is more necessary to be armed than on these plains. All round Wami hill and as far as you could see over the plains, the country was alive with literally thousands of hartebeest, wildebeest, zebras & gazelles ..."

Alfred broke off during the thirteen-mile ride to Theki, to look over a herd of eland while Nellie, Lavender and their escort went ahead, and the Boer wagon trundled on slowly in the rear. Selecting a bull in the herd, he dismounted, following which his horse bolted as did the bull, leaving Alfred to walk the remaining nine miles in the heat, and uphill to his farm at Theki.

"I could not imagine where the end of my journey was going to be, as you do not see my 2-roomed house, nor anything to indicate a settler till you are within a few hundred yards of the house. The house, I found to my surprise, with its two rooms, was in the occupation of the two Hills and Hall, the latter an Afrikaaner whom they had got to help with the ostriches. There were also two decent huts built. Below the house are the ostrich boma and sheds, where there are 25 fine young birds of mine, and 50 or more belonging to the Hills. There are about 20 acres of roughly enclosed land, with a patch of it cultivated, or rather ploughed out - also a spring & a dam - beyond is a plain & low hillside (looking west) covered with hundreds of kongoni & zebra ...

The outlandishness of it all is rather a shock to Nellie and Lavender ... Neither the air, the scene, the sun nor the teeming game seems to give either of them any pleasure, and from the first moment of arrival they took a dislike to it & began to become homesick - it was unfortunate that the wagon did not turn up till midnight, & they had to sleep in Hill's two beds &c &c. Now they have made up their minds to hate it - I feel rather beat."

From his house, in addition to those already mentioned, he could watch giraffe, eland, lion, leopard, cheetahs, wild dog, hyaenas and jackals while the birdlife was just as bountiful - falcons, buzzards, eagles and vultures, secretary birds and partridges - an absolutely marvellous wonderland - there was nothing more to say about it.

19th Jan. "Began furnishing our two long grass huts, much roomier & cooler than tents - one is our dining room, the other Nellie's & Lavender's bedroom; opposite their door is a bell tent where I sleep to protect them from lions - the Hills &c have killed 7 here - one broke through the boma and killed 2 ostriches one night a short time ago."

21st Jan. "I went a walk round the base of the hill as we want meat, being now on our own & the Hills, up to today, providing us with everything. Our boys are a poor lot, but such as the country produces & we cannot yet speak enough of the lingo to make much of them. The ticks are awful - when I came in for lunch, I changed. I took 37 ticks off myself - my record - the after irritation is bad."

The Hills had returned to their adjoining farm at Wami, south of Kilima Theki.

22nd Jan. "Moved into the house - Ladies scared in the huts & had sort of D.T.'s - saw snakes, lions, rats, ticks & generally had the horrors."

27th Jan. "Lavender seems seedy, & both she & Nellie are worried frightfully with ticks, & we are covered with their bites."

29th Jan. "Evening - the Hills & Hall dined with us & letters arrived from Slatter - they arrive next month."

Alfred had persuaded Captain Arthur Slatter to pack up in South Africa and make a fresh start in Kenya, and Slatter, fired with the spirit of a pioneer, had now completely pulled himself out of his depression of last year.

31st Jan. "I was preparing after lunch to write for the mail tomorrow, when H. Hill came running in to say there were lions near the house - we soon spotted 3 in some bushes, but Percival[3] riding up after us started them off. They went off at a gallop 200 yds. below us making out into the plain. I hit the leading one in the foreleg with my Mannlicher & H. Hill hit him again; he lay down in the open & watched us; I gave him 2 with the 10 bore at 50 yds. Hill gave him one with ·404 & we left him dead & ran for another one which C. Hill, (on my Arab), & Percival on the 'weary one', were holding up 2 miles away - he was horribly vicious & made for the horses several times - I hit him at 300 yds. with the Mannlicher & Hill hit him with my ·404 & he then seemed worse than ever. We were short of ammunition & we held our fire during an hour or more, while Hall went home for more. He arrived before sundown, & when we approached every time he charged (4 times) either Hill or I landed him one & saw him die.

C. Hill & I (the sun setting) went off to skin lion No 1 & while doing so we were watched by 2 other lions on the hill by the house - & as we came home, the last mile close to home, one of these, a big one walked parallel with us 400 yds. on our right till it was too dark to see it."

1st Feb. "At 2 a.m. we were invaded by ants & driven out of the house. We removed into my tent for the rest of the night."

3rd Feb. "The Wakamba seem bad workers, the good boys on the place are Kikuyu."

Theki our first home in B.E.A

30. Our first home in B.E.A. (Sketch by Alfred Edward Pease.)

17th Feb. "I tried in the midst of interruptions to reply to letters ... Nellie called in Hill to flog Malinga for not being content to wash clothes with half a piece of soap. Hill gave him a dozen & a kicking with the result I foretold, that they would never get any more work out of him - he went off - this is the 3rd of our boys Hill has sjambok'd, & each time with the same result - I think they are the worst hands at making boys good servants I ever came across, and they will never have really good servants or ones that will attach themselves - However, Nellie seems to approve of the system, & as she has the management with Lavender of the house department she can do as she likes - It is not my way ... A most irritating day, & I was glad in the evening to go out a long walk with Chungo & get a steinbok far off for the pot ... "

20th Feb. "The Slatters & their child arrived - we have installed them in one of the huts & one of my bell tents. Hill & Hall are in the other tent & the other of my bell tents."

21st Feb. "Loder turned up ... he wants me to start at once on a trip with him."

Alfred and Loder set out and were joined by Arthur Slatter. Whilst on the hunting trip, and passing by Kilima Kiu, Alfred pointed out to Slatter the land that he and Hill had selected for his farm, and Slatter seemed very pleased with the chosen site. Kilima Kiu was further to the

270

south from Kilima Theki and Wami, and nearer to Machakos. 28th February, and being still on the trip with Loder:

"Last night, some lions raided some zebra just above our camp. The zebras all but stampeded our camp; the men woke up yelling 'Simba' (lion). When I started off at daybreak there were the lions' footings down the *(Uganda)* railway for two miles. They could only just have gone, as the footings were clear on the dew on the sleepers, & the wet soil was freshly lifted & the track dry underneath. I saw 2 more fresh tracks of lion, one, a very large one in a river bottom where we had drunk last night. I cannot think why Jackson & Percival sent Loder down here, I could give them more to hunt in an afternoon down at Theki than we have had all week."

29th Feb. "Marched 20 miles from Sultan Hamoud to Simba - arrived 1.30 - good marching - very hot - 95 in our tents at 3.30 ... got a wire from Nellie to say she was spending Sunday (1st Mar) at Naivasha, & Monday & Tuesday at Nairobi, Norfolk Hotel & that they were enjoying themselves ... I have had only one English mail since December."

5th Mar. "We left Simba at 4 a.m. and reached (by train) Kapiti Plains Station early, and made Theki at 1 p.m. ... Found all well at Theki - Hill is making a nice mess of all my expensive 10-foot corrugated iron sheets, which I have imported to make an ostrich boma with, for the protection of the Hill's and my birds from lions & hyaenas - he is bending and hammering most of them out of shape to save himself the trouble of a neat job - it is wasteful, and will not make a good fence at the finish. However, he knows something about ostriches, and they both know how to get a start themselves out of me. Their energy and spirits are great, but H.H. like many South Africans cannot handle other natives than kaffirs - & not always kaffirs - the natives here dislike them and H.Hill's hot temper, & will not work with him, or for long; but they have confidence in themselves & believe if they can't do a thing, no one else can, & this pays in the end."

7th Mar. "With Lavender & Slatter, they riding, I walking, to look at my far northern boundary up on the hills. I was delighted with the country up there, and the trees, the bracken, brambles like at home, & the great bushes of wild jasmine - plenty of timber & water & splendid views; South is Kilimanjaro, and North to Mt. Kenia. It was a spot from which we could see these, that I selected as the site of a future house - there is lots of game there, and many native villages of huts in the bush and among the trees, where it all looks park-like - Off my ground, a little more to the north are some rocks and caves where some more natives are living in & under the rocks ...

It is an advantage to have natives so near, & I like to have them, but I hear that the ... government authorities will very likely turn them out, & not allow them to live on land taken up for white men, & gradually evict them from their pretty places & good pastures. It is a policy that saves the government trouble - but what they ought to do, is to reserve some good land for natives among the settlers, & see that the settlers do not make bad use of the natives nor take advantage of them."

9th Mar. "Went with Arthur Slatter to have another look at the site for my house - the site I want is just beyond my last beacon which took a lot of finding."

31. Alfred's ostritch chicks at Kitanga.

The following day, Alfred went to Nairobi, to seek out the official attitude to his selection of the site for his new house. Sir James Hayes Sadler, the Governor, thought that from the map, it looked as if it went a bit into the Wakamba Reserve, so he could promise nothing until a report had been made. Elsewhere, he got a sympathetic hearing from the Commissioner for Lands and Barton Wright the Land Officer, and he was told he could plant and cultivate without fear of disturbance.

"I bought a plough (the only one in Nairobi) for Rs150[4], 2 hoes, 1 spade, ordered stores, & put up at the Norfolk Hotel; quite comfortable. I dined with the Hayes Sadlers at Government Ho. & met there Mr & Mrs Talbot Smith. Loder left Theki today on safari - Nairobi is a poor sort of place & built on a silly site - The Government Offices are like kaffir stores - Game swarm right up & into the town - there were kongoni & zebras right up to the Railway Station."

11th Mar. "A hard morning trying to see officials - they do not get to their offices till 10 - they should do as in India - get up at 6 & do the best part before 11 a.m. ... met Delamere. Not changed much since our Somali days - I bought an Abyssinian pony from him for Rs. 350 - engaged a cook boy & got back to Theki at 5 p.m."

13th Mar. "I went with the wagon & oxen to Kapiti Sta. - it is a long six hours there, and lions all the way, & when you are overtaken with night, a jumpy business getting the oxen safe home - Here they can keep lions off with lanterns, fire & even by striking matches - that would not be the slightest use in Somaliland."

272

A leopard was grunting all night near the house."

14th Mar. "We all went to look at my new site - the spot is called Kitanga by the Wakamba, after the native name for a white man who was killed on this spot by a lion a few years ago ..."

Alfred now wrote to the Lands Department, asking for a 300- yards extension in his boundary, in exchange for the surrender of an equivalent area elsewhere, so as to build his house where he wanted it. Then he wrote a long letter to Capt. Dick Allsop at the Mines Department at Barberton. This was to invite Allsop to come to Kilima Theki, where, following a period of guidance and training from Harold Hill, he would become the manager of Alfred's farm.

In writing to Allsop, he outlined what had been accomplished by Harold Hill; that in addition to the 5,000 acres he, Alfred, leased, he had taken up a further 1,000 acres freehold in the Mua Hills; that the farm should run 500 ostriches and over a 1,000 when sufficient area was under lucerne. He elaborated on other possibilities for the land; it was suitable for fruit trees and all kinds of crops.

As to terms, Alfred was to provide the development capital (somehow) but offering Allsop ¹/₃rd of profits, and after a term of 5 years, an entitlement to ¹/₃rd of the livestock, or its cash equivalent, the exercise of such option resting with Alfred. He concluded by giving Allsop the chance of first refusal, but asked him to do it quickly by cable, as he was returning to England on 10th April.

Gerard Gurney arrived on 19th March with an army of porters, who pitching their tents made the farm look like a settlement. The following day Lord Delamere came for lunch and an overnight stay.

21st Mar. "Lavender, Slatter & I, after breakfast 5.30 a.m. & seeing Delamere off, rode round to Lukania and saw Prinsloo ... where he & three or four Boers have settled. It was a real bit of South Africa transferred to this country, the same people, the same clothes, the same surroundings, the same sort of tin shanties, the same dirt, the same mucky children, the same spitting on the floor as I used to have to be among at White River. We negotiated with Prinsloo, who is a nice businesslike young fair Boer, about the building of our new house."

26th Mar. "I wrote ... to the Land Officer thanking him for his letter of 18/20 March, confirming his telegram, giving me permission for my new site, & saying the Surveyor had instructions to give more than 10 acres if reasonably necessary. In my letter I told him Slatter wd. look after the site while I was away & have funds for purchase - Hill *(to)* continue to act generally for me - I stated that 10 acres wd. do for house, garden &c, but I wanted the site to join up with present boundary ...

I handed the original letters, (as I previously did the telegram), to file with my papers to H.D. Hill; he was annoyed at my giving the supervision of this site to Slatter, but as he has far more than he can get done here, I am sure it is the best plan - he is very behind plan with ploughing, & I shall lose another season thro' his doing so much himself, & having no competent natives or coolies to assist him. Finally, I think he was satisfied; at least he said he was."

With arrangements fairly well in hand for the running of Theki during his absence, and the building of the new house at Kitanga, Alfred started to pack up for the journey home, and on 6th April left Theki at dawn with the Boer wagon loaded up. At Mombasa, he picked up a cable from Dick Allsop, accepting the proposition, and as Alfred set sail for England, leaving Nellie in Italy for a holiday with an aunt, Allsop made preparations to set out for a new life in Kenya.

Notes:
1. Theodore Fox, brother-in-law to Sir Joseph Whitwell Pease had been the latter's tenant at Pinchinthorpe House for a few years before Alfred and Nellie's marriage.
2. Winston Spencer Churchill.
3. Philip Percival, who except for Alfred's and Hill's farms was the only other settler on the Kapiti plains, his farm being at Potha, east of Wami.
4. Rs150 was equal to £10 Sterling.

CHAPTER THIRTEEN

An Ex-President's Visit &
The End of a Phase

3rd May, 1908 "Here I am home again - Welcomed by Flunkey, Togo & Tyke *(the dogs)* Theresa, *(Sudan parrot)* - the peacock - & Long *(the gardener)*. I arrived 6.30; the thrushes singing & cuckoos too - but it was cold - however vegetation is not much behind France - the daffodils are out & things getting green - no one here. Christopher in London ... Got a post card from Nellie to say she is coming back."

12th May "Bench - Lunched with Jock Clarke & met Medlicott[1] who has come to be Agent at Wilton - a nice man, he knows the Buxtons."

20th June "... Nellie persuaded me to take Lavender up to London for the King's Garden Party at Windsor - We went up by the evening train, & London being frightfully full, I only succeeded in getting Lavender a bedroom at the Great Central Hotel, I myself sleeping on the floor of the ladies' cloakroom - a horrid hole without a window, & a stuffy night.

At breakfast Sat. morning, behold Ted Leatham arrived from New Zealand with his attractive wife. I spent the morning with him & Lavender - went to prepare for the Windsor 'show' - We went to Windsor & met many friends. Lavender looked charming & I was proud of her. The King & the Royal family moved about amongst people all the afternoon after 4.30 - particular pains were taken to present Labour M.P.s ... to the King, which is a way of 'getting at' them that is very amusing to me, & very effective! - such is human nature & our national character."

Through June and July, Edward was home on leave. He had been accepted for work in the Persian Consular Service, but had then been told he was just over age for the examination. During his leave, he went with his mother and Lavender to Bayreuth, while Alfred, having commitments at home, remained behind.

There was a meeting in London in late July with Taylor Hallett. No coal has been unearthed since last we heard of the search operations at

Komati Poort in October, 1906. But a flicker of life still beats in the heart of The Delagoa Eastern Transvaal Coal Syndicate Ltd.:

16th Aug. "I have been worried the last few days. H. Samuel M.P. wrote asking me to take part in the Liberal Demonstration on 5th Sept. I have declined - I am so disgusted with some, with many of the doings of the party, & their departure from the principles & traditions of true Liberalism ... They propose all sorts of things that aim at crippling individual enterprise, & promote the corrupt methods of municipal & state industries & trades - which fetter the rights & liberties of people to work as much as they like, & harass them with multitudes of laws & regulations - They have packed the Benches with party men & persons quite unfitted to dispense justice, & ignorant of procedure, & the most elementary knowledge of magisterial law. They have trafficked in titles & sold offices.

Having denounced the Ho. of Lords, they have created dozens of peers - & Jno. Morley who has posed as against the Ho. of Lords & for ending them, has taken a peerage ... But it is all too long a business to discuss in a diary - Anyway, I am sick at not seeing any clear way to act - though as I need not come out of private life it should not worry me much."

Herbert Samuel's kind invitation having evoked from Alfred a torrent of invective, he went off to Scotland to shoot with Arthur Francis Pease.

"Arthur talked to me about several things, including Christopher - he is I think pleased with him - he said, and I wish to note it, that he *hoped* to get him put on the board of P. & P. this next year, but as it was not in his power to promise it, I had better not say so. I told him *(Arthur F.P.)* that if he *(Christopher)* got a hint of this, it might be a great encouragement to him - & he cd. not expect to have the self reliance & authority for good work unless he had some assured position - If this is done, my greatest grievance will have almost vanished viz:- the keeping me, the senior of the family, & the longest connected with P. & P. off the board, after asking me to retire, 'just for the form of the thing, to be put back again as soon as possible'."

In October Alfred was back in London with Taylor Hallett, where they set about trying to get an option on Breyten coal in the Transvaal. Breyten lies about 80 miles SW. of Barberton, and is in a different search area to Komati Poort. Nothing is reported on progress, or more to the point, the lack of it, in the original 15,000-acre claim. This latter would seem therefore to have been abandoned after two years of sinking shafts.

20th Nov. (London) "To the City & saw Hallett. Dicey has cabled he will inspect Breyten ... Then to lunch in Berkeley Square with Rosebery - he was very nice & amusing & asked me to go in Dec. & stay with him at Rosebery Cottage - Looked

at his wonderful portrait of George Washington by Stuart, the only one he ever sat for & priceless to America - he said "I keep it as a sort of hostage."
9th Dec. From Pinchinthorpe. "Went up to London ... My thoughts very much on the interview I had to have with Secty. at the Colonial Office, where they want me to go out apparently to meet the Mullah[2] & try to square him before tackling the brute, who is at his old games raiding & murdering in Somaliland.
Went first to 52, Q.V. St. Annual Delagoa Co., Meeting, in spite of whipping up shareholders, only Hallett, Vinck & I present - Drew up a temporary Report, went thro' accounts & pass books, & postponed issuing a Report & Accounts till Dicey reports on Breyten -
Afterwards met Secty. & Reid in Secty's room H. of C. & had a long talk *(about the Mullah)* - the result of wh. is summarised in a memorandum I made after."

Alfred's memorandum has not survived.

"My whole feeling is mixed - It would bore me to go, but I wd. cheerfully undertake a doubtful, & perhaps dangerous mission to effect a solid peace in Somaliland, but honestly think that Cordeaux's views shd. be expressed on the subject, & that the policy is very doubtful, & the means of carrying it out more so, & possibly might only lower our position & improve the Mullah's in the Somalis' eyes - besides, I cannot see how any subsidy, which is the Colonial Office idea to buy his neutrality, can do anything but strengthen him."
11th Dec. "Got home - Nellie here ... Wrote fully to *(Colonial)* Secty. & also if decided, to send an envoy or only a letter from the King - suggested the lines on wh. H.M.'s letter should run."

1909

7th Jan. "Christopher has been selected unanimously by P. & Partners Board, to be recommended as a Director at next Annual Meeting. I am very glad indeed - Jack writes & says it is the place I ought to have had - This is so, & nothing is meaner than the way I have been treated in this matter, but of that I have said enough, & I would *far rather* see Christopher there than myself - The question arises, how are we to get him qualified - I have only 25 shares & this is the only free security I have in the world except my furniture & one Life Policy - so that in case of trouble I have nothing to fall back on except my farm in B.E.A."

During February, he started making preparations for his return to British East Africa, and left London on 9th March. Sandy Medlicott was joining Alfred, Nellie and Lavender on this trip. Sandy had been much at Pinchinthorpe during the preceding nine months, and he very much shared with Alfred the same keen interest in natural history, and was a regular rider to hounds.

It was on 1st April that they all arrived at the railway station at Kapiti Plains.

"We were met by Dick Allsop and H. Hill with the Ox waggon ... We lunched at Theki, where I have Dick Allsop installed, & reached my new house up at Kitanga before dark - the ox waggon made a good journey and arrived about 9 p.m. - The house, in spite of patience, and greater cost than I ever intended, is not nearly finished - only two rooms habitable, but it is very nice & will soon be comfortable."

The original estimate for building his house had been set at about £400 on the top side. The cost now looked to be running fifty per cent over this figure.

4th April. "Went over to Theki to see my birds & to go into prospects & accounts - saw my wheat - it is splendid stuff - If I had capital I could grow it, & it would pay - With capital I should add to my cows, get marinos & implements and make some money."

5th April "Walked up the valley with Sandy & Lavender among the now deserted shambas. I have already had a melancholy walk on the beautiful hill with Nellie, where we were very sad at the sight of the native villages, all destroyed by the Government, & all the pretty sights of native homes, shambas & cattle gone, which made this hill forest country so attractive. We picked up native stools & things among the ruins & ashes."

8th April "I had planned to ride over today with Nellie & Lavender, to see the Slatters at Kilima Kiu, where they are now established - but they did not feel up to it - it is a hot 19 miles. As Nellie does not like me riding through lion country alone, Huie *(Chaloner)* came with me - We reached Bondoni Water about 11.30 where Slatter met us, and we got to his new place about 3.00, & found Mrs Slatter & the 2 infants awaiting us. The scene of our first camps there when I spotted this place, was strangely changed - houses, huts, bomas, & a bit of ploughed land. Slatter is absolutely tied to the place, being the only white man between Ulu & us, & finds he is handicapped in his work, having only one arm, but he enjoys the life & is fairly hopeful, though having got through his little capital & no near prospect of returns, the outlook is not bright & the fate of most pioneers may be his & mine too."

9th April. "Slatter & I did accounts & found the result worse than we thought. However, we went out a nice walk in the evening round the Melia Crag. There were roan and bushbuck there while other game swarms."

11th April "I must go to Nairobi to fix up Roosevelt's plans & find horses for him."

This is the first hint Alfred has given, that the former President of the United States, Theodore Roosevelt and his son Kermit were coming out to stay with him at Kitanga - and only two rooms of the new house habitable!

13th April "Sandy & I got on to our horses & left at 6 a.m. for Nairobi ... it is a very dreary ride over the plains ... we did well to reach the Norfolk Hotel at 12.30,

32. Harvesting Alfred's wheat, Kilima Theki.

having averaged 6 miles an hour over, some of it, rough ground. Saw Cunninghame who is to be Roosevelt's white hunter & camp commandant, & arranged a mass of details with him - he is practical & experienced, & is the right man for the job - I selected 3 horses from the Boma Company for Roosevelt's riding."

15th April. "We had a meeting today of the Ulu Settlers' Association of which I am President - all the Committee were present, namely, Bunbury from Donya Sabuk, Webber the Secretary, Slatter, C. Hill, Allsop, & Laws-Humphrey as Dist. Commr. was there, also Piggott from Embu ... We passed various resolutions re Indian immigration, 10-acre lots for irrigating lucerne at Machakos for ostriches (chicks), railway & postal grievances. On his way to Theki, Slatter passed 2 very big lions by the Theki bushes ... & filled up with a Kangoni kill near by. It was tempting, but we are keeping all lions for Roosevelt now."

16th April. "Sandy & I spent all day painting the house - it is hard work & not easy to do neatly."

17th April. "Sandy & I painting the house all day; we nearly got the whole of the verandah done in the day - I received a ridiculous letter from Cunninghame today, saying that as there were so many ticks on my place, he did not intend bringing any of Roosevelt's horses here. I must put this right at once - does he think I can mount all Roosevelt's party, & that we are to round up lions on foot, & that Roosevelt is going to sweat all day on foot on the equator."

279

19th April "Sandy & I worked hard all day on the house, painting, joinering &c - today we got into our dining room - it is all white paint & a nice cool duck egg blue or green distemper I brought out from home."

The preparations & arrangements for Roosevelt's visit, & the constant hard work from the day he arrived at Kapiti Plains Station on April 23rd. until he rode away from our house at Kitanga on May 13th quite prevented me from making many notes; far less was it possible even to keep this imperfect journal. What I set down is from memory fresh after his departure.

The Government Officials & Cunninghame were rather fussy & troublesome about the coming of the great man. Cunninghame's anxiety was natural - but I got rather fed up with all sorts of suggestions, some of which were obviously stupid, & others to me appeared simply idiotic. I had quite a struggle over the horse & tick question - which was, comparatively, a small one. Then Humphrey, our District Commissioner came over & told me that the authorities had instructed him to put before me, the suggestion that I should place askaris, to be provided by Humphrey, 'on every hill top to watch for lions' - I asked Humphrey to tell them not to fuss; that I wanted lions on the hill tops & not askaris, & that I promised to find the big man lions enough to keep him busy shooting for as long as he liked. Then everybody who fancied himself wanted to come & show me how to do it. Percival[3], the Game Ranger, wished particularly to come to me & to bring his Masai & show me *how* to provide sport - this was natural - as he is the chief game official at the moment, & of course has had much experience, but still, I know my bit of country better than anyone else except the 2 Hills who are at hand, & I do not want so many bosses about - If anyone wants to take the job out of my hands it must be Cunninghame.

The Press ridiculed his coming to 'Pease's Ostrich Farm' for lions, & said all he would find with me would be ticks! ... I was most loyally helped & supported by Cunninghame & my neighbours without a trace of jealousy ...

Colonel Roosevelt arrived at Kitanga on Sunday, 25th April & left us on May 13th - 17 days with me - several of which were taken up with marching to camps, & others given up by Roosevelt to writing for Scribner's Magazine ...

Among the many charming & interesting letters I have had from him, I prize the following little note the most, written the evening of the day he left us.

The Juja Farm,
Nairobi, B.E.A.
May 13th, 1909

Dear Sir Alfred,

How can I ever tell you how much I enjoyed the three happy weeks I owe to you! I shall have none others so pleasant in Africa. Give my warmest regards to Lady Pease; Kermit sends his love to you both; We look forward eagerly to seeing you a year hence. Tell Miss Lavender that her lunch was delicious and so abundant that I shared it with Harold Hill and there was ample for both.

With renewed thanks, believe me, most affectionately and faithfully
    Your friend,
       Theodore Roosevelt.

Tonight, May 13th, I am really tired though very fit with the incessant work, for I have not only had to manage R's big show, that is to say the detachment told off to me here, from his big base camp at Potha, wh. is under Cunninghame, but have had to make his plans & carry them out each day, & when everyone was in bed at night, & before anyone was awake in the mornings, I was busy fixing up things, sending notes & arranging for horses, meals, & all details - so that with Nellie's & Lavender's splendid help, our guest has never had to worry about a single thing but his sport.

Roosevelt was a very delightful guest, most appreciative, understanding, sympathetic, easily pleased, simple in his habits & wants - always kind, genial, courteous & tactful - He understands intuitively the people he is with, has a versatile mind, deeply interested in everything, not only in nature, but everything which touches mankind & 'all sorts and conditions of men.' He is able to express himself extraordinarily well, & has his head stored by a most retentive memory with the results of his own experience, & from those experiences, of the many interesting people whom he has had the advantage of knowing ... To me he opened out most freely, even expressing his likes & dislikes of men & nations, of statesmen, politicians & kings ... His strong prejudices are many, but I found them corresponding to true instinct & generally my own. He is a man undoubtedly with a great love of distinction, & every day showed that *one* of the reasons he wished to succeed in whatever he was at, was what the world would say, write or think about his success or failure - He told me, 'Of course I like to be a big man - *every one likes to be important and to have power and influence - it is a pleasure to have power.'* Though a great man, he knows how to be a boy & to enjoy things like a boy. I guessed he knew me & my tastes very quickly. Now with Nellie's help from her diary, I shall put down our days as I remember them.

22nd April "I got my Nedj Arabian horse, my tent boy & my faithful Chungo, & with a few things in my saddle bag, my ·256 rifle & ammunition, off I started for Kapiti Plains station at 2.30 & arrived in the dark at Roosevelt's camp ... they have got some 50 tents pitched & over 250 porters & men ready."

23rd April "Clifford Hill kindly came to help today, as I wanted him to get this army and camp to Potha & to act as guide - It was the place I had fixed for R's base camp, the only place within 20 miles with sufficient water. In the middle of the day the train arrived at our station with Jackson who is Acting Governor as the Hayes Sadlers have gone to the Windward Isles, Mrs Jackson, Selous[4], Kermit R., Wilson (Lord John) & some newspaper people were on the train. The other three white men with R. are Dr Mearns, Loring and Heller - they are the scientific department & collectors &c.

We had 300 camp followers drawn up in parade order at the station, & before the arrival of the train, practised them in 'howls of welcome.' Owing to the enormous masses of stores & boxes & cases of ammunition, Cunninghame was unable to get this unwieldy camp moved to Potha for several days. The first trouble was that Cunninghame had forgotten to order any bread or flour. I went to the station & found Lavender's week's supply of bread had arrived, so I put that trifle & some others right, & after dining with the Roosevelts, Clifford Hill & I went to the station & passed the night in the waiting room."

25th April "I got R. & K. off as early as I could with their gunbearers, syces & some porters for Kitanga - I took them via Chumbi. After they had killed kongoni, granties & tommies we drew Chumbi blank for lion & reached Kitanga at 3 p.m."

27th April "Roosevelt has mapped out his time & allotted me three days for him to get his lion - I thought before going for certainties, that I would give one of these days to getting the big black-maned one we had seen between Chumbi & Lukania if possible ... We went accompanied by Nellie & Lavender to the Chumbi Donga - away went Kermit after Hyaena - he had a most desperate & long gallop, but shot him at last after about a 10- mile run - this delayed us, but we had time to try the Lukania Donga. This Donga is thick in places, but not wide & often holds lion, but I found the boys would not face it alone, & I had to go in with them & go through the middle of it before they would try for lions - I had posted Sandy & the Colonel together at the Kitanga end of the Donga ... I walked onto a 13-foot python which I shot with my little rifle as I jumped out of its way - I told Roosevelt, who asked what I had shot, & he said he would like to have it, so we went back & took it home. I did not think it worth bothering about, as I have seen one killed ... at Kaap Muiden 27 feet, & have killed them up to about 20 feet or over."

28th April "Roosevelt I noticed began to doubt whether he was going to see lions as easily as I led him to expect, but I did not say more than that I would be as good as my word. Sandy took Kermit on to the Mua hills for Impala where he had lots of shots at them, but got nothing all day but a zebra in the evening close to the house. I sent the Colonel on to the plains where he got, if I remember right, zebra, granti, & steinbuck."

Shooting zebra and giraffe for sport was something for which Alfred could generate no enthusiasm, and on his own account he did not molest them, though he had at one time in the past taken zebra. But his object now was to provide for Roosevelt. Even so, he took no part in this day's events.

29th April "I intended before the day was over, Roosevelt should see lions, & took him first to Theki hill - the others, including the ladies, beating the bush below for lions - I took the Colonel first on to reedbuck & klipspringers. He did not get the klipspringers, but he got two Chanler's reedbuck - I then told him that the best chance to get lions, was to leave the men & noise & to just come with Nellie, Lavender, Sandy & me & Philip Percival who had just turned up, & I thought I could find one. He fell in at once with the idea, & I felt with Percival there, who is first class, & Nellie & Lavender who understand the game, & Sandy quite staunch & a good shot, that I was running less risk for them than with a big party when one is always bothered by other people's ideas.

We went to the Cheetah bush - it was blank - but I found fresh spoor in the Donga. There were several tracks, but only one big one - 'Ben,' the dog, set at a small bush at the moment the ladies were in an awkward place, & as soon as we got within 5 yards of the bush, there was a loud double grunt, & out belted two lion cubs in the direction of N. & L. but the Colonel killed them both at about 20 yards, though I

282

think Kermit got a ball into one.

I was very disappointed at their size, but our guests were pleased to have already got a couple of lions - I set out now to find their mamma or parents - but in vain. As evening was drawing on, I set off with Sandy at a canter, to have a look at the wild dog Donga, but Lavender & the Roosevelts would not be left behind & followed us - Nellie remaining behind with Roosevelt's gunbearers & syces, the only boys out with us.

Before getting to the Donga, I saw from my horse the fresh spoor of two big lions apparently - & the sand damp in their track. I knew they were not far off - the first single bush ahead looked likely. So placing the others, I fired a shot in - but they were not there - I pushed on to the last bush with our little party, & saw again the fresh double track. I took the Colonel & Kermit to within 10 yards & whispered to them to dismount - they had quickly got off as the first volley of grunts came to stir their blood - real good grunts. I seized Kermit's horse, & Sandy & I waited to shoot or to gallop. The Colonel got a good chance, & quickly gave the left hand lion a nasty one high up in the ribs, & I saw his back was touched but as he wanted 'to come' I shouted 'give him another,' & his next shot laid him out. I was responsible for the Colonel, & Sandy for Kermit. Kermit had not hit the right hand one, & now he & his father pumped lead into him till he was 500 yards off - this prevented me getting a good start, but I then started & called on Kermit to join me, & told him to do as I said & we would get him.

One of the nice things about the Roosevelts is that they do not mind being told what to do & what not to do - & followed my instructions not to go within 200 yards of a lion mounted, & to keep if dismounted, an extra 100 yards to remount in; though a lion, never in my experience, charges from 300 yds. Kermit came with me, & in less than a mile, we bailed him up & he took his stand - I held him there, & Kermit waited as I asked him to, till Sandy & Lavender joined us, & Nellie came up to help the Colonel with his horse.

We now advanced, Kermit to 150 *(yards)* when I told him to shoot him; the Colonel came with Nellie close to, to about 120 yards at right angles to us & about 200 yards from us - thus the lion did not know which way to face, & Ben turning up, gave him another enemy to divert him by baying at him. The Colonel I saw, stuck on his horse, & kept shooting from the saddle & missing. Nellie got R's syce to take his horse & then R. got to work properly - he missed him the first, but knocked the lion out of action with the second. Meanwhile I was getting uneasy as the thing lasted about ten minutes & I had never seen a lion so bombarded without charging; but every time he 'set' to charge, a shot from the other rifle, or a yell from me distracted him. Kermit fired some 20 shots ... & though with Sandy there, I felt we were safe enough even if he charged us, I got fidgety about his father. We photographed the lion & then dispatched him ... We reckoned this last lion had 35 shots fired at him before he succumbed - not very re-assuring for the man who is responsible for the safety of his guests, but I feel we can make things fairly free from danger."

Roosevelt, at the end of his stay, wrote a letter of thanks to one unnamed organiser - a letter which was shown to Nellie, who made a

33. U.S. ex-President Colonel Theodore Roosevelt and son Kermit, with his first buffalo, Kenya, 1909.

34. Roosevelt with warthog. (Photography by Alfred Edward Pease.)

copy, and who felt it very nice to know that he could write to a third party in the following terms:

> "Well your thoughtfulness has borne the most ample fruit of success for me, a success in which my own prowess has played but a small part! The Peases are among the most delightful people I have ever met, and Sir Alfred got me 4 big lions ... I hope the Peases are permanent friends, I am devoted to them. Kermit has really done very well; I am proud of him, I have done no hard work; I am afraid I couldn't do any real work now; but no man has ever had more fun! I have enjoyed every minute."

After his guests had left, Alfred got back to the business of finishing the painting of his new house. Within a few days, Sandy Medlicott got word to return to England.

Adjoining Alfred's farm in addition to the previously mentioned Hill's at Wami, and Philip Percival's at Potha, there was a more recent arrival, a German Afrikaaner named Werner. His farm was Spring Vale, and was situated on the western boundary of Alfred's farm. After eleven months' very hard work on his 3,000 acres, Werner decided to sell up at a loss and return to South Africa.

284

He wrote to Alfred on 14th May asking him if he would be interested in purchasing the farm. After some consideration, he took an option to purchase. There was a possibility that Gerald Buxton might be interested, and if so, then together with Kilima Theki (5,000 acres), Kitanga (now increased in area by an additional ten acres, to make it twenty acres), and Mua Hills (1,000 acres), they would have between them some 9,000 odd acres.

Going by train on 1st June, from Kapiti Station to Nairobi,

"I had hardly got into the train in a 2nd C. carriage with Prinsloo & Werner & an English youth, than the latter began to ply me with what I thought were rather impertinent questions. Where was I going to; did I know the country; how long &c &c, & then he said 'Do you by any chance know Sir Alfred Pease?' - He was much taken aback when I told him I was the man - he had a letter of introduction from Fitzgerald Wilson to me & his name was Algernon Cartwright.

The following day I had a long talk with him as he sought my advice as to how he cd. best invest his £500 of capital, & what I recommended him to do. I was sorry for him, as he came out with the idea he cd. make money easily farming in this country - I explained to him it was a long rough uphill job, taming wild country, & one only fitted as a rule for Boers & hardy farmers - that a pioneer by himself must be willing to toil hard, & expect but little return for years, that a small percentage of even this class survived or reached success - and that I counted success for a pioneer to be able to enjoy the simple necessities of life ...

I advised him on no account to touch his capital, or let people know of it, but look round, take a billet with a good farmer on the terms 'work for keep,' & decide after a year's experience.

This young fellow had never been out of England, had no idea what anything was; asked me what 'those' were, pointing to zebra ..."

Leaving Algernon Cartwright, and upon arrival at the Norfolk Hotel, Nairobi, Alfred was seized by Kermit Roosevelt and taken for lunch, dinner and breakfast the following day with Theodore Roosevelt, after which

"Kermit came to the station to see me off & gave me an Indian silver chased cigarette case. He is a nice warm hearted boy & I like him very much - Got to Athi River 1.30 & home 4.30 - all well at Kitanga, but H. (Hill) behaved very badly & like a brute to his gunbearer yesterday, & upset both Nellie & Lavender - N. had to separate them in a free fight - our boys are all mad with him."

In mid-June, Alfred started to pack up for the return to England, booking passages for 28th June.

29th June "My birthday, 52 years old - & I have not been in such good health for years - & am less worried than in the days of wealth when its cares, business engagements & public life were, combined with all my varied pursuits, more than I could stand - My only worry now-a-days is how to make ends meet, but I feel at the worst, I can return to Kitanga & live the simple life there - Africa still fascinates me, but I am not sure that I do not look back to the years spent in Algeria, in the desert & in the Aures mountains, as the ones most full of charm & wonder - The invasion of brutish British ideas into B.E.A. & S.A., taints those lands in a way that is hardly felt in the desert, & those red bare but beautiful mountains of the Atlas Range."

After arriving in London and a short stay at Birch Hall, Theydon Bois to see Gerald Buxton, and discuss the "Spring Vale" purchase option, Nellie, who was tired after the journey, went off on a round to see her sisters, and Alfred alone arrived back at Pinchinthorpe on 19th July.

"At Pinchinthorpe all looked delightful - the roses the most ravishing sight."
22nd Aug. "Time & inclination have been wanting, hence my journal has been irregular since our return home, & indeed I think I shall drop the regular entry of my doings, they do not get more interesting as I get older & there are so many volumes of them that no one will ever care to read them ...
Since Sunday, 1st, the subject which has occupied my mind most has been Lavender's engagement. Solicitude for her future has been uppermost, & though it will be a great giving up to me to lose her, I do not know any man I would rather give her up to than Sandy Medlicott - But it is an anxious business, and he is hardly in a position to provide for her as I think she ought to be ...
I have heard from Edward this last week, & am very disappointed to think we shall not see him this year, but he writes happily about his work."

Alfred picks up his life at home again as though he hasn't been away. He also, sometime during the last two months, has decided to try and sell Kitanga - and it is assumed that it was that property alone, and not the Kilima Theki and Mua Hills Estate that he wanted to sell. But he gives no reason for this sudden move. Probably it was an attempt to raise some development capital. Whether or not, Kitanga was advertised, but in the event, no purchaser came forward.

14th Nov. "At Birch Hall - Talked B.E.A. with Gerald who takes my offer to him of Werner's *(Spring Vale)* & finds £1,500 - £500 this next 12 mos. if required - I am really giving him a present of hundreds of pounds in Werner's - but I want him, as he has volunteered to join me, to have a good thing & I cannot get on with the business unless more capital is put in."

A farming partnership is now established between Alfred, Arthur Slatter and Gerald Buxton, on terms not spelt out in the journals but in supplementary fragments. Slatter had been having a struggle at Kilima

Kiu, and it was out of friendship that Alfred made the partnership offer to him. The main terms were:

1. Slatter takes over the management from Dick Allsop with effect from 1st November, 1909. Dick Allsop had had enough of this pioneering business and wanted to return to South Africa.
2. Slatter to have residence at either Kitanga, Theki or Spring Vale.
3. Interests as follows:-

(1) Sir Alfred E. Pease, Theki,
Kitanga & Mua Hills, computed at ...... £2,000 = 4/9ths

(2) Capt. A.A. Slatter, Kilima Kiu,
computed at .... £1,000 = 2/9ths
(to receive a salary £98 p.a.)

(3) Gerald Buxton, Spring Vale, cash capital ... £1,500 = 1/3rd

£4,500

(Gerald Buxton pays £350 purchase money for Spring Vale and £500 working capital for the first year - the balance (£650) of the £1,500 later, if needed)

Partners to remain individual owners of land until some other scheme mutually agreed upon.

This autumn he had many days out with hounds, a few days shooting and entertaining friends, among whom was Oscar Staten visiting from the Transvaal. The New Year opened out for him in much the same way, with hunting, shooting and visitors.

1910

This January there was a General Election. Undecided how he should act, Alfred, after posing three questions to each candidate, satisfied himself that he could no longer support Samuel, and declared publicly that he was going to support the Tory candidate, Lewis.

Herbert Samuel was once more returned as Liberal M.P. for Cleveland, but his majority was halved. Herbert Pike Pease lost his seat at Darlington, and Jack lost his at Saffron Walden:

"I have heard with sorrow of Jack's defeat at Saffron Walden today - Now there is not a Pease in the House for the first time since 1865."

30th Jan. "To Guisboro' Meeting with Kit & Nellie. Lavender never goes now & is going to join the established church - Her mother is less in sympathy with her doing this than I am, for I think it is best if young people *care* to be as much 'one' in these matters as possible when they marry - & tho' I cannot understand, just as Nellie cannot, how anyone, without a sacrifice of sincerity, declare their belief in such terms as are prescribed - yet I am not prepared to say, that others cannot at least deceive themselves, into either believing, or at least into believing in the necessity of declaring, that they believe them - and for most women, there is something that appeals to them, to being messed about by Clerics &c - Let those who persuade themselves that it is the right thing, to do it; if they live long enough, & are honest with themselves, they will see through a great deal of the nonsense ere they finish their course - & yet unity is worth something too, & give & take."

10th Feb. "30th Anniversary of our Wedding Day. Nellie & Lavender have gone to Bishopthorpe today, to stay a night in order to get Lavender baptized by the Most Revd. His Grace the Lord Archbishop. He kindly asked me to come too, which was tolerant for a Church of England dignitary, but I have no use for them - & their pretensions to magic & supernatural control of the destinies of souls only give me cerebral irritations - Hounds met at Ayton Firs & there was a large field out but a poor day."

11th Feb. "N & L returned from Bishopthorpe. Lavender enchanted with the Archbishop. Nellie rather sad that she should find such comfort & pleasure from this, & that all her own efforts & views have had no impression compared with an hour's talk with a young ecclesiastic - but she herself was young once & was influenced by these things, & only life has taught her that what matters is what we are, & to be true to our best knowledge, & not what we label ourselves - Sincerity is better than any creed."

Lavender went to Bishopthorpe with Nellie for her confirmation towards the end of March. Alfred was laid up in bed following a hunting accident.

"I was left in bed to nurse my leg & had all the windows open. A lovely sunny day with the song of birds, the cry of gulls & wheeling peewits & the cooing of cushats in the plantation pouring into my room - I lay there alone with my reflections."

19th May "I was much occupied during April over many things - lectures - papers - correspondence - & local duties - that I kept no diary during April. I did my usual round of Bench, County Council Committees, Ayton School, Cleveland Bay Meeting, lectured at Newcastle & other places - hunted a few days - attended Richardson's Charity Meeting - Wilson Pease Board & many such things.

Nellie wished us to turn out for spring cleaning at the end of the month - & she went to London about April 24th - & Lavender a few days earlier went to the Medlicotts - I was left alone here - & fixed to go to Algeria with Christopher for a fortnight & have a week after larrowi - & last night I got back here - & am again alone - Nellie is at Murren & Lavender in the south - I left Kit in Paris on Tuesday *(17th May)."*

288

He then sets down an account of his fortnight in Algeria. He and Christopher had arrived at Algiers on 2nd May and left immediately for El Kantara, and on 3rd May,

"Arr. at Hotel Bertrand, El Kantara where many years ago we stayed when Lavender & Kit were little children - it was a poor little pub then; now it is a clean hotel - M. Mertrand (Eugene) is still there; he came there in 1864 - I found all the arrangements I had made by letter complete - but as our time is short, there is no use trying to get to my best places for sheep."

4th May "Marched through the gorge by starlight & *Comet* light (Halley's Comet is brilliant here) at 3.30 a.m. - with tents, baggage & provisions on 6 mules - Kit & I on foot with our little party."

5th May "Off at 4 a.m. after a cup of coffee. Kit took the East I took the West & worked hard & nearly got to Turkeh without seeing many fresh tracks of sheep ... & Kit had the same sort of day, but captured one of my old friends the Elephant Trunk Rat. After inspecting him, we let the little fellow go - We caught several varieties of rats & mice, but I would not kill any of them, as I have not the brutality necessary for scientific collection of small mammals - though I have done some bloody work with birds, when collecting seriously - still, not without violence to my nature - & as I grow old I am not so anxious to kill as to see things - yet the thirst to get even with a wiley old ram returns to me when they have defeated me day after day, & hard work has made me bloodthirsty."

6th May "Marched before light by Comet light towards Turkeh & camped about 10 at the entrance to the fine gorge of Shabah Hadeid - In the evening hunt saw nothing but tracks of a few mouflon, & admi, & a jackal or two - It is 17 years since I was in this mountain when I camped alone with Ali bel Kassim in the Turkeh Gorge - among the oleanders."

An attack of sciatica the following day distracted Alfred for the rest of this trip and

12th May "Had a bad night, & could not at 3 a.m. look at breakfast - I had to make up my mind to march on an empty stomach in great pain with sciatica to El Oulaia station - At 4 a.m. I had made up my mind that if any man could bear the agony of walking 21 kilometres over rough ground, I would do it, & did it, covering the distance before 8 a.m. How I did it I can't think, only that I am very fit & when determined, things can be done - glad to throw myself on a table at the restaurant by the station, & then on a bench at the station till the train arrived at 8.50 - & we got to El Kantara in time for déjeuner there, & our mules came in a little later."

13th May "I determined to stick to our plan of going to Biskra today - Wound up things at El Kantara & left at noon, each with a hat box for luggage - arr. Biskra at 2 - & went to the Hotel Victoria - welcomed by the Osers - there is no one else here, nor has been for some time ... we had No. 27 room, the room Nellie & I occupied when we first were at Biskra in 1892 - just the same, the same furniture, carpet curtains & stencilled pattern on the walls - I could not walk about but managed to stand a drive all round the oasis into my old haunts - was hailed by two of my old Arabs as I passed the cafés near the Oulad Nail quarter - El Arbi & another one. Heard of the death of my old Arab hunters & friends, Ali bel Kassim ben Chergui Saharoui, & Mohammed ben Said - & of others too - found Ahmeda ben Houbi, who was magnificent & profuse in his expressions of devotion - & I was everything, for had he not gained thousands of francs by my recommendations - he was now rich."

They left Algiers on 15th May. Upon reaching Paris, Alfred left his son there, while he carried on homeward, passing through London where preparations were taking place for the funeral of King Edward VII.

"Alone at home - at least 300 letters waiting for me, took me from 9 p.m. to 12.20 a.m. to open them & see what they were."

On 27th May he was back in London, and there met Nellie and Lavender who had just returned from Murren. From London they went to stay with Edward North Buxton at his home at Knighton. Theodore Roosevelt was the principal guest there over the week-end.

28th May "The other visitors to meet the great man were Selous, Sir Wm. Garstin, Lord Warwick, Rhys Williams - Gerald & Ethel, & Col. Paterson came on Sunday ... a very pleasant & interesting party - Roosevelt was really pleased to see me and gave me a good deal of his time, taking me into E.N.B.'s room on Sunday (29th) afternoon to have a quiet chat - rather to the annoyance of our host I fear, but I tried to escape monopolising any more of his time than I could help ..."

On 6th June, Alfred was back in London, where, at the Savoy Hotel,

"I dined at the Fauna dinner to Roosevelt. I sat by George Grey[5] & near many old friends - saw Kermit who really hugged me & Roosevelt took me aside after dinner awhile - to tell me he had read my Lion M.S.[6] & that it must be published & that it was 'quite admirable.' He said, 'you would notice I quoted from you (I had noticed) in my speech,' though he did not mention me save 'as one who is one of the greatest lion hunters in the world'."

8th June "Nellie & I lunched with the Leas in Chesterfield Street to meet Mr & Mrs Roosevelt - It was a farewell luncheon party as they sail on the 10th - There were there - Lord Selborne, Lloyd George, Jacobs, Johnny Millais & a few others. It was funny to sit between Lloyd George & Kermit - It is the first time I have met Selborne since before he went out to S. Africa - he has not changed much - Roosevelt sat bet. Selborne & Lloyd George - Had a good talk with R which I enjoyed more than talking to Lloyd George. The latter is pleasant enough, but understands nothing outside his little world."

In late June Alfred went to the Royal Show at Liverpool to judge the Cleveland Bay horse classes, and soon after he returned home Nellie and Lavender went off to London to buy the trousseau for Lavender's wedding, leaving Alfred, who had much to do, behind. Two days later,

> *6th July* "About 11 a.m. I got a telegram to say that 'Nellie unwell. General condition excellent' - a diplomatic telegram always makes me ten times as nervous as the bare truth - I wired back for full particulars - & just when Bertie & Mag Barclay & Mrs Humphrey had come for lunch I got one from Sir Thos. Barlow, 'slight haemorrhage - advise you don't come till tomorrow' - but I packed up & got off at 3.30 & arrived at 23, Bentick St. soon after 11 to find as I expected, that Nellie was very ill ...
> Since then till today July 11th, I have been there ... & she has, with her pluck, struggled through some bad days & nights but is progressing. She said to me she could not have struggled back to life except for my sake - & I think the awful state I should be left alone in, with my sons & daughter gone, was her chief incitement to live."

Christopher was now engaged to be married to Margaret Phillipa Johnson. Phillipa was aged twenty-three, ten months younger than Christopher, and their wedding was planned for December. During the coming five months, with two weddings ahead, there would be great changes coming to family life. Edward was still in the Sudan, and Lavender's wedding was settled for October. By the year end there would be just Alfred and Nellie remaining at Pinchinthorpe.

On 15th July, having got past the initial crisis, Nellie was considered sufficiently improved to be able to withstand a rail journey in an invalid saloon back home.

> "It was very easy & comfortable, leaving her room in London at 10.40 & being in her bed before 6 p.m. at home - better rather than worse for the journey."

Nellie made slow but certain progress, and by the end of the month, when there were some lovely sunny days, she was able to sit about outside in the garden once more.

During this time, Alfred had a lunch visit from Tom Parrington. Now aged 93, his memory went back to the time when the site of the town of Middlesbrough was nothing but green fields, he having been born at the farm there.

> "The old gentleman was very fit & bright, most interesting & amusing in his conversation & anecdotes - his memory is perfectly good as to names, dates & events. He is rather blind, lame & deaf - He told me many stories of old times - He drank sherry during lunch & drank 5 glasses of '47 Port after lunch - I had 3 bottles

in the cellar laid down by my father in 1854 ... Tom Parrington said he owed his health & age to following the maxim 'moderation in all things'."

Alfred made no entries during the whole of August, and his next appears on

2nd Sept. "This is the first time for more than a month that I put down anything - my terrible anxiety increased at the beginning of August, & Sir Thomas Oliver was summoned. He gave me hope that I should keep Nellie, & did not despair at all of her reaching a certain point of recovery. And now I see little hope. How long I shall have her I cannot tell, but she is going to leave me ... and as *all* my happiness has been in her & with her & through her, I cannot bear it ..."

As his anxiety increased, he sent a cable to Edward who arrived home from Khartoum in nine days.

4th Sept. "I cannot get away from myself; every corner of the world I know speaks to me ... every creeper on the house, every plant, tree, field, road, hill is full of the 34 years of her never changing love & being. I can see nothing & touch nothing without tears & gripping at my heart ... The most precious hours to me are in the afternoons when I lie beside her on the bed & have her hand caressing mine & feel she still is there."

A month later, 5th October was Lavender's wedding day, at Guisborough Parish Church.

"I rose at 5 after a very sleepless night, and at 6 a.m., Lavender, knowing I was up, came into my room and sat awhile on the hearth rug by the fire I had lit at 4 a.m. & chatted to me. She gave me a photograph of herself in a little silver frame dated this day - I gave her a prettily bound Prayer Book in which I had written some verses which I feel are the greatest help to those whose faith is weak ...
It was a lovely sunrise and the day was more beautiful than any day this year - I had made all the arrangements for the day & all worked smoothly - Nellie had had a good night, & was as sweetly calm & bright & perfect as any mother ever was - When all but Lavender & I had left the house, she in her lovely but simple bridal dress, & I went in to her mother for a minute or two - they 2 had been together before - & I had been alone too with Nellie - she to give me courage - then over rose leaves spread by those about the door, she & I went off, and arrived exactly at the time. Up the long Nave behind the Choir, slowly up to the Altar rails, & then I handed my child over to another.
It was a very pretty sunny wedding, but I felt the strain very much. There is just sufficient Pease in me to get through such ordeals.
I arranged for Sandy & Lavender to arrive here before any of us, so that Nellie should receive them. This she did - We then all gathered in the garden ...
A little later, the ... motor came round to take them to Askrigg - I went up to fetch Lavender - I found her in Nellie's room - Nellie sitting in a pretty dressing gown in

the big chair, & Lavender on her knees saying loving things with her head in her mother's lap - I had my parting on the stairs & off they went."

After 16th October, with all hope for Nellie lost, Alfred's journal entries for this year cease.

Nellie died on 4th November, 1910, just one month before her fifty-second birthday, and was buried close by Alfred's sister Effie, in the little churchyard at Newton-under-Roseberry.

On 20th December, he faced up to what was for him the final ordeal of these last few months; his younger son Christopher's marriage to Margaret Phillipa Johnson at Arncliffe Church near Northallerton; had Nellie been with him, it would have seemed so much less the almost final act of family dispersal. Then four days before Christmas, Edward took leave of his father and his father's home, and returned to the Sudan. Now there was no one but Alfred, alone with his thoughts as he turned back into his empty and silent house.

In a letter he wrote to Edward he said,

"... You must not think I am lonely *because* I may be by myself - the kind of loneliness I have is not all pain, & it is sometimes more felt when not alone. I cannot describe it, but one of the great weights in it is this - that we who have had no secrets from each other - *now she* holds - has solved the great secret - & I am in the dark guessing - I could not bear that she should suffer without me ... she is still close as close can be, and she did believe 'Life cannot end, so love has no farewell'."

Notes:
1. Walter Sandfield Medlicott.
2. Hadji Mohammed Abdullah, known as the Mad Mullah. It was not until 1920, that the Mullah was finally brought to submission, and then only by means of aerial bombardment.
3. A. Blayney Percival of the Kenya Colony Game Department, was the brother of Philip Percival who farmed at Potha on the Kapiti Plains.
4. Frederick Courteney Selous, the adventurer and big game hunter.
5. Brother of Rt. Hon Sir Edward Grey, Bt., K.G., M.P.
6. *The Book of the Lion* by Sir Alfred E. Pease, published 1913 by John Murray.

CHAPTER FOURTEEN

The African Farm Fiasco &
to Switzerland in Secret

1911

"During the 30 years of my married life, I have kept a Journal with fair regularity. In it I have entered all sorts of things besides my own passing thoughts & personal experiences. When my darling was taken from me out of sight, much of what hitherto seemed of importance in this world seemed, & will continue to be very trivial & worthless - I will not say there is no happiness left to me however lonely I may be, however much I miss that voice which was the sweetest music I have known, and those true sweet eyes.

I am not unhappy, but have no anchorage here ... Yet I shall try to continue a record as descendants may find some things of interest to them, for the old order changes ..."

2nd Jan. "Left Pinchinthorpe I hope in good order, & all my affairs settled."

On 5th January, Alfred left London for Marseilles with Howard Pease and George Grey, bound for British East Africa. Leaving Naples it was quite dark when the boat passed his old island Villa home on Capri where a few months of life had been shared with Nellie five years ago.

Upon reaching Port Sudan, Alfred was there joined by Edward. He had resigned his appointment he said, on health grounds, and was going with his father to Kitanga, his father's house, before returning home. After leaving Port Sudan,

"An exquisite soft tinted sunrise - calmer & warmer 80° 7 a.m. - Last night a most, (if not the most) perfect & exquisite moonlit sky & sea I ever looked on. The moon sailing through vistas of feathery purple & green & red clouds, & across soft purple cloud masses. Behind these great & bright edged dark heaps of loveliness she cast silver paths on the calm deep blue & glistening sea."

19th Jan. "This afternoon I dreamed of N. the 2nd time only since Nov. 4th last - She was walking with me in a grey walking dress & hat and talking eagerly and

294

happily and emphasised what she had to say in the old sweet way by pressing my hand, but alas, I remember not what she said - we turned in at a garden gate, she turned round to close it and then went on talking to me and gave me a kiss & I awoke."

28th Jan. "Arrived at Athi River - we were met by Slatter - George *(Grey)* bicycled up - we rode ponies - arrived before sundown at Kitanga. Great alterations and improvements ... *But."*

It must here be explained that a number of changes have taken place since last year, both in the partnership and in the land being farmed.

In the first place, Gerald Buxton had retired from the partnership as from 31st October, 1910 but retained a £500 interest. Alfred was buying the 3,000 acre Spring Vale farm from Buxton, and had also taken an option on 1,000 acres at Chumbi which lies to the south of Spring Vale, and from which it was separated by the public road to Machakos. Alfred still had his 5,000 acres at Kilima Theki, the 20 acre Kitanga, and 1,000 acres at Mua Hills.

Arthur Slatter had sold his 7,000 acre farm at Kilima Kiu to a man named Archie Lambert. In place of Kilima Kiu, Slatter had bought cheap 2,000 acres west of Spring Vale known as Klopper's, and 1,000 acres north of Spring Vale known as Botha's. Slatter also had 2,000 acres at Lanjoro to the east of Kilima Theki. The combined acreage in the partnership was therefore 15,020 as to:-

Alfred	9,020
and Chumbi under option	1,000
	10,020
Slatter	5,000
Total	15,020
	acres

It is nowhere stated, but is presumed that the cash difference received by Slatter from the sale of Kilima Kiu and that paid out for Klopper's and Botha's was retained in the partnership capital.

Alfred and Slatter were equal partners with 4/9ths each, the other 1/9th being Buxton's retained interest. The stock was joint and equal, and upon termination of the partnership, for which a year's notice was agreed, the stock and proceeds were to be divided equally. On these new terms, Slatter was to give up his salary (increased sometime last year to £200) and management remuneration, and must build his own residence within three years.

Because the farm ostrich stock was in danger from lions two of which had been heard grunting close to Kitanga the night before his arrival, and four others were known to be prowling about Theki, a decision was made the day after Alfred's arrival to pre-empt the probable slaughter of livestock, and an immediate start after lions was made. Alfred wanted to give George Grey the chance he had been longing for, but he wanted also that both his own son, Edward, and Howard Pease be kept under the guidance of a reliable man. Harold and Clifford Hill were anxious to settle accounts with the lions. Harold Hill was to take charge of the drive, Clifford Hill to stand by Howard Pease, Slatter to support George Grey, and Alfred, keeping Edward with him, was to bail up on the plains any lion that broke away.

George Grey was no novice at big game hunting. He had spent some years in South Africa where he had killed many lions. He had spent years in Uganda where he had hunted elephant. He absolutely revelled in the most dangerous moments and from fighting his way out of a tight corner. Particularly, he took delight in deliberately increasing the danger, raising the stakes and shortening the odds. For him, nothing compared to the thrill of hunting elephant in the long grass of Uganda, because it was longer and thicker than anywhere else, and 'the danger and excitement increases in proportion to the length of the grass'.

George Grey had brought out with him a ·280 Ross single-barrelled magazine rifle which was new to him and untried.

"The meet was at Lanjoro at 8.30 - There we fixed to drive Theki Hill first ...
A lioness was found in a bush on the S. end of K. Theki & Howard had a good chance to bag it, but could not see it, or was too slow - it then broke back towards Slatter & Grey - Grey had a fair chance at her standing below him in the open at 180 yds. but missed her, & from the plain, Edward & I watched her gallop through the bush.
To Slatter's surprise, and in spite of his protests, Geo. Grey ran into the bush after her down the hill, & Slatter followed. Meanwhile I saw her lie down in a small bush with longish grass round it, about 400 yds above where Edward & I were watching on our horses. I told Edward to keep his eye on the bush & not to move - & if she broke towards him, to let her pass him before firing, & I galloped up to where Slatter & Grey were standing & told them I had her marked down, intending them to wait till all came up, & till I got back to Edward & my post, but to my disgust, George set off running as hard as he could to the bush I had pointed

to, as the one in wh. she was. I cantered after him as well as I could, over the rough ground & bush calling him to wait, but he paid no attention to me - he had only his ·280 rifle & I had only my ·256 - he ran right up to the bush, & I had no alternative but to abandon my pony & run up too, for I felt almost certain she would charge, & I thought it unlikely that either of us would stop her at 10 yds. range - In fact I never felt more sure of a bad business - but he would not listen to me, or even speak to me - To my intense relief, just as we got within 3 yds of the bush Edward shouted that she had left the bush & gone up the hill.

After this display of rashness, the Hills, Slatter & I decided to leave her & find something in the open. What happened after this I have set out with great care elsewhere. It is an illustration of the danger to all there is, in any one man acting on his own, & in defiance to the rules after every disposition for safety had been made. It was a display of suicidal courage, & a terrific but wonderful sight to see George take those great brutes on - He had no business to be there at all, he had no business to ride after the lions, nor to get within 200 yards of them, but he did all a brave man could do when he had made a mess of everything, to save his life by coolness & valour."

Two lions were seen by Clifford Hill and Alfred, just after they had swept down the main donga and were on a right-handed turn away from it. From the point where the two lions were sighted, Alfred and Clifford Hill followed behind the lions on the outside of the turn, whilst Howard Pease and George Grey were following at some distance on the inside of the sweep, the two lions moving back up towards the main donga. Alfred started to follow the slower of the two lions on the inside from Hill who was following the faster of the two.

"I was a minute or two watching the spot where he had gone into the donga, and then saw that he had come out further down, and was rapidly catching up the leading lion, and Hill was now half a mile ahead of me, so I just pushed on & caught up with Hill.

Both the lions were now turning off Wami, and my lion had now passed Hill's lion, and I was thinking of nothing else but where they would stand, and guessed it would be in the little donga (towards Theki), when Hill called my attention to Grey and Howard Pease who, I saw to my surprise, galloping hard directly behind the lions perhaps 350 yards behind, but gaining on them. Hill shouted to me 'They will drive them right up Wami. We must get ahead. For goodness sake stop them.' We were still galloping, and till that moment, never thought of anyone else having anything to do with *us*.

I felt certain we had both lions collared and safe, and that we should hold them till the main party came up. I could see no one else in sight besides these two who had appeared suddenly upon the scene. I yelled, waved and blew my whistle as hard as I could, but Grey who must have seen my frantic efforts and heard the noise, paid not the slightest attention, and to my surprise, I saw him gaining rapidly on the rear lion, Howard Pease coming across to me. Still, I never dreamt that Grey was

297

going to literally try and ride them down, and was more annoyed than anything else that the lions were being pressed up the hill just as we had begun to turn them. Then Hill called out 'Grey is getting too near.' Then what happened all took place in about 4 seconds, and as quick as you can think and see. I put the facts down as they flashed on me:-

Moment 1. Grey galloping hard 100 yards directly at the tail of the rear lion, the other lion some 60 to 80 yards ahead of the rear lion. *(At this moment)* Hill cried out to me some despairing exclamation such as 'My God they will have him for a certainty,' and leaping from his horse said 'shoot him shoot him.'

Moment 2. The rear lion whipped round and stopped for a moment & the other stopped and faced round. Grey some 80 to 90 yards directly below him on the hill side.

Moment 3. The lion charged at once.

Moment 4. Grey leapt from his pony in a flash and stood in shooting attitude all at the same moment, the lion then say 40 yards from Grey. (Hill positive that Grey dismounted before the charge began).

Moment 5. Lion at 25 yards. 1st shot from Grey. No effect.

Moment 6. Lion at 5 yards. 2nd shot immediately after 1st. No effect. Lion on top of Grey.

That is what I saw in say 4 seconds of time.

At moment 1 I was bewildered with horror, and hearing Hill's appeal to shoot pulled up dead, and had got to the ground when I saw the lion prepare to charge and charge all at once. I had just got my rifle to my shoulder and had cried to Hill 'it is too far; it is over 300 yards,' when Hill said 'shoot, shoot 200 yards,' and he fired his bullet which fell short by about 10 feet.

Realising the position, conscious that Howard Pease was either on his feet or on his pony close by, I leapt on my horse and galloped over roughish ground in the hollow dividing me from Grey close by. Pease, with my eyes fixed on the horrible scene in front of me. The 300 yards seemed like half a mile, and the lion lifted his head when we got within 50 yards and ceased mauling Grey.

At about 20 or 25 yards we left our ponies, and hardly got to the ground and ran in when C. Hill, who had not stopped to remount, but ran with great speed was there too. The rest of the story is not what I seek to dwell on - Hill gave the lion the knock out shot with his ·404 before it jammed. I fired 3 shots, including the final one in the brain & Howard Pease two shots.

The position was rendered worse by the other lion preparing to charge and grunting 60 yards above. Hill begged me to shoot it. It flashed on me that he too will be down on us if I do not kill him. Hill was unarmed and this was Howard's first sight of lions. I begged them not to look at the other lion - and he got up and walked away.

My feelings were awful ...

When the lion was dead and the other lion moved away from us, I knelt down by the mangled body thinking he was dead, but though he was one sheet of blood from head to waist, he opened his eyes & said to me, 'I am afraid this is a bad business Alfred,' and after a few words from me he said, 'Remember, whatever happens, that no one but myself is to blame for this. It is all my own stupidity and

298

foolishness.' I said something more & he said, 'No, but I wish you to remember that I said, no one but I am to blame for this.'
I was in a great state of alarm about Edward - he alone was missing of the party, and the lion which had moved off soon after we had disposed of his companion was a great big savage brute ... and would certainly go for anyone he came across. Slatter kindly went in search of Edward & found him on Hill's mule, watching and following this brute, quite alone and quite ignorant of the accident."

Edward was sent to Machakos, some twelve miles distant, and men were sent two miles to Potha to cut trees from which to fashion a stretcher, and an old stretcher was brought from Wami and a travelling litter made, overlaid with grass, and shaded from the sun, and after Grey's wounds had been dressed with pure carbolic acid, and morphia given, he was taken some hours later by special train from Kapiti Plains to hospital at Nairobi.

"I was in a most dreadful mess when Howard and I arrived at Nairobi in the early hours of Monday, 30th January, - I had been drenched through with George's and the lion's blood while giving first aid - had no clothes to change into, and neither Howard nor I had *(had)* a meal since 6.00 a.m. *the previous day,* - We had helped to carry George part of the 13 miles, and after getting him to the hospital, we walked, (it is a long way) to the Norfolk Hotel *(at)* about 2.00 a.m. - it was locked up - Knowing the premises, I found a way in - but could find no one - the manager's name is Blanc - I tried to get into the kitchen - it was locked -
I saw from the corridor, one could climb about ten feet and get over the partition, and so into the kitchen, and I had just got to the top of the partition, and Howard looking on, when Blanc appeared in his pyjamas with a candle - I was afraid he would shoot, and hurriedly explained - but it took some explaining why I was trying at 2.00 a.m. to get into his kitchen, all covered in blood.
When I had got some idea of the situation into him, and calmed his anger, he went and got us two bottles of soda water, some biscuits and a box of sardines, and we ate them and then rested in the sitting room, till daylight revealed to us the disreputable condition we were in - the hotel was full, but before the day was over, we got rooms and got washed - a visitor kindly lent me a jacket, and Edward having sent a runner with clothes, by Tuesday we were more respectable."

For three days George Grey made progress, and his wounds, all except his upper left arm showed signs of healing, but on 3rd February, with blood poisoning he became delirious, and died that evening, and was buried the following day in the cemetery at Nairobi.

"My recollection of the funeral is chiefly the weight of the coffin, and the pain of it on my shoulder as we carried it the long distance to the cemetery, and of the heat ...
After George's funeral I was tired out, and spent the next day, Sunday 5th February at Nairobi ..."

Alfred telegraphed news of the tragedy to Sir Edward Grey, and returned to Kitanga two days after the funeral.

11th Feb. "As we were going to Kilima Kiu between K. Theki & Potha near the river, there was a stampede of about 3,000 kongoni, zebra, & wildebeest from Machakos side towards Theki & Wami - we were in the middle of it. Three wildebeest bulls charged me - I stopped the two leaders & they all turned - they were about 30 yards off when I knocked them both down - Howard polished off one & got an excellent head."

On 25th February, Alfred, his son Edward and Howard Pease left Nairobi for Lake Victoria. At Entebbe they met and talked briefly with Lord Kitchener who was on his way from Khartoum to Mombasa, and after parting from Howard Pease (who went home), and seeing the Ripon Falls and Lake Victoria, returned on 6th March to Kitanga.

Following the tragedy, Alfred felt that the extra cautions he took with Edward frequently disappointed the latter, but during the next three weeks they had further sorties after lion and other game and then packed up, boarded their ship at Mombasa and started on the journey home.

15th Apl. "Crossed via Boulogne & Folkestone. Edward went straight on to Pinchinthorpe where Xpher & Phillipa are, & I went to spend Sunday (16th) with Edward Grey - We had many hours of close converse about our dead, our pain, our hopes & many things nearest our hearts, he has learnt many of the same lessons - & we find comfort in many of the same thoughts - Lavender came up late last night to meet me - I loved seeing her sweet face. She is a lovely daughter to me, and I find a tenderness & gentleness in her that I never guessed was there - My Nellie did not slave, suffer & die in vain - I see this in all my children."

18th Apl. "Lavender came with me to Pinchinthorpe, met by Edward, Xpher & Phillipa - but I listen for a footstep & long for the smile & blue eyes I shall never see again - Yet alone in the familiar room I slept well - where am I in my dreamless sleep? I sometimes think I have spent that time with her I wake so quiet in my mind."

24th Apl. "I felt very ill all the morning with very bad palpitation & intermission of the heart - Today I heard the first cuckoo & nightingale."

After a further visit to London to see Sir Edward Grey, Alfred turned to the problems of his own affairs. He was hard pressed to pay his taxes, and the expenses of last year had made things difficult. Edward now at Pinchinthorpe was starting a new career at Normanby Iron works *"to learn something, but of course earns nothing."*

6th June "Up early after a bad night & out into a glorious morning of sun, shadows & singing birds ... then to Headlam Hall & a most charming afternoon with Jack,

300

Elsie and Joe in their delightful old garden & in the fields. Elsie's taste is very pretty, her flowers & house very lovely - but it is curious to see the old common things that Nellie & I had to discard as too common for the servants such as blue willow pattern earthenware now the fashionable craze - I remember our servants refusing to use pewter which was the serviceable servants' hall stuff when we married, & we turned ours out into the dog kennels & poultry yards - now it is run after!"

23rd July "Since I last made an entry in my journal *(15th June)* I have been at home and the time has passed somehow - most days Edward has been at Normanby where he is interested in his work & in the evenings we are together - The weather has been glorious & the garden lovely, save 2 days' rain it has been unbroken perfect summer, with afternoon temperatures indoors often about 80, but seldom more than a degree higher - just what Edward & I like - but it's strange to go round my garden & eat so many meals alone, & to come into empty rooms decorated with flowers for no one to see."

During September, Alfred went up to Drumochter to shoot with the Albrights, and went on from there to Cowie, near Stonehaven to shoot for six days with Gerald Buxton, from where

"Ethel & Blanche took me in the motor with them. This day *(28th Sept)* we went via Deeside to Corndavon - lunched with Mrs Lundie, & saw the places made familiar for ever during 20 years of my life - How few are left of those I tramped the heather with - I thought of my father & mother, Uncle John, my uncles, Willie Barclay, Frank Lockwood, Gurney Buxton, John Gurney, Henry Birkbeck, John Dent, Isaac Wilson & many more who were there.

It is most wonderful how little Corndavon has changed - & even the road, the river pools are much the same - then via (Balmoral views) 'Queen St.' to the Deeside Road, past the places where we drove the woods, & where I first went after deer with my father, to our old Cluny haunts - where I spent the sweetest of autumn days & evenings by the Dee in the forest or among the craggs with my little Nellie in 1878 & 1879 - & so to Braemar.

Then we were to go by the Spittal of Glenshee to Perth that night - but a mile the north side of the Devil's Elbow, the motor collapsed & Ethel, Blanche & I walked to the Spittal of Glenshee Inn (8 miles), slept there & drove in a trap to Blairgowrie (29th) & so I got home to Pinchinthorpe by train."

Alfred had commissioned a stained glass window memorial to Nellie in Guisborough Parish Church, and preparations for the dedication had occupied him a great deal. All his family gathered at Pinchinthorpe over the first anniversary of Nellie's death.

"I think the window is beautiful & the service too, & *(Rev.)* John Flynn *(Nellie's nephew)* said what I liked about the window & Nellie - It was cutting to me at times - & the unanswerable question always there - How fares it with the happy dead? ..."

301

During November he underwent an operation. Phillipa was expecting her first child and was at Pinchinthorpe for the birth.

19th Dec. "I am more than convalescent, but Nurse Cryle still most kindly attends to me - & when at 10 p.m. she brought me a cup of Benger, she gave me a hint that the event we have waited a month for was imminent. I was awake at 2 & saw a light through my door & going outside, I met the Nurse. I heard the Dr. arrive about 3.45 & at 5.15 or 5.20 the Nurse put her head into my room & said 'a little girl' - I heard its voice as the door opened, & rejoiced to hear a child's cry again in my house - Soon after 6, Nurse Cryle brought the little thing to me in my bed, & I saw the 6th generation that I have seen of my family - a nice little thing & it peeped at me.

Phillipa got off cheap (if it can ever be called so) 2 to 5.10 - but Christopher was ridiculous, sleeping like a pig, & when the nurse pummelled him & told him, he just muttered that 'he knew all about it,' & turned over & went fast asleep again. At 5.45 I went & woke him up properly, & drummed the fact into him, when he quickly woke to a sense of his responsibilities as a husband & father."

The baby was named Rachel Hebe Phillipa Pease.

21st Dec. "I put on my red coat & hunted for the first time since (1909-10 season) - there have been many times when I thought I could never do this again - but I must make the effort."

1912

2nd Jan. "Went to Falloden to stay with Edward Grey till Friday *(5th)* I enjoyed my time & spent much of it with him & had some very close talk with him - about our past & our hopes - we fed his ducks in the evenings. On Jan. 3rd we shot together in the morning - in the afternoon we went to Howick & spent some pleasant hours with Albert & Lady Grey & the young people ... Jan. 4th Edward Grey & I went across to Embleton & I visited some of my old haunts - I had not done this for over 30 years - the Church has its new & very effective Memorial windows - all the old black hatchments have been taken down - the village is much improved - The Creighton Memorial Institute a very nice one - Edward stopped to speak to a lady in the village - when he had done I said, 'Surely that is Mary Jane Appleby who sang in the choir when I did as a boy, he said, 'yes, she married the Doctor!' - I was pleased to find my memory so clear."

20th Jan. "Decided this week to clear out of farming at Kitanga & if possible to sell the property to do so - it is a blow - but Slatter has broken down, & is quite hopeless about doing any good without a large expenditure of capital. Besides, the delight of it passed away with Nellie & Lavender's companionship. My sons, one has had a surfeit of hot countries, & the other hates the heat, & neither will ever want to live there."

Slatter had appealed to Alfred to be relieved of the partnership.

This was acceded to, and Slatter was asked to try to sell Theki, Kitanga and the Mua Hills land as one lot.

By early February, Alfred and his son Edward were alone again at home.

18th Feb. "I have been very ill since the Feb 1st - and in bed a week with my heart terribly bad & myself prostrated - The Doctor came twice a day. I had oxygen from a cylinder every hour & digitalis till my stomach was upset - Twice I thought the end was near - Lavender (who had now come) a constant comfort - On 14th I was downstairs again & on Thursday 15th Lavender took me to London to see Dr Mackenzie, 133, Harley St., a heart specialist - I like him - he said nothing could be done to cure an attack - something might be done to ward them off. Friday 16th I had my heart electrophotographed by Dr Lewis & Lavender brought me home on Friday evening."

Lavender left on 19th February.

22nd Feb. "I tried to hunt a little at Ayton & rode in a fast run from Newton Stell to Newham, & was bad after it & came home - Dr Stainthorpe came in the evening & said Mackenzie wished me to stay in bed for a month, & take lots of digitalis - the uncertainty of whether I am going to get better or worse worries me - I refuse to go to bed for a month. Apparently I am a physiological freak as the auricle of my heart beats 210 to the minute & the ventricle 112 - it is a very uncomfortable thing to be."

28th Feb. "Dr Stainthorpe on Dr Mackenzie's instructions ordered me back to bed."

During March, Alfred went with Gerald and Ethel Buxton to San Remo:

"Gloriously fine - the Riviera most unattractive in everything except climate - one long pretentious town from Cannes to this place."

He returned home in mid-April.

17th April "To Darlington to Wilson Pease Board Meeting - Amalgamation with Pease & Partners & Normanby *(Iron Works)* announced i.e. all to be P. & P. now."

21st April "Today, *(and)* yesterday have been just like mid- summer - quite perfect - all is delightful to look on - but I never come home now without the awful drag at my heart."

14th May "Archie Lambert came, being in England for a short time from Kilima Kiu. He gave a hopeful account of things there, & confirmed my view that Slatter was off his head, & had made a dreadful mess of my affairs at Kitanga - he has done nothing for a year & is quite ill - the place is practically derelict with his neglect, & though I don't know what to do about him, things have come to a crisis

303

- I have sacrificed my own interests in every direction there to assist him - & with a not unusual result."

22nd May. Pinchinthorpe. "It is cold after lovely weeks - I attended the first combined Normanby *(Iron Works),* & Wilson Pease, & Pease & Partners board. It is privately announced today that P. & P. will pay 8% on Ordy. shares & 4% on Deferred - I know little of what is going on in the colliery & mines depts. but imagine there are serious difficulties at Thorne."

Thorne Colliery was one that had been bought by Pease & Partners in the Doncaster coalfield area.

In June, Arthur Slatter came to England to try farming here, and before setting himself up, arranged to meet Alfred.

"On June 20th, I met Slatter at Doncaster - but could not make much out of his information, as to how he could claim that he had done a proper thing, in taking, besides all the money he had got for Klopper's and Bothas's farms, *half* the money paid for Kitanga - In my opinion a morally wrong proceeding - his only excuse was that 'the money was of more importance to him than to me' ..."

The Kenya farming venture, entered into with high hope, thus ended in a fiasco. Alfred never did discover what had happened to his furniture and equipment at Kitanga. Slatter came out of it at a profit, Gerald Buxton got his £500 back and Alfred stood the loss. The reason he gave for not insisting on the rightful return in the partnership wind-up, was that

"Slatter was really partly off his head."

It may be added that since the Delagoa Coal Syndicate has now completely disappeared from view, we can close the book on all Alfred's various enterprises in distant places.

As far as business was concerned, he now concentrated on his directorships of Wilson Pease & Co., (now renamed Pease & Partners Foundries Ltd.) and O.M.E. Ltd.

24th July "To Iron Works Board at Darlington & then to see Bowden Close Colliery new works. A great outlay on Coke Oven & electric &c plant - it is extraordinary doing all this at this old colliery, but I suppose they know what they are doing - motored home with Jack."

During August, Alfred had a few days driving grouse with Howard Pease in Northumberland.

The next entry appears:-

"October 11 - 1912 - Pinchinthorpe.
A great deal has happened to me since my last entry. Here is the outline:-
Aug 27 Bench at Guisborough, then to London & lodged at St James's Place -
Aug 28 To Dorney Ho. Toplow to see the Ferris's.
Aug 29 Left London at 2 p.m. and arrived at Le Pont, Friday *(30th)* afternoon. Saw
Laure - & very soon arranged to be married.
From the moment she knew I was coming, she began to recover - & was able to
motor from Lausanne to Vallorbe."

There is nothing to indicate the nature of Laure Sugnet's illness, or for how long she had been ill, and with certainty Alfred had not seen Laure since he had last been in Switzerland in 1898. The only clue to the course of events comes, in a letter he wrote in pencil to his elder son from Le Pont and dated 31st August, 1912:

My dear Edward,
I did not tell you that I was going to pay France a flying visit or what I was about, because I was shy about it, & feared my visit might miss its object, but now that I have succeeded in my quest, I want you to know as soon as possible all about it - I do not think anyone but Lavender had any suspicion that I was *thinking* of marrying again, nor do I think anyone will understand so well as she does why I have decided to do so, if I could secure the one person, who seemed to me the one who would not clash with my past, & all my sacred associations with home -
I came here to ask Laure Sugnet, who you will remember at Les Avants, to marry me, & she has accepted me - I am sure she will bring much light & music into our desolate home - & do it with a real understanding of what the past has been to me, & how I cling to everything that belongs to the sweet & sacred memories of my years with your mother -
I need change nothing of this - indeed I could not do it - it is part of my being, & if there is 'for ever' it is there too -
Of course Laure Sugnet is 20 years older than in those far off days, but she is still bright & happy natured, & full of music & can sing well too - I want her not only for myself, but to make Pinchinthorpe a sweeter & happier place for you all - She brings no fortune of any sort in the material way - she is of a poorer family even than I am, but of good family ...
We have provisionally fixed Oct 19 for a very quiet wedding in a protestant Church near here - She is a protestant. I am sure you will like her - though I anticipate that people who have seen less of the world than you, will think her too French for an Englishman's wife.
Finally I should like to tell you that your mother told me I should not live alone, & wished me not to, & I know how she admired & liked Laure Sugnet - & loved to have her with her -
Your ever affectionate father,
Alfred E. Pease

2nd Sept. "To Lausanne & made acquaintance of Laure's sister Berthe Clerc & renewed my old acquaintance with Jeanne Sugnet & received a most kind welcome."

The wedding date was advanced by three weeks to 28th September.

6th Sept. "Our Promises of Marriage - recorded at the État Civile."

10th Sept. "Permission to marry given. After this our banns were published at Montmagny & at the H. de Ville, Lausanne.

My children have been loyal & sweet to me about my marriage - I hope they understand that it is what their mother hoped for me, & that Laure knows & understands the past - They cannot know how true her devotion is to me & mine - Edward, my most loyal son & who has been my companion & help in the dark days, came out to the wedding - he arrived on Fri. 27th & was the greatest help."

28th Sept. "Edward & I got up early at the Hotel Mirabeau. I went on to the Marronniers early - the sitting room there was prettily decorated with flowers - & the guests arrived about 10 - 11 - but only the following were of the party for the Civil Marriage. Laure & myself - Laure looked very sweet in her mauve dress - & had a bouquet of white roses & heliotropes - her brother Gustave came to give her away - & Edward as a witness & Armand Thiraud as the other - We drove there, but had to walk through the market to the Hotel de Ville. It was soon over - & we returned to the guests at Les Marronniers ... Then we drove down to Ouchy & were married in Church - the service was simple & very nice - & then we all went to déjeuner at the Royal Hotel & Laure & I left for Paris at 3.00."

29 Sept. "We left Paris & arrived at Princes Hotel, Jermyn St. late - after a fine morning in Paris - Jack & Elsie came to dinner & were charming to us."

Laure, at the age of forty-three, was eleven years younger than Alfred. He brought her home to Pinchinthorpe on 4th October, 1912, and from this time through to late November, in addition to his own home routine, he took Laure around the district to introduce her to friends and found again the contentment of a shared life.

24th Nov. "I have bought a Chalet &c at La Tour de Peilz for Laure for £800, leaving 12,000 francs on mortgage in addition. When I am gone, I hope she may have a happy home there."

1913

3rd Feb. "Hounds at Gribdale Gate - a very windy day, poor scent - I rode Kitty & hounds ran across Lounsdale from Nanny How to Ayton Moor and back. I took a heavy fall jumping into boggy ground in Lounsdale, lost a spur, twisted the other & lost a shoe - got it put on at Dale's at Kildale - heart bad after fall - but stayed out to the end - drew Hutton blank in afternoon ..."

11th Feb. "Today I heard that Capt. Scott had perished with others after reaching the South Pole last year. A year or two ago he came to see me. A nice cheerful big man & I told him I could not understand the desire to go to the Poles - one knew there was nothing there but ice & snow & cold - all useless - no scenery worth seeing, no pleasure - & much discomfort - pain & risk - & a dirty existence - & so much more wonderful things to discover in other parts - he laughed & could not understand my not thinking it worth while - I wonder during his last conscious hours whether he thought it had been worthwhile - perhaps it is worthwhile to do a brave useless thing & to show others how to die in any attempt."

Nine days later, Alfred and Laure left Pinchinthorpe for La Tour de Peilz, Switzerland and returned in April.

Alfred's journals from this time until May, 1919 were destroyed. That being so we can only sketch in the main events from suriving scraps until we can return to the journals.

At some time during 1913, Alfred's elder son, Edward, for undisclosed reasons threw up his job at Normanby Ironworks and went out to North West Rhodesia with the intention of getting some experience in farming there. Whether there was in this move some intention to lay a foundation for Alfred's return to Africa, cannot be stated. For the time being however, life at Pinchinthorpe continued quietly and routinely.

1914

For seven weeks from early February, 1914 until the end of March, he and Laure were again in Switzerland, and during their absence Alfred's first grandson, a brother for Rachel, was born to Phillipa and Christopher. He was christened Ingram Edward Pease.

Alfred had provisionally booked passages to British East Africa for himself and Laure. His expressed intention was to take another look, and possibly, if the life suited Laure, to settle there. These plans were upset by the outbreak of war.

From the outset of the "Great War", Alfred's life became one of intense and unremitting activity in war work. Extra to his now being acting Managing Director at O.M.E., a magistrate, a North Riding County Alderman, a Deputy Lieutenant for the North Riding and also for the City of London, he lists his other appointments as being:

"Took on horse purchasing for the Army (Remount Service), became District

307

Officer in charge of Food Production, recruiting for Yorkshire Hussars & Northumberland Hussars, Chairman of War Pensions Committee, Chairman of the Emergency Committee, Divisional Commandant of Special Constables, Acting Chairman of the North Riding Police Committee, Chairman of Military Tribunals and Appeal Tribunals, Chairman of the local Board of Agriculture and a host of other things."

At some time in 1914, Captain Arthur A. Slatter, having failed at farming in England, went out to Rhodesia, and in a fit of deep depression, committed suicide.

When war broke out in August, Edward immediately returned from Rhodesia and presented himself at the War Office, offering his services as an interpreter. Told that interpreters were not wanted, he enlisted as a trooper in the 2nd King Edward's Horse, and in a few weeks was in the trenches as a machine gunner, his regiment having been unhorsed.

Alfred's younger son, Christopher, joined the Yorkshire Hussars and was commissioned in 1914, while Lavender's husband, Sandy Medlicott was commissioned in the 2/1st Northumberland Hussars.

1915

Edward was severely wounded at Neuve Eglise this year, and spent seven months in hospital.

In December, Arthur Pease's widow (Alfred's Aunt May, Mary Lecky Pease) died, and, it should not pass without notice that in her will, after some small bequests, she left the residue of her estate amounting to some £20,000, to the creditors of J. & J.W. Pease (the Counting House) "in such amounts and in such manner as the trustees shall determine."

This is mentioned, simply because there was no obligation whatsoever for her to do anything, and what she did was made with the full knowledge and approval of her sons, and as an act of honour, to make a further contribution towards the discharge of creditors of the Bank in which her late husband had been a partner. The fact that adequate provision for her sons had already been made, in no way diminishes the magnanimity of this gesture.

1916

Edward was ordered to report to the War Office, where by now, there was a growing need for interpreters. He was retained there for six months as censor in Oriental languages, on a pay of 1/2d per day with rations - or 1/4d per day without rations. As a private, he was ordered to wear mufti so as not to offend the dignity of the officers and officials with whom he had to associate.

In consequence of his joining the Army, Christopher was 'disowned' by the Society of Friends. For some reason, the fact that Alfred's elder son had also enlisted, appears to have escaped the notice of Friends, there being no evidence that he too had been drummed out. However, with Christopher disowned, Alfred in sympathy resigned his membership on 3rd July, 1916, and belonged to no religious sect for some time to come.

Christopher was sent to the Western Front.

1917

Alfred's brother Jack, after a successful political career, being in turn Liberal Chief Whip, Chancellor of the Duchy of Lancaster and President of the Board of Education, was elevated to the peerage this year, taking the title Baron Gainford of Headlam. He had been made a Privy Councillor back in 1908.

Edward was commissioned, and in May this year he was sent to Mesopotamia in the Intelligence Section and became an Acting Deputy Military Governor and then a Political Officer.

Christopher was in Flanders and at the Battle of Arras.

Alfred gives us a view of his own position in relation to his two sons having taken up arms:

> " ... I have often felt very much, the fact that my two sons have had to do what I have escaped from doing, taking part in the actual fighting & operations of war - with a realisation of the fact, that as long as a soldier plays the game, he is but the faithful instrument of his country, & when his country's cause is righteous & just, his conscience is clear. I have enough Quakerism in me to be glad that I have not to be one of the executioners, but I feel it a mean gladness, & in my heart take on myself a full share in every deed of my sons & of my country & hope, if I am called to account, to be judged as if I had myself borne the sword."

On 4th December, 1917, Newton, sixth Earl of Portsmouth died aged sixty-one at his home, Hurstbourne Park. The marriage had been childless. Alfred, being Beatrice's next of kin, wrote to her - the first communication since before the law-suit of 1900. What he said in his letter we shall never know, but she replied:

Hurstbourne Park,
Whitchurch,
Hants.
Dec. 11. 17.

My dear Alfred,

Of all the letters that have reached me these sad days, not one has been the solace that yours has been. I keep turning to it in thought with a feeling of deepest thankfulness to God & I thank *you* from the bottom of my heart.

My experience of the last parting has been very different from yours - a strong life suddenly called away at a moment when it was busiest & apparently most useful - a few days only of illness that did not appear alarming, & not a moment for last words - but the many years of happy companionship have been the same for both, & I - like you, am grateful that it is not he who has to drink this cup of sorrow -

You will like to know that the nephew (Oliver Wallop's boy) who has made his home with us for the last eight years, will be a real son to me if he lives. His turn may come any day to be sent to France but I would not have him miss it.

Thank you again for all you say, & for your offers of help if I should need it. I hope we shall meet some day -

Yours affec.ately,
Beatrice Portsmouth.

Nothing more needed to be said in this exchange between Alfred and Beatrice. There had been contact in place of silence, and to this extent minds were rested. It should be said however, that Alfred never made a point of meeting Beatrice again, though during all those intervening years, Alfred's sister Helen Blanche Pease kept contact and saw Beatrice from time to time.

Sylvia Hamlyn too, having promised her father that she would keep contact with Beatrice *"in her unhappy marriage - because she had a rotten life with Portsmouth,"* at times went over from Bridestowe to the Portsmouths Devonshire place at Eggesford.

1918

Edward applied for transfer to regimental duties in France, but was instead transferred to the 6th East Lancashire Regiment and eventually sent to Marsh Pier, Salonica where he was kept with seven thousand Turkish prisoners nine months after the war ended, burying and re-burying the corpses of men and horses washed out of the marsh with each flood.

35. Edward Pease.

Christopher was home on leave in February, 1918, and during the March offensive, when he had returned from leave he wrote to his father:

"It isn't so bad, rather a nervous strain always and sometimes fatiguing and uncomfortable, but there is much one positively enjoys. All the joys of life come from the great moments. Only one looks back at them. At the time one is too busy to think much ... You need not worry about me, I don't want to be on home service or away from the war."

On 9th May, 1918, Christopher was in the front line at Givenchy. At 6.00 p.m. the British raided the German lines and the Germans retaliated with a heavy bombardment. Four hours later, Christopher went to the advance posts to hearten the men and to warn them to be prepared for a gas attack by the British at midnight. With his orderly, Private Owbridge of the 9th West Yorkshire Regiment, placed under Christopher because he required a little discipline, and *"who was a nice, bright-eyed spare good looking intelligent man,"* they went along the trenches, and often in the open to the advance posts, and a little before midnight he had completed this round.

Owbridge gives an account of what happened next. The shelling of the British lines was particularly heavy during the two hours before midnight, but Christopher "was very cheerful & happy and talked ... pleasantly a great part of the time. He went about and chatted just as if there were no shells falling about us ... he went out often into the open and in front of the lines to look at the wire and see that it was standing.

Having finished our round, we were getting across the open when he made the last remark. His words were, 'I do not know what we have done to them, but they seem very vexed tonight.' We had just got near the parapet of the trench ... when a shell burst about 5 yards from us, it blew us both into the trench - we were just going to jump down into it - and at the same time I heard Lieut Pease say 'I am ...' and he fell dead on top of me in the bottom of the trench ... I think he was going to say 'I am hit' but it was instantaneous and he was dead before he could say it."

Four days later Alfred writes:

"We had begun dinner at 9 & the telephone rang - there were maids taking down the message making a good deal of fuss, & Laure left the table & did not come back quickly, so I began to be afraid it was bad news about her sister Jeanne who is failing.

After a while she came back agitated, & I said I hoped it was not bad news - she said it was bad news about Jeanne but that the cook was copying it - I said 'Is she dead?' and she said 'No - I do not know what to say - it is about Christopher' - I went to the kitchen knowing what I had to face ...'"

Christopher's Captaincy had been gazetted just before he was killed.

Writing to Edward immediately after this crushing news,

" ... a son is a big thing in a father's life, and the future largely loses with a son the support and hope for things here - when I come to think of Kit's life, I have lost him over and over again, & my other children too - he was a charming child, & that *(which)* disappeared in the boy I found delightful & that again in the man, who had become not less a joy & still more a comrade & son ... my heart aches for you - you become very nearly all I have hope in now ... dear Kit - his last words to me were 'keep calm'."

This September, Alfred joined the Church of England. He wanted more than anything now with Christopher's death, to be at one with Phillipa and Lavender in matters of religion.

"Laure & I joined Lavender & Phillipa at York on Wednesday evening *(25th Sept)* & went to Bishopthorpe for the night. There was no one there but ourselves and the Archbishop & his chaplain. It is a beautiful old place. After dinner, the Archbishop saw Laure & Phillipa alone & there were prayers in the Chapel. I had half an hour's talk with the Archbishop & he was very kind and very sympathetic - I told him then & before what I felt, & how in the main I held by my Quaker views; of the reality of religion being in the spiritual attitude of the soul - he is a really

312

36. Christopher York Pease, from a painting done posthumously.

good & devout man & understands our & others' point of view ... the ceremonies of Baptism & Confirmation were performed very quietly in the Chapel, but quite ritually - these rites do not affect me, but the Archbishop's remembrance in his words to & prayers for us - touched me - remembering all we loved here & There, our children ..."

By December and following the Armistice,

"I myself *(am)* suffering from some reaction & mental inertness after 4 years of incessant drudgery & anxiety. I feel that if I was sure of 10 years of life, I could not get the things done even of a simple kind that I wish to do - however hard I worked - but I suppose as long as one has a wish to work at things, one is not really a 'dead beat'."

Alfred was now permanent Managing Director of O.M.E., and it was his hope that as soon as Edward (still at Salonika) had his discharge from the army, he could find a place for him in his office.

Shortly after this he wrote to Edward saying,

" ... Lavender thinks I am doing wrong to try and get you into 'business,' that you are not cut out for it, & that with your brains, experience of countries & knowledge you would be much better at a superior job in London or at Cambridge (or a European or Consular post?). I am rather worried about it, as I feel there is a great deal of truth in what she says - I think you have generally a desire to do the things other people can do rather than the things you can do and others cannot do ..."

Edward's decision, made now or later, was to be on home ground and join his father in the Middlesbrough office.

1919

On 6th January, Theodore Roosevelt died, which moved Alfred to write,

"I have been much affected by Roosevelt's death - I was very fond of him - he was the sort of fearless, downright, upright, just, humbug-hating man I love - he was always very affectionate to me - he was younger than I am - He was a strenuous man, but took far greater care of himself than ever I have - he was younger - yet he has gone before me."

During the winter, Alfred had been doing what he describes as a "stiff bit of work":

"A Mrs Stuart Menzies ... who was fond of Father as a girl, & who has written curious gossiping breathless kind of books, wrote to me that she was writing, or

314

going to write my father's life - & asked me a whole lot of questions, ending up with questions about the Portsmouth case & the 1902 smash - I told her I did not think his life would make a popular interesting book, or part of a book - However, she said she did not agree with my view - so I was almost obliged to send her material ... My own idea is that full justice to him cannot be done in the last phases till one can speak out about those who did him down by foul means - & by then no one will care about the rights and wrongs - As it is, a whole lot of the swine are dead, as well as those who were only cowards ... Anyway, it is a bit of work which made my blood boil again with righteous indignation against injustice, however much I accept the results to myself - & that I have long since done - it is a cruel story ..."

As soon as it was possible once more to travel abroad, Alfred and Laure went to La Tour de Peilz for two months, returning to Pinchinthorpe at the end of May, at which point we again pick up the story from his journals.

8th June. Pinchinthorpe. "The Spring here has been most beautiful & the hot fine weather continues. Laburnum is still lovely but the lilac, blue bells & most spring beauties & spring bird songs are over, or nearly so -
The arrears here & at my office are worries that pay rather dear for our change. Laure is much better, but I am tired, depressed ... Our home here is clean & sweet - it had not had any cleaning through the 5 awful years of strenuous war work - Things are better in England now - a little more sugar, & things rationed ..."
7th July "This is the National Thanksgiving Day for the Peace. I have recorded nothing for 2 to 3 weeks ...

A new terror has come into my life, & my nerves, strength & age make me almost unable to bear it - I wonder if I have done all I could have done to avoid it. I am sure I did not realise that I must give up every other thought, save how to save Laure from every worry & trouble, & that her nerves & brain were in a most critical state - now I dare hardly leave her an hour - and the tragedy of it all, her mental malady is due to her intense love and anxiety for me - it takes the form that I am persecuted; that everyone is working against us, & trying to get us down - & to kill us & take our places - she has her brain drumming with horrible thoughts and horrors of the last 5 years ..."
13th July. "Dr Stainthorpe ... has prescribed for her - he regards all this brain affection & nerve condition as it now is - to change of life - he agreed with me, that it might be best to take her to Switzerland, where she would be in more congenial surroundings - I had promised L. this and had begun to plan it - when her obsession took the form of its being a plot to get us out of Pinchinthorpe."

Peace Celebrations. 19th July, 1919.

"We went over to the Hutton & P'thorpe Celebrations & Sports, for the children & parishioners at the Hutton Schoolroom - It was a perfect hot afternoon & evening,

& Laure enjoyed seeing the children & tea, & gave away the prizes for the sports very nicely, & I took her round part of the familiar Hutton grounds, down the old avenue, by the stream & by the overgrown and neglected paths so full of memories; then we met Mrs Penry Williams & walked up by the site of the old Hall, & the old rose garden & by the now ruinous & untidy paths in the Home Wood, & back to the festivities - It is 18 years since I trod these places in my old home ... L & Mrs W. were astonished at the beauty of the place; they had no idea of the loveliness of the views & splendour of the trees - but it is a melancholy abandoned paradise to me ...

Phillipa is pouring out tea today at Cloughton, with thoughts I know where - Lavender doing the same at Normanby, (Scunthorpe, Lincs) with her hair turned grey before 30 - Edward at Salonika - & Kit & his sweet mother - Where are they?

There being no trains, no work, no one on the roads all day, and not a sound except a bird's note at times, or a rook's or pigeon's or plover's and the flapping of the big St. George's flag on the house (Pinchinthorpe House) top - it was most strangely peaceful in the garden of roses & sweet peas - the contrast with the last 5 years of strain & noise. No firing at sea - no aeroplanes whirring overhead, no rattle of rifle & machine-gun fire of the men at training ranges - all the clatter & rush of troops & trains & motors & lorries over - after 4 long years of it.

In the evening Laure & I walked in the fields & saw no one till we passed Ward's farm[1] - Harry *(Ward)* was there alone with his mother (aged 93-4) ... Harry Ward told me the Pickerings had left Hutton 'for good.'

Warley Pickering, who had bought Hutton Hall and the Hutton Estate in 1905, had left, but the Hall remained furnished.

10th Aug. "I had a cable Aug 7th from Edward saying he was sailing on the 5th Aug. (from Salonika). This is an intense relief to me, & I hope soon to see my only son return from the wars ... "

31st Aug. "Edward crossed 25th from Boulogne he wired me - I should have liked to have gone to meet him, & felt much the way I am tied by Laure's mental state, tho' I did not know quite where to find him, Crystal Palace or where - he has had a most miserable homecoming so far, tho' very weak & ill he managed to see his Molly[2] who was also ill & cross with all the trouble of arranging a meeting - he got away and to Lavender's on Friday 29th collapsing twice that day ... & today he writes that he will be able to come here by Tuesday *(2nd Sept.)*. I feel anxious about him, but more indignant than I can say; he is packed ill in a troop train 6 days' journey to Boulogne & dumped in London, his cheque refused & *no pay* forthcoming since May, 1917 ... 2 years & then chucked at the end like rubbish - it makes my blood boil."

2nd Sept. "I went to Egton Show ... I got back here at 3 via Battersby - to prepare for Edward's arrival - he arrived at 6.20 -

I was dreadfully shocked to see him so emaciated, & very weak - I drove him up to the house & gave him a bath, put him to bed & sent for the Doctor - he thought more seriously of the case than I did - I had been thinking, well, he is a terrible wreck, but now care, rest & time will put him right. Dr Stainthorpe gave me a great shock, in saying that he rather feared it was not malaria & dysentery only, but that it might be his lungs - He, Edward, had a temp. of 104° at Salonika & stuck the last 4 days to his duty setting his teeth - to report sick was to go to hospital & not to get home ..."

3rd Sept. "An anxious day - Laure in a dreadful state at my having to leave her tomorrow for one night - I wired for Lavender to spend Thurs night, & come to çare for both my patients -"

4th Sept. "Left at 8.30 Middlesbro' - Lavender comes to Pinchinthorpe for tonight - went at 1.06 to London - slept at Brooks's ... & was called up at 1.45 a.m. to receive a wire from Laure."

Alfred had gone up to London principally for a meeting with T.W. Newcombe (The Secretary of the Middlesbrough Owners) and Lucas (Darlington Solicitor) at Somerset House, believing with Jack, that they had a case for reclaiming the shareholdings in O.M.E. which they had lost in 1903. Counsel's opinion was generally favourable to their case, but after reflection, they stepped back from the brink of initiating fresh litigation, preferring peace and quiet to all the risk, worry and expense this would have entailed.

Edward's condition deteriorated during the following three weeks. His malarial and dysenteric condition was complicated by infection from direct contact with putrid corpses. His fiancée (Molly Lawrence) was sent for, and both she and the doctor lost hope, though never ceased their efforts.

In this crisis, Alfred sent to London for Sir Ronald Ross, the foremost medical expert in malarial disease. Ross came immediately, being met by motor at York and arriving at Pinchinthorpe at close to midnight on 17th September.

"... he at once said the first enemy to attack is 'malignant tertian malaria' & said fr. the chart, Stainthorpe by giving quinine has arrested the worst. 'He shall not have another paroxysm & I will not speak of a "fatal termination".' He began with quinine that night - a dose of 90 grains of quinine, & every day 30 grains for 8 days - then 20 grains. Ross took the greatest pains - commended Stainthorpe - Molly has been wonderful & I think kept him alive with salines ... Now I think he has turned the corner ..."

During the following weeks, Edward made wonderful progress.

In November, Edward and Ida Mary Lawrence were married at a quiet little ceremony in London.

"I hope Edward & Molly feel that Molly is now taken fully into our family circle -

317

Molly was dressed in white, looked pale, tired & quite happy - she did not look her best. She is much more attractive & pretty in everyday clothes - & her hair is a lovely colour & that did not show at all."

1920

Alfred was hoping to take Laure out to Switzerland again for Christmas, but there were very long delays in getting visas, and Laure's nervous state added difficulty to his plans. It was not until 17th February, 1920, that they got to his Chalet Blériot, La Tour de Peilz, where they remained until 16th June. Writing on 24th March from Chalet Blériot:

> *24th March* "... It was an expensive year, 1919 for me, & this place with its impecunious inhabitants is a drain on me."

This was a reference to two of Laure's sisters who were staying at Chalet Blériot on what seemed to be an indefinite basis.

Alfred continues his 24th March entry:

> "My financial situation is a perpetual worry to me - & I can not make Laure understand the value of money & the necessity of being careful. This question is mixed up with the immediate future - What I intend, without any serious setback in her condition, is to leave on Monday 29th *(March)*. She goes frantic when I hint at this & cannot reason & understand that it is impossible to let things rip at home or to live boxed up with invalid women with no object and no future, but I feel though my first responsibility in life is her health & her happiness ..."

Alfred came back alone to Pinchinthorpe and work, but within a week was begged to return to Swizerland - immediately - by his sister-in-law Jeanne Sugnet - because, as she explained to him after his re-arrival:

> " ... the gas thing in the bathroom nearly blew up while Laure was there & that Laure had a very narrow escape from being burnt to death, & that Laure never once turned out the light at night in her room after I left & did not sleep at all, & fretted all day, & that she (Jeanne) got terrified & ill & could not be responsible any longer."

Whilst in London, on his way back to Switzerland, Alfred had written to Edward saying,

> "If I have time, I will write to Arthur about Monday's Board - you might say to him that I understand all the questions on the topics; that you will keep me posted up & that I can do something even by correspondence & by writing - for I should

318

like my billet kept if possible for some months at least - as I might be back sooner than just now seems possible."

Fearful that absence from his office would bring about his removal from his managing role, if not from the board, by regular correspondence with Edward he tried to maintain at least some kind of direction over the conduct of affairs, while at the same time trying to handle the highly charged situation at Chalet Blériot.

On 19th April:

> "It is as well that I came back, for Laure's sisters, being neurasthenics were driving her ill - I cannot write about all the complications with them - but I have had to tell them that Laure is here for repose, & not to be their prey & their nurse & to be made generally useful - besides, these excited women are always scrapping & making scenes - just the very worst thing for Laure - Thank Heaven they have taken the sulks & I hope they have them chronic - Laure is alright quietly with me ..."

From Switzerland by constant correspondence, Alfred conducts the management of O.M.E. affairs, and returns to Pinchinthorpe in mid-June (this time with Laure) after a two month absence:-

> *21st June* "O.M.E. Directors' Meeting - I have now, in 5$\frac{1}{2}$ years work raised the dividends gradually from 4$\frac{1}{2}$% to 8%, added greatly to Reserves & Investments, paid off all the £120,000 Debenture Stock & carried forward £10,000 ... "

Edward was elected a director at the General Meeting in July.

> *1st July* "I was 63 on Tuesday *(29th June)* & entered my 64th year - it is curious that I have always regarded 64 as the limit of my hard life - I have felt my heart getting weaker & my bodily vitality less, but I am full of the things I still want to get done & in order before I die - I know I cannot ever get them done - but I have worked off some arrears ..."
>
> *30th July* "- O.M.E. - afternoon walked as L & I often do together - but my heart bad & slow & intermittent ... (Laure) sent for Dr Stainthorpe after tea - he told me to remember that my heart was about 100 years old with what it had gone through, & to be careful - Of course I know he is surprised I am still alive ..."
>
> *4th Aug.* "Met J.H. Pease[3] at *(the)* office. He, after some discussion agreed to my purchase for O.M.E. of Claud's *(Pease's)* Cliff House & 6 cottages &c property for £4,000 - he thinks I shall find it hard to sell."

Cliff House, Marske-by-the-Sea, had once been Alfred's grandfather's summer residence.

> *9th Sept.* "To Marske to meet Sir Arthur, Charlie & Lady Dorman - I sold them

Cliff House property for £8,000 - not without regret to see it go out of the family - but it is for a good use. Claud ... had been trying to sell it for a year, & could not get a bid of more than £3,000 - I might have done a good deal for myself - for in 48 hours I found a likely customer."

22nd Oct. "O.M.E. - I think I shall show twice as good a result as this time last year - but I don't suppose I shall get any benefit from my success - I am not sure that my success does not annoy 2 of my colleagues - for they never did anything like it, & had far better chances, & have always treated me as if I was not capable of managing affairs ..."

In self-criticism, what Alfred saw perhaps as a drawback in his make up, he expressed in a letter written to Edward a year or so earlier:

"I know that you, and Kit in a less degree, inherited a certain kind of modesty or shyness, mixed with a certain kind of pride, perhaps from me - which prevents you being assessed at anything like your real value."

This character-trait in himself as observed by others, had been remarked upon by Sir Arthur Lawley when Alfred was in the Transvaal as follows:

"'In these Colonies & places, people take you at your own value, and you can assume superior knowledge and experience, and they will credit you with even more - You *(Alfred)* are too unassuming -'
and he inferred, which is true, that in this world if you want to get to the top, you must pose & not be modest ..."

But Alfred was never a poser and never competed for position, and though modest and ever reticent in company where he thought his own likes, interests and tastes were not particularly shared, he had great self-confidence in situations over which he had full charge.

One of his great loves and lifetime interests was in Cleveland Bay horses, and he bred them at Pinchinthorpe. He was a founder member of the Cleveland Bay Horse Society and for many years its President.

1st Nov. "Blakeborough[4], Sec. C. Bay H.S. came to lunch & we worked at the new volume of the Stud Book to which I contribute the introduction upon which I have spent some time & pains - I am the last man now living who could have written it, & I consider it a good bit of work - it will *(be)* recognised hereafter as such *if* the Cleveland Bay comes again into its place as the most wonderful clean legged draught breed in the world - *it is this -*"

4th Dec. "Nellie's birthday - put flowers in her room - meant to take some to Newton but wind & rain discouraged me, & it upsets Laure. At 12, in mufti, I got on to Missonnette ... I found hounds about 1 at Upleatham ... & ran fast over by

Soapwell to Dunsdale Bridge to below Court Green via Greyhound Course. I had at this point a bad heart attack, & was in front, Ramsden M.F.H. close behind - I let him & all the rest go past & watched them go over the hill at Court Green, & could hear hounds in full cry as far as Eston Lowther Plantations.

As I made my way home by Barnaby Moor, on my charming little Missonnette, who is also a thoroughbred of my own breeding & now 5 y.o. ... I made up my mind that my hunting days were over - the body in which I live cannot live with hounds - for 55 years I have *'ridden to hounds'* - not to be with hounds would be no pleasure - I have had my day & a delightful one - & hunting too passes out of my life ... I owe prolonged zest for living, health, friendships, delightful memories of comradeship with man & horse, my wife & children & with Nature to this great pleasure in my life. I leave it with intense regret but with intense gratitude."

1921

Almost seven months elapsed before his next, a collective entry:

26th June "On Dec. 11th, 1920 (Laure being most anxious to spend Christmas in Switzerland, & also much concerned with the accounts of her sister Jeanne - I consented to go for 3 weeks, but on the understanding I should be home within a month), we left home for Switzerland & arrived at our Chalet Blériot Dec. 13 - ... I omitted to keep my journal - being ill & worried - What I went through in May I don't want to remember, but I was on the verge of a nervous breakdown - due to my constant worry about loosing my billet at Middlesbrough; my difficulty in facing the expenses I have been let in for in Switzerland, anxiety about Laure, the trouble of moving into Villa Gounod[5], the confusion of affairs at home - the Doctors, servants & bills and a most dreary difficult life contrary to my nature - Twice (in March & May) I had taken my place in the train to come home, & twice I had, owing to Laure's state & the Doctors, had at the *last moment* to give it up - in my state of nerves, and with bad nights & taking Bromidia - I got very ill - Nothing I could do would induce Laure to return home with me, & I was terribly anxious about her condition & most anxious to do *all* I could for her happiness & health - But for me to become a nervous wreck, to lose my salary & die would do nothing for her.

At last, after many kind efforts of Jack and those at home - Gerald Buxton came out to me, arrived at Vévey at 8 p.m. Sat. 11th June & we left together at 5.58 the same afternoon - When it came to the point, Laure was, as I had told the Doctors she would be, charming & quiet & came to the station with us - my heart aches for her - but what can I do."

Laure remained in Switzerland while Alfred returned to Pinchinthorpe.

13th June "I got home ... I still have touches of 'the horrors' in the night & in the evenings - chiefly due to my distress of mind over my Laurie's condition."
(Still writing an up-date on 26th June) "The accounts of Laure are as good as I

could expect - but there is no sign of her wanting to come back - her heart is set on my going back to Switzerland - a thought that I cannot yet entertain - I should get *very ill* & her duty & mine is here - she writes me most loving letters imploring me to come back ..."

Within a few weeks Alfred went out to Switzerland yet again, to try to persuade Laure to return with him to England.

16th Oct. "Laure having promised to leave with me from Vévey on 2nd Oct. - I had all ready & packed on 1st - she had been with me on 20th Sept. when I took tickets & places in the Simplon Express & ordered rooms in London - I had agreed to the expense of taking her maid with her ... & for 2 or 3 days begged her to get ready -
When the 2nd came, it was only when I was ill with the worry occasioned by her determination not to go, & her excited state, & said I was going in any case, that with Dr Isler's help she said she would go on Thursday 6th - I went off & booked places again & she really began to make a move - I had to find more money & had endless trouble, but we got off on the Thursday evening & had a good journey home which we reached on Saturday 8th October ... Ever since getting our faces turned home I have begun to pick up - tho' I am not up to much."
26th Oct. "County Council at Northallerton ... I got home later than Laure expected - she was very much upset & very excited all the evening & night because I was going to see Lavender at Doncaster & leaving by the 7 a.m. train ..."
27th Oct. Doncaster. "... I went... she looked very pretty & bright & happy to see me ... I am ... most unhappy to know that the Dr. has found her lung touched - this news I have dreaded for many years & the thought of her ever getting like her mother in this way is terrifying to me - my troubles are unending - Edward has seen Sir R. Ross who finds him still ill with malaria."
6th Dec. "I have felt ill for more than a week ... If I die now, I do hope my family will take care of Laure & not let her be treated like a lunatic - I wonder if I ought to give up everything here & go & live in Switzerland ..."
21st Dec. "Very windy & I kept thinking of Lavender (and Sandy) having a bad crossing of the Channel on their way to Biskra - It is curious to think of her returning to those familiar haunts of mine ... after 25 years."

1922

Alfred's opening entry is:

"Phillipa & the children are at Crabbes Hill, Essex & go to St. Moritz on 12th. *(Jan.)* - Lavender & Sandy are at Biskra & enjoying it - Edward & Molly are at Saltburn, - Laure & I are at Pinchinthorpe."
20th Jan. "I have lost count of days - I have had influenza badly - Laure nursed me most beautifully and tenderly - & then fell ill herself - With her spirit & courage she struggled against the idea of being ill ... and now she is most dangerously ill

with pneumonia & I am in such a state of distress & terror I do not know what to do - I am with her day & night ..."

25th Jan. "My sweet & spotless Laurie was torn from me this morning at 5.10 a.m., so warm & so precious in her love for me ... the last days & hours was the most fearful battle for breath that can be conceived - she clung to me all through pouring between her gasps loving words & tender names for me 'her darling 'oney' - 'Reste prés de ta Laurie' - till weakness stilled the voice & with her last conscious efforts within a minute of the end poured a torrent of little kisses on my lips & then came a few quiet moments when her face became peaceful ... I am now desolate ...

All the evening *(24th)* as I lay with her head on my shoulder she kept asking when Gustave ('Gut') would arrive - he arrived in time & we held her between us & she was happy, & cooed away to us both ... Blanche has been most sweet in being with me the last 2 days - & saw my Laurie die - & I think she, at least can now guess how & why we loved each other.

She was lovely in death as she was in life - Time will never spoil what my living Laurie was - she was by far a being of life & beauty, the loveliest & most graceful being I ever saw - As Margaret Tuillens said, *no one* when she was young, could look on her without being transported by her charm and loveliness."

Notes:
1. Alfred's tenant at Pinchinthorpe High Farm.
2. Ida Mary (Molly) Lawrence who had nursed Edward in hospital in 1915 after he was wounded, and to whom he was now engaged.
3. John Henry Pease, son of Gurney Pease (Alfred's uncle) who died in 1872.
4. J. Fairfax-Blakeborough, journalist and author of many books on sporting subjects.
5. Bought on mortgage this year for SF75,000 (£3,000) in substitution for Chalet Blériot.

CHAPTER FIFTEEN

Tying up Loose Ends

1922 continued

11th Apl. "I have been very ill since my last entry - and during my illness, when I had turned the corner, Gustave left *(23rd March)* ... Lavender came here on 17th - far from well - I do not remember when I fell ill again - I had never recovered from influenza, & had a relapse & it turned to pneumonia. I was very well nursed, & Dr Stainthorpe attended me at least twice a day -
I did not want to recover ... but now I am up & about again - my nurse left a week or two since ... my illness is a very hazy memory - a sort of nightmare - so strange being so ill, & not one of my family to see me die or live - Edward was in Algeria - Phillipa at Innsbruck - Lavender & Sandy in the South of France ... Everybody & everything goes on as if nothing had happened - and everything has happened to me - I seem to care for nothing here at all any more ..."

23rd Apl. "I have financial worries & much trouble over Swiss affairs & correspondence - I have destroyed enormous quantities of papers - It seems to me incredible the work I got through during the war - The masses of papers I have destroyed & thrown away this week after a first weeding in 1919 - astonished me."

28th May "3.30 a.m. ... I am not much better than a month ago. April 24 Nurse E.E. Smith who was so nice with Laurie & whom Laure loved to have by her, & who took care of me in the awful first days & nights after Jan. 25 - came back to look after Lavender & me as neither of us was well enough to look after each other, Lavender wanted her to go south with me when I went on 10th May, for I get nervous at time*(s)* as I sleep very little - scarcely ever after 2.30 a.m. - but though she is most soothing & gets me through the nights & I am fond of her, I must not get dependent on such things - she left 8th May."

22nd June "I am worn with work & worry & sleeplessness so I went to bed at 3 p.m. & slept till 8 when Blanche arrived - she was very sweet & though no one can know except those who have been near it, what it is to be near a nervous breakdown on the top of so much trouble - she sympathises with me - I really try to appear cheerful & normal ...
Really it seems strange that my little, wild, red haired nurse, with her gentle soothing & happy ways is the only being whose sympathy & care did me good - I have got into a state & to an age when I really do want someone to look after me a little - ..."

Nurse Emily Elizabeth Smith, short in height and with fine auburn hair was aged twenty-five. She had trained as a nurse during the war, after which she had gone into private nursing.

Six months elapse before Alfred's next entry:

17th Dec. 1922 "I am home at Pinchinthorpe once more ... & most of (the time) absent from home. These months have been strange ones in which life has brought yet new experiences and many more unexpected ones - Few men can have had all the main & natural anticipations in life entirely wrong & off the mark."

Filling in the intervening period, he continues,

"... I had a terrible night on 25th June & did not know how to bear myself. In the morning I asked Lavender, who was very poorly through all these weeks & who did not know of, or could have realised my deplorable condition, to send for Nurse Smith - She thought it was quite the best thing, but she was engaged at Barnard Castle nursing an old lady.

The next night I could not sleep at all and had the horrors - I saw I was on the edge of a bad nervous breakdown & made up my mind that at my age, and misery ahead, no ordinary ideas counted, & that if I could not have Betty qua professional nurse to look after me, I would try & give her the right to, & ask her to marry me some day.

I went straight to Bd. Castle, & we walked in the woods - She said it was impossible for me to marry her. She never said she would, but I knew she cared enough to do it - & on 29th she came here *(to Pinchinthorpe)*.

On 28th *(June)* I told Lavender, & L said I had done the very best thing I could have done, & told Betty the same & gave her a most affectionate welcome.

Phillipa came ... & did the same & said the same - Then they both begged me to marry Betty *at once*. We had no such ideas, but spoke of next Spring. Betty was to be with Lavender while I was in Scotland, & then, as they pressed it, we spoke of marrying in October ...

Then, one day, all changed; everyone turned nasty - I was begged to leave P'thorpe, that my presence endangered Lavender's health. I was requested to tell Betty to go home ..."

Alfred, absolutely indignant, refused, though

"... Betty, outraged in every sentiment went away at once - & I had no other course but to arrange our marriage as soon as possible. I was bombarded by all my relations & family except Edward, Molly & Sandy - What they said & did I wish to forget. I took it all lying down - but was not to be turned for a moment.

We were married at Holy Trinity, Darlington on August 1 ... & motored to York - & then went to the Alexandra Hotel, Hyde Park Corner ...

On 1st September we went into the little house of Commr. Boyles at Sleights - 'Silverdale' - We had engaged 2 servants but they did not turn up - the house was filthy & much dilapidated & badly equipped, no linen, little glass, no towels - &

325

damp; had not been lived in for more than a year or attended to - the garden similar ... Betty was splendid, cooking & doing all the household work almost - I doing what I could - coals - messages - cleaning flues - & washing up &c. We had everything to get & many loads from the station - but we got through. We were there till Dec. 2, 1922 when we came home ...

During my stay at Sleights, I attended to my office at Middlesbro' & to my duties at N'allerton (I am still Chairman of the Standing Jt. Cee,) & at York - To get to Middlesbrough, I often had to be up at 5.30 & left at 7 & returned at 7 - & Betty was always at the station to meet me with 'Ben' *(his Labrador).*

Alfred and Betty became totally ostracised by all but a few members of the wider family.

> "... I have all through refused to be driven into reproaches and words which I feel would be true & just ... We shall I hope, be able to live quietly & happily here - I am very grateful for having such a very dear wife as my companion and helper, & that I am not alone - nothing could be so sweet and capable as her management of my home under every difficulty."

1923

31st Jan. "Sandy & I shot together here. We got 5 pheasants, 1 woodcock, 2 hares, a few rabbits - He spent one night - & gave a good account of his family ..."

12th Feb. "Maud *(Alfred's sister)* came to us for 2 nights - looking very well - we enjoyed her visit very much. Before she left, she told me the horrible and infamous lies which have been circulated about B - I have never been up against such wickedness & cruelty."

Alfred nowhere elaborates on the circulating gossip.

25th Feb. "With Howard *(Pease)* most of the day - kept Betty's birthday - she is only 26 tomorrow - I gave her several little presents & a sewing machine. I have given her a cream coloured pony by Sunburst out of an Arab mare 5 y.o."

26th Feb. "Betty's birthday - she had no letters & no presents but mine - I have become everything to her & enjoy making her happy."

3rd Mar. "Betty's 'father' James Smith[1] died peacefully at 5 a.m. today - She went there. She has the greatest admiration & love for her grandparents who have cared for her all her life, and whom she has always worked for ... such men as he, loving, faithful, hardworking & doing his best for his home ... are the salt of the earth, & his wife a wonderful woman I should say."

29th April "Dr Burnett came ... all goes well - A lovely day - sat & walked in the garden with Betty among daffodils, cherry blossom - with puppies, peafowl & birds on the lawn - A peaceful evening - with hopes of happiness & that the evening of my life after all the storms & catastrophes may be thus quiet - not in selfish repose."

On 4th May, Betty presented Alfred with a daughter who was christened Anne Phillida Pease. Alfred notified the near relations with the exceptions of

"... Jack & Phillipa *(who)* have never taken any notice of us since we married, at least not of Betty, so I left them alone especially as Phillipa ... warned me not to force my wife on people - She & I are the last people in the world to dream of advancing a step towards imposing ourselves..."
13th May. "I have the greatest admiration for Betty - she has had a hard time bravely borne - leaving her own world, treated with contempt in mine, such a poor wedding for a girl ... all our sacrifices for others & all our devotion to them purchasing only wounds & nasty attitudes.
Betty now has the sweetest little child & is happy; 10 days have gone & not a soul has come to see it - I wonder if a child ever arrived in our family before under such conditions ... I have had nice letters from my sisters ... and to my pleasant surprise, a letter from Jack - Edward has always been very nice - Phillipa has not broken silence ... Lavender ... wrote to Betty & wired congratulations ...
I have been looking through Laurie's music. It brings back to me her favourite pieces as she alone in this world interpreted them with her acute feelings & sensitive touch ... Not a soul in England ever took the trouble to know her, or to listen to her - her soul was beyond their reach & their sense of music too dull - Among women it was partly jealousy of her powers, her ways - It was so striking that Betty knew & felt what Laure was at once - it was the first flash I got of Betty's being no ordinary nature & soul, but full of that intuition, perception & sympathy which was part of Laure's nature."

Alfred was in London on 7th June, for the Shikar Dinner held annually at the Savoy Hotel:

"I took Ferris as my guest to the Savoy to the Shikar Dinner - On the other side of Ferris sat R.J. Cunninghame who was with Roosevelt with me at Kitanga 1909, he has no big black beard now & he recognised me before I did him. On the other side of me sat Sir Alfred Sharpe (Nyasaland) - I had some conversation with Delamere who has aged & looks as if he had no teeth & is very bald - I enjoyed meeting him again after more than 11 years ..."
27th June "Jack came for 2 nights ... & gave me family news & news of the world - very nice to see him."
7th July "This week I have had a correspondence with Phillipa - another attempt to change her attitude towards us, but she remains obdurate & all I get in return for my devotion to her & her children are insulting & absurd letters - She says anything but the most formal intercourse is impossible, & that my society would be uncongenial - Her conduct is most offensive towards Betty & has been so for 10 months."
15th July "I am sorry I made this last entry for although it is true that she will not come here or recognise Betty, Phillipa has written to me & said, what comforts me, that the bond of affection & devotion between us will never lessen - The only

road to peace is that Betty or Phillipa should sacrifice their injured pride or feelings - for me - I cannot ask this - but hope for it."

30th July "I got a telegram saying poor suffering Jeanne Sugnet had gone to her rest on 29th Sunday morning in the Villa Fernande, Lausanne - where I provided for her - she was neglected by her sisters & Gustave, & clung to me - she was difficult to manage, but so many memories of her with Laure & myself at the Chalet & at the Villa Gounod make me feel it the death of a sister."

The next journal entry is one at the end of December, and skims over the five months of neglect.

3rd Sept. "I went over to the Hollins for lunch with Phillipa & saw Ingram & Rachel - Ingram going to school for the first time soon - Phillipa will not bring the children here, & Betty will not go there - so it is difficult for me to see these dear children - & to be loyal to Betty who has been treated very unfairly."

Throughout the Autumn, Alfred had many day's hunting. There is no more talk of giving up this pleasure.

17th Dec. "... Betty & I & little Anne spent our Christmas very quietly alone - We never saw a soul through Christmas week in our house, but Anne was a source of infinite pleasure to us ... I have worked steadily at my office, County business & things at home - I have had, in spite of some sore thoughts, the quietest & perhaps the happiest year of my life - not happiest in the sense of having achieved anything much, or done anything interesting, but in peace of mind & comfort in my home - I know I have done my best ..."

328

1924

9th Jan. "I had a wire to say that Edward N. Buxton had died peacefully at Knighton & asking me to Birch Hall for the funeral - but with infirmities, I dislike leaving home & my little family alone - but decided to go - as he was a dear friend of mine."

14th Jan. "Home - found Betty in low spirits - she had not seen a soul to speak to since I left - Phillipa & the children had stopped at our door for the first time for over a year - but finding I was away - P would not come in and see Betty - This is a cruel thing - but only in a piece with P's efforts to wound."

19th Apl. "Betty motored me to Alnmouth to spend Easter Day with Aunt Helen & Ella at Nether Grange. It was fine weather. We found Aunt Helen very bright & interested in everything & I thought, not quite so feeble as last year - I think she is 87. We had a very pleasant visit - Miss Kitty Redmayne was there. A very nice person, & an extraordinary creature called Mrs Phillimore. She is one of the wealthy persons who affects Socialism & looks as if she wanted a hot bath & grooming. She was pleasant and amusing in her way. She is an authoress of a book that has had a certain vogue *By an unknown Disciple* - a sort of modernised colloquial version of Christ's Life - for my part I find no gain in these concoctions - there is all that is required in the New Testament, & nothing I have read responds to the search for Truth, or yields the same satisfaction to the human soul when confronted with what appeals to its apprehension of spiritual & eternal verities."

May, 1924. "Anne's birthday on the 4th ... No one came - we are very happy together - & if few care for the sweet child or for us, I still am blessed in my home & these possessions."

10th May "Cyril Pease[2] came to tea - it is quite an event to see anyone here."

16th June "Directors Board, O.M.E. at Darlington - I have I know done well in very bad times & after making various liberal provisions - we decided on a Dividend of 7% making 10% for the year."

16th Oct. "Edward Grey *(by now Earl Grey of Falloden)* came here to stay the night ... it was very nice to have a good talk with him ... takes a pessimistic view of politics & the future - considers Lloyd George has been a corrupting influence in the Public Departments & in public life - I did not discuss Asquith with him - but it is Asquith who has ruined the Liberal Party - Anything more shocking than his putting in the Socialists was never done by a Liberal - Ed. G. made a speech that any Unionist could have made as far as party colour goes."

Alfred elsewhere states in reference to Herbert Asquith:

"I do not feel I am competent to judge or to criticise him, for a personal question has affected my opinion of his character and possibly warped my judgement. It is during my long life the only experience of a man, who had been on terms of personal friendship with me, withdrawing that friendship purely on account of my political views. From the day I left his party Asquith never spoke to me again, nor would he recognise me when we met by so much as a nod. In my experience of gentlemen this behaviour is unique."[3]

1st Nov. "Hounds at Hutton - Betty went in her car - I rode Mananga - Anne went on her donkey ... We found Pinchinthorpe side, ran fast via Bousdale, Brown's Intake, Little Roseberry, Hutton & Ayton Moors to Gribdale Gate to the Kildale side of the Monument & lost - I took a toss on the moor with Mananga who got both her forefeet in a hole & came over the top of me, but I never let go of the reins & was none the worse tho' galloping hard - we found again Roseberry Road Hutton, ran across Bousdale, P'thorpe, past my house, over the railway by the signal cabin & then very fast over Barnaby Side to Moredale & Court Green top & to Eston Banks, & they came back across Barnaby Grange fields, Grove Hill, Harrisons Close & I came in having given Mananga who is only 4 y.o. 3 good days this week."

10th Dec. "Phillipa came for the night ... enjoyed having Phillipa here once more."

24th Dec. "Edward & Molly came for Christmas ... Anne has her nursery very pretty with a Christmas tree of her own, an enormous Santa Claus Stocking full & garlands & holly."

25th Dec. "Christmas Day - Went to Newton Church with Molly to Holy Communion 9.30 ... about 40 communicants - walked home with Molly & Miss Ward - Betty is too near her time to do more than she is doing for others for Christmas ..."

1925

4th Jan. "Phillipa, Rachel & Ingram came to lunch - the children are growing fast & as attractive as ever - I enjoyed this Sunday - & feel our family troubles are over."

5th Jan. "To Rowland Hugill's funeral - I went to Hemble Hill, & though I purposely arrived at 1.0 when the funeral was due to start - I was taken into the house & the coffin lid 'unscrewed' that I might have 'the last look' - it is an awful Cleveland custom, & I have seen some dreadful & almost unrecognisable distorted faces as in this case."

14th Jan. "Maud came here for the day 11.40 to 3.50 - Very nice - Immediately Maud left Betty began with symptoms of labour - The next 48 hours are a nightmare to me. She had a dreadful time ... The Baby was not born till *4.15 pm on Friday 16th Jan.* & was only got after a great struggle ... and weighed fully 13lbs on the scales - The Dr said 'no confinement could be worse,' but when he left, was satisfied with the condition of Betty & the little girl - the latter has been injured a little, left eye, head & shoulders with the forceps, but both Dr & Nurse say it is not serious ... I am deeply thankful it is all over ... A lovely short, sunny, calm January day.

I went upstairs feeling suddenly the world had changed, that I loved everything and everybody more ... the room looked deliciously comfortable, with shaded lights, the chintz curtains drawn & the glowing fire. I watched my new daughter, & saw she was very fair with dark hair."

28th Feb. "I have heard of Oliver's death, my father's faithful butler - when the smash came in 1902 & my father had to give Oliver notice, he declined to go & said he would stay and did till my father died."

25th Mar. "Without knowing quite how far we should get this day, Betty & I started ... in the car about 11.20, picking up Phillipa ... on an expedition to see the Grand National ... After the race we had tea comfortably, got away soon after 4, landed Phillipa home about 8.40 & got home here to dinner at 9.20 - 139 miles - It is strange to think that with one's car one can see the Grand National run & be home to dinner. A most enjoyable time away & found our little ones very well."

8th Apl. "... afternoon I spent outside with Judy as I heard her cry - I went to her near the cucumber frames and thought she looked pale. I soon made her happy & wheeled her about the gardens till she slept 3 - 4.30 - I asked if she was quite well - & was assured she was perfectly well."

It was on 10th April,

"... Good Friday morning at seven o'clock, just as we were dressing to go to early service at Newton, that Judy's mother ran to me and said, 'Judy is ill.' I cannot forget her voice nor the fear that immediately clutched my heart. Of the twenty-four hours which followed I cannot write. All that could be done was done for our little Judy then, as it had been throughout her life. Neither doctor nor surgeon could find any cause for her sudden illness till late at night, when symptoms of acute meningitis developed. In the presence of Dr Burnett, her devoted nurse and myself, she quietly yielded up her sweet little life on her mother's knees, just as the old clock on the stairs was striking seven o'clock on the morning of Easter Eve. I saw a little knitted boot with its undone silk ribbon lying on the floor; the sight of that little thing brought more anguish in its silent proclamation of the meaning of what had happened than all words or thoughts ..."

14th April "It has been a perfect Spring day. In the garden and the churchyard at Newton, which we have just left, the daffodils are dancing in the grass, the sun is shining ... upon the snow-white blossom of the sloes. Larches are all but green, and glossy golden buds are gleaming on the chestnut tree. Thrushes and blackbirds are singing everywhere, the pigeons are tumbling in the air above the white dovecote on the lawn, as they did on the day our little Judy was born, the peewits are crying over the fields, and we have just come back to a changed home ... It is dreadful leaving her there ..."

As Alfred approached his sixty-eighth birthday, he could not afford to retire, but neither did he wish to. He thoroughly enjoyed, and was keenly interested in every aspect of his company work. Business and correspondence was regularly attended to from home in the evening and after dinner, so that any days spent in hunting, were never at the cost of neglected work.

9th June "Directors' Meeting at Middlesbro. O.M.E. Annual a/cs & Balance Sheet - I had a very good showing for these unprecedentedly bad times - and we were able again to make the Dividend 7% for the half year i.e. 10% for the year."

12th Nov. "In spite of frost I rode Mananga & we hunted from Grey Towers & had a fair day - I had a near shave of a fall - Mananga is scarcely a made hunter yet but is very keen. I took her in a run from Blackmoor (Stanley Houses) over some new rails (& wire) into a plantation; it was not high but an awkward take off, & very stiff - she did not quite understand & got right up to the rails breasting them, (I had taken my feet out of the stirrups to fall free thinking this might happen) when she bucked clean over the rails without touching them or moving me. A very clever performance but a lucky one too!"

1926

5th Feb. "In *(the)* afternoon I went over to Hutton *(Hall)* with Betty to see the contents which are to be sold next week. The interior of the old place is very shabby - There are some good pictures ... Met Charlie Ward Jackson there whom I had not seen for years - he is getting grey - He told Betty I was looking better than he ever remembered. In old days he said, I 'was always dying,' but 'bless me, you could not kill Alfred with a hatchet!'"

Warley Pickering (senior) of Hutton Hall had died two months earlier.

21st Feb. "At home with Anne & Betty - Kermit Roosevelt just returned from an Asia expedn. after sheep & ibex came to see me ... I had not seen him since 1910 - he was not much changed from the time we hunted together with his father at Kitanga in 1909. It was very nice talking over old times and the intervening years which have removed most of those we knew in B.E.A. ... "
2nd Apl. "A disturbed night - as Betty began with pains at 3.15 a.m. ... "

This day a son, Alfred Vincent Pease, was born.

3th July "Betty & I went up to London ... Dined ... with Jack, Elsie, Miriam & the Novars[4] at 18 Mansfield St - & had a pleasant evening. I was glad to see Novar again - Elsie as usual talked a lot of fantastic rubbish - but was in good temper."

At dinner, Elsie, in conversation with Lady Novar was overheard referring to *"our little Yorkshire shooting box"* i.e. Headlam Hall, Gainford, that place being neither little, nor a shooting box, nor in Yorkshire, but a mansion in County Durham. Any mention of 'County Durham' would have conjured up a vision of colliery winding gear and slag heaps. To avoid *that,* Elsie pushed Headlam Hall south and over the River Tees into Yorkshire, transforming it on the way. Alfred listened to this "fantastic rubbish" in amused silence, while Miriam gave Betty a knowing kick under the table.

"When we were in London I took Betty to see the House of Commons & the Lords
- I found to my astonishment Sir James Agg Gardner M.P. *still* there - & he took us
round - I could hardly believe it - for he was there in *1874,* & when I left in 1902, &
is still there - that is, he has been there with one or two breaks, 52 years ... Curious
in the Lords to see Jack & a few old stupids I was in the House with, composing
the opposition - Selborne, a worthy dull contemporary of mine was holding forth -
only one official in the H. of C. knew me & came up & chatted with me."

22nd July. "Ld. Lascelles gave (he is President of the Yorkshire Show) luncheon
to 30 or 40 people, all men, on the Council &c &c and Princess Mary was there -
rather to my surprise & alarm, Lascelles put me by Princess Mary at the top table -
she is a very nice little person, simple & natural in her manner, with pretty
colouring and light blue eyes - I quite enjoyed talking to her - on various subjects -
Hunting, Yorkshire, Dee Side - her children, gardens, Cleveland Bays, Forestry -
she seems surrounded by old people. I am sorry for her, but people around her
home are very fond of her."

The trustees for the widowed Mrs Warley Pickering were at this
time trying to sell the Hutton Estate. The asking price was £60,000 for
1,626 acres. But these were funny times. When the contents of the Hall
had been auctioned in February, many of the fine pictures had fallen
under the hammer for little more than the price of wallpaper. At that
time, Alfred had bought a large seascape painting by E.W. Cooke, R.A.,
for fifty guineas, a birthday present for Betty. If the contents had sold at
rubbish prices, and the trustees were serious about selling the estate,
there was an outside chance that Alfred could buy back what had been
lost in 1903. He was not in the least daunted by the complete absence of
the wherewithal to accomplish a purchase.

8th Oct. "I wrote to my Solicitor Winterbotham asking his assistance, & sending
him a memorandum about the Hutton Estate
- If I can raise £30,000 to 35,000 on 1st Mtge I could bid this - I have had the
Timber valued £17,000
There is about £1,000 Rev. from Agricultural land.
There is about £1,000 Rev. from Minerals.
There is about £500 Rev. from Village &c.
The Grange shd. let at £150.
The Hall is speculative.
The gardens let for 190 - say 100.
& there are houses &c in hand - & shootings - say the Hall is worth 5,000 break up,
or could be let at £500 - I put this as a speculative margin - but say there is but £200
a year from shootings, Hall & Stables &c, there is about Gross 3,000 a year
@ 10 years purchase = 30,000
Timber   = 17,000 *(£47,000 calculated value)*
A great deal can be developed for Villa residences Nr. Hutton Station."

In the event, there being no buyer at or around £60,000, the estate was withdrawn from sale for the time being.

On the 6th November, Alfred went to the funeral of his nephew Henry (Harry) Alfred Pease, a son of his sister Blanche, at the Friends' Burial Ground at Darlington.

" ... Friends' funerals are dreadful, & get more so as they have now no Ministers, say anything they like, & do everything in any way they fancy - they do not even wait for inspiration & guidance of the Holy Spirit (the foundation of Quaker Ministry) but arrange that some one should say something, & the some one holds forth a prepared address - more or less suitable - You never know what you are in for - the silences are briefer & disturbed by not knowing how soon or in what way - you cannot really get into quiet religious meditation or forget your surroundings - It is all most uncomfortable & comfortless.

On this occasion, as soon as we got to the grave, my brother Jack *immediately* elbowed himself past me and began a prepared oration 'suitable for the occasion' - it no doubt satisfied himself - but no one less fitted to lecture us on death, sorrow and the consolations of our religion is to be found ..."

A month later Lavender's son, Stephen Christopher Medlicott died aged nineteen months:

9th Dec. "Betty & I went over early on this day of his burial. It was a perfect sunny quiet day & the moors beautiful & the sea & hills too ... After a while, we 4 followed with the nurse as they carried him away on foot, up from his playground the garden & by the rocks & over the hill to our car, near the gate out on to the moor road - L & S went with him in our car to the Church ...

We had a perfect little service for a child in the Church ... & then we laid the little simple coffin with great tenderness in our hearts in his little grave. I felt it all dreadfully - Sandy & Lavender were calm & sweet - I watched them walking away to their changed home over the hill fields over the moor, just they two alone.

Lavender had ordered tea for relations & friends from Cleveland & Darlington *if they came* - but no one did - these little lives and these greatest of sorrows to parents are of small account to the world. But I liked it all as it was, without any posed sympathy and sententious addresses - When I compare the beautiful little service in this beautiful little moorland place, with the depressing & ugly proceedings at poor Harry's funeral in that dank catwalk of a yard, I am sorry to think that they can have no memories that are happy & sweet of an affecting day - L & S would reach home in the most glorious sunset of the year in the West, & the crescent moon high in the East - I shall not forget this day."

Within three months of his seventieth birthday, Alfred resolved once more to enjoy the thrill of a fast race, and entered for the Cleveland Hunt Steeplechase. The week before the event, he gave his horse

"Skinny" a good testing gallop over fences, making the observation that,

"He is fitter than I am to ride him."

It was seven years earlier that he had been told by his doctor that his heart was "100 years old", that he should remember this and, by clear implication, lead a quiet life without excitement. In the intervening years all his keenness and zest for living had been rekindled. Even so his intention to race a course of four and a half miles, at break-neck speed, jumping twenty or more fences was considered foolhardy by some, though not by Betty.

This year, the races took place at Pinchinthorpe and on 14th April,

"A beautiful warm Spring day with hot sun ... People would not believe I was going to ride in the Hunt Members' Steeplechase, (for which there were 11 entries - 9 of which went to the post) considering my horse is old, & I getting to the close of my 70th year.

It was a very fast race & I was in my element - I am told that no-one but Sir Claud de Crispigny has ever ridden a steeplechase in their 70th year. I do not know if this is so. I did well, & I know no one who would have done better on old Skinny - The winner was a high class Newmarket horse & was ridden by 'Gunner Welburn' from York, a professional rider. My 'Dragon Fly' 4 y.o. was 2nd & I was third - 'Miss Ethel,' a winner of *(the)* 3 mile Hurdle Race &c I had beaten at 2 miles, & she fell.

Betty was pleased & she was quite sure I would stay the course, but I doubt if she quite knows that you are going a terrific pace all the time & having stiff posts & rails with big ditches & drops beyond, with queer 'take offs.' It is not like a 'made course' - it is a question of eye & head as much as of riding -

Ld. Gisborough wrote to me & said 'I cannot let the day pass without saying how much I admired your pluck in riding today & finishing 3rd. It was a wonderful performance ... it was a great feat.' I received a great cheer as I came in."

In mid-November another son, Joseph Gurney Pease, was born, and Alfred now had a surviving second family of a daughter and two sons.

A week later, Alfred learned of the death of his cousin Sir Arthur Francis Pease, eldest son of his late Uncle Arthur Pease. A.F. Pease had been created a baronet in 1920.

" ... some had heard that I had died suddenly in the night & had been 'awfully shocked!'"

2nd Dec. "Middlesbro' - had our half-yearly Board Meeting & a/cs - Passed Resolution re-Arthur's death - & sympathy - I was elected Chairman ... "

335

1928

4th Feb. "Hunted Mananga at Cross Keys - Betty went with Anne on 'Tiny' there; a bitter strong wind ... had a lot of running between Normanby & Yearby - I got a nasty fall on Barnaby Moor galloping fast. She got her feet into a mine crack and went heels over head, a real proper one, & then over the top of me knocking me out for a minute & spoiling my only good hat, tramping on my foot, thumb & back - went on to the end with a stiff neck.

I am cutting down all expenses ..."

9th Feb. "Betty took me to the meet at Nunthorpe Village - a high cold wind & bright day - Drew all Dorman's coverts blank, found at Seamer New Whin a fine fox (2 went away), ran to Tanton Majors, Stokesley & Skutterskelf Road, back N. Side of Stokesley & lost at Blackmoor Plantn. - I got a nasty fall with Mananga trying to cross the River Tame W. of Stokesley - banks rotten & mud 4 feet deep - Trying to get out, Mananga fell backover with me & I landed on my back in deep mud! She then got out having broken the reins & *broken the bit*. Cobbled things up & went on to the end ..."

In September this year, Betty took Alfred to Devon and Cornwall, their first holiday for three years.

In Cornwall at Treworgan,

" ... it is a lovely place & valley - and the badgers are there *in numbers* in the grounds just as they were 40 years ago when Jack & I used to dig them out."

The next day,

1st Oct. "... then to Glendurgan⁵ for the day ... were most kindly and warmly welcomed ... & in the afternoon B. & I went down to Durgan - once ours - & the village owing much to what my father did in the seventies for the people & fishermen - but there are no fishermen now!"

1929

4th Mar. "I am going on Thurs. 28th (March) for 16 days' voyage to Madeira with the Peats⁶ - Betty has arranged this over my head - I was not keen to leave home. My wife & kids are all I want - but have to go it seems."

He returned on 13th April well and rested:

" ... it has done me good, though I should have enjoyed much more had Betty been there - in fact I hated her not having the holiday & not sharing the experience."

Alfred, who in earlier years had put his own life expectancy pretty low, is seeing friends, contemporaries and relations dropping out one by one. His brother-in-law, Gerald Buxton, had died in March last year and

336

now, while in Madeira, his sister Lottie Hodgkin suffered a stroke and died a few days later. Then on 21st May,

> "Heard of the death early this morning of my dear old friend and leader Lord Rosebery - I feel it - all my memories of him are delightful - he always had an affection for me & if circumstances had allowed me to remain in public life after 1892, he would have made a career for me."
>
> *29th June* "My 72nd birthday - it is strange to live on and to feel as if I had more life left ..."

1930

> *1st Jan.* "My 73rd New Year's Day ... Of course I am sensible of a decline in physical activity - 4 hours out hunting about fits me now, & 6 hours tires me - I work hard - & am interested in many things which I shall ere long say goodbye to ... I am blessed in my home, children & grandchildren as few old men are, & my home is a great happiness and comfort to me ... We have ... 2 cows, 1 pig, 2 ponies, old Skinny, Mananga & foal, poultry & dogs."

In March, Alfred's horse, Skinny, was entered for the Cleveland Hunt Members Race -

> " ... but have not made up my mind to ride - I get chest barred ... In the run last Thursday I felt this badly - but it was quite as hard work as a race - with much pulling and quick turns - The course is a fairly stiff one - 4 or 5 lots of timber, & a good many of the 22 fences you cannot chance - & 3 with considerable 'drops' on landing."

In the fortnight before the race, "Skinny" became lame and was withdrawn.

> "I should love to have had one more ride ... I dare say I should not have had wind for it - so I suppose I shall never do it any more."

Frequently during the fine, warm, August evenings, Alfred went riding with Anne (now aged seven):

> "We have had some delightful ones - on to the top of Highcliffe & on to Ryston Nab & Hanging Stone another - she rides well & I have bought 'Tiddleywinks' for her - a good pony. I am glad to be able to do this & hope I may be able to start the little boys before I die ..."
>
> *28th Sept.* "P*(ease)* & P*(artners)* in a *very* bad way - Jack *(who was Chairman)* in a great stew over it - & there is a row between Headlam & Selaby *(Jack and Claud Pease's respective homes)* - the charge against Claud being deserting the ship in difficulties, but this is not just - The *fault* is with Arthur *(Francis Pease)* who

expanded instead of hoarding in the good years, paid great dividends instead of husbanding extra profits & paying off Bank & Debentures ... I suppose it will mean I loose my little all ... they banked with Barclays who are a mean lot ... & will wreck the concern if it pays them to - they ought never to have banked there - after their dirty work in 1902, 1903."

1931

19th Jan. " - Had a great day with Anne - Hounds met P'thorpe - found in Bousdale at 1 - ran hard down Bousdale, round this side to Mount House, over Bousdale, under Hanging Stone - flew across Middle Gill - Anne & I first across, caught tail hounds going into Hell Gill - raced across to Codhill, over High Cliff, Guisbro' Moor, Potter's Rigg, Sleddale bottom (Anne & I first across) & to the Piggeries - Frank *(huntsman)* & 5 others there out of a big field ... & we rode home - really a wonderful fast run for Anne & she will never cross all that quicker, 50 minutes' hard galloping & much of it very hard going, bang up shale tips, through woods, becks & moor."

Towards the end of January, Betty went out to Leysin where, since early 1928, with only brief spells in England, Lavender had been receiving treatment for her tubercular condition. In mid-June she returned from Switzerland and came to convalesce at Pinchinthorpe.

"L. was tired but looked well and was very cheerful & she was put in the new room & sun box made for her in the 'corridor' with opening out into the rose garden - Betty has been very clever & has worked hard to make things nice for her."

1932

11th Jan. "Hounds at Upleatham - a cold v. fine day ... plenty of foxes - some galloping about - but no good run - In one gallop, Skinny refused twice a *low* gate chained & wired up - this means he is, like me, growing old for the game, (over 20 y.o.) for he was very good at timber - 10 years ago I should have *made* him do it 'coute que coute,' but now a cropper over timber is a thing only to be faced in the best of runs - so I funked it - with humiliating reflections - 4 or 5 others behind me jumped it ..."

The previous year Alfred had written a book of political reminiscences which was published that January, (1932). During the Autumn and Winter he had written another, *Half a Century of Sport* which was published in March that same year. With the cut in dividends, his shortfall in income had to be made up somehow; this he did with his pen, which enabled him to stay on at Pinchinthorpe through 'another evil year.' During an earlier financial crisis, in 1928, he had compiled and had published *A Dictionary of the North Riding Dialect*. He could write with authority on dialect, drawing upon childhood experience from his nanny, Sarah Wilson, from the Hutton miners, blacksmiths, joiners, farmers and especially old Blanchard, the molecatcher who taught him natural history in dialect, before ever he knew it in English.

In May, Harold Hill came to England from Kenya, his first ever visit. Alfred had last seen him in 1911:

"But he had not changed beyond that his hair is grey - he is as nervous & incoherent as ever - but I enjoyed seeing him again & knowing how prosperous he is ... I think anyone who can live in Kenia & does not is an ass, including myself, tho' I have not now enough to do it & am far too old - My old place is more or less derelict - Curiously enough, the game & even lions are there still - but he says, none of us hunt lions 'since you left' - & are thankful to be survivors - if they have to kill lions they take a motor lorry & shoot from safety! - He says there are many giraffe round my place & Chumbi - They have roads, cars & electric light & water laid on!"

29th June "My 75th birthday - I had a very happy one - it was a perfect summer's day and before 7 Betty greeted me with loving wishes and the three children came wishing me many happy returns with presents ... I arrived at the end of the day feeling few men at my age are so blessed in having still a home & young life about them - Yet it is a very solemn thought that I have outlived so many, & reached an age older than all but one of my Pease forefathers."

Hutton Hall being empty,

28th July "In afternoon we took all the children over Hutton - all over the house - & had tea in the remains of the Billiard Room - Little Vincent had written to Mrs Pickering for leave, & she wrote him a very nice letter - the children enjoyed it all tremendously - I took them even on to the roof. A very strange & curious feeling for me - going over this immense house, once crammed full of life & people - It is curious to have brought back on one the profusion and abundance of my early days - It seemed the natural thing to have 20 servants - to be waited on & valeted and to do everything without need of considering cost - not that there was wild extravagance, only things done on a big scale.

These rooms were in a shocking state of filth - lots of dead birds & jackdaws in them, & our playroom had not only dead birds, but swallows in their nests in the room - the trees & shrubs are beautiful, but it is all a wilderness, & we had to wade through high stuff on the main paths - Ichabod."

In August, Alfred went to see Edward, Earl Grey.

11th Aug. "I went by the little changed roads & villages of Lesbury, Long Houghton - past Howick to spend the afternoon and evening with Edward Grey - I

339

had a delightful time & he knows every inch of the house & grounds so well that one forgets he is nearly blind - The house is smaller than the old one was, but much the same - the trees have grown up & are very fine. He took me all over the house & we spent hours until 10.10 p.m. with his ducks; there are I should say over 200, mostly wild bred ... which are extraordinarily tame - teal, widgeons in variety, mandarin, pintails, caran back, tufted &c &c - they feed from your hand & even pull at you, & sit on his head. His squirrels come in at the windows as they did in Dorothy Grey's days before 1906 ...

I mentioned in the wall garden his grandmother taking me round & wearing black gloves too long in the fingers & telling me the names of things, & he took me to a bed of scarlet lobelia & said 'do you remember that bed?' I said 'No' - & he said they had always amused themselves by asking the name & she always replied 'Lobelia Cardinalis fullgins' (fulgens)."

On 25th November, 1932,

"Today the awfully drastic reconstruction scheme of Pease & Partners came out - it means 95/100ths of all my own capital has gone - I have other worries - Sir Timothy Eden's Solicitors have notified that he is going for *me*(!) as the surviving signatory in 1890 to the Lease of Windlestone! I have had nothing to do with the concern since 1902 ..."

The threat from Sir Timothy Eden's lawyers came to nothing. Two days after this, Warley Pickering (junior) died, giving rise to the question,

"I wonder what will happen to Hutton now ..."

1st Dec. "A cold fine likely hunting day - Hounds at Marton - Anne came with me ... Anne's performance today was extraordinarily good and plucky for a child - we did not find till after noon at Seamer 'New Whin' - but we then had 50 minutes' *top pace* racing past the old covert, Antelope & West of Severs with the first half dozen who could go the pace - then her mare ran away for two big grass fields level with hounds in the next fields, then I got her pulled up, wasted time opening a chained gate & from there to Thornton Road, & on to Hilton Plantations we were in the second division & luckily so, as the few in front had broken some stiff fences, but one was a rough one which we got over safely.

We then galloped *all out* & did not catch the first squad till South of Falklands Whin, where we were well up till they finished on Leven Bank S. of Hilton Village, by running the gallant little fox to ground. In the last field Anne's mare, Firefly, slipped & swerved in a gateway & Anne came off & got a dirty jacket ...

We passed in the last 10 minutes, pumped horses, riderless ones & people with dirty coats running about after their horses - the last place we jumped was a blind small stell where others came down.

... I put this all down for Anne to read when I am no more. I am glad she will have some memories of happy & exciting runs with her old father. I think my little boys will remember me and my red coat, but alas I shall not live to gallop across country & show them how to do the trick - nor be what I would have so gladly been, a help to them in everything."

1933

26th Feb. "All the Directors except Dick[7] & Jack have been dismissed from the Board of Pease & Partners - & Jack is put out of the Chairmanship."

15th Mar. "A very fine day - I hunted at Yearby Bank ... Hounds went away fast with a fox from Yearby Bank ... Hounds raced past the West end of Yearby Village & I was taking a line of my own when, at a fence of extraordinary dimensions, with a field road & some rough stuff on the take off side, I pulled Skinny up to half pace for several reasons; the take off was rough, the top of the fence thin & because at the beginning of a run if I let Skinny have his way, he jumps so big that it is a bit risky with his old legs & if you cannot see the other side; he knew what I meant & did it as I intended, jumping through the thin top - I got the most awful toss as he turned heels over head & landed me an awful smack on my head & came over the top of me & I think trod on my face, but though I had a closed eye, & nose cut & black eyes, the very hard (Scott's) hat & my doubled up spectacles saved me a lot, but I was in great pain from a twisted neck & shoulder ... I left Skinny at Thompson's Farm - Though I was nearly knocked out, a drop of whisky at home put me right enough ..."

22nd June "A hard & worrying day at home ... & examining my own financial position which is appalling, and, it is plain - we must abandon living here & get into a small house - I am not going to describe what I have gone through over this - & being in a worse position than when I was first ruined in 1902 - I must use all my strength & courage to face the job & to save what I can from the wreck before I die."

29th June "My 76th birthday ... It was a day of many serious thoughts - & with great anxiety as to whether I have the strength to make the great change we have *decided on* of living in the 2 cottages hard by ..."

A few months earlier to this, when ideas for further economy had been floated, Alfred had suggested shutting down half Pinchinthorpe House, and living in the remainder, a scheme which would give more room, without the cost involved in Betty's preferred alternative now settled upon; that of converting two estate cottages into one house of five bedrooms.

Alfred now produces a rationale, for his having thus far held tenaciously to the home that had been his since his first marriage - his home once lost and then regained.

"Taking the view that long possession of even a small estate with an acquired standing with position of public service in one's county, with a reputation won by one's forefathers in a district is an asset for one's descendants, I have even under

341

misfortunes and adverse conditions endeavoured to maintain it.

I am confident, that even if my children are, after all my struggles, left in circumstances even worse than mine have been since the war, *that it is of value to them to have had even these associations in their childhood,* that they will have a better chance in the battle of life, *and things will be more possible for them to do,* not only because of the record, and to retrieve misfortune and to conquer difficulties.

I cannot convince myself, that even if it eased one's life to scrap all this, and abandon what has been my object, *(and)* to live in a cottage, *that the gain in available means would equal the loss of the rest -*

... in the meantime, the children have a happy time and plenty of room and all they can desire. As I know, with many years' hardship and difficulty, it has been a great thing to have had a happy country life during the first 11 years of my life - It does not follow, that because I have had to bear severe reverses of fortune, ill fortune will pursue those who come after me ..." *(Author's italics)*

3rd July " ... We are now on the eve of a great change having decided to vacate my home for 53 years & where I had hoped to end my days; it is I hope, the final catastrophe ... and the last step in my descent from the abundance and wealth of possessions to poverty - It is only a catastrophe to me ..."

6th Aug. "The alteration of the cottages began last week."

The cottages being converted were, as part of the entailed estate property, put on lease to Betty for fifty years.

Edward, Earl Grey died on 7th September. This blow, the loss of another old friend, lowered Alfred's morale further. But then quite suddenly and unexpectedly, fate once more intervened.

Phillipa was ill and alone, her family away - Rachel in Bavaria and Ingram at Oxford. The outcome of a family discussion in early September resolved two problems - at least temporarily - that Phillipa would come to live at Pinchinthorpe for six months where she could be cared for, and that this for Alfred would be a reprieve from turning out of the house for a time.

31st Dec. "And now I have got to the end of another year in which I am sensible of going down hill and yet unreconciled to the inevitable hour."

1934

9th May "O.M.E. - Tom Donking, one of Warley Pickering's Exors. came in on Mon. (7th May) with the offer of the Hutton Estate - This is interesting & I have asked for particulars ... I calculate without having the particulars, that it would be *(a)* good purchase at £40,000."

342

This, unlike the exercise he went through in 1926, was not Alfred considering a purchase on his own account - such was no longer possible - but the offer was being put to him as Chairman and Managing Director of O.M.E. which, in his own reduced circumstances was the next best thing.

26th May "Had a long time with Mrs Pickering & Tom Donking at Hutton - finished it by seeing, after I get an outside opinion such as Sandy Medlicott's, what kind of an offer we can make my own valuation is £46,000.
Hutton looked exquisite - I took the 2 little lads with me - Mrs Pickering's new house on our old cricket field is a charming little residence built out of the ruins of my father's greenhouses."
6th July "Directors' meeting 4 p.m. - home 7 p.m. - Have Reports & valuation of Hutton Estate. We are paying 8% Dividend for the year ... and carrying forward £15,000 of undivided profits - The Auditor, Challands (of Price Waterhouse) told me he thought I had been extraordinarily successful - it is something for him to say."
14th Aug. "Went to see Mrs Pickering ... She wanted me to make an offer from the Middlesbro' Owners for the Hutton Estate. Tom Donking was there - he is a very straight & pleasant man to do business with - but very, as he should be - very business-like - It was evident that she wanted to be rid of the bother of the property - I gathered they expected to get about £46,000 - but I pointed out that the place was not in the condition it was in 1903 or 1905 - about 200 acres felled & not replanted - grounds & the Hall derelict - Farms & cottages not painted - pheasantries & kennels gone."

The offer made by Alfred on behalf of O.M.E. was £30,000 for 1,654[8] acres, including the Hall, five farms, the village of Hutton with twenty-eight cottages, and development land.

Two weeks later,

" ... Mrs Pickering accepts our offer of £30,000 for the Hutton Estate - It is undoubtedly a bargain - I am of course very interested in the prospect of after 32 years, being again associated with Hutton, but I have mixed feelings, as it involved me in much anxious thought and extra labour - & in my own impecuniosity no advantage to me or mine that I can see."

1935

1st Jan. "The children are well ... & at any rate I have succeeded, although a ruined man, in giving them a home here & a happy childhood so far - the future I dare not think of, as all I have struggled to do has gone 'West'."

In May, and in Cornwall for an early "economy from home" holiday, Alfred took his family to Falmouth where once again, looking about Bosveal he was overcome with melancholia:

> "There are no donkeys on the cliffs and the donkey stables my father built are empty.
> It is curious that my father never thought of settling an acre of land here or in the North on me ... However, I have gone about with a sense that I must be near the end of my journey, & yet I have no wish to leave what I know & have loved for anywhere else. I don't even long to see all those I have lost in any other world or to meet them changed - I loved the past & I cannot love an utterly unknown future - I have never craved for rest."

He cut his holiday short by a few days and went to Oxford to see his grandson Ingram Edward Pease.

> "I love being with Ingram. He is my sort & reminds me very much of his dear father in many ways, and is of a delightful and happy nature."
> *12th June* "... arrived at P'thorpe at 5.30 *(from Cornwall and Oxford)* - Everything looked beautiful, laburnums, lilac, rhododendrons, may, guelder roses, masses of clematis, montana all in full bloom together with the pea fowl amongst the tulips which are not over; woodpigeons about the house - It is something to have lived to see this once more - the children enchanted to get home - I feel for them it has been worth while all my struggle to preserve my old home & to give them a memory of all this."

Hopes of preserving this a little while longer were strengthened when later Betty found a tenant for the cottage she had on lease.

> *29th June* "I was 78 this day - a most perfect summer's day spent with my dear wife & children mostly in the garden ... my family gave me what I like, a wire haired terrier pup."
> *14th Sept.* "For the first time since 1903 I shot at Hutton - going to the moor with John Fry[9] ... we had 3 drives ... in a gale. There were lots of birds, but they went wrong with highwind, but those which came were high twisters - I got 8 with 8 cartridges ... It is years since I had shot at grouse & was satisfied ... lunched in the conservatory at Hutton."

Alfred neglected his diary for some weeks, but as the year drew to a close, he turned to it to cover the period missed.

> *29th Dec.* "Beatrice Portsmouth died 13th Dec. the day after I had given my approval as her 'next of kin' for the appointment of a Receiver by the Court, owing to her being mentally & physically incompetent to act in any way. Thus ends her anything but happy life - No Pease attended her funeral, though Ethel went ..."

He here attaches a letter from his sister Blanche which reads:

"Dearest Alfred,

Thank you very much for writing ...

I went up to London on Sunday to go to Beatrice's funeral with Ethel as I felt I wanted to see the end of that sad little body, but instead I developed one of my miserable sick headaches ... & came home ...

I too hated the Lymington engagement & remonstrated both with Mother & Beatrice & my worst fears were realised, for besides all he made Father & you & indeed all of us suffer, he subjugated and repressed her, until her soul & spirit were like the drawers he made her always lock up. *(Everything* at Hurstbourne was locked) but I always kept up with her, because knowing the cruelty of it all, I felt I must keep a door open for her where she could find family love & something steadfast, and to a good measure, after Portsmouth's death, we could talk & resume the old footing.

Gerard Lymington was her one happiness ...

Well, there it is, as you say, the end of a sad chapter. I wonder what the next world holds for them all, B., Father, Mother, Uncle & Aunt Edward ... what a vivid picture we could make.

Beatrice made good use of her years of freedom. The Y.W.C.A. people loved her & she had good judgement about policies for them, and she was a good friend to Hurstbourne people.

That lovely Park - I wish it held cleaner & brighter memories.

I am nearly ready for Maud tomorrow & what I hope will be a very peaceful family Christmas. I hope you & Betty & the children will be able to enjoy it thoroughly. We can love the children's joy even with old hearts - much love, Blanche."

1936

On 21st January, the day of the death of King George V, Anne went off to boarding school at Sneaton Castle, Whitby. This for Alfred was a most *"terrible giving up,"*

"... for ever since she was a babe she has been a delight & the closest companion in old age ..."

As the children grew, Betty had more time to develop outside interests - as well as being involved in those she shared with Alfred. She did much voluntary work, with the Red Cross, Personal Service League and other bodies. Alfred, still doing much work at home at his writing table in the Museum, regularly disturbed by his children coming and going, often playing noisily at his feet. Once only can it be remembered, that with his children making so much noise, he felt driven to stand up and shout *"WILL - YOU - CHILDREN - BE - QUIET ---!!"* - and the effect was immediate, stunning and puzzling - Alfred had never before been heard to shout like that.

When soon, all his children were away at school, he wrote to them twice or even more times a week, frequently adding coloured illustrations, painstakingly executed, to depict the domestic animals about home, or a caricature of some event he had attended. Doing this lessened the pain of separation.

> *29th Mar.* "Went with Betty to lunch at Headlam - Jack is very fit & cheerful, Elsie never stops talking and is very indiscreet & wild in her remarks about people - but was very hospitable ... One Potts & his wife were there & Elsie apologised to us for having such 'middle class' people. It is better to be middle class than vulgar! - We had a very pleasant afternoon, spent by me tête à tête with Jack - the others went to the Bowes Museum."
>
> *24th June* "In the evenings we watch the badgers ... with glasses - about 9 p.m. they come out from the earth in the hill opposite ... When the last snow was on the ground, Woardby[10] tracked a badger from this earth over Hanging Stone to Percy Cross Plantation & *back* - a good 7 miles ramble in the snow."
>
> *27th July* "A day I have longed for when Betty went to bring Anne home from Sneaton for the holidays."

Before Anne had returned home, Alfred collapsed in the garden while waiting for his friend Percy Aylmer who was to call, and who found him lying on the gravel path.

After prolonged rest, he began his routine again, attending to his office, the Bench, County Council, Guisborough Grammar School Governors' meetings and in the pursuit of his other interests.

> *16th Nov.* "Gurney's 9 y.o. today - his first birthday away from us - he says 'knowing' things - when he came to see me ill in bed - to console me, he said 'Father, dying is only like having a birthday; you don't know *what* you are going to get - it may be just what you want - or something nicer'."

Throughout the winter, though it was a cold one, on better days Alfred was able to take Anne's pony for a look at hounds on a few occasions.

1937

During February, Betty took him to Wiltshire and elsewhere, to look at Cleveland Bays at different studs, and this, despite the blizzard conditions in the South, he enjoyed.

29th June "My 80th Birthday.
This was a surprising day for me - I knew that Betty had arranged for Edward &
Molly, Sandy & Lavender, Ingram & Rachel ... to come to my birthday tea party,
& had arranged all beautifully, but what I never expected was presents & shoals of
letters & telegrams & notices in the Press ..."

Betty's present was a pigeoncote and fantail pigeons erected in full
view from their bedroom window.

Alfred decided the time had now come when he should start to shed
some of his outside responsibilities, and he resigned as Chairman of the
Standing Joint Committee on the North Riding County Council. When
Autumn came round, he tried to get a few days out with hounds.

27th Nov. "I tried to ride Anne's pony & find hounds at Guisbro' Park - the pony
was mad fresh & what with its buck jumping & the bitter wind I was soon pumped
& had to go home ..."

1938

On 26th January, Alfred resigned as Chairman of the Cleveland
Hunt Point to Point Race Committee but the Committee absolutely
refused to accept it, so he carried on.

28th Jan. "I had a Directors' Meeting at M'bro' this morning & got through well -
Claud *(Pease)* said to me 'I am very pleased with the way that all the properties are
being managed' - I know - I never cease giving the subject my labour &
thought."
27th Mar. "The weather has been wonderful - the best March I can remember -
many days of sunshine & some like Summer - Today the ribes, japonica &
daffodils are in full flower - cherry & plum blossom out - & even chestnuts in
leaf."
11th Apl. " ... On Sat (9th) I rode with Vincent & was unlucky to strike the coldest
day for weeks past & caught cold - this means much coughing & asthma."
25th Apl. "1st swallows here."
29th June "My 81st Birthday ... 2 peacocks arrived."
24th July "Lymington came - & spent the next 2 days seeing all our properties and
activities."

Gerard Wallop, Viscount Lymington, Beatrice's nephew, who had
spent so many of his early years living at Hurstbourne Park with the
Portsmouths, stayed at Pinchinthorpe for three nights. This was the first
time any of that family had set foot in the district for forty years or more.
A difficult thing for Lymington without doubt, and just as much for
Alfred, with the remembrance of such bitterness all those years ago.

347

Lymington was heir both to the Portsmouth Earldom, and also to the Portsmouths' substantial interests in O.M.E. - and his coming to Pinchinthorpe the final banishment of the past to family history and the vaults of time.

In August, Alfred and his family were in Ireland - at Gweedore and then by Loch Corib. Though the fishing was poor, he played the water with his fishing rod, and John Malloy, a local fisherman, taught the children to dab for trout.

25th Aug. Ireland " ... A most perfect day - & tho' unwell I really enjoyed it, as we went through beautiful scenery to a Show at Carna, of ponies, cattle, industries, produce &c - It was very amusing, interesting & entertaining - & I have written an article for *Horse & Hound* on the Connemara Ponies - about 250 ponies shown & about 140 mares & foals - all on a quaking bog."

15th Sept. Pinchinthorpe "A beautiful day - Stokesley Show - I went with B. & the children for 2 hours in the morning & watched the Clevelands & Hunter Brood Mares being judged ... our swallows left."

23rd Sept. "Anne was packed up & ready to return to school - We had arranged for her to leave St. Hilda's at Xmas - & I had some correspondence with the Prioress - & got a letter this morning - which made it easy to put our plan for her to attend the Friends' School at Ayton as a day girl at once - So - to my great delight - she now lives at home."

"December, 1938. - I sent a Christmas Card & a little message to *Rosie Wake* and was startled to read of her death in *The Times*. She died (suddenly) on Dec. 20 - she was 76 ...

I loved her dearly when I was a boy at school, and she was as devoted to me - It is strange how this very distant romance of youthful days comes back to me -

When she & her family settled in Br. Columbia, & George, & May (her sister) joined them - we still corresponded regularly - but as the years rolled on it came to an end - & she married her first cousin & I married mine - & I destroyed all traces of this early attachment which was of the purest and nicest kind -

It caused her sister May & my mother some concern - & when I was questioned as to whether I got letters from her, & whether I wrote to her - I deliberately *lied* to my mother for the first & last time in my life - & would always have done so for the sake of any woman who trusted me -

I have kept this to myself - tho' Nellie & Lottie knew all about it - One cannot ever say we *forget,* those who were worthy of our love & who loved us -

We spent a very quiet happy Christmas, just by ourselves - It was a green Christmas and open - In the South they had snow, storms, frost, blizzards & fog ...

I am grateful for being spared to be able to enjoy my children but am surprised to be still here - my little boys are my chief companions now."

38. Rosie Wake.

1939

17th Jan. "A sad day for me - parting with the little boys off to school ... I feel the little boys love me & will miss me."

February
"I do not know how to write about the desolating calamity which befell us this month -
On Sunday morning, *Feb. 19th* I was writing in the Museum when Betty came in sobbing - & for a minute or two could not speak - then she said *'Something terrible has happened'* - my heart stood still, and my thoughts flew to our little boys - & Anne who had gone out riding - then she told me *Ingram* had been *killed* flying the evening before at 6.10 p.m. near Kinross - I was paralysed - I loved him dearly & he was the greatest comfort & hope in my old age - my pride & most precious helper.
28th Feb. "Ingram's Birthday - had he lived 10 days longer he would have been 25 y.o.
God knows what I have suffered since he died - I have thanked for some 150 wonderful letters about him, & could not read or answer many of them without tears - But I have attended regularly to my business & office."
18th Mar. "Cleveland Point to Pt. Races were today - but altho' I am Chairman & a Steward I could not face the bitter cold ... I did not *want* to go - Ingram rode last year over this course at Easby."

In mid-April Alfred wrote to his son Edward saying that he was himself now packed and ready to depart for the greatest adventure of all,

349

and just as the swallows returned, he set out on the morning of 27th April, 1939.

"Let the World proceed as it will, and let each generation born into its own environment be as pleased as mine is, to have lived when it has lived and be as thankful, that I have seen and touched the things of my own, and not of any other day." - *Alfred Edward Pease.*

Notes:
1. James Smith of Thornaby and his wife Sarah (née Pickering), grandparents of Emily Elizabeth Smith, had adopted her as a baby. Betty's forbears were Quaker, her great-great grandmother was Elizabeth Flounders, sister of Benjamin Flounders of Yarm, a Quaker railway pioneer and founder of the Flounders Institute at Ackworth. The Flounders family were connected by marriage to the Waterhouse family who in turn were connected by marriage to the Fowlers and Peases. Alfred's first wife, Nellie, used to speak of her 'Aunt Flounders' (née Mary Waterhouse) who m. 1817 Jonathan Flounders.
2. Cyril Pease, son of Alfred's sister Helen Blanche Pease.
3. *Elections and Recollections* by Sir Alfred E. Pease, p.302 published by John Murray, 1932.
4. Lord Novar was formerly Ronald Ferguson, Liberal Whip.
5. Glendurgan was the Fox family home where Alfred's mother was born.
6. James Barclay Peat and Ethel Peat, friends and neighbours of Alfred and Betty.
7. Sir Richard Arthur Pease, son of Sir Arthur Francis Pease.
8. It has not been possible to reconcile the difference between the 1,626 acres given in 1926 and that of 1,654 given now.
9. Sir John Pease Fry, son of Sir Theodore Fry sometime Liberal M.P. for Darlington.
10. William Woardby, Hutton Estate gamekeeper.

EPILOGUE

Following Alfred's death, Betty received over 350 letters of sympathy, and to each of which she replied personally.
Among them were these three:
From Lavender Mary Medlicott, written after the funeral.

Dearest Betty,
So many thanks for letting me have those Service papers & for your dear letter. It must have been hateful for you going through all of Father's papers. As you say, "he was so dear to everyone"; we all need sympathy in our different ways & the world is a great deal poorer without him - that I shall always feel there never was or could be another spirit like his. Am certain his spirit will always be near you & that our mother will always bless you for your wonderful care & help to him during these last years. She absolutely worshipped him always, as I expect you realise & am thankful, for her sake, she was spared the awful parting and blanks which faces all of you & us. I know you must be overwhelmed too by all these letters,
Your loving Lavender.

From Phillipa Pease, Alfred's daughter-in-law, written from Cotaghy, by Kirriemuir after the funeral.

My dearest Betty,
We got here safely on Monday night; it is a charming place but the fishing is very bad as the river is too low. I have thought a great deal of you during this last week; you have all my sympathy and my admiration for your splendid courage. In spite (of) your grief, you are as capable as always. I do hope you can find comfort in the knowledge that by your loving care, (you) made Father's life longer & happier, & we & all his friends know it. Though it must always be there, the time passes & the sorrow gets easier to bear. Don't answer this, but I feel I must tell you that I am thinking of you & that I respect & admire you & that your courage will not fail, always your(s) with love,
Phillipa Pease.

From Gerard Vernon Wallop, Viscount Lymington (Later 9th Earl of Portsmouth):
Writing from Freiburg, Germany, 3rd May, 1939.

My dear Lady Pease,
This morning a letter was forwarded to me from George Jenyns telling me your very sad news. I am so distressed to hear of it. It came as a complete shock to us as

we had seen no English papers for days.

A very great landmark has disappeared from the North. Sir Alfred seemed to me to typify not only all that was so remarkable in the Pease tradition, but all the courtesy of a vanished world. He carried the tradition of the very finest type of country gentleman in everything he did. If I may use a contradictory metaphor, he seemed to be always the Quaker who wore lace ruffles & a sword. He combined the Friend & the Cavalier.

I need hardly tell you how much my sympathy goes out to you & the children. It is not easy to express but please remember it is there.

I do hope that when you are in the South, you come to see us,

Yours sincerely,

Lymington.

Betty remained a widow, and having reached the same age as Alfred, she died on 26th March, 1979 - one month short of the fortieth anniversary of his death.

Pease & Partners Collieries, Mines and Quarries Operating between 1857-1902

County Durham

(a) In the area around Bishop Auckland:-
1. Adelaide Colliery
2. Deanery Colliery
3. Eldon Colliery
4. St. Helens Colliery

(b) In the area around Crook:-
5. Peases' West Colliery
6. Bowden Close Colliery
7. Stanley Colliery
8. Tindale Colliery
9. Wooley Colliery
10. Waterhouses Colliery
11. Esh Colliery
12. Ushaw Moor Colliery
13. Sunniside Colliery
14. Brandon Colliery

At Ferryhill:-
15. Windlestone Colliery

Cleveland Ironstone Mines
1. Hutton mines
2. Upleatham Mines
3. Loftus
4. Skinningrove
5. Lingdale
6. Brotton
7. Tocketts

Quarries Co. Durham
1. Broadwood (Weardale)
2. Frosterley (Weardale)
3. Rogerley
4. Tut Hill

Other operations
1. Bankfoot Coke Ovens
2. Lingdale Brick Works
3. Roddymoor Firebrick Works

In 1898, the average annual output from the collieries, Ironstone and Limestone mines is given as:-
1. In excess of 1,300,000 tons of coal
2. 715,000 tons of coke
3. 1,196,000 tons of Ironstone
4. 260,000 tons of limestone

INDEX

Jackson, (Acting Governor B.E.A.): 281
Jackson, C.W.: 120-121, 132-134, 165, 179
Jackson, Charlie Ward: 332
Jackson, Ralph Ward: 23n
Jenyns, George A.B.: 352
Jobson, Alfred: 201
Johnson, Phillipa (Margaret Phillipa): 291, 293, 300, 302, 307, 312, 316, 322, 324-325, 328-331, 342, 351
Jones, O'Connell: 123

Kaiser, Emperor of Germany: 114
Karoly, Szitagyi: 242
24, Kensington Palace Gardens: 3, 8, 22, 23n, 28, 33, 38, 45, 52, 60, 62, 65, 66, 69
Keogh, Capt.: 56-57
Keogh, Judge: 57
Kerris Vean, Falmouth: 8, 34, 217, 221
Keyser, Arthur: 176, 182-184, 186
Kidderminster (constituency): 45
Kilima Kiu: 270, 278, 286-287, 295, 300, 303
Kilima Theki: 264, 267-269, 271-272, 274, 278-279, 285-287, 295-296, 300, 303
Kitanga: 273-274, 278, 280, 282, 285-287, 294-296, 300, 302-304, 332
Kitchener, Lord: 300
Klopper's Farm: 295, 304
Kolhapur, The Maharaja of: 199-200
Kurslake, Preston (solicitor): 31

Lambert, Archie: 295, 303
Lambton, Lord: 14
Lascelles, Lord: 333
Lawley, Sir Arthur, (Joe): 214-215, 219-221, 234, 237, 320
Lawrence, Molly (Ida Mary): 316-318, 322, 323n, 347
Leatham, Charles Albert: 24n, 75n, 150n
Leatham, Rachel, née Pease, - see Fowler, Rachel
Leatham, Ted (Edward Aldam): 50, 73, 75, 75n, 118-119, 159, 275
Lewis, Dr.: 303
Liban: 188

Lockwood, Sir Frank, Q.C., M.P.: 28, 35-37, 42, 45, 47, 62, 67, 83, 85, 100, 113-114, 136, 301
Loder, Sir Edmund Giles: 95, 97n, 103-106, 112, 116, 122, 125, 128-129, 133, 219, 268, 270-272
Loder, Marion, Lady: 116
London, City of, (constituency): 14, 48n
Long, Harry: 232, 259
Lowell, Russell (American Ambassador): 28
Lowther, James: 177
Lucan, Lord: 55
Lucas, Arthur: 30-32, 102, 108, 111, 116, 119-121, 131-132, 144-145, 171, 180
Lundie, (Corndavon gamekeeper): 73
Lundie, Mrs: 301
Lymington, Gerard, Viscount: 345, 347-348, 351-352
Lymington, Newton, Viscount - see Portsmouth, 6th Earl of
Lyttleton, General Neville: 220

Mackenzie, Dr.: 303
Mahony, Pierce, M.P.: 63
Makonnen, Ras: 128, 150n, 185-186, 190-191, 195, 200
Malloy, John: 348
18, Mansfield Street: 332
Marchmont, (Editor, *Yorkshire Chronicle*): 62, 95
Mariam, Hailo: 192-195
Marjoribanks, Hon E.: 44
Martin, C.B.: 46
Mary, Princess: 333
Massoutier, Captain: 161
Mathews, Colonel: 249
Maxse, Ernest George Berkeley: 89
May, Sir Thomas E.: 28
McIndoe (Hutton Hall head gardener): 179
McKelvie: 189
Medlicott, Lavender Mary - see Pease, Lavender Mary
Medlicott, Sandy (Walter Sandfield): 275, 277-280, 282-284, 286, 292, 308, 322, 324-326, 334, 343, 347